POLICE IN A MULTICULTURAL SOCIETY

An American Story

POLICE IN A MULTICULTURAL SOCIETY
An American Story

David E. Barlow
Melissa Hickman Barlow
University of Wisconsin-Milwaukee

WAVELAND

PRESS, INC.

Long Grove, Illinois

For information about this book, contact:
    Waveland Press, Inc.
    4180 IL Route 83, Suite 101
    Long Grove, IL 60047-9580
    (847) 634-0081
    info@waveland.com
    www.waveland.com

Photo Credits—© Bettman/Corbis: 4; 164
            Minnesota Historical Society: 122
            Minnesota Historical Society/Edward H. Meier: 222
            Serena Nanda: 274
            Shasta Phillips: 98
            © Reuters Newmedia Inc./Corbis: xiv; 288
            University of Wyoming/Richard Throssel: 208

Copyright © 2000 by Waveland Press, Inc.

ISBN 1-57766-129-X

Printed in the United States of America

9 8 7 6 5 4 3

Dedication
to Atticus Finch

for Kaitlyn
with hope for a more just world

Acknowledgments

First and foremost, we owe a debt of gratitude to the many authors whose primary research made it possible for us to tell the story told here. At Waveland Press, we thank Neil Rowe for encouraging us to write the book we wanted to write and Carol Rowe for understanding what we wanted to say and helping us say it. We are in awe of her skills as an editor. We are grateful to our parents, Marilyn and Bill Barlow and Ann and Bob Hickman, for their love and support.

Contents

Preface

The United States is multicultural. United States history and its institutions are multicultural. To deny this social fact is to deny ourselves. To construct explanations of events or descriptions of social formations without incorporating multicultural perspectives produces a one-dimensional picture of a multi-dimensional reality. The more dimensions that we explore and integrate, the closer we approach a reflection of reality. This process is what we refer to when we use the term multiculturalism.

The purpose of this book is to inform students of criminal justice about the role and function of the police in the United States in relation to the society in which police operate. Most of the chapters in this book primarily focus on the interaction between African Americans and the police, because African Americans represent the marginalized group that has most consistently and continuously been involved in conflict with municipal police throughout the history of the United States.

The book's uniqueness is in its presentation of traditional police-related topics from a multicultural perspective. We contend that to grasp the complex realities of policing in the United States is possible only from such a perspective. Too often police scholars dismiss the personal experiences of minority citizens as "anecdotal" (Mann, 1993). The assumption is that the personal accounts are not scientific and, therefore, are inherently inferior to the findings of systematic research.

The bias in favor of scientific evidence and statistical analysis is profound in the European-American academic tradition. It stems from the Enlightenment period when "scientists" insisted that the path toward truth must travel through the scientific method, with its equations, variables, systematic observation, and data collection. Oral histories and personal accounts are discounted as subjective and selective observations. Despite this tendency to favor scientific accounts, police scholars do acknowledge the limitations of science in instances of personal police "war stories." In these situations scholars admit that, although scientific research is one method for capturing an important part of the social reality of policing, it is incomplete.

Just as systematic observation and statistical analysis sometimes fail to depict the real world of policing reflected in personal accounts of police officers, these measures commonly fail to capture the "minority experience." They are simply incapable of providing us with a complete picture. To understand policing in the United States, it is essential that we not exclude information simply because it does not "fit" our own biased perspective. We must seek out historically marginalized voices to fill in the missing information. Our intention in this book is to achieve new insights into police theory, research, and practice by tapping resources that have previously been ignored. The traditionally neglected viewpoints which inform this book shed a penetrating light on the topics of the role of police, community relations, rebellion, and marginalized police officers.

Part 1 explores "The Role of Police" in U.S. society from a multicultural perspective. Chapter 1 challenges some of the more traditional perspectives on what police do in our society. Chapter 2 presents a historical analysis of the development of municipal policing in the United States, with a focus on police history in relation to various racial and ethnic groups. We focus on interconnections between the historical development of the modern police institution and racial, ethnic, and class power relations. This historical analysis traces the strategies and forms of policing from the earliest municipal police in the United States to the advent of community policing.

Next we explore the most visible manifestation of race, class, and cultural conflict: police-community relations. Part 2 continues the discussion of historical development with a look at law enforcement practices in minority communities. The three chapters in this section describe the impact of majority-controlled law and law enforcement on police-community relations and police training efforts to resolve conflict between police and minorities. Chapter 3, "Underpolicing," describes the failure of U.S. law and law enforcement to protect the rights, property, and lives of marginalized groups in our society. Chapter 4, "Overpolicing," documents the oppressive and often brutal treatment of marginalized groups by police. Chapter 5 explores a number of the efforts which have been initiated to improve the relationship between the police and marginalized groups.

The single most significant sequence of events concerning police and society in the last twenty-five years was the videotaping of the Rodney King beating, the first acquittal verdicts, and the subsequent riots in South Central Los Angeles. Part 3, "Police and Rebellion," places the 1992 Los Angeles uprising in a larger social, historical, and multicultural context. Even more importantly, Part 3 demonstrates the very active and critical role that society has had in the formation of police and police practices. It illustrates precisely how the more marginalized groups in U.S. society have utilized whatever means available to overcome domination by the majority through the law and its enforcement. Chapter 6 begins this analysis by investigating the efforts of slaves to resist their legal oppression. Chapter 7 documents the continuing struggle by African Americans after slavery to transform the legal racism which forced them into second-class citizenship. Chapter 8 describes the "Modern Urban Rebellions" from 1965 to 1990 in relation to previous struggles. Finally, chapter 9 brings the reader back to the Los Angeles Riot of 1992 and contextualizes its significance in terms of preceding events. It is our contention that the understanding gained by exploring these events in context provides critical insights into the major racial rift that continues in interpretations of social interactions, the role of the police in urban minority communities, and the role of society in the functioning of the police.

Part 4 on "Marginalized Police Officers" is especially important to understanding the concept and process of policing in a multicultural community because it deals with the intersection of multiple cultures. Part 4 emphasizes the multicultural nature of police agencies and describes the unique perspectives that "minority" police develop because of their particular vantage points. The experiences and perspectives of traditionally marginalized police officers who occupy places in both majority and minority cultures make them invaluable "cultural contacts." They can provide special insights on police, minority communities, and their interactions.

Through a concentration on Native American Tribal Police and African Americans in policing, chapters 10 and 11 explore the long history that racial minorities have had in policing in the United States. Of particular interest are the motivations and social efforts of racial minority communities to obtain representation of members of their own race on police forces, the motivation and struggle of individual racial minority police officers to work in these traditionally racist agencies, and the motivations of police executives and political officials to hire or recruit racial minorities onto the police forces.

Chapters 12 and 13 focus on "Gendered Police," exploring those groups that have been marginalized on the basis of gender or sexual discrimination. Chapter 12 explores the historical development of the role of women in policing and their struggle to have an impact on police and police practices. Chapter 13 explores what is currently the most marginalized group in policing: gays and lesbians. It looks at issues gay police officers in the United States face, noting similarities and distinctions in the problems of both gay police and other marginalized police.

There is an unfortunate tendency in police scholarship to overlook views of the communities that are policed. Police textbooks traditionally focused on what police do and how they do it. Society was discussed only in terms of its interaction with the police, and not in terms of real people in real communities as agents of change and power. The traditional focus on the professional police model has shifted recently to discussions concerning community policing. The role of community members, however, is sometimes simply transformed from an obstacle to overcome to another element in the fight against crime. This change fails to question the fundamental premises about the role of police in U.S. society. This textbook focuses on the communities within society because they have the most at stake in the ongoing development of the police and police practices.

At times in this book the authors use a first-person account to refer to the first author's professional experiences. David Barlow provides a number of examples to help illustrate specific points. These examples come from his personal observations as a correctional officer, deputy sheriff, university police officer, and a police training instructor.

Part One
The Role of Police

The historical development of the police and their role in the United States has not been an evolutionary process in which the police have steadily improved along a progressive course. Such a view would suggest that the police were brutal and corrupt in the nineteenth century but improved in the twentieth century through various reforms in a steady march toward professionalism. Now that professionalism is reaching its limits, more and more cities are experimenting with community-oriented policing. An evolutionary view of police history does not capture the intense ideological and political battles surrounding each of these developments. Each police reform was not, in fact, preordained by the natural progress of civilization.

An evolutionary view of changes in policing limits our ability to imagine the possibility of a different course or sequence of events, either in the past or in the future. The presentation of police history as evolutionary does not reveal that it is a history in which political battles were fought and in which decisions were made by real people in real social and political contexts. Linear presentations stifle the potential for creative innovation by sanctioning the status quo. As Loewen (1995) put it, "feeding students rosy tales of progress helps keep them passive, for it presents the future as a process over which they have no control" (p. 263).

The very concept of "reform" (an implied improvement on an existing foundation) depicts each new development or change in policy as a progressive step on the road to perfection. Police innovations, transformations, and new techniques are traditionally considered police "reforms" and, thus, are seen as part of the advancement of civilization. Police problems such as corruption, discrimination, and brutality are likewise thought of as historical legacies that will eventually be overcome. It is commonly assumed that police leadership is dedicated to correcting these problems.

Such a view provides no framework for analysis of those police chiefs and police reformers who are themselves corrupt. Further, it provides no framework for understanding discrimination and brutality as endemic to policing rather than simply the acts of a few bad apples. Within this evolutionary framework, resistance to police policies or conflicts between the police and the public are reduced to "misunderstandings" in which the police and the public are only experiencing the growing pains of progress toward a better

1

police department. Individual people or policies may need adjusting, but the system is basically sound and must be preserved. We believe that the starting point for an understanding of police in society is to question the very role of police—not to begin with the assumption that their role is to fight crime.

Police institutions are commonly assumed to have functional necessity and to have changed because of the intellect and will of a few good men in history, such as Sir Robert Peel, August Vollmer, or O. W. Wilson. However, the actions and influence of everyday people (e.g., immigrants, union organizers, workers, racial and ethnic minorities, and women), of ordinary police officers and administrators, and even of political and economic reformers have been extremely important to the nature and character of policing in our society. If police departments formed out of necessity and police officers are steadily becoming more humane and just, then how can we explain tensions in police-community relations, which are particularly strong along racial lines? And, why do these tensions seem to ebb and flow in more of a cyclical pattern than in a linear progression of improvement?

Evolutionary views of police history cannot answer these questions. We need a dynamic, multicultural perspective. Indeed, class and race are rendered invisible by evolutionary accounts of the history of police. Policing appears to be a neutral crime control operation. The fact that officers are primarily from the working class might be assumed to suggest that the police are more likely to identify with the working class. However, one of the primary activities of the early municipal police officers was to break strikes. This is an anomaly that requires explanation.

Students of policing must not shy away from examining the influence of class and race in their analyses of police. Our government structure was established by rich white men who envisioned the government as providing the foundation for private property, commerce, and free enterprise. The U.S. Constitution clearly states that the duty of the government is to protect the "life, liberty, and property" of [white] male property owners. Therefore, in a capitalist society it should not be hard to imagine that the role of the police has been shaped by economic forces.

Overwhelming evidence attests to the important benefits to wealthy industrialists from police efforts to bust unions, to keep open the channels of commerce, to control immigrant groups, and to protect private property. Even politicians and government leaders are often very clear about developing policy and constructing political institutions designed to enhance the private sector's ability to make a profit. Thus, an important part of our analysis of the role of police in society is to consider the relationship of police to the economic system. A tradition in U.S. education of treating the political system (a democracy) and the economic system (capitalism) as separate entities fails to capture the reality that we live in a capitalist democracy. The interconnectedness of our political and economic system is a reality that cannot be ignored if we are to understand any aspect of our lived experience in U.S. society, including that of police in society.

Along with class relations, race relations are central to understanding the role of police in society. Much of the history of race relations in the United States, particularly with regard to police, is shameful. It is difficult to confront and explain this negative side of U.S. history, especially with an audience of students eager to embark on a career in law enforcement or some other aspect of criminal justice. However, leaving race out would be even more problematic than the omission of class.

The class bias in the criminal justice system is in many ways more complex and subtle than the long history of racism in policing. The issue of race permeates every aspect of police study and research. At a conference on "Racial Issues in Policing," sponsored by the National Organization of Black Law Enforcement Executives (NOBLE), the Police Executive Research Forum (PERF), and the Reno (Nevada) Police Department, Gerry Mendez explicitly addressed this point: "Let's be honest here. When we say 'police-community relations,' we mean 'race relations.' And when we say race relations we mean 'African Americans!'" (personal communication, 1992).

Of course racism, particularly against African Americans, is not exclusive to police history. It is a fundamental element throughout the history of the United States. From the moment that Christopher Columbus initiated the transatlantic slave trade in the Americas to the 1995 O. J. Simpson trial and beyond, race has defined who we are as citizens and as a nation. The police play an important role within the dynamic of race relations, as they are often the principal mechanism for maintaining a system of racial discrimination. We must understand this dynamic in order to understand current racial rifts in police-community relations. Facing the troublesome sides of U.S. and police history, along with the positive sides, is the only path to an understanding of the racial divisions that all too often destroy the lives of both police officers and citizens.

The following two chapters investigate the role of the police with an expansive and multicultural focus. Chapter 1 presents multiple perspectives on U.S. society, criminal justice education, and what police do. It challenges the restrictions of the rules of science and monocultural biases. Chapter 2 searches for an understanding of the fundamental role of police in the historical development of municipal policing with an appreciation for the racial, ethnic, and class power relations and community actions that shaped its form. It ends with a review of the history and role of police in the United States.

1 Multiple Perspectives On The Role Of Police

The communities of the United States in which the police operate have been constructed by people from many "different shores" (Takaki, 1993, p. 2). European-American history and culture have traditionally overshadowed the contributions of non-European cultures. It is particularly telling that Eurocentric domination of culture has subjugated the indigenous people of the Americas to the status of an ethnic minority in the United States. According to Loewen (1995), almost all U.S. histories begin in 1492 with the arrival of Christopher Columbus. Not only are the pre-Columbian civilizations of Native Americans ignored, but so are their remarkable contributions to medicine, food and agriculture, military tactics, and political philosophy. It is as if history did not exist or was unimportant until a white Western European stumbled onto the scene.

Furthermore, as U.S. schoolchildren across the country put on plays in celebration of the Pilgrims' first Thanksgiving in 1620, few are taught that Africans were brought to Jamestown as indentured servants a year before the Pilgrims set foot on Plymouth Rock. Even fewer are presented with the evidence that Afro-Phoenicians may have come to the shores of America in their own ships as early as 1000 B.C., that West Africans may have done the same in A.D. 1311, or that the first non-native settlers of the area now called the United States were about one hundred African slaves in a South Carolina settlement in 1526, who rebelled against their Spanish masters, killed some of them, and escaped to live with the Native Americans. The extensive settlements of Spaniards throughout one-third of what is now the United States, beginning in the early1500s, are also rendered invisible in most U.S. history textbooks.

According to Loewen (1995), even the term "settle" masks the true nature of the first Thanksgiving, which was an event in which the original settlers of this land (Native Americans) made it possible for the first white European settlers to survive. Takaki (1993) pointed out that the romantic vision of Ellis Island and the Statue of Liberty welcoming huddled masses yearning to breathe free has blinded many of us to the other ports and passageways through which immigrants have entered the United States from lands other than Western Europe. Students of traditional U.S. history are deprived of a clear view of the Asian gateway of hope at Angel Island and the horrors of the African slave ports in Charleston. Contemporary images of illegal immigrants from south of current U.S. borders obscure the geopolitics that created those borders in the first place.

Multicultural Mosaic of U.S. Society

From the beginning and throughout its history, the United States has consisted of multicultural communities. For instance:

> a single northern Ohio town, "the Glaize," was made up of hundreds of Shawnee, Miami, and Delaware Indians, British and French traders and artisans, several Nanticokes, Cherokees, and Iroquois, a few African American and white American captives, and whites who had married into or been adopted by Indian families. The Glaize was truly multicultural in its holidays, observing Mardi Gras, St. Patrick's Day, the birthday of the British queen, and Indian celebrations. (Loewen, 1995, p. 100)

Native Americans cultivated the land and established the first agricultural communities, which both whites and Blacks[1] then occupied after the original tribes were removed through disease and war. Native Americans served as guides, supplied food, provided clothing, and rendered medical assistance to European and African people from the moment they set foot on the soil that would later become the United States. Benjamin Franklin even attributed the rationale for the famous Albany Plan for the confederation of the colonies to the organization of the Iroquois League.

The influences of numerous cultures on the formation of U.S. society are nearly unprecedented in world history. The contributions of Western and Eastern European immigrants have been so well documented that the contributions of others have been eclipsed. Perhaps the most significant contribution of a non-European culture was the African slave labor that built the South (Genovese, 1976). The merging of Africans and Native Americans as both slaves and free people produced much of southern cooking, otherwise known as soul food (Loewen, 1995; Genovese, 1976). In addition, Africans and Native Americans, together with Europeans, developed new tribes of people, such as the Creeks, the Seminoles, and the Lumbee (Loewen, 1995; Genovese, 1976).

The first martyr of the American Revolution, Crispus Attucks, who was killed in the Boston Massacre, was of both Native American and African descent (Loewen, 1995; Bennett, 1993; Genovese, 1976). African Americans and Native Americans fought in U.S. wars from King William's War (1689–1697) to the Gulf War (1990), and they made up at least twenty-five percent of all the cowboys of the West (Loewen,1995; Bennett, 1993; Katz, 1992; Quarles, 1989). People of Spanish descent had tremendous influence on the construction of the so-called "American West," from the creation of the cowboy to contributions to food, language, and culture (Loewen, 1995).

In Ronald Takaki's (1993) words, "America has been racially diverse since our very beginning on the Virginia shore, and this reality is increasingly becoming visible and ubiquitous" (p. 2). In 1990, one-third of the people in the United States had an ancestry other than European. Groups whose numbers in census polls indicate that they might be described as racial/ethnic minorities already exist as majorities in most major U.S. cities. In the year 2056, it is anticipated that the white European majority will officially become a statistical minority in the United States (Takaki, 1993). Already more than half of the U.S. workforce consists of minorities, immigrants, and women. "White males will make up only 15 percent of the increase in the workforce over the next ten years" (Thomas, 1990, p. 107).

Multicultural perspectives on policing are essential. The premise of this book is that education must prepare students to live and work in a truly multicultural environment. Criminal justice educators must begin the process of conducting, disseminating, and promoting police research and theory based on an understanding and appreciation of cultural diversity. This effort is not an ideological exercise or a question of being politically correct. Failing to recognize the relevance of multicultural diversity is not only short-sighted and unfair, it can be dangerous.

Criminal Justice Education

In a *Time* magazine essay, Barbara Ehrenreich (1991) described the legacy of monocultural education:

> American history, as it was taught to us, began with Columbus' "discovery" of an apparently unnamed, unpeopled America, and moved on to the Pilgrims serving pumpkin pie to a handful of grateful red-skinned folks. College expanded our horizons with courses called Humanities or sometimes Civ, which introduced us to a line of thought that started with Homer, worked its way through Rabelais and reached a poignant climax in the pensees of Matthew Arnold. Graduate students wrote dissertations on what long-dead men had thought of Chaucer's verse or Shakespeare's dramas; foreign language meant French and German. If there had been high technology in ancient China, kingdoms in black Africa or women anywhere, at any time, doing anything worth noticing, we did not know about it, nor did anyone think to tell us. (p. 84)

Multicultural education has begun the process of filling in some of these gaps. "More than ever before, there is a growing realization that established scholarship has tended to define America too narrowly" (Takaki, 1993, p. 6). While recognition of previous ethnocentrism is a crucial beginning, continued vigilance is necessary so that multiculturalism is not limited to a few extra pages on Martin Luther King, Jr., Susan B. Anthony, or Frederick Douglass.

In the years immediately following the Rodney King beating and subsequent riot, criminal justice agencies aggressively pursued cultural diversity awareness training for their employees (Barlow & Barlow, 1993; 1994). Police officers have been particularly targeted by government administrators, as well as various community groups, as needing cultural sensitivity or diversity training. University outreach programs and college faculty often become involved in the process of training police officers. To respond to this need in the profession, it is logical that universities should take the lead in providing multicultural police education.

As long as criminal justice education simply reflects dominant ideologies, it fosters a stagnant learning environment:

> Because monoculturalism is ill-equipped to explain the complex and contradictory phenomena of crime and justice, monocultural criminal justice education is unable to provide students with explanations of crime and justice which are superior to the ideological interpretations with which they enter criminal justice and criminology courses. (Barlow & Barlow, 1995, p. 114)

Interpretations of Events

The fact is that different parties experience social relations in very different ways. Through an investigation of both slave diaries and slaveholders' diaries of the pre-Civil War southern United States, Genovese (1976) illustrated that the same event or relation can be described sincerely by both parties in completely different terms. They simply do not experience the event in the same way. Loewen (1995) used Columbus to illustrate the same point:

> Columbus's conquest of Haiti can be seen as an amazing feat of courage and imagination by the first of many brave empire builders. It can also be understood as a bloody atrocity that left a legacy of genocide and slavery that endures in some degree to this day. (pp. 60–61)

Both of these interpretations are valid, but for various reasons we have traditionally been taught only the former. Without the second interpretation, however, we do not get a complete picture of the event and our explanations of subsequent developments are insufficient. Who decides which interpretation is the truth? According to George Orwell in his classic novel *1984*, those who control the present control the past. It is critical that social scientists and historians actively resist relegating control of historical knowledge to only those with power and authority in society. Multiculturalism seeks to include those perspectives that have been pushed to the fringe.

Criminal justice offers fertile ground for vastly different interpretations. The Rodney King beating and verdicts and the O.J. Simpson case are merely the best documented examples. Deciding "truth" is no simple matter. Barak (1991) observed that:

> Justifiably or not, blacks' and whites' perceptions and experiences of crime and justice in the United States are as different as the racial and ethnic compositions of the people themselves. Thus it is important that the disciplines of criminology and criminal justice stop reproducing a literature that attempts, consciously or unconsciously, to cover up the differences by blending them unsuccessfully into a uniform experience. (pp. 180–181)

Improving the cultural competence of police officers and their agencies can improve law enforcement effectiveness, enhance officer safety, and reduce civil and criminal liability (Barlow & Barlow, 1994; Benson, 1992; Weaver, 1992). For the individual, developing good cross-cultural communications skills in a diverse workplace may improve performance evaluations, make a line officer a better candidate for promotion, and reduce fear and stress (Barlow & Barlow, 1994; Soloman & McCarthy, 1989). For managers, the desire to recruit and retain women and racial/ethnic minorities in their workforce, as well as the desire to reduce potential lawsuits based on discrimination and harassment, provides further impetus to develop an agency that is sensitive to multicultural perspectives (Blakemore, Barlow, & Padgett, 1995).

Race and Criminal Justice Issues

The need for multicultural perspectives is clearly enhanced by the powerful connection between race and a number of criminal justice and police issues. The lifetime risk for an African American male to be arrested hovers around 80 to 90 percent (Miller, 1996). While drug use among racial minorities, including African Americans, is roughly proportionate to their percent of the population (12 percent), they make up 35 percent of all drug arrests, 55 percent of all drug convictions, and 75 percent of all prison admissions for drug offenses. They are 18 times more likely to be arrested for a drug offense than a white person.

Walker, Spohn, and DeLone (2000) noted that racial and ethnic minorities are more likely than white Americans to be arrested, stopped, questioned and searched, victimized by excessive physical force, and shot and killed by the police. There is also evidence that a defendant's race continues to affect decisions regarding bail, charging, jury selection, juvenile justice processing, and sentencing. While African Americans make up 12 percent of the population, they represent 31 percent of federal prisoners and 51 percent of state prisoners. In 1993 they represented 55 percent of all state and federal prison admissions as compared to 42 percent in 1981, even though the percentage of African Americans arrested for violent crimes has dropped since 1976 (Miller, 1996).

The proportion of people under correctional supervision in 1994 was 1-in-37 (Irwin & Austin, 1997). For young white men, it was 1-in-15, 1-in-10 for young Hispanic men and 1-in-3 for young African-American men. In 1993, the incarceration rate for African American males was 3822 per 100,000 in the United States and only 815 in South Africa (Walker et al., 2000). How can we adequately address these issues without the help of the individuals and groups who are directly affected by them? Neither critical issues in policing nor the basic day-to-day realities of policing can be fully understood or properly addressed without placing them in a multicultural context.

The omission of race from the historical analysis of police does not reflect the real experience of police officers on the street. It fails to prepare students for what they will inevitably encounter on the job as a police officer. My own experiences help illustrate this point. I am a white, middle-class male who grew up in a suburb. I had just received my undergraduate degree in Administration of Justice and Sociology when I began working full time as a correctional officer in a maximum/medium security prison in 1980. The textbooks that I read in no way prepared me for the racial dynamic that I encountered in the criminal justice system.

At the South Carolina prison where I worked, approximately 60 percent of the employees were African American, as were my two immediate supervisors and the chief correctional officer. Approximately 80 percent of the inmates were African American. Racial disparities and racial tensions were apparent to everyone. The adjoining minimum-security prison often had a majority of white inmates, as well as a much higher ratio of white officers. The inmates were violently divided along racial lines, and no fight of more than four persons was intra-racial.

The primary question that the chief correctional officer asked me during my job interview was, "What are you going to do when one of these inmates makes a racial slur toward you?" I was dumbfounded. I could not even imagine racial slurs in reference to me. I did not have a race or an ethnicity. I was white; I was normal. My race quickly became very clear to me. When I asked a Black correctional officer about playing basketball with a regular "after work" crowd, I was told, "Sure. We're not like that. We don't mind letting white people play." Everyone talked, joked, and argued about race. When I disagreed with a racial stereotype expressed by a white officer, I was told, "You may not be prejudiced now. I wasn't when I started. But if you stay in this job very long, you will be."

When I went to work in 1981 as a deputy sheriff (still in South Carolina), race relations were much meaner and more dominated by white officers. Race was the primary topic of conversation, and most racial talk consisted of very crude and hateful jokes. Our shift lieutenant and desk sergeant would tell racist jokes in front of the entire squad during roll call, usually associating being African American with being a criminal. My field training officer took me to the side of a river where a nine-year-old African-American boy had drowned. He told the emergency medical team to unzip and open the body bag so that I could see a dead body. When they opened it, my field training officer leaned over to me and whispered in my ear, "Another good nigger." I was absolutely speechless at the time. After a while I began to voice my disagreement with their assessments of people of color. I was quickly ostracized and found myself always riding alone. At one point, I spoke up in the squad room during roll call and told the desk sergeant that his comments were racist; he called me a "communist!" My fellow officers even went so far as to (unsuccessfully) request that the shift lieutenant deny me the opportunity to attend the police academy so that I could be fired. Police officers were required to graduate from the academy within a year of employment, and I was not sent until I had already been working the road for six months (four months solo).

When I left the Sheriff's Department and went to a university police department in Florida I found a much more progressive department. Yet race was still a primary topic of conversation and a continual subject for jokes. It was obvious to me that police officers typically responded differently to African Americans than to whites. With some officers, race was a remarkable predictor in reference to their ticket and arrest decisions. Officers would frequently use "black-dialect" when they wanted to sound ignorant or when they referred to a criminal's conversation. By this time, however, I was much more adamant about opposing racism in policing. On nearly every annual evaluation that I received after my first one, my sergeant wrote that I was "too opinionated." I asked him what that meant and he said that I was "too sensitive about race." I asked him to give me a specific example. He referred to the time that an investigator sergeant walked into the squad room and asked me if I wanted to hear a racist joke. A common tactic of police officers is to announce ahead of time that the joke is racist under the assumption that this admittance makes it okay. I told the sergeant, "No." The sergeant just chuckled and continued telling the joke. At that point I left the squad room. My shift sergeant told me that the investigator was offended by my behavior.

The above experiences took place over fifteen years ago in the South, but the situation is similar for police officers working in an urban police department in the Midwest in the late 1990s. Melissa Barlow interviewed police officers for a research project on the media role in police-community relations. Invariably, officers described situation after situation in which race and racism are central to their day-to-day activities and interactions. When asked if he had expected race to be such a dominant theme in his life as a cop, one white rookie police officer said that although he had expected racial issues to arise from time to time, nothing could have prepared him for the degree to which race and racism permeate every aspect of the job.

The strong grip of Eurocentric bias in criminal justice has long restrained the expansion of knowledge and the development of innovative ideas. What is needed is a more rigorous effort to incorporate previously marginalized voices and perspectives. Multiculturalism produces a more holistic understanding of criminal justice issues. Achieving greater insight into social issues of critical significance is possible only by including multiple views. This process enhances our understanding and stimulates critical thinking and self-reflection.

What Police Do

Moore, Trojanowicz, and Kelling (1988) expressed the white, middle-class perspective on the role of police in U.S. society when they wrote that "[t]he core mission of the police is to control crime. No one disputes this" (p. 1). For most police scholars and for the white, middle-class majority, this view of police officers as "crime fighters" reflects their personal experiences. White, middle-class suburbanites rarely encounter the police in the performance of their duties. When they do interact with police, it is typically because a crime has been committed. Suburban children learn to think of the police officer as their friend and protector, a safe haven from "stranger danger." Because of the relatively rare interaction between police officers and white, middle-class suburbanites, most of these citizens receive the vast majority of their information about crime and the criminal justice system from the media. Media portrayals of police tend to perpetuate a one-dimensional perspective on police as crime fighters.

Even much scholarship on police uncritically incorporates the white, middle-class view of police as crime fighters. For example, in a widely used book on police supervision, Iannone (1994) states that the proper way to evaluate the success of a police department is "by its ability to suppress unlawful activity" (p. 201). Problems in policing are often attributed to a failure, among police and those who control their activities, to adequately embrace and fulfill the crime-fighting role.

No Safe Haven

The personal experiences of racial and ethnic minorities, abused children, immigrants, and battered women who have frequently failed to find a safe haven among the police expose the ethnocentrism of the assumption that the role of police is to fight crime and thus protect the citizenry from harm. Richard Wright (1945) described a scene in his autobiographical novel, *Black Boy*, which provides a different perspective on the role of the police in our society:

> My life now depended upon my finding work, and I was so anxious that I accepted the first offer, a job as a porter in a clothing store selling cheap goods to Negroes on credit. The shop was always crowded with black men and women pawing over cheap suits and dresses. And they paid whatever price the white man asked. The boss, his son, and the clerk treated the Negroes with open contempt, pushing, kicking, or slapping them. No matter how often I witnessed it, I could not get used to it. How can they accept it? I asked myself. I kept on edge, trying to stifle my feelings and never quite succeeding, a prey to guilt and fear because I felt that the boss suspected that I resented what I saw.
>
> One morning, while I was polishing brass out front, the boss and his son drove up in their car. A frightened black woman sat between them. They got out and half dragged and half kicked the woman into the store. White people passed and looked on without expression. A white policeman watched from the corner, twirling his night stick; but he made no move. I watched out of the corner of my eyes, but I never slackened the strokes of my chamois upon the brass. After a moment or two I heard shrill screams coming from the rear of the store; later the woman stumbled out, bleeding, crying, holding her stomach, her clothing torn. When she reached the sidewalk, the policeman met her, grabbed her, accused her of being drunk, called a patrol wagon and carted her away.
>
> When I went to the rear of the store, the boss and his son were washing their hands at the sink. They looked at me and laughed uneasily. The

floor was bloody, strewn with wisps of hair and clothing. My face must have reflected my shock, for the boss slapped me reassuringly on the back.

"Boy, that's what we do to niggers when they don't pay their bills," he said. (p. 157)

What was the "core mission" of the police officer in this event? There is no evidence that he was acting in a deviant manner; rather he was performing what he perceived to be his normal duty. His normal duty, though, was not to protect the Black woman from crime; it was to maintain the social order and to preserve current power and race relations.

More recently, in an autobiography, *Monster*, Kody Scott (a.k.a. Sanyika Shakur) referred to the Los Angeles Police Department as just another gang. According to Scott's (1993) accounts, even the police refer to themselves as a gang identified by their precinct, as in the "Seventy-seventh Street gang." In the following excerpt, Scott described police activities during a "war" between the "Eight Trays" (Scott's gang) and the "Sixties" that are nearly unimaginable to white, middle-class Americans:

Our missions were successful largely because we had logistical help from the LAPD CRASH units. For four nights in a row now, we had been getting helpful hints from "our friends" in blue—as they liked to refer to themselves. "But," they'd quickly add, "we are from the Seventy-seventh Street gang, which just happens to not get along with the Rollin' Sixties.

Ignorant, very eager, and filled with a burning hatred for the "enemy," we ate that shit up. We never realized that the Seventy-seventh Street gang didn't get along with anybody in the New Afrikan community.

"Hey, Monster," a tomato-faced sergeant said, "I tell you them goddamn Sixties are talking about murdering you on sight."

"Oh yeah, who?"

"Peddie, Scoop, Kiki, and a few others. If I were you I'd keep my gun close at hand, 'cause those boys seem mighty serious."

"Yeah, well fuck the Sixties. They know where I'm at."

"Yeah, but do you know where they are? I mean right *now*?"

"Naw, you?"

Then, calling me to the car in a secretive manner he said, "They on Fifty-ninth Street and Third Avenue. All the ones I just mentioned who've been bad-mouthing you. I was telling my partner here that if you were there they'd be scared shitless. If you get your crew and go now, I'll make sure you are clear. But only fifteen minutes. You got that?" he added with a wink and a click of the tongue.

"Yeah, I got it. But how I know you ain't setting me up?"

"If I wanted to put you in jail, Monster, I'd arrest you now for the gun in your waistband."

Surprised, I said, "Righteous," and stepped away from the car.

We mounted up and went over to Fifty-ninth and Third Avenue. Sure enough, there they were. And just as he had said, we encountered no police. (pp. 175–176)

Although even to many police officers across the country this type of police behavior seems unconscionable, Scott's (1993) experiences are no less real than the experiences of white, middle-class, suburban dwellers. His perspective on the role of police based on his personal experience is no less valid than that of mainstream society. Scott simply provides us with a different window through which we may view a side of the police role that many of us are not "privileged" to experience.

Primary Activities

Ironically, even the scientific evidence does not support the claim that the key role of police is to fight crime. Most studies indicate that law enforcement comprises no more than 15 percent of a patrol officer's time. In a thoughtful cross-cultural analysis of police in four different democratic societies, Bayley (1994) calculated this percentage at under 10 percent. Even if the figure is as high as 15 percent, what are the police doing with the other 85 percent of their time—and why do these other duties not define their mission? The answer to the first question is clear. Police spend most of their time "maintaining the social order."

As a white, middle-class, male suburbanite I became a police officer for reasons which are probably like those of other demographically similar officers: to fight injustice and protect the innocent, to be a "crime fighter," and to catch bad guys. However, it did not take long to see that little of my time as a cop was spent enforcing the law. During my first year as a deputy sheriff, I made two arrests, both for "drunk and disorderly" conduct. The first arrestee was a female restaurant patron who had become drunk, was loud and belligerent in a public restaurant, and then refused to leave at my sergeant's request. The second was a person who was trying to take a taxicab home, but had no money on him and was too drunk to remember where he lived. What was I doing? I was maintaining order and keeping the lines of commerce open. These arrests temporarily resolved disruptions in the normal business activities of the day. Most of my "law enforcement" involved taking theft and various damage reports to facilitate the processing of insurance claims.

If the Sheriff's Department was serious about "fighting crime," then it would have developed an entirely different approach to handling our most common calls for assistance from victims of violence—domestic violence. I handled an average of two domestic disturbance calls per shift in my first year as a deputy sheriff. Not only did I make no arrests during this time, I wrote only one report.

This report was written only because the survival of the victim (in this case, a male) was not assured. This particular incident developed because a more senior officer responded to an earlier scene in a federally subsidized housing project. An African-American woman called for assistance because her boyfriend cut her across the thigh with a razor blade. The senior officer refused to provide any assistance and told her to see the magistrate on Monday morning. He never even filed a report. Eventually the victim got frustrated and angry and told the officer to leave. She would take care of the problem herself. Satisfied that his duty was done, the officer left. I received the next call about five hours later. The original suspect, now a victim, had been stabbed twice in the back with a 9-inch butcher knife while he lay sleeping in his bed. When he jumped up, she slashed his face nearly in half. The woman met us with the knife in her hand, explaining that she had taken care of the problem. The man stated that he did not want to press charges. Therefore, after the paramedics transported him, we left the scene of this attempted murder and submitted a short incident report. No arrests, counseling, or further investigation required.

The lack of law enforcement in domestic violence cases was common throughout the state in the early 1980s. I saw cases involving other officers, such as one where the victim had both her arms and several ribs broken and a disfigured face, in which no arrest was made until the victim physically went down to the magistrate's office and filled out a warrant for the suspect's arrest. I saw cases where victims were beaten, cut, shot at, and cracked in the head with a Coke bottle, with no report filed. Why? The deputies were under specific direction from the administration not to make arrests in cases of domestic assault. Because of this policy of inaction, reports were rarely filed. The most common method for settling disputes of all sorts was to tell one of the parties to leave (usually the victim) and to advise the victim that "if you really want to have your husband arrested, you can go to the magistrate on Monday morning and see if he'll issue you a warrant."

This policy was strongly endorsed at the statewide police academy, attended by all police officers. This particular state's legislature refused for many years to pass a spousal rape law and contained an "in-presence" rule for all misdemeanors, including aggravated assault! If it didn't occur in the officer's presence, it didn't occur. Like other police work, these actions, or inactions, also maintained a social order—a patriarchal and repressive social order, one which is particularly hard on people who are poor and thus more susceptible to becoming trapped in abusive relationships. My training officer explained to me his justification for never making arrests or even providing counseling in domestic assault cases in which the parties were African American. He stated, "They're like cats, they have to fight before they can fuck."

Sympathy, compassion, and protection were rarely given to any abused spouse, particularly if that spouse was poor. If the victim was poor and Black, she was even less likely to receive protection from the police. It should also be noted that this sheriff's department was the most prestigious local police department in the state. As deputies, we were the highest paid and the most educated officers in the state, because a four-year degree was required before an employment application would be considered. Also, we were the largest sheriff's department in the state with the most populous county, surrounding the capital city.

My experience is anecdotal, but the available scientific research suggests that my experience may be much more common than most of the public is led to believe by the media and by police themselves. According to Bayley (1994), "the myth of the police" is that the police prevent crime and "if they are given more resources, especially personnel, they will be able to protect communities against crime" (p. 3). Neither increasing nor decreasing the number or ratio of police to citizens, area, or violent crime has a substantial impact on the crime rate. In addition, there is no evidence to demonstrate that the three core strategies of policing (patrolling, rapid response, and investigation) prevent crime. "The plain fact is that police actions cannot be shown to reduce the amount of crime, and the police know it" (Bayley, 1994:9).

Understanding this helps explain the common experience described by Anthony Platt (personal communication, 1995). He said, "If you go to your local police department and ask them what can be done to reduce the crime in your neighborhood, they hand you a pamphlet on Neighborhood Watch." In response to the question of what police do, Bayley (1994) notes that only between seven and ten percent of their time is spent handling requests involving crime. Even less of their time is spent in the battle against violent crime. Most of their time is spent "restoring order and providing general assistance." Rather than invoking the criminal law, officers most commonly use their "intervention authority" (pp. 18–19). According to Bayley, the overarching mission is to be prepared for war. The prime directive of police managers is to have enough officers available on patrol to respond to major disturbances. Although in small ways each police officer is continuously maintaining order in their own area of patrol, the quantity and quality of police responses to citizens' requests and to everyday street crime are secondary to the ability of the police department as a whole to respond in force to primary threats to the social order.

Preserving the Social Order

In a sense, each action by individual police officers, as they exercise their intervention authority, resolve conflicts, and keep open the lines of commerce is part of the larger effort to preserve social order. Thus, if we develop a single definition of the role of police based on what they *do*, as identified by Bayley's (1994) research, as known to police officers, as experienced by white, middle-class suburban dwellers, and as described by Richard Wright (1945) and Kody Scott (1993), *the primary role of the police is to maintain order*. However, as we review the history of police in the United States, we will see that the police do not preserve just any order, but *the* social order, with all its current class, race, and gender power relations. Police departments are the domestic repressive apparatus of the state and are designed to prevent social rebellions that threaten the status quo in relations of power. Moreover, they have played this role throughout U.S. history.

Although it is true that one element of the order-maintenance activities of police is to fight crime, definitive statements by police scholars that the *core* mission of the police is to control crime deny the historical and cultural controversies surrounding this issue. The phrase "controlling crime" masks the most consistent core mission of the police, which is to maintain the status quo. Maintaining the status quo, of course, includes protecting and preserving current power relations in society. Historically, the order maintenance activities of police have largely regulated the activities of particular "problem populations." Therefore, the police do not continue to endure as a vital and growing component of our society because they have failed, but rather because they have been largely successful at their core mission of order maintenance. To understand the role of the police in our society, we must look beyond the rhetoric. We must look at what police do and have done throughout the history of our society. We must also look closely at what they do in all segments of society and how their activities vary depending on the location, time, circumstances, and population.

The Value of Historical Perspective

It is only through a historical examination of police that we can identify the role that they play in our society. The view that the role of the police is to control crime is exposed as inadequate when we examine the historical formation and development of the police institution in the United States. If the primary function of the police is crime control, how can we explain the disproportionate hatred and fear of the police in minority communities? How can we explain the fact that most police activities have little or no effect on the crime rate? How can we explain the massive transformations which have historically occurred in the way that police perform their job, from what police scholars have traditionally described as the Political Era to the Reform Era to the Community-Oriented Era?

We must allow history to inform our understanding of the police, rather than allow our assumptions about the police to distort our historical perspective. We must critically evaluate our assumptions about police to ensure that they are consistent with the historical facts. We must also recognize that the particular role of the police at any precise moment is historically specific. That role varies across time and in different circumstances. Recognizing this leads us away from the assumption that "crime control" is the core mission of the police and toward an understanding of the primary task of police as "social control." Moreover, we find that social control by police has historically focused on particular problem populations, usually distinguished by race and class.

Conclusion

What is needed is a description of the role of municipal police in the United States that can explain not only the lived experiences and observations of white, middle-class citizens, but also the lived experiences of Richard

Wright, Kody Scott, and police officers themselves. It is essential that this description be historical, not because we have changed so much, but because we have changed so little. To explain current police agencies and policies, it is essential to explore their historical transformations and to analyze how and why they have developed as they have. We need to utilize the historical development of police in the United States to bring understanding to the current institutions as they now exist and as they proceed to change. We need to break from the evolutionary assumption that history represents a steady progression from savagery to barbarism to civilization.

Change and innovation do not necessarily mean improvement. Police organizations and strategies are created by human actors with specific intentions, motivations and strategies that are not necessarily, or even typically, altruistic or noble. Police institutions and policies are forged within political, economic, and social contexts. Furthermore, historical analysis of police must confront head-on the impact that class, profit, and race have had on the specific formations of police in the United States. These factors impact every aspect of U.S. life, including the institutions and policies of policing. Chapter 2 explores the formation and development of publicly-funded municipal police agencies and the forces that shaped the role they would play in society.

Notes

[1] We use the terms African American and Black interchangeably; however, during the time when people of African descent were forced into slavery and denied recognition as human beings by the U.S. government, it sounds strange to refer to them as African *Americans*. We also capitalize the term Black to demonstrate respect for their intense and united struggle. At other times in the book we quote terms that are clearly racist, and our intentions are to accurately illustrate the mood and the intent of the language and the speaker.

2 A Historical Analysis of Municipal Policing in the United States

Our historical analysis divides the formation and development of publicly funded municipal police organizations in this country into four distinct periods. The first period, "Preindustrial Policing," includes police organizations that emerged before the formation of large industrial urban areas. "Industrial Policing" describes the formation of municipal police organizations in large cities after the Industrial Revolution between the 1790s and the 1820s. The "Modern Policing" period begins in 1873 and encompasses changes in public police that resulted in the formation of the police agency of modern society. The final period is called "Postmodern Policing" and refers to the most recent innovations in police strategies that began to emerge in the late 1960s.

These phases are marked by distinct and identifiable changes in policing strategies, organization, and technology. However, the transition from one period to another is not abrupt and distinct. Borrowing terms used by Gordon, Edwards, and Reich (1982) to describe long economic cycles, we observe that each period in policing has overlapping stages of "exploration" (during which a new approach is explored and experimented with) and "decay" (during which a particular policing strategy shows signs of failure). Between exploration and decay of a form of policing is a "consolidation" phase, wherein the distinctly new police strategy is institutionalized and becomes prevalent. Although remnants of previous stages can be found in all police agencies, and some agencies can be found that simply do not adopt the new strategy, a dominant strategy for policing in urban America emerged during each of the periods we delineate.

Preindustrial Policing

The very first publicly funded municipal police departments were constructed in Southern cities, and their primary role was to preserve the racist social order and to maintain slavery.

Slave Patrols

Walker (1999) referred to slave patrols as a "distinctly American form of law enforcement" and as the "first modern police forces in this country" (p. 22). According to Genovese (1976), the slave patrols were made up of mostly poor whites who frequently "whipped and terrorized slaves caught without passes after curfew" (p. 22). In the following excerpt, Williams and Murphy (1990) described the extensive power granted these patrols:

> "Slave patrols" had full power and authority to enter any plantation and break open Negro houses or other places where slaves were suspected of keeping arms; to punish runaways or slaves found outside their planta-tions without a pass; to whip any slave who should affront or abuse them in the execution of their duties; and to apprehend and take any slave sus-pected of stealing or other criminal offense, and bring him to the nearest magistrate. Understandably, the actions of such patrols established an indelible impression on both the whites who implemented this system and the blacks who were the brunt of it. (p. 4)

Slave owners and slaves themselves frequently commented on the vicious behavior of slave patrols, including arbitrary brutality and excessive beatings. Some plantation owners actually attempted to protect their slaves from the patrols, while others used the patrols to discipline slaves who resisted their masters. The patrols were very successful in accomplishing their main pur-pose: "they struck terror in the slaves" (Genovese, 1976, p. 618).

As part of a larger effort to control the growing slave population, public offi-cials in Charleston, South Carolina established a mounted daytime patrol in the 1740s. The formation of slave patrols is not a trivial event in history, and their origin in Charleston is not inconsequential. According to Genovese (1976), the most common problem for slave owners was runaways. Without secure borders, the institution of slavery could not long endure (Loewen, 1995). Much like the Berlin Wall for East Germany, defensible boundaries were needed—not to keep people out but to keep them in. Native American slaves at one point made up approximately one-fourth of the slaves in South Carolina. However, the slave owners found it almost impossible to construct a defensible boundary to inhibit runaways because of the vast border with Native American controlled areas.

African slaves also found refuge in the areas controlled by American Indians. According to Loewen (1995), almost every pre-Civil War treaty with the Indians made demands for the return of all runaway slaves. Entirely new tribes, such as the Lumbees in the Carolinas and the Seminoles in Florida, were created through the merging of Native Americans, runaway slaves, and even some Europeans. The Seminole Wars were not about the control of the worthless everglades but about destroying a haven for runaway slaves. The United States demanded the return of all Africans, and the Seminoles refused. To reduce the potential for slaves finding a safe place to escape, whites often shipped Native American slaves to the West Indies while Afri-cans were shipped to American Colonies.

Institutionalizing Slavery

In the following passage, Loewen (1995) described a remarkable trading route that helped to institutionalize the enslavement of Africans, within which Charleston, South Carolina played a pivotal role:

> The center of Native American slavery, like African American slavery, was South Carolina. Its population in 1708 included 3,960 free whites, 4,100 African slaves, 1,400 Indian slaves, and 120 indentured servants, presumably white. These numbers do not reflect the magnitude of Native slavery, however, because they omit the export trade. From Carolina . . . colonists sent Indian slaves (who might escape) to the West Indies (where they could never escape), in exchange for black slaves. Charleston shipped more than 10,000 Natives in chains to the West Indies in one year! (p. 98)

Africans became the primary race to be enslaved in the southern United States, not because they were better equipped to handle the work or because they were more docile, but because they frequently had no sure place to run and, thus, were easier to keep subjugated. Through various wars and treaties, Indian borders were pushed back to make it more difficult for slaves to escape.

When the Dred Scott decision legally denied sanctuary to runaways who escaped to the northern states, thousands of free Blacks went to Canada, Mexico, and Haiti (Loewen, 1995). In fact, one of the primary duties of the Texas Rangers (the first organized state police force, established in 1835) was to retrieve runaways attempting to or succeeding in escape to Mexico (Samora, Bernal, & Peña, 1979). Slavery was never a practice accepted by the enslaved; therefore, a powerful police force was needed to suppress this large population.

The following excerpt from a letter from South Carolina sent in 1720 to London illustrates the fear produced in those who attempt to contain a large number of people with brute force:

> I am now to acquaint you that very lately we have had a very wicked and barbarous plot of the design of the Negroes rising with a design to destroy all the white people in the country and then to take Charles Town in full body but it pleased God it was discovered and many of them taken prisoners and some burnt and some hang'd and some banish'd. (Zinn, 1980, p. 36)

There was a relatively large rebellion in Stono, South Carolina in 1739, shortly before the formation of the Charleston slave patrols. According to Zinn (1980), about eighty slaves participated in this armed revolt. As they marched to the beat of two drums and shouts of "liberty," they broke into warehouses, stole guns, burned buildings, and killed whites. The militia responded and fifty slaves and twenty whites were killed in the ensuing battle. Williams and Murphy (1990) quote an excerpt from the South Carolina legislation that established the slave patrols, and suggest that the primary motivation for the creation of this new form of policing was the fear that the militia was unable to control slave rebellions:

Forasmuch as many late horrible and barbarous massacres have been
actually committed and many more designed, on the white inhabitants of
this Province, by Negro slaves, who are generally prone to such cruel
practices, which makes it highly necessary that constant patrols should be
established. (p. 3)

According to Takaki (1993), the fear of slave insurrection was particularly strong in cities. Whites feared that slaves could more easily congregate
and conspire amongst themselves and with free Blacks who often worked in
the cities. In the cities, African Americans assembled into groups and became
much bolder in their interactions and even confrontations with whites.
"Whites feared free blacks in the towns because they suspected them of foul
play and conspiracy among the slaves" (Hawkins & Thomas, 1991, p. 69).
The structure of work was dramatically different than on the plantations.
"Urban businessmen needed a more skilled and flexible black labor force that
would not accept the harsh discipline and social controls so common on
plantations" (p. 70). With a population that had more slaves than whites, no
city was more threatened by potential revolt than Charleston, South Carolina. According to Zinn (1980), fear of social disorder was so prevalent that
during the American Revolution South Carolina "could hardly fight against
the British, her militia had to be used to keep slaves under control" (p. 76).

First Municipal Police Department

Considering Charleston's critical role in the slave trade, its large slave
population, and the highly unstable nature of a slave economy, it is not surprising that Charleston was the site of the first public municipal police force
in the United States. By 1837, the Charleston Police Department had one
hundred officers, and the primary function of this organization was slave
patrol. The largest item in the Charleston municipal budget was the cost of
police (Williams & Murphy, 1990). Police officers regulated the movements
of slaves and free blacks, checking documents, enforcing slave codes, guard-
ing against slave revolts, and catching runaway slaves. Both for mental peace
and for physical safety, Charleston created a police force whose primary mission was to maintain the social order—that is, to preserve the current relations of power, which were primarily characterized by racial domination.

Even the creation of the new police force did not erase public fear. The
following excerpt was published in a South Carolina newspaper in 1848:

We present that the Negro law is not put into strict execution, and that
the slaves of Charles are not under good regulation, and that they at all
times in the night go about the streets rioting, that they do often gather in
great on the Sabbath day and make riots where it is not in the power of
the small number of watchmen to suppress them, which may without any
precaution prove the utmost consequences to this province. (Hawkins &
Thomas, 1991, p. 70)

Police as Guardians of Status Quo

From their inception in this country, police have played a pivotal role not just in maintaining social order, but also in preserving the status quo—a status quo that was extremely unequal, racist, and unjust. Williams and Murphy (1990) argued that this legacy is a critical element in understanding police history, and for understanding contemporary police.

> The fact that the legal order not only countenanced but sustained slavery, segregation, and discrimination for most of our nation's history—and the fact that the police were bound to uphold that order—set a pattern for police behavior and attitudes toward minority communities that has persisted until the present day. That pattern includes the idea that minorities have fewer civil rights, that the task of the police is to keep them under control, and that the police have little responsibility for protecting them from crime within their communities. (p. 2)

At this early stage in the history of police in the United States, the role of the police appeared in its crudest form—the maintenance of order. When placed in this historical context, the maintenance of order can no longer be viewed as a neutral function for the equal benefit of the general public. As long as that order contains immense inequalities, the maintenance of order is inherently repressive to those on the bottom and enormously beneficial to those at the top. This pattern of policing continued with the emergence of organized municipal police in the North and Midwest, although the problem population in need of control was not African slaves, but free poor immigrants who filled the seacoast cities during the Industrial Revolution.

Industrial Policing

Although slavery, except as a condition of punishment for a crime, was systematically eliminated from the urban areas in the North early in the nineteenth century, these large urban areas had their own "problem populations" with which to contend, namely free Blacks and recent immigrants.

Different Locale, Different Populations to Control

These populations were the by-products of an emerging industrial society whose growth began to stagnate in the 1830s. In the mid-1800s, it was increasingly difficult to escape urban poverty. Society had no organized system of providing for economically marginalized populations.

Surplus populations are an important asset to a capitalist society that relies on keeping labor costs down, for they provide an available pool of labor from which industries can draw during periods of labor disputes, strikes, or even contract negotiations (Adamson, 1984). They are also a critical liability to the economic and political system because they are at the bottom of the social stratification system and therefore receive the least benefit from the social order. If the police are to maintain social peace in a society with such sharp and wide class divisions, their efforts must logically be directed toward these economically surplus populations. When we review this period in history, that is precisely what we observe.

From the 1780s into the 1820s, the United States experienced an industrial revolution with the large-scale introduction of machines and the steam engine into the manufacturing of goods (Wright, 1979). With accelerated growth and the formation of a world market for industrial goods, the rate of profit for industrialists was very high, which in turn led to high levels of investment and production (Mandel, 1978). To produce the products, industrialists needed a large supply of laborers. The growth of competitive capitalism slowly expanded the industrial proletariat, the class of people who sell their labor for a wage (Gordon, Edwards, & Reich, 1982). A massive number of immigrants, often the very poor and destitute, were attracted to the United States to build their lives and livelihoods as wage laborers. In the eighteenth century the merchants, lawyers, and political leaders established night watches to protect property, but they lacked popular support or any kind of efficiency, training, organization, or regular pay.

From the late 1820s until the 1840s, economic growth in the United States stagnated. The three previous decades of unprecedented growth in urban centers had created a host of social problems which the leaders of the young nation were either unable or unwilling to address adequately (Gordon et al., 1982). Serious concerns about the social order arose among political and economic leaders and the public.

This period in U.S. history was rife with signs of decline, unrest, and fear. Rapid population growth (due to continuing high levels of immigration), increasing class distinctions, high levels of mobility, and increasingly impersonal human and work relationships all contributed to widespread feelings of unrest and disorder. But it was not until these elements were combined with a severe economic depression in the world economy that official and organized action was mobilized.

> American cities and towns of the eighteenth and early nineteenth centuries had their problems of crime, vice, and disorder, and some men complained strongly about the extent of prostitution, brawling, and robbery. Yet few cities felt compelled to make substantial changes in the traditional pattern of nightwatch and unsalaried police officers before the 1830s. (Richardson, 1974, p. 19)

In the context of a declining economy, an important element of concern about social disorder was fear of and anger toward the most recent wave of immigrants.

The "Dangerous" Classes

The fear and hatred of poor immigrants was accompanied by the popular opinion that these "dangerous classes" lacked the proper level of discipline and thus required control. The establishment of an organized police force closely paralleled the influx of immigrants and fears of social disorder. The previously established European immigrants, particularly the Dutch and English who had done well in the early stages of capitalist development, were threatened by waves of new immigrants as industrial jobs became more scarce in the declining economy. The following excerpt from Gurr (1980) illustrates this very real threat and the concern for an orderly society containing "industrious" workers:

> A major consequence of the early stages of industrialization was rising demand for the protection of private property. When only a few benefitted from the wealth . . . property was at risk—the more so since it so often took the form of portable goods and money, which were more readily stolen than the holdings of wealthy rural gentry. The upper middle classes were typically the most ardent advocates of tougher more consistent laws, enforcement, and punishment for property offenses. There was a parallel concern, shaped by the middle classes and the political elite, for regulating the new urban working classes, and especially the unassimilated, unskilled people at the very bottom of the class ladder . . . (There were economic reasons for regulating the activities and movements of these people, since they were a potential source of labor—hence statutes against vagrancy, which have a long European history.) Many of the historical characteristics of criminal codes, police services, and penal systems in western societies derive from the desire of those who devised them to control a dangerous underclass. (pp. 34–35)

This fear of social disorder had very different meanings to different people. To wealthy industrialists, preserving the social order meant preserving a good business climate by maintaining a stable and disciplined workforce, keeping open the avenues of commerce, and increasing the potential for a high rate of return on investments—profits.

The social order was threatened by the escalation of rioting in the 1830s. The riots were generally by large numbers of the unemployed protesting monopolies, the high cost of food, and exorbitant rent.

> In the 1830s an unprecedented and frightening wave of riots swept over urban areas. Philadelphia and Baltimore competed for the dubious title of "mob city." . . . New York experienced three major strikes in 1834 alone. Nor was the problem confined to the east; Cincinnati, St. Louis, and Chicago had their own riots. To many Americans, the survival of the new nation was at stake. In 1838 Abraham Lincoln warned about the "increasing disregard for law which pervades this country. (Walker, 1980, p. 57)

The mob violence centered around recent immigrants. Either they were the object of attack, or they were participants. Boston's Broad Street Riot demonstrates the centrality of immigrants to social disorder:

> [The riot] broke out when some volunteer firemen, returning from an alarm, clashed with an Irish funeral procession. While the Irish had at first the advantage of numbers, more fire companies were summoned, and they were followed by others with grievances against the immigrants.

It was a Sunday so few men were at work, and residents of the Irish tene-
ments all along the street, were driven out and beaten by a mob eventually estimated at fifteen thousand, more than one-sixth of the city's
population. It was nearly two hours before Mayor Samuel Eliot was able
to get help from a cavalry regiment of militia and restore order at the
head of eight hundred horsemen. (Lane, 1971, p. 33)

After 1830, immigration jumped substantially, which made the dangerous underclass more numerous, more identifiable, more mysterious and,
therefore, more frightening (Richardson, 1974). Private security companies
were formed to insure the safe transportation of gold, money, and other valu-
ables (Lipson, 1975). The earliest forms of police were primarily private and
hired by industries, but a movement began toward the development of a more
public, efficient, and organized police system.

"Respectable" citizens grew increasingly intolerant of crime as they
demanded more effective and less corrupt police forces that could control
unseemly behavior in public places.

The chaos and disorder of a changing America evoked demands for more
effective social control. The crisis was mostly in the growing cities. . . .
The urban ethos demanded order and tranquility, and these demands led
to the creation of the modern-style police. (Walker, 1980, p. 59)

The Public Salaried Police

Of particular concern was that the earlier watch systems were unable to
suppress the riots, demonstrations, and strikes that became frighteningly frequent during the 1830s without the aid of the militia. The industrial police,
along with a number of private police agencies such as the Coal Police, the
Railroad Police, and company town police agencies hired by specific industrialists, were used against Irish and German immigrants in the urban seacoast
slums to break strikes (and would continue this role into the 1870s) and to
suppress hunger riots. "They also enforced anti-immigrant ordinances on
liquor, gambling, and Sunday closing" (Platt et al., 1982, p. 22). Many state
legislatures passed laws to regulate drinking habits, particularly targeted
against the poor. For example, in 1838 Massachusetts made it illegal to sell
alcohol in any amount less than fifteen gallons (Richardson, 1974).

The exact dates are subject to debate, but a general period is clear. Richardson (1980) locates the creation of the public salaried police department
between 1820 and the 1840s. Philadelphia created a modern-style police
department between 1833 and 1854 (Walker, 1980). The culmination of the
movement toward public municipal police was the development of the first
uniformed day and night watch unified into one unit of the New York Police
Department in 1845. Platt et al. (1982) noted that "[t]he bureaucratically
organized and partially trained police forces, first established in New York in
1845, differed from their predecessors primarily in their great size, higher
level of armament, and other institutional forms" (p. 23).

The primary role of these newly developed policing agencies was to maintain *the* social order, including social stratification as it existed at the time of their formation. The greatest perceived threats to that social order were labelled the dangerous classes—those who derived the least benefit from the current social order.

The Intersection of Race and Class

These agencies also played a critical role in maintaining the stratification of society along racial lines by regulating and suppressing the activities of free Blacks living in urban areas. It should not be assumed that because slavery was eliminated in the North that African Americans were treated as equals in the various forms of criminal justice:

> In 1830 Alexis de Tocqueville toured the United States to study prison reform. Unfamiliar with American norms, he was surprised to discover that there was more overt hostility and hatred toward blacks in the North, where slavery did not exist, than in the South, where it did. (Williams & Murphy, 1990, p. 5)

The rights of Blacks were only somewhat less restricted in so-called "Free States":

> Every new State admitted to the Union after 1819 restricted voting to whites. Only five States—Massachusetts, Rhode Island, Maine, New Hampshire, and Vermont—provided equal voting rights for black and white males. Illinois, Ohio, Indiana, Iowa, and California prohibited black testimony in court if whites were a party to the proceeding, and Oregon forbade Negroes to hold real estate, make contracts, or maintain lawsuits. Massachusetts banned intermarriage for whites with blacks and enforced segregation in hotels, restaurants, theaters, and transportation. (Williams & Murphy, 1990, p. 5)

Police, of course, were responsible for enforcing these racist "Jim Crow" laws, which actually began in the North and were transported to the South with the abolition of slavery. The municipal police departments that emerged in the industrial North played an important role in maintaining the status quo in relations of power by controlling the perceived dangerous classes.

Throughout the 1830s, vigilante actions against the anti-slavery movement occurred in Boston, Cincinnati, Philadelphia, and other cities (Walker, 1980). Abolitionists suffered verbal and physical abuse in northern cities resulting in a number of race riots in the mid-1830s. The conflict illustrated the intersection of race and class relations in urban industrial centers.

> Philadelphia, the "City of Brotherly Love," experienced severe anti-Negro riots in 1838 and 1842. . . . Baltimore experienced a total of nine riots, largely race-related, between 1834 and the creation of its new police in 1857. In a desperate attempt to cope with the social disorder brought about by this conflict, America's major cities resorted to the creation of police departments. (Williams & Murphy, 1990, p. 4)

Specifically Tailored Social Control

"Preindustrial Policing" and "Industrial Policing" were two distinctly different forms of municipal policing operating in the United States during the first half of the nineteenth century. The slave patrols in the South served an important social control function that helped to preserve their particular political economy—a feudal slave economy. The experimental phase of the slave patrols took place during the Colonial Era and moved toward consolidation by the early 1800s and continued to operate until after the Civil War. Industrial policing primarily developed in the large cities of the North and Midwest to preserve the political economy of competitive capitalism. Industrial policing went through an experimental stage between the 1820s and 1840s, and efforts were consolidated by the 1850s. Both systems of policing were dominant within their particular political economic system and both worked to protect property and facilitate the accumulation of wealth and benefits enjoyed primarily by the upper class.

The South eventually adopted industrial styles of policing after the Civil War, but they often operated in ways that were reminiscent of the slave patrols. During Reconstruction, Northern occupation of Southern cities led to the formation of the type of Industrial Police agencies that existed in the North. The "problem population" of southern cities was comprised of the large numbers of recently freed African Americans, soon transformed into a multitude of severely poor and unemployed. According to Adamson (1983), "Crime control in the antebellum South was subordinated to race control. With the abolition of slavery, alternative forms of race control had to be found, and race control naturally became a major aim in crime control" (p. 558).

Even the Freeman's Bureau, which was organized by abolitionists who were dedicated to helping Blacks obtain full civil and political rights, "emphasized that the transient black population needed discipline and control" (Adamson, 1983, p. 559). A series of state and local laws were passed throughout the South, often referred to as the Black Codes, that essentially restricted African Americans to being propertyless rural labor. The few political and legal rights that were promised by the radical Republicans were either not forthcoming or were meaningless given the virtually universal economic destitution shared by newly freed slaves.

Through both formal and informal racial discrimination, African Americans were either systematically forced into becoming sharecroppers or convict laborers. Blacks who refused to become sharecroppers were relegated to living in severe poverty and in debt to the landowner. They could be arrested simply for having "no visible means for support" and then sentenced to work as free labor at the same plantation (p. 559). Even freedom of movement was essentially eliminated by the many restrictions in the codes. The role of the Industrial Police forces that emerged in the South was to enforce these laws and to preserve the severely racist social order.

Whites in the North were very apprehensive about the tremendous flood of freed slaves into northern urban areas (Hawkins & Thomas, 1991). Northern police supported many racist legal codes and social norms, although they were somewhat less notorious than the ones in the South. As African Americans moved into Northern cities they were "relegated to the worst jobs and housing along the red light districts teeming with vice and crime" (p. 72). Relentless poverty and racial oppression pushed many of the newly freed African Americans into crime and vice, which were then attributed to the innate character of Black people rather than to the horrible social conditions. Many government officials and police departments used crime by Blacks as an excuse to create racist legal codes and to harass, arrest, and jail African Americans at a much higher rate than whites. The Industrial Police of the North thus systematically preserved their own racist society.

Resisting Supervision

The initial move to create a policed society was quite a remarkable innovation and should not be viewed as an automatic or necessary response to the historical conditions. The establishment of these police institutions occurred only after intense ideological struggle. Silver (1967) noted the revolutionary nature of this innovation:

> The policed society is unique in that central power exercises potentially violent supervision over the population by bureaucratic means widely diffused throughout civil society in small and discretionary operations that are capable of rapid concentration. (p. 8)

As Richardson (1974) explained, the decision to establish a New York City police agency was controversial and succeeded only because of fear of riots:

> These events, plus the existence of a model in the London Metropolitan Police, encouraged the formation of organized police forces whose primary job would be to control riot and disorder. The old opposition to the police as an instrument of despotism did not give way easily, and the organization of police forces proceeded hesitantly and fitfully. (p. 22)

There was definite resistance that continued for some time, even among the wealthy elite, but the benefits of having a legitimate bureaucratic and apparently neutral group enforcing the class-biased laws eventually became obvious to at least a majority of those influential enough to affect the outcome.

The connection between the London Metropolitan Police Department and the New York Police Department is often greatly exaggerated in police textbooks. The police institution, as it developed in the United States, is often presented as if it were a logical and inevitable adoption of the police system that first emerged in England. Such presentations often ignore the tremendous differences that existed between the United States and England. They also have a tendency to separate police from the conditions of their formation, which leaves us with an evolutionary perspective, void of analysis and explanation.

Opportune Conditions

The police suppressed strikes and regulated the lower classes in England, but they did not face the same diversity of languages, cultures, and races. The extremes of racism and slavery were fundamental to U.S. society. The police became *the* symbol of social control, as authority could not come from long held traditions or class position. Authority and legitimacy were based on economic, political, and physical force.

The differences between the New York and London Police were fairly pronounced. The New York police were much more decentralized and responsive to the community. Unlike the London police department, which was a highly centralized agency of the national government, the New York police force was decentralized and administered at the neighborhood and ward levels. While the London police officials were highly professional in that they were chosen for their ability to manage a police force, the New York police were administered by amateurs with little police experience (Miller, 1977).

A major motivation behind making the police responsive to the community was to secure votes for the local politicians who controlled the police. Police jobs were handed out as political favors, and the officers retained their jobs as long as they were able to get the "right" votes from the people in their ward. Beginning with the hiring process, corruption was an integral part of policing, just as it was for entire municipal governments. Community responsiveness, political favors, and corruption were interconnected. Sir Robert Peel and the London police department abhorred this type of political influence as well as the inherent intimacy that developed between the police officer and the people being policed. In the United States, however, this intimacy was not only accepted, it was strongly encouraged.

The vast diversity and large immigrant population, along with the desire to win votes from the immigrant populations, led to even greater intimacy between the police and public. In order to achieve greater legitimacy and thus enhance social control, police officers were often recruited directly from the neighborhoods that they policed. This familiarity made it easier for police officers to regulate the recreational activities of the recent immigrants, but at times it also made them somewhat sympathetic and more easily corrupted, which was precisely why Sir Robert Peel felt that police must remain professionally and socially detached from those whom they police.

Immediately following the Civil War, local politics in most large northern municipalities and southern county governments were dominated by political machines ruled by powerful bosses (Ostrom, Bish, & Ostrom, 1988). The formation of political machines in the South was largely an effort to maintain white supremacy as African slaves were set free and granted citizenship. The political machines adopted a patronage system whereby government officials, political candidates, and even law enforcement officers were carefully chosen by white Democrats. Under Reconstruction, the Republican party elected a number of African Americans, but through political corruption and terrorism the white Democrats regained complete domination of southern politics by 1877 (Bennett, 1993; Katz, 1995; Loewen, 1995).

In contrast, the development of northern political machines was a result of the complexities of providing municipal services and utilities in an environment filled with high levels of urbanization, industrialization, and technological innovations (Ostrom et al., 1988). These technological and social changes in the political economy not only made it highly profitable for a corrupt political organization to secure complete control over government contracts and utilities, they made it technically possible for the political machines to dominate the process. In his study of the Chicago Police Department between 1890 and 1925, Haller (1976) provided a vivid illustration of the critical role that the police played in supporting the political machines, as well as the impact that the machines had on the organization and operation of the police. The primary task of the police officer on the beat was to ensure that the dominant political party secured the votes needed to stay in power. As opposed to controlling crime, police spent most of their time providing various services to loyal supporters, maintaining a reasonable level of social order necessary for the city and local businesses to operate smoothly, and seeking out every opportunity available to them to make money. The police, as well as prosecutors, judges, and other government officials, were appointed for their political patronage and they maintained their jobs by keeping their benefactors in power. At the same time, they personally participated in highly corrupt money-making ventures to benefit themselves financially (Haller, 1976).

The perception of "dangerous classes" consisting of the urban poor, recent immigrants, and free Blacks contributed to widespread use of curbside justice and police violence. Miller's (1977) analysis of the New York and London Police Departments determined that the amount of discretion was another major difference between the agencies that contributed to both corruption and brutality. In New York the police officers were granted much more discretion than in London, allowing the officers in the United States greater freedom to handle legal and extra-legal issues informally. This informality offered the opportunity to bargain with the criminal and to exercise immediate "justice." The police in the United States were also given greater authority to use violence, including the use of firearms and other weapons. Platt et al. (1982) argue that this wide discretion was granted to the police precisely so that they could more creatively and selectively enforce regulations against the so-called dangerous classes.

Another important characteristic of nineteenth century policing in the United States is that private police agencies dominated the social control function until the late nineteenth century. Harring (1983) observed that the public police agencies remained relatively small, fragmented, inefficient, and, most importantly, unreliable. Sometimes the intimacy between the police and the public, as well as their loyalty to political machines, made them unpredictable during periods of intense poverty and labor strife. With private police, industrial capitalists could ensure their biased support to break the power of labor and to maintain the policing agency's commitment to the accumulation of capital (Spitzer, 1981). Private police were a much more profitable investment until the late nineteenth century when Industrial Policing began to show signs of decay. Spitzer and Scull (1977) referred to the loss of the ability to guarantee "the kind of stable, predictable, orderly environment that alone permits sophisticated forms of markets to flourish" (p. 276). Between 1875 and 1900, a new form of public policing was developed to take over the role of preserving the social order.

Modern Policing

The small public and private organizations that emerged during the period of Industrial Policing were unable to preserve the social order in the late nineteenth century, particularly during the 1870s. Beginning with the devastating depression of 1873, social unrest and discontent spread throughout the cities of the United States. With many industries introducing new, labor-saving technologies, millions were left unemployed. "Public relief was usually nonexistent, and private charity either insufficient or offered only on the most demeaning terms" (Dubofsky, 1975, p. 20).

In New York, between 1873 and 1879 demonstrations by the unemployed often drew ten to fifteen thousand people who had to be dispersed by mounted police (Piven & Cloward, 1971). During this same period in Chicago, "mass meetings of unemployed, organized by anarchists under the slogan, 'Bread and Blood,' culminated in a march of 20,000 on the city council" (pp. 43–44). Dubofsky (1975) identified 1877 as the most violent year in the late nineteenth century. The major threat to the social order in the United States in the late nineteenth century was the class warfare that ensued between industrialists and workers. This time period represents a critical crossroads for social stability, the labor movement, capitalism, government, and the police.

Targets of Violence

From 1865 to 1897 some of the most violent industrial conflicts in U.S. history took place. "The ability of the powerful few to dominate the society left the masses frustrated" (Dubofsky, 1975, p. 31). Strikes, lockouts, and worker rebellions were commonplace throughout this period. Class struggle grew in scope and intensity largely due to the fact that workers had become powerful enough to pose a real threat to the status quo. Police departments in every major city were on the front lines of the struggle because they were charged with maintaining social order.

Much of the violence on the part of workers was directed at the destruction of the factory, which was viewed as the cause of unemployment and job insecurity. However, it was often the most recent wave of immigrants who were blamed for the violence and social unrest during this period. "The American ruling class perceived newer immigrants as particularly prone to violence" (Dubofsky, 1975, p. 8). Business owners often used African Americans and recent immigrants as scabs to break union resistance and then blamed these same people for causing unemployment among union workers.

While the factory symbolized the greed and power of the owners, the fury of the working class also found other targets. According to Harring (1983),

> Studies in late-nineteenth-century labor history have shown that the working class was highly class conscious, and there can be no question that the bourgeoisie were acutely aware of their social position and of what was required to defend it. (p. 7)

Workers had become angry and afraid of the intense competition for jobs brought about by the economic depression of the 1870s. Many in the labor movement began suggesting that poor people, social radicals, African Americans, and recent immigrants were instigating the violence and economic insecurity of the time.

The Workingmen's Party had been formed in San Francisco in 1877 to organize "poor and laboring men" to fight against big business, monopolies, and the railroads (Morgan, 1982: 33). However, they clearly excluded Chinese laborers. The Workingmen's Party blamed the Chinese for poor economic conditions and fought hard for exclusionary laws and other anti-Chinese legislation. Some of this legislation made it illegal for Chinese Americans, along with many other Asian Americans, to live in certain areas and to work at certain jobs. Oregon lawmakers, for example, made it illegal for Chinese people to move to their state.

Most significantly, a common recreational activity of the Chinese, opium smoking, was made illegal while all other forms of opium use remained legal (Liyama, Nishi, & Johnson, 1976, p. 10). Labor leader Samuel Gompers opposed the hiring of non-union Chinese workers. He used their opium smoking as a means to demonize the Chinese. "There are hundreds, aye, thousands, of our American girls and boys who have acquired this deathly habit and are doomed, hopelessly doomed, beyond the shadow of redemption" (p. 10). The organized assault on Chinese laborers by Gompers has been characterized as "a stroke of brilliance" (Latimer & Goldberg, 1981, p. 207). He excluded the Chinese from labor membership and then condemned their non-union scabbing.

When the American Federation of Labor (AFL) was officially chartered in 1886, the delegates called for the immediate expulsion of all Chinese from America. Gompers accused Chinese laundries of being filled with "white orphans and kidnap victims, tiny lost souls forced to yield up their virgin bodies to their maniacal yellow captors" (Latimer & Goldberg, 1981, p. 212). Gompers even convinced California cigar factory owners to place on each box the original union label, declaring "White Labor." This label went on to specifically state that the factory which produced this product has committed itself to "neither buy nor sell *Chinese made cigars*" (p. 207).

Through the criminalization and enforcement of various victimless crimes from vagrancy to opium smoking, an assault was launched against the "dangerous classes." It was the police officer's job to enforce these racist and class biased laws (Walker, 1980). The racism took two forms. Racist laws against the Chinese were enforced, while other laws that would protect them from assault were ignored. When whites raided Chinese camps in Los Angeles, Eureka, Jacoma and Rock Springs, Wyoming in the 1880s, "scores were maimed and lynched" (Latimer & Goldberg, 1981, p. 209). The police did nothing to protect the Chinese.

Possibly the two most significant events in the formation of Modern Policing were the Great Strike of 1877 and the Great Upheaval of 1886. The first signified the decay of Industrial Policing, and the second signaled the success of the social experiment of Modern Policing. Sidney Harring (1983) has argued that "beginning with the 'Great Strike' of 1877 and the 'Great Upheaval' of the mid-1880s, the urban police institution was transformed into an efficient, well-organized, and disciplined system that was capable, for the first time, of asserting a powerful regulating effect on urban life—of *policing* urban society" (p. 27). The "Great Upheaval" of the mid-1880s actually refers to several social upheavals which took place in the 1880s: the 1884 Longshoreman strike in Buffalo, the 1884 street car strikes in Chicago, Columbus, Detroit, and Indianapolis, and Chicago's McCormick Strike and Haymarket riot in 1886. In the following excerpt, Piven and Cloward (1979) describe the Great Strike of 1877 and identify some of the problems that emerged in reference to the ability of Industrial Policing agencies to maintain social order:

> In 1877, when four years of severe depression had led to sharp wage cuts and left perhaps one million industrial workers unemployed, a strike on the Pennsylvania and Baltimore and Ohio railroads led to riots that swept through a dozen major rail centers, escalating to open conflict between workers and troops. When local police and state militia were unable to handle the disturbances—in Pittsburgh, for example, police and militia were openly sympathetic with the mob that was burning railroad property to the ground—3,000 federal troops were rushed from city to city under the direction of the War Department. Order was finally restored, leaving twenty-six dead in Pittsburgh, where the mob openly resisted; thirteen dead and more than one hundred wounded in Chicago. . . . Property damage reached about $5 million. (p. 103)

Most industrialists continued to use citizens organized into militia to put down strikes. The civilian militia were very prone to violence and often became more riotous than the strikers. The inefficiency of these militias moved industrialists to hire private police (such as Pinkertons) whose brutal forms of repression often inflamed the workers to even greater resistance and violence. In many places, such as Pennsylvania, they were given full police powers, like the "coal police" or "iron police." More often they were deputized for guard duty or for the duration of a strike (Platt et al., 1982).

These strategies proved insufficient in putting down the Great Strike of

1877. Eventually the U.S. military had to be called in to maintain domestic order. Police departments from the era of Industrial Policing lacked the technology, organization, and sheer numbers to handle such large disputes effectively. In addition, their familiarity with the people in the community and their extremely informal and personal approach to law enforcement sometimes led the officers to ignore certain laws as they became sympathetic with the struggle for better pay, living conditions, and job security. According to Harring (1983), it was during the 1877 strike that the industrialists first began to recognize the need for a better disciplined, more efficient, and better organized police force. The social experiment often referred to as the professionalization of police (Walker, 1980; Kelling & Moore, 1988), took place in the major cities in the United States, particularly in the North and Midwest. Harring (1983) noted that, in contrast to the failure of local police during the Great Strike of 1877, many reformers interpreted the relative success of local police agencies in maintaining order during the Great Upheaval of the mid-1880s an indication of the value of the changes they were making. Modern policing was still in an embryonic form, but its improved ability to handle the strikes and riots of the 1880s without the use of the military helped to cement the municipal police as the major instrument of social control in urban areas. Because of a variety of organizational, administrative, and technological changes, modern police departments responded to the threat of social disorder with a stronger, more unified, and more effective force of officers than the industrial police system. In sum, the revolutionary transformation in the structure, design, and technique of urban police to the modern, professional style was in part due to the failure of police to maintain order during the Great Strike of 1877. The successes attributed to police professionalism, as indicated by increases in technology, discipline, and the size of police departments during the Great Upheaval of the mid-1880s, helped to solidify the transformation and to establish municipal police as the first line of defense for the social order.

Revolutionary Reorganization

One aspect of this radical transformation in the nature of policing included a move from the use of private police to the use of public police as the dominant social control instrument for breaking strikes, suppressing riots, suppressing the dangerous classes, regulating the activities of the poor working class, and protecting property. The transition from the use of private police to the use of public police was not smooth and linear, but rather took place in spurts. The first sign of this was in the 1830s and 1840s, but the transition was completed in the last three decades of the nineteenth century. According to Spitzer (1981), "[s]ocialized policing did not spring full-blown from the head of the capitalist class; it evolved dialectically through several imperfect and at least partially 'privatized' forms" (p. 331).

The expansion of the municipal police was part and parcel of an increase in an array of services provided by municipal governments. Industrialists had a vested interest in socializing the costs of reproducing the working class. This meant spreading the expense of education, training, housing, health and welfare, and the maintenance of the social order among a large number of people. In democratic countries, socialization is accomplished by shifting these costs from individual industrialists to governments through taxation. In other words, instead of a single mine owner in a company town building schools, training labor, and providing housing, sewage, water, and police protection, the workers themselves as well as other businesses are taxed to provide the funds to do these things.

The Shield of Legitimacy

A critical factor that helped convince powerful people that a strong municipal police department was superior to private police agencies, local militias, and even the military was the issue of legitimacy. For policing in a democratic society to be effective, it must be considered legitimate by the vast majority of the people. That is, the police must be seen as having the right to exercise force, because to do so represents the best interests of society in general. If a police agency does not have legitimacy, then it must operate by the use of brute force. In such a case, the society is no longer a democracy; rather, it is an authoritarian police state. The private police agencies that worked directly for industrialists, business owners, railroads, wealthy citizens, or mining, lumbering, and steel companies did not have legitimacy—particularly in the eyes of the workers in these organizations. Therefore, the private police had to rely heavily on brute force to obtain respect, discipline, and order. Their efficiency and effectiveness declined as more people resisted their efforts.

As people rebelled against this blatant repression by property owners, the severe brutality of private police often triggered more violence and destruction of property than the private police prevented. Spitzer (1981) described this situation in the following excerpt:

> Once it became apparent that the policing of workers' lives and the repression of worker organizations might give lead to a "crisis of legitimacy" if it continued to be carried out under the personal authority of individual capitalists . . ., and that this repression would have to become more and more "public" as the boundaries between capitalist enclaves and the rest of society began to dissolve, there were important political and ideological, as well as economic incentives to transfer the responsibility for this policing to the "public authorities." (pp. 331–332)

The attempt by Franklin B. Gowen, president of Reading Railroad, to break the Workingmen's Benevolent Association (WBA) strike provides one example of why this shift to public police took place. Gowen realized that the defense of law and order made a better public platform than anti-unionism. "Most industrialists . . . learned that opposition to violence and defense of law and order could be turned to their own advantage" (Dubofsky, 1975, pp. 38–39). Gowen only had to demand that the streets be kept clear and property not be damaged to set the "neutral" police in a frontal attack against the strikers. Although they were doing essentially the same job as private police had done previously, the public police were able to obtain legitimacy. The government in a democracy is defined as a neutral entity working for the best interest of "the people"; legitimacy was a by-product of that definition. Thus, the professionalization of police can be seen as a response to declining profits, a crisis of legitimacy in policing, and the threat of a social revolution.

Legitimacy was also sought by adopting rationalized formal structures as the basis on which to construct police departments, as well as entire municipal governments. Legitimacy was achieved in this process because widespread faith in theories of modernity during the first half of the twentieth century assumed that the rational formal structure was "the most effective way to coordinate and control the complex relational networks involved in modern technical and work activities" (Meyer & Rowan, 1977, p. 342). Police reformers who sought to retain, strengthen, or expand the role of police recognized that, in a rational-legal society such as the United States, adopting this modern model of efficiency operating under the rational rule of law would help police organizations gain legitimacy, stability, and resources (Walker, 1977).

In the twentieth century, modern U. S. society became filled with rationalized bureaucracies as formal organizations grew more common and more elaborate (Meyer & Rowan, 1977). As police leadership worked to achieve professionalization and modernization, police departments grew more rationalized, impersonal, and institutionalized. Discretion was restricted as the influence of individual police was reduced and the social purposes of the organization were represented as technical rather than social in nature (Walker, 1977). Therefore, the historical development of the large bureaucratically organized police department can in part be attributed to a larger movement by government officials to obtain legitimacy for their agencies by adopting the rational-legal formal structure which placed more emphasis on impersonal rules, laws, and discipline, than on individuals.

For many social reformers, the most important impact of this application of a rational-legal model to the operation of political organizations was that it would weaken the power and influence of political bosses and break apart the political machines (Ostrom et al., 1988). The desire of many participants in the Progressive Reform Movement was to dismantle the corrupt political machines that dominated local politics in the big cities (Ostrom et al., 1988). These reform efforts were often strongly supported by industrialists and opposition party members (usually native-born, Protestant, white Europeans), because the political machines were typically built on the support of poor, working class Catholic immigrants. Many industrialists worried about the loyalty of police officers and government officials in the case of massive strikes and felt more comfortable relying on legislators and the rule of law, which they could more readily influence. The police were a primary target of reform, partially because they were seen as the enforcement arm of the political machine.

According to Walker (1984), the police were not simply controlled by the political machine, they played an essential role in its survival. The police were "the means by which certain groups and individuals were able to corrupt the political process. These errands included open electioneering, rounding up the loyal voters, and harassing the opponents" (p. 85). Therefore, as social reformers sought to challenge the rule of the political bosses, the police became an obvious target for reform. Numerous changes were eventually implemented in most major cities to weaken the direct control of police by the political machine or to remove politics from policing. Central to these reforms was requiring police agencies to operate under formal, rational bureaucratic rules and laws. Many of these changes emerged as the dominant characteristics of the modern police department.

Centralization and Bureaucratization

Professionalization entailed a radical reorganization, including greater discipline for police, increased centralization, bureaucratization, a greater division of labor, new technology, and extraordinary increases in the sheer number of officers. Harring (1983) described the transformation that took place in the organization of the police institution:

> The two decades between 1880 and 1900 saw a profound restructuring of departments organizationally: strong downtown chiefs were backed up by strong centralized administrative bureaucracy; definite standards of recruitment and training were applied; highly specialized units were established; standards of professionalism and discipline were enforced. In short, police departments assumed the outline of their current form. (p. 30)

By 1905, most urban police departments had grown from six to ten times their size in 1865. This increase was not due simply to increases in the size of cities. Many police agencies grew to twice the number of officers per capita.

New Technologies

The innovations which characterize the shift to Modern Policing included the introduction of new technologies. The most significant technological developments were designed to make the police department more responsive, capable of responding more quickly and in greater force to potential trouble spots. For example, in 1878 the telephone was applied to police work for the first time in Cincinnati, Ohio. This made it possible for police officers and the central command station to communicate directly and in detail about events occurring on the street. This communication also helped the central command to coordinate the police response.

Probably the most significant technological innovation was the patrol wagon and signal system, which allowed officers to respond quickly to potential riot situations or to the early stages of a strike involving large numbers. The system was set up to allow police to respond much like modern firefighters. A number of officers stayed at the central station in barracks. When a signal came in for help, a large number of officers responded in a horse driven wagon.

Civil Service

Harring (1983) argued that the major innovation in the rights of police officers as employees was the introduction of civil service. Some of the major problems of earlier police departments were high turnover rates, poor working conditions, and political corruption. A movement to solve these problems and to reduce the influence of powerful politicians brought the first civil service protections for police. Two of these movements occurred almost simultaneously in Milwaukee and Brooklyn in 1884. Another move toward the professionalization of police was the first school of instruction, which was established in Buffalo, New York in 1893 (Richardson, 1974). According to Harring (1983):

> [t]here was an unmistakable trend toward increased stability of tenure and decreased day-to-day political control after the 1880s . . . police work became a very attractive occupation. . . . By the 1890s, however, police work featured shorter days, regular days off each month, and attractive pension and benefit systems. (p. 42)

Both the rhetoric of being "professional" and the reality of being more separated from the "people on the beat," and under less direct control of local politicians, reduced the likelihood that individual police officers would falter in the performance of their duty because of sympathy for the poor and unemployed people that live in the community.

The first test for Modern Policing occurred with the Great Upheaval of the mid-1880s. Modern Policing was still in an embryonic form, but it had responded to threats of social upheaval with a strong, unified, and effective force of officers. It handled many of the strikes and riots of the 1880s without the use of the military. During the Great Upheaval, police successes (attributed to the increases in technology, discipline, and size) helped to establish the municipal police as the first line of defense for the social order.

As we have seen in the previous stages of the history of policing in this country, innovations in policing were triggered by the failure of police to effectively fulfill their primary role, the maintenance of *the* social order. The professional model of policing that emerged during the first half of the twentieth century, firmly established "crime-fighting" as the dominant approach to understanding the nature of police work. According to Walker (1980), "by the late 1920s and 1930s, the crime-fighting model of policing moved to the forefront" of police departments throughout the country. Much of its technology, such as the radio, patrol car, airplanes, and psychopathic laboratories, reflected the desire to make the police more efficient.

Throughout the 1920s and 1930s, the police were a popular focus of reform; however, this reform was almost exclusively centered around making the police more efficient and effective. The answer to reforming the police was almost always increased professionalization: greater training, management, technology, discipline, and autonomy from political machines. Even reform efforts which sought to reduce police corruption and brutality viewed professionalism as the answer. This form of policing dominated law enforcement in the major cities of the United States until the mid-1980s. Signs of decay in Modern Policing emerged during confrontations between police and demonstrators supporting various social movements in the 1960s.

Postmodern Policing

As police clashed with demonstrators seeking to change the social order, the "traditional" style of policing came under serious criticism. It was viewed as too repressive or too ineffective, and sometimes both. The criticism came from both the left and the right, from practitioners and academics, from activists and politicians, and from the inner-city poor to middle-class suburbanites to the business community. The police themselves began to recognize the limits of Modern Policing as they started to experiment with new forms of policing.

Just as postmodern theory critiques faith in modernity as a panacea for social ills, these new approaches to policing were often based on a critique of professionalism as a panacea for failures in policing. As police departments began to reject more bureaucracy, more advanced technology, and more efficient management techniques as solutions to the complex problems of policing in a media-dominated age, they transcended Modern Policing and began to construct something entirely new. What has emerged is what we call Postmodern Policing. However, the impetus for and the consequences of this radical change in policing are consistent with each previous historical transition—the preservation of *the* social order.

Turbulent Times

In the 1960s the police came into direct conflict with numerous, and often overlapping, social rebellions that challenged the social order. For example, the civil rights movement exposed inequality and unfairness as it challenged the forms of social control placed upon African Americans. The student movement challenged the "establishment" and its traditional forms of social restraint. Accompanying this rebellion were flagrant use of drugs, changes in sexual mores, and contempt for traditional styles and appearances. Student protests increased with demonstrations to stop the Vietnam War. These challenges often came into direct conflict with the legal system, and the government did not appear to be able to control the situation. Ohlin (1973) suggested that the 1960s were characterized by a "rising tide of public insecurity and fear of crime in the streets" (p. 6). Walker (1980) described the social conditions that helped to create a national crisis of confidence:

> The 1960s was the most turbulent decade in American history. Never before had so many different crises engulfed society simultaneously.

> There was racial polarization, with protest and violence on both sides; militant protest against an unpopular war; three political assassinations; the emergence of a youth counterculture that rejected the values of established society; and the development of both radical and underground sects and a systematic pattern of illegal actions by authorities themselves. (p. 221)

The social disorder of this period produced real fear among the public, as it appeared that family, church, school, and particularly the police were losing their grip on society. As defenders of the social order, and as the most accessible and visible instruments of that social order, the police were an integral part of these social conflicts.

The most violent and disruptive movements of this period were the protests by African Americans stuck in an oppressive white society and the reactionary response of White America.[1] In 1960, many of these protests began with sit-ins which swept across the country. Fifty thousand people participated in at least one demonstration or another in that year, and 3,600 demonstrators spent some time in jail. A wave of civil disobedience took over with sit-ins, freedom riders, etc. Marches in Selma, Alabama resulted in 1,250 arrests in just two days (Piven & Cloward, 1979). Social disorder reached unprecedented heights between 1964 and 1968, as riots engulfed every major city.

Most were sparked by incidents involving the police. The Harlem (1964), San Francisco (1966), and Atlanta (1966) riots and several others were each triggered by the shooting of a black teenager by a white police officer. The riots in Philadelphia (1964), Watts (1965), and Newark (1967) escalated from routine traffic incidents. The Detroit (1967) riot developed after a police raid on an after-hours bar in the ghetto. Walker (1980) described the summer of 1964 as follows:

> The spark that ignited the riots occurred on July 16, 1964, when a white New York police officer shot and killed a black teenager. . . . On July 18th, demonstrators marched on the twenty-eighth precinct headquarters. Police efforts to break up the crowd only aroused the seething passions. Looting and burning erupted that night and lasted for two full days. . . . When the Harlem riot was brought under control disorders broke out across town in the Brooklyn ghetto of Bedford Stuyvesant. When it was all over, the toll included one person dead, more than one hundred injured, almost five hundred persons arrested, and millions of dollars worth of property destroyed. . . . Rochester, New York experienced disorders the day after peace returned in New York City. In the summer of 1964, rioting erupted in Philadelphia, Jersey City, and a few other cities. (p. 223)

The riots continued into 1965 with the Watts riot in Los Angeles, which resulted in twenty-four dead, one thousand injured, and $35 million in property damage. Chicago and San Diego also experienced riots in 1965. In 1966 riots became even more frequent, affecting forty-three cities including Los

Angeles, Chicago, Cleveland, Omaha, Dayton, San Francisco, and Atlanta (Walker, 1980).

Militancy within the Civil Rights movement grew even more pronounced in 1967. The violence of the Watts riot was exceeded in Newark and Detroit:

> Disorders engulfed Newark for five days, leaving twenty-three dead and more than $10 million worth of property destroyed. The Detroit riot a week later lasted nearly a week and resulted in forty-three deaths. Initial accounts reported property damage as high as $500 million, but later reports lowered the total to something in the neighborhood of $90 million. (Walker, 1980, pp. 223–224)

In the aftermath of the Newark and Detroit riots, President Johnson established the National Advisory Commission on Civil Disorders. According to the Commission's investigation, the number one grievance identified by communities was "police practices." In the first nine months of 1967, there were 164 disorders involving "Negroes acting against local symbols of white American society, authority, and property in Negro neighborhoods" (Harris & Wicker, 1988, p. 6). The police were deeply implicated in these disturbances as they came to symbolize "white power, white racism and white oppression" (p. 11). The police were well known for their inappropriate and often violent reactions, which escalated disorder rather than ending it.

The initial police response to civil disorder was confrontation, using physical force to repress activities. When brute force was insufficient for suppressing insurrections, the dominant solution was to strengthen the fundamental elements of Modern Policing—a fallback to the longstanding commitment to the professional model of policing. Authority was centralized, and the chain of command was tightened (Walker, 1980). The 1968 Law Enforcement Assistance Act (LEAA), for example, can be understood as a final massive effort to fortify Modern Policing. According to Platt et al. (1982), the LEAA was "devoted primarily to standardizing and centralizing the police and other criminal justice agencies, and to funding the development of new and increasingly sophisticated police strategies" (p. 7).

Federal Involvement

Taking Modern Policing's commitment to centralization to a new level, the federal government became heavily involved in the activities of the local police. The federal government sought to increase the efficiency and effectiveness of local police by coordinating their activities, enhancing organization and planning, and investing in new technology. "The primary focus was on technology and administrative problems, and the overall thrust was toward reorganizing the police as an effective combat organization" (p. 36).

The ideal police institution in the country became the Los Angeles Police Department with its widespread introduction of new technologies and strategies, such as computers, electronic surveillance, undercover infiltration into militant organizations, new weaponry, advanced training, and the Special Weapons and Tactics Teams (SWAT). Quinney (1973) described this effort by the federal government to salvage Modern Policing:

> Whereas crime control was formerly in the hands of local police, crime control in the 1960s and 1970s became a primary concern of the federal government. Although funds for crime control are allocated to states and local governments, the overall system is designed and dictated by the federal government. (p. 111)

In sum, the initial reaction to the failure of the police to control crime and disorder in the 1960s was to increase its professionalism and militarization. That is, attempts were made to mobilize the police, nearly at a national level, into a better trained, educated, armed, disciplined, specialized, and technologically advanced fighting unit, capable of suppressing any insurrection. However, an undercurrent of resistance to this approach was emerging.

Community Relations

In the title of their book, *The Iron Fist and the Velvet Glove*, Platt et al. (1982) identified the expansion of two distinct forms of policing in the United States. The "Iron Fist," as a commitment to Modern Policing, is designed to create an elite and very "professional" military organization to wage war on crime and disorder through the effective and efficient use of physical force. On the other hand, the "Velvet Glove" approach to policing emerged as many observed that "a key lesson from the riots of the 1960s was that purely repressive or overly mechanical and distant forms of official control were usually counter-productive, tending to aggravate the already volatile nature of the urban poor" (p. 128).

The "community relations programs" which were largely developed beginning in the late 1960s were the initial experiments into a radical revolution in policing that is being consolidated today.

> Because of criticism in the late 1960s that the technical and managerial approach to policing would alienate large sectors of the population, the need for the closer police ties to the community were stressed. . . . Community relations programs are another method to persuade people that the police really do exist to serve them. (Balkan, Berger, & Schmidt, 1980, p. 104)

Speaking at community centers and in schools was one of the first attempts to improve community relations. These programs eventually expanded to include neighborhood storefront offices, ride-along programs, fear reduction programs, police academies for citizens, cultural diversity training, police-community athletic programs, and Drug Abuse Resistance Education (DARE).

For proponents of Modern Policing, the major threat of the police-community relations movement was that it initiated efforts to dismantle the wall between the "professional" police crime fighter and average citizens. The fear was that the police were giving up some of their autonomy and professional status by soliciting citizens for support, assistance, and guidance. According to Walker (1999), these police-community relations programs were largely marginalized from what was considered "real" police work, as they were considered "essentially public realtions rather than a change in basic police operations" (p. 175). As we will see, image management has become the critical characteristic of Postmodern Policing.

Another challenge to the structure and organization of Modern Policing was the effort to decentralize policing. One of the first such efforts following the late 1960s was the strategy called "Team Policing." The fundamental thrust of team policing was to decentralize and despecialize the police so that they could work as a coordinated and relatively self-sufficient neighborhood unit. According to Walker (1999), one goal of team policing was to improve police-community relations by assigning officers to particular neighborhoods for extended periods of time. Largely due to poor planning and limited commitment by the departments, the team policing experiments were not a success. However, the movement to decentralize police decision-making and to localize efforts to confront the problem of crime and disorder was revitalized by a scathing critique of Modern Policing and the formation of a new policing strategy called "problem-oriented policing."

Goldstein (1979; 1990) criticized Modern Policing's preoccupation with efficient management and its commitment to the rational military bureaucracy. He argued that police departments needed to decentralize their efforts, to develop a more fluid management style, and to allow more creativity and innovation among the rank and file. He also critiqued Modern Policing's "professional" approach that distanced the police from the public being policed. Goldstein argued that in order to identify and solve problems in the community it was necessary for the police and the public to become much more connected. This rejection of modern professionalism by Goldstein, however, did not fully usher in Postmodern Policing until it was merged with community policing and its total commitment to image management.

The most significant differences between Modern Policing and community policing are that the philosophy of community policing encourages the scrutiny of the police by the public, enhances the accountability of the police to the public, provides customized police service, and shares the responsibility for resolving the problem of crime with the public (Brown, 1984, August). Part of Trojanowicz and Bucqueroux's (1990) definition of community policing described it as "a new philosophy of policing, based on the concept that police officers and private citizens working together in creative ways can help solve contemporary community problems related to crimes, fear of crime, social and physical disorder, and neighborhood decay" (p. 5).

According to proponents of community policing, involvement of the community in policing is designed to ensure that the police effectively meet the needs of the community. The police now openly admit that they cannot solve crime on their own, and they need the community to help them. If community members are more involved in the crime-fighting process, they will be more supportive and cooperative with police. The idea is to convince the public that the police are in their community to help them. Therefore, to interfere with the police and the performance of their duty is self-defeating and illogical.

The phenomenon called "community policing," which emerged in the 1980s and now dominates the rhetoric of nearly every major police department in the United States, fully integrates image management as an essential component of policing. The logic of community policing is often based on a classic article by Wilson and Kelling (1982) called "Broken Windows: The Police and Neighborhood Safety." In it, the authors argue that image management is not only an important crime prevention tool for the police, but it is essential for communities as well. The basic argument is that if a community presents the image that it is in a crime-ridden state of disrepair and disorder, then the reality will soon match the image. As the analogy goes, if a broken window is left unrepaired, then soon all the windows in the building will be broken. Therefore, working together, the police and the community should aggressively address the signals (i.e. untended property and untended behaviors) that send the message that a community is in a state of disorder.

Wilson and Kelling (1982) go on to suggest that, even if this effort does not really reduce crime, it improves the quality of life among the citizens by reducing their fear of crime. Wilson and Kelling strongly recommend foot patrols as an important police strategy even though they admit that evaluations of this strategy clearly demonstrate that it does not reduce crime. Their reasoning is that foot patrols manufacture an image:

> These findings may be taken as evidence that the skeptics were right—foot patrol has no effect on crime; it merely fools the citizens into thinking that they are safer. But in our view, and in the view of the authors of the Police Foundation [of whom Kelling was one], the citizens of Newark were not fooled at all. They knew what the foot patrol officers were doing, they knew it was different from what motorized officers do, and they knew that having officers walk beats did in fact make their neighborhoods safer. (p. 358)

Based on such logic, community policing blurs image and reality to the point that they are inseparable—distinguishing between the two is unimportant. This approach fits perfectly with the postmodern concept of "hyperreality," where media images and reality are so intertwined that our images become real and reality becomes an image (Schwartz & Friedrichs, 1994). The police become a commodity to sell to the public, much like any other product on the market.

Community policing is image-management policing. Evaluations of community policing often concentrate on the public's image of the police. The most common measurements have involved "soft direct indicators" of the public's perceptions about the police and crime (Bayley, 1994, p. 98). In other words, under the guise of treating the citizen like a customer and being more client-oriented, the police often use evaluations that focus on the public's satisfaction with the police. These measures of the image of crime have become particularly important as most community policing strategies appear to have little effect on the reality of crime. Thus, under the rhetoric of improving the quality of life, Postmodern Policing is rapidly declaring war on the image of crime rather than crime itself. Bayley warns that "police must not be allowed to make performance a 'con game' of appearance management" (p. 98).

Conclusion

Postmodern policing is essentially social control through image control. By convincing the public that they are going to receive a police department that is responsive to their specific needs and that is going to be an advocate for the improvement of the quality of their lives, the police hope to produce a public that will provide them with intelligence information, grant them greater flexibility in the dispensing of curbside justice, and offer less resistance to their efforts to maintain order. In an analysis of a community policing program in San Diego in the 1970s, Balkan et al. (1980) wrote:

> One might expect some impact on crime rates with a program that involves substantial changes in police technique; but perhaps the primary function of COP was not crime control, but social control. Profiling, for example, can be another name for infiltrating and gathering information on leaders and potential movements so that the police can be ready for (and maybe even direct the course of) the next social uprising. (pp. 106–107)

This is precisely what happened in Reno, Nevada in 1992. In preparation for a riot in Reno following the acquittal of the Los Angeles police officers who beat Rodney King, the success of the Reno Police Department's community policing program was that it was able to prevent a social uprising by organizing their own protest march through the streets of Reno with the police chief leading the procession.

Under the surface, the image-management of community policing is a new and potentially powerful social control mechanism. Manning (1991) referred to community policing as a "new tool in the drama of control" (p. 28). Klockars (1991) stated that community policing "is best understood as the latest in a fairly long tradition of circumlocutions whose purpose is to conceal, mystify, and legitimate police distribution of nonnegotiable coercive force" (p. 240). Therefore, the power of community policing is that "it wraps the police in the powerful and unquestionably good images of community, cooperation, and crime prevention. Because it is this type of circumlocution, one cannot take issue with its extremely powerful and unquestionably good aspirations" (p. 257). In other words, community policing evokes powerful positive images that tend to insulate the strategy of social control, and the police operating within that strategy, from critical analysis. Who is against a more responsive police force and stronger communities, greater cooperation between the police and public, and the prevention of crime?

An argument by Balkan, Berger, and Schmidt (1980) in reference to the earlier police-community relations programs is equally relevant to community policing: "the police were interested not in a real transfer of power from the police to the community, but in more effective management of the community and information gathering. Community-police programs glossed over the continuing repression and arrest of people in poor communities" (p. 104). The logic is that a police department that appears to be more responsive to the community can be a more effective agent of social control. In a democratic society, the police are most effective when they do not have to rely on force or the "Iron Fist." They are most effective when the Iron Fist is cloaked in a Velvet Glove. In other words, effective policing in a democracy requires the police to be seen as legitimate in the eyes of the people being policed.

Manning (1991) suggested that community policing is the latest police strategy to secure legitimacy through the manipulation of public opinion. The common thread that links the early police-community relations programs to the adoption of community policing is image management. These programs seek to persuade people who have every reason to believe that they are being repressed by the social order that the police are their friends. But no matter how many town meetings are held, no matter how many baseball cards are handed out, no matter how many "officer friendly" robots appear in inner-city classrooms, the police are mandated to preserve the social order and to maintain the status quo. When they stop doing this one task, then they have transformed into something different—they are no longer "police."

Notes

[1] We use the term "White America" to refer to a nebulous category of citizens in the United States. The term is utilized to refer to the general feelings and perspectives of the majority of white people living in the United States. We recognize the ethnocentrism and the ambiguity of this term, but we believe that its connotation captures something unique.

Part Two
Police-Community
Relations

In order to maintain the social order in a democratic society, it is essential that the police achieve a certain level of legitimacy in the eyes of those being policed. Democratic governments gain their right to rule and their right to suppress certain behaviors from the "rational" ideology that the government's actions are in the best interest of the people being governed. When people believe that the current social order serves their interests, they generally consent to police action. On the other hand, if segments of the population come to believe that the current social order does not serve their interests, they may withdraw their consent for the authority of the government. When this occurs, police agencies, the most visible repressive apparatuses of the state, experience a crisis of legitimacy and find it increasingly difficult to preserve social order.

In the absence of legitimacy, the police must rely on crude physical force to prevent social rebellion. Such actions are not only much more dangerous and less effective than rule by consent, they seriously contradict the concept of democracy. In order for the government to fulfill its first responsibility, the preservation of civil peace, a delicate balance must be maintained between coercion and consent.[1] This is particularly true in a society such as the United States, which is based upon democratic ideals of freedom and consent.

Rule by consent requires that even those who benefit the least from the current social order believe that it is in their best interest to maintain the status quo. This problem is particularly acute in a society with substantial social, economic, and racial inequality. The self-interest of subordinate groups in an unequal society may motivate them to try to change current social and power relations. For this reason, such groups are frequently viewed by those in power as the "dangerous classes" or "problem populations."[2] The social processes that foster consent to the established order are powerful. Even in communities populated almost entirely by the so-called dangerous classes, most residents support the police and the government. However, when social inequalities become especially acute, rebellions against the social order become

49

more likely, particularly in these marginalized communities that do not share in the prosperity of the U.S. political economy.

The police are charged with preserving the social order. This includes suppressing rebellions and protecting current social, economic, and racial inequalities. The police are thus placed in a precarious situation. They must physically confront angry, frustrated, and desperate people who see the police as the source of much of their pain and suffering. The police are often bewildered by such confrontations with hostile citizens or groups and are unable to grasp the magnitude of the problem of legitimacy. As a result, they often initially approach such confrontations with brutality and oppression. However, in the postmodern era of policing, we see a growing movement to construct mechanisms and strategies within police agencies to secure a greater level of legitimacy. These mechanisms and strategies often take the form of image management or public relations designed to increase public support for the police. They may also be genuine efforts by police to apply democratic ideals such as freedom and equality to police-community relations.[3]

For us, community relations encompasses all of these social interactions as they relate to the police. However, as we explore police-community relations, it becomes obvious that the community relations that are particularly problematic are race relations and, in particular, relations with African Americans. The legacy of racism in the United States permeates every social institution, but it often takes its most blatant and violent form in the legal segregation and oppression of racial minorities. Throughout U.S. history, the police have had serious conflicts with racial and ethnic minorities. The most consistent, widespread, and violent confrontations have been with African Americans.

Discussions about the improvement of relations between the police and the public often substitute a variety of terms—inner-city residents, gangs, urban youth, the urban poor, and marginalized groups—for racial minorities. Efforts are made to speak in generic terms so as not to offend, or perhaps in order to diminish the ubiquitous nature of racism in our society. Police officers know what is being said, no matter what rhetoric is used. The police have a problem, and that problem is race. "Police–community relations refers primarily to *relations between the police and racial and ethnic minority communities.* The police have never had the same kinds of conflicts with the white majority community as they have with minorities" (Walker, 1999, p. 212).

The law and its enforcement by police have a long history of racial and cultural conflict within communities primarily populated by racial and ethnic minorities. The racism of U.S. law was blatantly obvious when the United States Constitution granted voting rights only to white male property owners. In the postmodern era, however, explicit references to race in law are often removed. Still, the effects of institutionalized racism in the law and its enforcement continue to present obstacles to racial and ethnic minorities. The most common concerns expressed by racial and ethnic minorities regarding police involve both "underpolicing" and "overpolicing." Throughout U.S. history, and across several racial and ethnic cultures, underpolicing entails the failure of police to protect the lives and property of racial and ethnic minorities. The problem of overpolicing has meant that racial and ethnic minorities have experienced less courtesy, greater scrutiny, and harsher treatment from the police.

According to Walker (1992a), "the major complaints voiced by minorities include: the lack of efficient and equal service; harassment and discourtesy; discriminatory arrests; excessive use of force (physical brutality, unwarranted use of deadly force); and racial discrimination in police recruitment" (p. 813). The investigations following each of the major periods of race rioting in the twentieth century have found evidence to support all of these allegations. Although police actions did not create the social, economic, and racial inequalities of U.S. society, they have the effect of magnifying and sustaining these cleavages (Bittner, 1996, p. 116).

In the following excerpt, Williams and Murphy (1990) explain the most fundamental conflict between African Americans and the police:

> The fact that the legal order not only countenanced but sustained slavery, segregation, and discrimination for most of our Nation's history—and the fact that the police were bound to uphold that order—set a pattern for police behavior and attitudes toward minority communities that has persisted until the present day. That pattern includes the idea that minorities have fewer civil rights, that the task of the police is to keep them under control, and that the police have little responsibility for protecting them from crime within their communities. (p. 2)

This basic contradiction—that the police in our democratic society enforce laws that are clearly undemocratic, biased and repressive—reverberates in a series of contradictions throughout the development of the police. African Americans, Latinos, Asian Americans, and Native Americans rarely enjoy the benefits of the so-called "progressive reforms" that are touted as advances in democratic policing. Two very different "worlds" of policing exist in our society, one for the majority and one for minorities. Members of the majority population often find it difficult to comprehend the deep-seated conflicts between the police and communities of color. The contradiction of democratic rhetoric in a society that is infected with severe economic inequality, racism, and sexism exacerbates contact between the police attempting to preserve the social order and the people who are marginalized from that society.

In Part 2 we challenge the myth of police as champions in the fight against crime and as protectors of the weak and innocent. Chapter 3 explores underpolicing, i.e. the historical failure of police and the U.S. government to protect racial minorities from white violence, violations of their civil rights, and criminal activity. Chapter 4 investigates overpolicing by reviewing the police and government efforts to control racial minorities through the law and its enforcement. Finally, Chapter 5 analyzes efforts by the police to resolve their community-relations problems through image management.

Chapter 5 primarily focuses on the historical development of various police-community relations programs, with a particular focus on sensitivity, race-relations, or cultural diversity awareness training for police officers.

Notes

[1] Hall et al. (1978) argued that while coercion is a necessary aspect of an orderly state, social life functions more smoothly when cohesion is established through popular consent. In cases where coercion becomes necessary, its effectiveness will be enhanced if it has the support of the majority of the population. The required popular consent for the social and political domination of one economic, racial, gendered, or social group can only be gained if certain costs are extracted from that class such that its interests come to look like the interests of all. Thus the liberal democratic state contains the mechanisms for the formal representation of subordinate group interests. The state represents itself as representing the general will of the people as it operates under the rule of law, all of which serves to conceal economic exploitation and discriminatory oppression.

[2] Adamson (1983; 1984) described problem populations as both an asset and liability to the political and economic social order. They often represent the fringe of the working class who provide the cheap manual labor necessary for economic growth and political stability. At the same time, they represent a continuous potential threat to that order because they benefit the least from the continuation of that social order and gain the most from its collapse. As the primary instrument of domestic social control, the police (as well as the entire criminal justice system) are largely focused on regulating the activities of these problem populations (Barlow, 1985; Barlow & Barlow, 1993).

[3] One example of such an effort is the adoption of the Kingian Nonviolence program to policing. Tallahassee (Florida) Police Chief McNeil and several members of his department have implemented a training program that incorporates the strategies of nonviolence as presented in the words and actions of Dr. Martin Luther King, Jr. The people within the department who are pushing for this new strategy are genuinely concerned about producing a police force that is more responsive to the community, less violent in its interactions with the community, and better equipped to produce positive police community relations (J. Scandone, Special Services Division, Tallahassee Police Department, personal communication).

3 Underpolicing

Police have denied equal protection to racial and ethnic minorities in the United States by failing to protect them from violent racist actions by whites, by declining to ensure their basic human rights, and by inadequately responding to problems of crime and neglect in minority communities. Police have historically enforced laws that are today widely regarded as violations of the human rights of racial and ethnic minorities. One may argue that the people who drafted these laws were a product of a specific time in history; however, such arguments are based on the assumption that human rights are relative and cannot be applied across time and place. We reject this assumption. We also believe that the United States, though great in many respects, must admit to its historical atrocities.

White Violence

Before the Civil War, the vast majority of people of African descent in this country were slaves. Therefore, most white violence committed against Africans before the end of slavery occurred on plantations and was officially authorized under various laws and slave codes. However, free Blacks in both the North and the South were frequently victims of white mob violence which police either condoned or ignored. Africans did not have the political clout to command responsive policing because of their small numbers and because they had not been enfranchised with the power to vote. Therefore, they "received virtually none of the benefits of policing that were directed to those with more political clout" (Williams & Murphy, 1990, p. 2).

Even as the North fought the war that would destroy the institution of slavery, free Blacks in the North continued to be victims of white violence. The New York City Draft Riots in 1863 were among the "bloodiest and most vicious lynchings in American history" (Skolnick & Fyfe, 1993, p. 27). In New York, unskilled Irish laborers resented the draft, which wealthy whites could avoid. They resented being pulled into a bloody war that they feared would free thousands of Africans to descend upon New York seeking their jobs (Bennett, 1993). For three days, white mobs roamed the streets attacking Black men, women, and children; so many were murdered that it was virtually impossible to count the bodies. "When caught by rioters, blacks were 'hung up to lampposts, or beaten, jumped on, kicked and struck with iron bars and heavy wooden clubs.' Homes were sacked and residents driven into the streets" (Skolnick & Fyfe, 1993, p. 27). On the third day, federal troops finally restored order.

When the Civil War ended the institution of slavery, African slaves were granted freedom, but they continued to be victimized by racial violence. Whites, particularly in the South, were determined to maintain white supremacy. Immediately following the war, ex-Confederate soldiers frequently attacked freed Blacks as they traveled along the roads. In Kentucky, the ex-Confederates robbed returning Black soldiers after local police forced the freedmen to surrender their guns (Katz, 1995). In 1865 and 1866, five hundred whites were indicted in Texas for murders of Africans. None were convicted. The military commander of the state of Louisiana, General Phillip H. Sheridan, observed that far from protecting Africans from heinous and violent attacks, the police actually participated in the brutal assaults. He described one such riot as follows:

> At least nine-tenths of the casualties were perpetrated by the police and citizens by stabbing and smashing in the heads of many who had already been wounded or killed by policemen . . . it was not just a riot but "an absolute massacre by the police . . ." a murder which the mayor and police . . . perpetrated without the shadow of necessity. (Harris & Wicker, 1988, p. 212)

Radical Reconstruction

In 1867 Republicans in the North began to recognize that the enfranchisement of freed Blacks was going to require the occupation of the South by federal troops. During Radical Reconstruction, the occupation of southern states by the Union army led to constitutions that ensured the right to vote for white and Black men.[1] This enfranchisement created a tremendous shift in political power. South Carolina and Mississippi voter registration records showed 80,000 black voters to 46,000 white voters and 60,000 black voters to 46,000 white voters respectively. The first Reconstruction state legislature in South Carolina included 85 African Americans[2] and 70 whites (Bennett, 1993).

As whites lost their political and legal dominance, they resorted to extra-legal methods of exercising power over Blacks. The Ku Klux Klan was formed and quickly spread throughout the South. Friedman (1993) noted that the Ku Klux Klan "was responsible for killing some four hundred blacks between 1868 and 1872" (p. 190). The Klansmen were night-riders who stopped at nothing to secure white supremacy: "they whipped, burned and raped; they were willing, even eager, to kill" (p. 187). Katz (1995) argued that anti-Black violence was designed "to prevent African Americans from holding office, voting and attending schools" (p. 254). The Klan specifically targeted African American officials, teachers, and successful farmers.

Conservative estimates suggest that thousands of African-American leaders were murdered during Radical Reconstruction. Northern whites who came south to help Blacks to achieve equality and southern whites who supported freedom and civil rights were also killed in this counterrevolution. Numerous examples of white terrorism against African Americans and their allies during Radical Reconstruction have been documented. In 1868, white Democrats killed nine African-American demonstrators marching from Albany to Camilla, Georgia; in the Opelousas Massacre whites killed two to three hundred Blacks at the St. Landry Parish in Louisiana (Bennett, 1993).

In 1869, in order to maintain control of the Tennessee state legislature, white conservatives used assassinations and widespread violence to suppress the black vote. In 1870, the same brutal techniques were used in North Carolina and Georgia to effectively end Reconstruction in their states. During the first six months of 1870, six men were murdered and more than 300 whipped in a single county in South Carolina (Bennett, 1993). Also in 1870, the Klan in Mississippi whipped a Black man for suing a white man; in Alabama they murdered a state legislator for being too influential; and in North Carolina they lynched an African-American leader of the Union League (Friedman, 1993).

When African Americans attempted to defend themselves, local police would disarm them (Katz, 1995). Finally, in 1871 the military arrested and indicted 930 members of the Ku Klux Klan in Mississippi, 1,180 in South Carolina, and 1,849 in North Carolina. President Grant was forced to declare martial law in many South Carolina counties that were under Klan control. In 1874, white Democrats killed more than sixty Blacks and whites during the Coushatta Massacre in Louisiana, and seventy-five Republicans in a massacre at Vicksburg, Mississippi. In 1875, white Democrats regained control of Mississippi after killing several Blacks in Vicksburg, one white and three Blacks in Yazoo City, and 20–30 African Americans in Clinton. The Mississippi State Senator, Charles Caldwell, was killed in broad daylight and his body was "grotesquely turned completely over by the impact of innumerable shots fired at close range" (Bennett, 1993, p. 245). In South Carolina, five Black Republicans were killed in Hamburg, and 2 whites and 39 African-American Republicans were killed in Ellenton in 1876 (Bennett, 1993).

Jim Crow

By 1875, northern whites had lost the will to continue the struggle to ensure the enfranchisement of African Americans, and Radical Reconstruction came to an end with the Compromise of 1877 (Loewen, 1995). The election of Republican presidential candidate Rutherford B. Hayes had to be certified by the vote of both Houses of Congress because of a dispute over electoral votes. The Democrats and the Republicans agreed to a compromise that granted Hayes the Presidency in exchange for "Home" rule for the South, withdrawal of troops, an end to agitation of the race question, and a tactical agreement that the South would be allowed to deal with blacks in its own way" (Bennett, 1993, p. 251).

White Democrats quickly seized power in the South and broke their promise to treat African Americans fairly. Southern Democrats moved to disarm the predominately Black state militia by raiding the homes of African Americans and removing their weapons. Through various methods, African Americans were systematically disenfranchised (Bennett, 1993). Voting was held at secret locations and at secret times. Armed whites and masked riders were stationed on the roads leading to the polls and, at times, actual gun battles ensued. Whites had superior firepower and economic power. General M. W. Gray, a South Carolina leader, stated that "Every Democrat . . . must feel honor bound to control the vote of at least one Negro, by intimidation, purchase, keeping him away or as each individual may determine how he may best accomplish it" (p. 246).

In addition to violent intimidation, most southern states developed various "legal" techniques for denying African Americans the right to vote. Some of these techniques, such as requiring literacy tests, property ownership, and poll taxes, could also have excluded poor whites. The "Grandfather Clause" stated that if a man's ancestors had voted on a selected date before any African Americans could have voted in the South, he would be exempt from the other tests.

The Supreme Court ruled in 1883 that the Civil Rights Act of 1875 was unconstitutional. Southern states began to enact a series of laws which segregated the races. In the following excerpt, Bennett (1993) illustrates the extent of these "Jim Crow" laws:

> Brick by brick, bill by bill, fear by fear, the wall grew taller and taller. The deaf, the dumb and the blind were separated by color. White nurses were forbidden to treat black males. White teachers were forbidden to teach black students. South Carolina made it a crime for black and white cotton mill workers to look out the same window. Florida required "Negro" textbooks and "white" textbooks. Oklahoma required "separate but equal" telephone booths. New Orleans segregated black and white prostitutes. Atlanta provided Jim Crow Bibles for black and white witnesses. (p. 256)

The laws were not just pieces of paper; they were strictly enforced by local police and established a "way of life" and culture in the South that lasted nearly 100 years.

The institutionalization of racism in state law, however, did not eliminate the use of violence by whites against Blacks. "Jim Crow" as a social phenomenon also had the effect of creating a social relationship of discipline, control, punishment, and humiliation between the races. Lynchings became both a material and symbolic threat to those who thought about challenging white domination. In fact, Friedman (1993) referred to the years after 1880 as the "golden age" of the lynch mob because "any threat to the ideology of white supremacy made a black man a candidate for lynching" (p. 191). Some estimates placed the number of people lynched in the United States between 1878 and 1898 at around 10,000. Black-owned businesses were attacked in broad daylight and African Americans were hunted and tortured.

Bennett (1993) likened lynchings to sporting events in the 1880s. They were advertised in newspapers, and crowds of people would arrive on chartered trains. Zangrando (1980) argued that lynching was used as a powerful weapon in the campaign by southern whites to reverse the impact of Reconstruction.

To attempt to appreciate the power and terror of lynchings, it is important to understand that they were primarily "a means to intimidate, degrade, and control black people throughout the southern and border states, from Reconstruction to the mid-twentieth century... men and women were flogged, dismembered, tortured with hot irons, and put to death by rope, flame, and gunshot" (pp. 3–4). The mobs frequently worked themselves into a ferocious frenzy, spending hours tormenting a defenseless victim and then fighting over body parts for souvenirs. A popular activity was to mutilate or remove the victim's sexual organs, particularly those of Black men.

In the following excerpt, Bennett (1993) identifies how pervasive, intrusive, and sadistic this form of social control was:

> Contrary to the generally accepted view, only a small percentage of the 1217 persons lynched between 1890 and 1900 were accused of rape. Others—the overwhelming majority—were charged with the "Crimes" of testifying against whites in court, seeking another job, using offensive language, failing to say "Mister" to whites, disputing the price of blackberries, attempting to vote and accepting the job of postmaster. (p. 271)

In 1898, in an attempt to eliminate any Black federal presence left in the state, the home of an African American federal postmaster was attacked by over 100 whites in Lake City, South Carolina. The Cleveland *Gazette* described the incident as follows:

> The postmaster was the first to reach the door and he fell dead just within the threshold, being shot in several places. The mother had their baby in her arms and reached the door over her husband's body, when a bullet crashed through its skull, and it fell to the floor. She was shot in several places. Two of the girls had their arms broken close to the shoulders and will probably lose them. Another of the girls was fatally wounded. The boy was also shot. (Bennett, 1993, p. 276)

The participants in these activities rarely made any attempt to disguise themselves and often advertised lynchings in advance in the public media, thus demonstrating their confidence in absolute immunity from the law.

Not only did police fail to protect African Americans from these ritualized murders by whites, they encouraged the intimidation. Much like the previously discussed riots, "law enforcement agencies occasionally abetted white mobs by a tardy response to the crisis, by a tendency to harass and punish blacks whether or not they actually fought their attackers, or by outright participation against black residents" (Zangrando, 1980, p. 8). Friedman (1993) observed that "local police almost never intervened; and it was practically unheard of to punish anybody for taking part in a lynching" (p. 191). The police provided no protection for African Americans who experienced such inhumane violence at the hands of whites and actually played an important role in preventing Blacks from exercising their right to equal protection of the law:

> And if a black protested, if he said enough, no more—what then? "If any black was fantastic enough," W. J. Cash wrote, "to run to the courthouse for redress for a beating or any other wrong, he stood a good chance (providing he was heard at all), not only of seeing his assailant go off scot-free, but of finding the onus somehow shifted to himself, of finding himself in the dock on this or some other count, and of ending by going away for a long time to the county chain gang and the mercies of persons, hand-picked for their skills in adjusting his sense of reality" (Bennett, 1993, p. 273).

Because African Americans were unable to vote, hold public office or serve on juries, less than one percent of white terrorists ever faced punishment (Zangrando, 1980). Some researchers have estimated that the police participated in at least half of the lynchings (Skolnick & Fyfe, 1993). "Lynch-mob participants hardly needed to fear prosecution with the machinery of justice firmly in white hands" (Walker, 1980, p.119).

Although white terrorists in the United States during this time period primarily controlled African Americans, other racial and ethnic minorities also experienced their brutality. Spanish-speaking minorities, Native Americans, and Chinese immigrants were popular nineteenth-century targets (Zangrando, 1980). Mexicans and Chinese were frequent targets of vigilante violence in California and other western states who had relatively large Mexican and Chinese populations. Frequently, these attacks were triggered by competition for jobs, business, and land.

In one attack in Los Angeles, mobs invaded the Chinese neighborhood, looting and killing twenty-one Chinese, including women and children. At least fifteen of the victims were immediately hanged from lamp-posts and awnings (Skolnick & Fyfe, 1993, p. 27). During the 1880s, white mobs invaded Chinatowns, burned homes and businesses, and killed Chinese in towns such as Rock Springs, Wyoming and Tacoma, Washington. Like African Americans, the fact that they were not permitted to testify in court against their attackers made them helpless against robberies and beatings (Mann, 1993). Another similarity with white southern treatment of African Americans was that the police and the entire criminal justice system commonly ignored or even participated in these assaults.

The "Progressive" Era

Ironically, the period often referred to as the Progressive Era in the United States (1900–1919) was characterized by "nearly uninterrupted racial violence, culminating in an orgy of riots in 1919" (Walker, 1992a, p. 814). Throughout most of the nineteenth century, the majority of lynchings and other forms of white terrorism were concentrated in the southern and border states, where the numbers of African Americans were larger. As African Americans migrated to northern cities in search of jobs and to escape southern oppression, they encountered a northern form of white racism and terrorism. The most serious confrontations were over housing, where racist laws, customs, and practices restricted African Americans from living in specific areas. In the following excerpt from "Fifth Avenue Uptown: A Letter from Harlem," James Baldwin (1961) eloquently describes the formation of the modern ghetto and the wave of racial violence that marked this period:

> I tried to explain what *has* happened, unfailingly, whenever a significant body of Negroes move North. They do not escape Jim Crow: they merely encounter another, not-less-deadly variety. They do not move to Chicago, they move to the South Side; they do not move to New York, they move to Harlem. The pressure within the ghetto causes the ghetto walls to expand, and this expansion is always violent. White people hold the line as long as they can, and in as many ways as they can, from verbal intimidation to physical violence. But inevitably the border which has divided the ghetto from the rest of the world falls into the hands of the ghetto. The white people fall back bitterly before the black horde; the landlords make a tidy profit by raising the rent, chopping up the rooms, and all but dispensing with the upkeep; and what has once been a neighborhood turns into a "turf." (p. 68)

African Americans moved in increasing numbers to northern cities, but their expectations for a better life were met by white racism and economic fears. Many northern whites resented and feared African Americans and had no interest in sharing jobs and resources with them. Most racial disorders erupted over jobs, housing, and recreational facilities. As in the nineteenth century, police were deeply implicated in the violence, either for their failure to provide protection to Blacks or for their active participation in the mayhem.

Although the Great Migration, when two million African Americans moved into northern industrial centers, is often said to have begun around 1915, white terrorist attacks against Blacks in the twentieth century began as early as 1900.[3] Racially discriminatory practices by the police, who were predominantly Irish and Catholic, intensified racial tensions (Walker, 1992a). Irish American civilians viciously attacked African Americans while the police did nothing to stop them (Skolnick & Fyfe, 1993). The inaction of the police encouraged terrorist assaults. Whites believed "it was 'open season' on blacks and that they were free to act with impunity" (Walker, 1992a, p. 815).

In a New York City riot of 1900, the police were active participants (Walker, 1980). Police were described as "swarming over the area 'cracking the heads of Negroes and doing nothing to restrain the Irish mob' . . . the police did not stop the white rioters, they joined them" (Skolnick & Fyfe, 1993, p. 73). This riot was "characterized as a 'nigger chase' in which both citizens and police officers chased and assaulted blacks in the streets" (Walker, 1992a, p. 815). The police were much more likely to arrest Blacks than whites during the riot. When whites were arrested, they were often summarily released.

The best known race riot of this period took place in Chicago in 1919. Racial tensions in Chicago steadily increased as more African Americans moved north to Chicago (Bennett, 1993). Although residential segregation had created a large Black ghetto south and east of State Street in Chicago, white concerns about African Americans moving into white residential areas led to violent attacks against African Americans. The spark that set off the riot was an incident that occurred when four African-American youths floated on a homemade raft into an all-white beach. Whites began throwing stones at the youths from the beach, and one of the youths was struck with a rock and drowned (Walker, 1980). His friends pointed out the man whom they had seen throw the rock to a white police officer. "The officer refused to arrest the man and would not allow his black colleague to do so" (Hawkins & Thomas, 1991, p.78). In fact, the police response to the complaints led to the arrest of an African American. A massive confrontation ensued, and later that day gangs of whites began moving through the city killing African Americans. In turn, African Americans began to organize to protect themselves.

> Gangs of whites swept into the ghetto to kill and burn. Blacks passing through white areas on their way to jobs were also attacked. Although the governor mobilized the state militia on the fourth day of rioting, lawlessness prevailed for more than a week. When it was all over thirty-eight persons were dead (twenty-three black, fifteen white) and more than five hundred were injured. Arson, meanwhile left more than one thousand black Chicagoans homeless. (Walker, 1980, p. 165)

The established pattern of inaction by the police was repeated in Chicago. Discriminatory law enforcement practices intensified the racial tensions, triggering hostility and anger. The police largely ignored white violence during the riot, "thereby persuading blacks that their only hope lay in retaliatory violence" (Walker, 1980, p.165). In other words, the Black violence was caused by police failure to protect Blacks from white violence. Also during the rioting, Blacks were arrested at a much higher rate than whites. In addition, "police officers became active rioters themselves" (p. 65).

World War I

As approximately 350,000 African-American soldiers and 1,400 Black commissioned officers fought "the war to make the world safe for democracy," it was vividly clear that the United States itself was not safe for democracy (Bennett, 1993, p. 352). African Americans fought hard and bravely in France, and the French people expressed their appreciation without regard to race. Bennett noted that the military frequently expressed concern that the experience of African-American soldiers abroad, particularly in their interactions with the French, might be "spoiling the Negroes" (p. 349).

The white racism in the United States was reflected in the military concern over the possibility of African-American men and white French women having sexual relations. The U.S. military police repeatedly arrested African

American soldiers for "walking down the street with Frenchwomen" (p. 349). In an attempt to dampen the expectations of African-American soldiers serving in France, Dr. Robert R. Morton of the Tuskegee Institute was sent to France by President Woodrow Wilson to "warn the black troops there not to expect French democracy when they returned to the United States" (Williams & Murphy, 1990, p. 6).

Fears that returning soldiers would insist on receiving equal rights ignited a wave of racial violence throughout the country to reinforce white supremacy (Katz, 1995). "Negro soldiers were mobbed for attempting to use facilities open to white soldiers. Of the 70 Negroes lynched during the first year after the war, a substantial number were soldiers. Some were lynched in their uniforms" (Harris & Wicker, 1988, p. 219). From 1917 to 1919, fears erupted into a homefront hysteria that resulted in numerous acts of white terrorism with the police implicated as either refusing to stop the violence or participating in it. "There were numerous attacks on blacks by whites supported by the police in New Orleans, Charleston, Tulsa, Omaha, Washington, D.C., Knoxville, Chicago, East St. Louis and other cities" (Platt et al., 1982, p. 40).

Concerns about empowered African Americans were strikingly evident in the 1917 riot in East St. Louis, where African Americans had been used as strike-breakers. White workers, concerned about African Americans taking their jobs, went on a rampage in the Black community and "killed from forty to two hundred blacks and drove six thousand from their homes" (Bennett, 1993, p. 349). In addition, 312 buildings and 44 railroad cars were burned as rioters set fire to the entire Black community. Thousands of white mobs roamed the streets beating, killing, and burning. Streetcars were stopped and "Negroes, without regard to age or sex, were pulled off and stoned, clubbed and kicked, and mob leaders calmly shot and killed Negroes who were lying in blood in the streets" (Harris & Wicker, 1988, p. 218).

The police and National Guard responded to these attacks either by fleeing the area, including entire police stations, or by assisting and encouraging the mayhem. "The few police officers who remained on duty actually encouraged white mobs to lynch blacks" (Hawkins & Thomas, 1991, p. 77). The committee appointed by the U.S. House of Representatives to investigate the riot found that the actions of the police and the Illinois National Guard demonstrated either a callous indifference or supportive participation (Zangrando, 1980). The critical role of the National Guard was illustrated by the following quotation from the committee's report: "It was a common expression among the soldiers: 'Have you got your nigger yet?'" (p. 37).

Although whites were rarely punished for their participation in race riots, nineteen African-American soldiers were hanged for their participation in a race riot that left seventeen whites and two Black people dead. Racial tensions in Houston in 1917 had become very serious because of conflicts between the local police and the African American soldiers of the 24th Infantry who had been stationed at Camp Logan near Houston. Rioting began when Black troops stormed the town after they had heard that an African American corporal had been abused by Houston city police officers after he sought to assist a Black woman. With the long history of the government's inability to successfully prosecute offenders of white-on-Black violence, it is especially telling that the government had no trouble identifying, arresting, prosecuting, and convicting the offenders of Black-on-white terrorism. The double standard in police protection was clear. In total, 114 African American soldiers were court-martialed, with the vast majority receiving life imprisonment (Katz, 1995).

Red Summer

The racial violence in the summer of 1919 at the end of World War I led to the designation "Red Summer" (Bennett, 1993). The first of twenty-six major race riots took place in May in Charleston, South Carolina (Waskow, 1971). In Phillips County, Arkansas "a white posse killed fifty African Americans and destroyed a Black sharecropper organization" (Bennett, 1993, p. 353). In Tulsa, Oklahoma whites "dropped dynamite from an airplane onto a black ghetto, killing more than 75 people and destroying 1,100 homes" (Loewen, 1995, p. 159). In Elaine, Arkansas, sheriff's deputies fired on a meeting of sixty-eight Black sharecroppers in a church (Katz, 1995). When the sharecroppers returned fire, one of the attackers was killed. Twelve of the sharecroppers were arrested and sentenced to death, while the others were sentenced to life or long terms in prison. Only after the NAACP provided lawyers and exposed the facts, including the torture of defendants to get confessions, were the sentences overturned. This action did not end the violence. The church "was later burned down by lynch mobs and in the reign of terror that followed 'men and women were shot down in the fields like wild beasts,' numbers were rounded up and 'penned in stockades in Little Rock'" (Katz, 1995, p. 370). According to the NAACP investigator in the case, not only did the police fail to stop this mob aggression, they joined it.

In 1925, an African American scientist, Dr. Ossian Sweet, returned from studying in Paris with Madame Curie. He bought a home in a white neighborhood in Detroit (Katz, 1995). The Sweets moved into their new home with a few relatives and friends for protection. The first night a small crowd gathered. On the second night it grew larger and more menacing. At one point, the white mob rushed the door. Shots rang out from an upstairs window, and a white man fell dead. "The police, who had done nothing to disperse the mob, arrested everyone in the house, including Mrs. Sweet. The entire group was charged with murder" (Katz, 1995, p. 381). The famous lawyer Clarence Darrow was eventually able to get the Sweets acquitted.

World War II

Another explosion of racial violence occurred in the 1940s, as a result of the massive mobilization of soldiers and workers that took place when the United States entered World War II (Walker, 1992a). A massive migration of

African Americans and whites to the cities occurred as workers sought jobs in the expanding war industries. Competition intensified for war-scarce consumer goods, housing, transportation, and recreational areas (Weckler & Hall, 1944). The flood of migrants, particularly into the industrialized cities of the North and West, caused severe shortages in each of these areas, aggravating racial tensions.

African-American soldiers from the North stationed in southern military camps encountered the institutionalized Jim Crow systems of the South (Walker, 1990). These soldiers had frequent conflicts with authorities in local communities. African-American soldiers were confronted with blatant racial discrimination in the Army and Navy as well (Walker, 1992a). All these forms of racial oppression appeared in sharp relief to the rising expectations for opportunities in a prosperous economy and the war-time rhetoric which framed the war as a struggle against political, racial, and religious oppression.

The worst riot of 1943 occurred in Detroit where 34 people died, 27 of whom were African Americans. This riot resulted in two million dollars in property damage and a loss of a million person-hours of production in vital industrial plants (Hawkins & Thomas, 1991). A major issue in the Detroit riot was housing. In 1942, whites had organized into armed mobs to stop Black tenants from moving into a new housing project. When police arrived, they never approached or disarmed the white mob. Rather, they stopped and searched the cars containing African Americans.

When the riot began, the discriminatory practices of police were even more evident. Mobs of whites terrorized the African American community—beating, killing, and burning. Police used persuasion rather than force in dealing with whites. To control African Americans, they used "nightsticks, revolvers, riotguns, machine-guns, and deer rifles" (Hawkins & Thomas, 1991, p. 80). Seventeen of the African Americans killed in this riot were killed by the police. "After the riot, Judge George Edwards, who became Commissioner of the Detroit Police Department from 1961 to 1963, told the riot commission investigators that there was open warfare between the Detroit Negroes and the Detroit Police Department" (p. 80).

The United States emerged from World War II as a world superpower and as the beacon of hope for democracy. This image was marred with another terrible wave of white terrorism against African Americans. Once again, local police agencies and the rest of the criminal justice system failed to protect Black citizens from these vicious attacks. In South Carolina twenty-eight *admitted* members of a lynch mob were acquitted of the crime (Walker, 1990). The NAACP reported that 1946 was one of the grimmest years in its history with "reports of blowtorch killing and eye-gouging of Negro veterans freshly returning from a war to end torture and racial extermination" (Bennett, 1993, p. 543). For attempting to exercise his right to vote, an African-American man was shot in the back in Athens, Tennessee (Zangrando, 1980). In Alabama, African American veterans returning from the war were assaulted as whites seemed determined to make sure that they did not "expect or demand any change in their status from that which existed before they went overseas" (p. 174). One of the most astonishing acts of brutality occurred in Batesburg, South Carolina by police officers themselves. Two white police officers took Isaac Woodward from a bus just three hours after he had been honorably discharged at a military demobilization center. The officers brutally beat him and then as he lay on the ground, they gouged out both his eyes with the blunt end of a blackjack and later threw him into a jail cell to suffer through the night without medical attention" (p. 174).

In Columbia, Tennessee racial attacks erupted into a full-scale riot with white mobs roaming through Black neighborhoods attacking African Americans (Zangrando, 1980). The initial incident occurred when a white radio repairman was pushed through a plate glass window during an argument with an African-American woman and her son. When eight white police officers entered the Black neighborhood to arrest the woman and her son, a crowd of African Americans formed to stop the arrest, and shots were fired. In response, Tennessee State Highway Patrol officers conducted an illegal house-to-house search and "fired indiscriminately into any building whose occupants did not open their doors on command" (Zangrando, 1980, p. 172). Eventually four hundred National Guard troops were called out and a dozen African Americans were arrested for attempted murder. Only two whites were arrested for disorderly conduct. Two of the African-American prisoners were killed with a machine gun by state troopers while in custody in the Columbia jail. The federal grand jury investigating the incident declined to take any action against the state or local officials involved (p. 173).

As we have observed, the police, along with the entire criminal justice system, have had a long history in the United States of failing to protect African Americans from the violent terrorism of white Americans. White vigilantism has played an important role in preserving white supremacy. For the most part, the police have either ignored this lawlessness or have themselves actually participated in the beating, torturing, murdering, and burning of African Americans and their property. "White persons exercised a sort of delegated police power. Local police and courts, as with slavery, were expected to assist in upholding caste etiquette" (Skolnick & Fyfe, 1993, p. 30).

The Civil Rights Movement

The modern civil rights movement forced the government to extend the same basic rights enjoyed by white men to women and people of color. Throughout U.S. history, the police have been instrumental in maintaining the status quo in power relations—sometimes through enforcing unjust laws and sometimes through failure to enforce laws that protect human rights. The role of police agencies in relation to the civil rights movement of the 1950s and 1960s is crucial to our understanding of the relationship between the police and racial minorities.

The civil rights movement is very recent in our country's history. It is particularly telling that the police in many instances had the legal authority to respond much differently than they did. Often the police did not support Constitutional laws. Instead they acted to preserve unconstitutional local ordinances and informal racist norms and power relationships. The police most often enforced local laws buttressing white supremacy in direct violation of the U.S. Constitution.

As early as 1944, the International City Managers' Association stated that it was the responsibility of municipal officials, including the police, "to protect legally prescribed civil rights of all the people in the community regardless of race, religion, or national origin" (Weckler & Hall, 1944, p. iii).

Throughout much of the civil rights movement, municipal, county, and state police directly opposed the efforts of African Americans, Latinos, American Indians, women, students, and their supporters to achieve equality. When the ground-breaking 1954 Supreme Court ruling in *Brown v. Board of Education*, (1954) struck down the *Plessy v. Ferguson* (1896) doctrine of separate but equal, many powerful and prominent southern whites began to mobilize to prevent integration.

A new wave of white violence erupted in the segregated South as whites attempted to prevent this ruling from dismantling white supremacy (Bennett, 1993). Tom Brady, the intellectual leader of the resistance to integration and a Yale-educated circuit court judge in Mississippi, stated, "We say to the Supreme Court and to the northern world, 'You shall not make us drink from this cup' . . . We have, through, our forefathers, died before for our sacred principles. We can, if necessary, die again" (Bennett, 1993, p. 377). The Ku Klux Klan increased its use of terror and violence to silence the voices that called for peaceful acceptance of the *Brown* decision (Katz, 1995, p. 441). The resistance was largely concentrated in the South but other pockets existed. "Chicago in the early 1950s was the scene of a near civil war as white residents fought integration with vigilante violence on a neighborhood-by-neighborhood basis" (Walker, 1990, p. 238).

Local police ignored their legal obligations to protect the civil rights of African-American citizens. Efforts by southern whites to oppose integration and voter registration by African Americans through violence were unopposed by the police. For example, when Little Rock's Central High School was integrated, the 101st Airborne Division had to escort nine Black children to class because local police failed to stop white mobs from attacking Black children as they attempted to attend class. The Kentucky National Guard escorted African-American children to class through howling mobs in Stugis and Clay. In Mississippi, two NAACP leaders were murdered for failing to take their names off voter registration lists. The Hattie Cotton Elementary School in Nashville was destroyed by dynamite; it had 388 white students and one Black student (Bennett, 1993). When the local police did take action, it was typically to bring the law down on African Americans. For example, on December 1, 1955 when Rosa Parks refused to give up her seat on a bus to a white man, the local police responded by arresting her (Bennett, 1993). The

1960s are littered with examples of efforts by the local police to prevent African Americans from peacefully exercising their civil and human rights.

Local Police Reaction

Sit-ins by African Americans and white students at lunch counters designated for whites were one example of nonviolent efforts to achieve the end of discrimination on the basis of the color of one's skin. Local police typically responded with force directed to block such peaceful attempts (Bennett, 1993). Ruby Doris Smith, a seventeen-year-old sophomore at Spelman College in Atlanta, was inspired by sit-ins in Greensboro, North Carolina.[4] She described her experience when she volunteered to participate in a similar protest:

> I went through the food line in the restaurant at the State Capitol with six other students, but when we got to the cashier she wouldn't take our money. . . . The Lieutenant-Governor came and told us to leave. We didn't and went to the county jail. (Zinn, 1980, p. 444)

Forty-one students were arrested for demonstrating in front of Woolworth's in Raleigh, North Carolina (Walker, 1990). Eleven Black students were arrested in Tallahassee and sixteen in New Orleans for participating in sit-ins (Walker, 1990). In Columbia, South Carolina, 180 Black students and a white minister were arrested after an antisegregation march. In Montgomery, Alabama, police broke up a protest demonstration on the Alabama State campus with tear gas and the arrest of 35 students, a teacher, and her husband (Zinn, 1980). The police also used tear gas to disrupt another student protest in Tallahassee, Florida. In Baton Rouge, Louisiana, police used both tear gas and leashed dogs to stop a mass demonstration. In 1960 alone, over 3,500 people, mostly Blacks, were jailed by local police for participating in nonviolent efforts to exercise their rights as U.S. citizens. Despite these roadblocks, lunch counters in Greensboro and many other places were successfully integrated by the end of 1960 through the persistent efforts of people to obtain what the law promised.

Spurred by the success of the sit-ins, CORE (Congress of Racial Equality) organized the "Freedom Rides" in 1961. Blacks and whites traveled through the South to make sure that bus terminals were not segregated. The police and white vigilantes relied on the use of force to subvert such efforts. Those riders who were not beaten by white vigilantes were often arrested (Walker, 1990). The first two buses of Freedom Riders that left from Washington to New Orleans never arrived. They were beaten with fists and iron bars in South Carolina, and in Alabama one of the buses was burned. According to Zinn (1980), the local police did nothing to stop the violence. A second set of Freedom Riders was organized by the Student Nonviolent Coordinating Committee (SNCC), which was formed by veterans of the sit-ins. The racially mixed group traveled from Nashville, Tennessee to Birmingham, Alabama where they were promptly arrested. After spending the night in jail, they were transported to the Tennessee border. When they made their way back to Montgomery, Alabama they were beaten by a white mob with fists and clubs. When they resumed their trip to Jackson, Mississippi, Attorney General Robert Kennedy agreed to allow the Freedom Riders to be arrested in Jackson in order to protect them from white mobs, ignoring their civil rights.

In 1962, the struggle for civil rights for all U.S. citizens continued. In July, the local police of Albany, Georgia arrested fifteen Black teenagers after they knelt and prayed on the steps of the public library reserved for whites (Bennett, 1993). In August, seventy-five ministers and laymen, Black and white, from the North were arrested after another prayer demonstration in downtown Albany. "Of the 22,000 black people in Albany, over a thousand went to jail for marching, assembling, to protest segregation and discrimination" (Zinn, 1980, p. 446). Because of the failure of local police to enforce integration and protect African Americans, civil rights workers, and Freedom Riders, twelve thousand federal troops, marshals, and members of the National Guard were mobilized by the federal government to restore order in the South. Sheriff Z. T. Mathews of Georgia summed up the attitude of many whites, including police, in the South when he stated, "We want our colored people to go on living like they have for the last hundred years" (Katz, 1995, p. 452).

The most publicized confrontation took place in 1962 in Birmingham, Alabama. The demonstrators organized by Dr. Martin Luther King, Jr., were confronted by police with nightsticks, attack dogs, and fire hoses that could take the bark off of trees (Bennett, 1993). Within a month, almost 1,000 demonstrators were in jail or out on bond. When African-American children were mobilized in a similar demonstration, they were met with the same police violence. Eventually over 3,000 people were arrested by the local police. The public reaction to the television and magazine images of this overt police violence against African-American men, women, and children prompted the federal government to intervene. The youths kept coming, with more than two thousand participating in the demonstrations. Finally, a tentative agreement was reached to begin desegregation and upgrading Black employment. It was local white merchants, not the police or the government, who agreed to make these changes (Katz, 1995).

In 1963, African Americans struggling for their civil rights "faced police dogs and armored police tanks. They were clubbed, bombed, stoned, murdered" (Bennett, 1993, p. 387). More than 10,000 racial demonstrations took place in 1963, and more than 5,000 African Americans were arrested for participating in them. An old "John Brown Statute" which made it a felony to incite African Americans to acts of violence against whites was revived in Virginia. Another such law was revitalized in Georgia that made it a felony punishable by death to encourage insurrection among African Americans. In Alabama, African Americans who marched to the registrar's office to register to vote were repelled by heavily armed police officers and police dogs. While demonstrating in Orangeburg, South Carolina, African Americans were arrested en masse and confined in barbed-wire fenced compounds. In Plaquemine, Louisiana police officers "bombarded a black church with tear gas grenades and fire hoses. Black demonstrators said a state policeman with an electric cattle prod rode a horse down the aisle of the church at the height of the counterattack" (p. 408). Backed by machine guns and armored cars, police officers of Danville, Virginia crushed a demonstration by wading through the crowd swinging billy clubs. Over fifty protestors were treated at the hospital for broken heads and lacerations. In Savannah, Georgia when protestors laid down in the streets to disrupt traffic, police officers responded with tear gas and concussion grenades.

In 1964, the Student Nonviolent Coordinating Committee (SNCC) launched a large-scale assault on the caste system of Mississippi. This triggered white terrorist attacks and police resistance, including the bombing or burning of sixty-five homes and churches and the beating of eighty civil rights workers (Walker, 1990). In addition, the police arrested over 1,000 civil rights workers, often on trumped-up charges of disorderly conduct and vagrancy (Walker, 1990). "In a typical case in Madison, Mississippi, a civil rights worker was charged with improper parking. When he objected, a police officer said, 'Don't keep talking to me or I'll drag you out of that car and beat your damn brains out'" (Walker, 1990, pp. 265–266). In another case, Al Bronstein went to the Magnolia, Mississippi jail to bail out forty-two people who had been arrested for attempting to register to vote. He was beaten by the town constable and the jailer. The most infamous of these acts was the murder of two white and one Black civil rights workers. Goodman, Schwener, and Chaney were released from jail late at night. They were seized by Klansmen led by Deputy Sheriff Cecil, beaten with chains, and then shot to death.

White racist violence against African Americans accelerated in 1965 after the passage of the 1964 Civil Rights Act. In March 1965 Dr. Martin Luther King, Jr. led a march from Selma to Montgomery, Alabama to encourage voter registration. Jimmy Lee Jackson, an African American youth, and Reverend James Reeb, a white Boston minister, were murdered before the march even began. Rather than providing protection from violence, the Alabama State Troopers responded by using tear gas and nightsticks to stop the march (Katz, 1995). Eventually the federal government sent armed troops to protect the marchers from white vigilante violence and the local police. While driving home after the march, Viola Liuzzo, a Detroit housewife, was murdered on the last day of the march. Tom Gilmore gave the following account of his encounter with an Alabama state trooper in 1965: "He put me up against a gas pump and frisked me and unbuckled his gun. He said, 'I'm going to be in Selma tonight and I'll see you again. I'm going to blow your brains out'" (p. 538). Although not a civil rights worker at the time, Gilmore was motivated by the incident to join the Southern Christian Leadership Conference. Ironically, in 1970, Tom Gilmore replaced the Greene County Sheriff who had previously cane-whipped him for helping with voter registration efforts—the very type of reform that created opportunities to replace law enforcement officials who ignored the civil rights of citizens.

Throughout the 1960s, the police continued to refuse to protect African Americans struggling for their civil rights. In 1966, James Meredith, the first African American to attend Mississippi State University, began a "march against fear" across the state of Mississippi to encourage voter registration among African Americans. On the second day of his march, while surrounded by FBI agents, he was shot (Katz, 1995). Major civil rights leaders, including Martin Luther King, Jr., continued the march for Meredith. As they began they were "pelted with rocks and bottles and then charged by knife-swinging whites. At Canton, Mississippi, state troopers used tear gas to smash the march. It regrouped and marched on" (p. 474).

In another example, African-American students protesting the segregation of an Orangeburg, South Carolina bowling alley in 1968 were confronted on the campus of South Carolina State College by sixty-six state patrol officers, forty-five members of the National Guard with M-1 rifles and fixed bayonets, twenty-five State Law Enforcement Agents, and several members of the Orangeburg Police Department and Sheriff's Department. After much taunting from the crowd of students and a few thrown items, the police panicked and opened fire into the crowd with shotguns and a revolver. Three students were killed and twenty-seven were seriously wounded in the "Orangeburg Massacre" (Bass & Nelson, 1984).

The Federal Government

In popular media, such as the movie *Mississippi Burning*, and in many historical presentations, the federal government is presented as the great savior of southern Blacks. The federal government is shown as having infiltrated the South to protect civil rights leaders and to ensure the full enforcement of the Federal Civil Rights Act. The entire civil rights struggle is often portrayed as a struggle between a corrupt South and a noble and pure federal government. It is true that the Federal Bureau of Investigation (FBI), the Federal Attorney General's Office and, more importantly, the U.S. Supreme Court eventually played a key role in forcing integration and extending the civil rights of African Americans. However, federal authorities took these actions reluctantly (Loewen, 1995). In the 1950s and into the early 1960s, the Supreme Court began to extend civil rights to African Americans, finally enforcing the 14th Amendment to the U.S. Constitution nearly 100 years after its passage. The FBI was extremely slow to act; they took action only after being sued for essentially failing to do their duty. Both Attorney General Robert Kennedy and J. Edgar Hoover were successfully sued by SNCC in 1962 "to force them to protect civil rights demonstrators" (p. 225).

To understand the reluctance of the FBI to protect African American and other civil rights workers, it is critical to understand J. Edgar Hoover, the heart and soul of the FBI until his death in 1972. As Loewen (1995) documents, Hoover was a bigot and an avowed white supremacist. During the anti-Black violence in 1919 discussed earlier in this chapter, the FBI began an intensive surveillance of Black organizations, rather than working to stop white vigilante violence or investigating the Ku Klux Klan. Hoover blamed white terrorist violence on "the numerous assaults committed by Negroes upon white women" (p. 224). He opposed the 1954 ruling in *Brown v. Board of Education* and helped to prosecute Carl Braden, a white civil rights leader in Kentucky, for selling a house to an African American family in a white neighborhood. When asked about the violence associated with school segregation in the 1950s, "Hoover told President Eisenhower's cabinet that NAACP leaders and Communists were turning crisis into revolution" (Katz, 1995, p. 518). As late as the early 1960s, the FBI did not have a single African-American agent, although Hoover attempted to count his chauffeurs as agents. The agents who were in the South were often openly sympathetic to white southerners and local law enforcement. In Mississippi, at the time of the killings of Goodman, Schwener, and Chaney, the FBI did not even have an office in the state. They relied on the local police for information—often the very persons from whom civil rights workers most needed protection (Loewen, 1995).

Throughout the early 1960s, the FBI failed to protect civil rights workers. "Again and again in Mississippi and elsewhere, the FBI stood by, while civil rights workers were beaten and jailed, while federal laws were violated" (Zinn, 1980, p. 447). Reportedly, when FBI investigators did have contact with civil rights workers, it was to inquire about communist involvement rather than to investigate crimes committed against them (Katz, 1995). Andrew Young, former mayor of Atlanta and long-time civil rights activist, stated that "our experience with the FBI was that no matter what kind of brutality . . . all the FBI agents did was stand over on the corner and take notes'" (pp. 518–519). Hoover worked to prevent the prosecution of the four Klansmen who firebombed a Birmingham church in 1963, killing four African American girls. Hoover was twice sent the evidence and the recommendation for prosecution from the FBI office in Birmingham, and twice he rejected it (Katz, 1995). In the case of the "Orangeburg Massacre" of 1968 in South Carolina, the FBI falsified information in order to help state troopers charged with murder of African American students engaged in a nonviolent protest of segregation (Loewen, 1995).

When the FBI did become active in relation to the civil rights movement, it was typically to undermine the movement through spying, bugging, break-ins, infiltration, and the dissemination of false and defamatory information to the media (Bennett, 1993). The FBI activities included circulating false messages among activists making it appear that one of their comrades was a secret agent; mailing harmful information on individuals to the media; making sure that criticism of the Mafia by comedian/activist Dick Gregory reached the Mafia; and investigating African-American faculty members and Black Student Unions in colleges and universities (Katz, 1995). According to Loewen (1995), an agent of the FBI proposed to "neutralize" the entire Tougaloo College in Jackson, Mississippi, because its students had sponsored "out-of-state militant Negro speakers, voter-registration drives, and African cultural seminars and lectures (pp. 226–227).

The FBI also worked to destroy the Black Panther Party, which was dedicated to stopping police brutality of African Americans (Katz, 1995). Although Black Panther Party projects included a breakfast program for ghetto school children and legal aid to ghetto residents, it was their open display of weapons and their movement to stop police violence with a violent defense that caught the public eye. The FBI infiltrated the officers of the Black Panther Party, disrupted activities, and attempted to destroy their unity by manufacturing evidence that rival leaders were going to kill one another. "By 1969, 28 Panthers had been slain, 750 had been jailed, and some leaders had fled the country. The party was finished as a political force" (p. 534).

J. Edgar Hoover's favorite target was Dr. Martin Luther King, Jr., whom he referred to as "burr head" (p. 518). Hoover first opened a file on Dr. King in 1947 when he was a college student. He had previously kept files on King's father and grandfather. Loewen (1995) argued that in "August 1963 Hoover initiated a campaign to destroy Dr. Martin Luther King, Jr., and the civil rights movement" (p. 225). Hoover ordered FBI agent William Sullivan "to come up with proof that King was a Communist. Sullivan later revealed how his men concocted 'a lot of nonsense [on King] which we ourselves did not believe'" (Katz, 1995, p. 520). Under the direction of Hoover and with the approval of Attorney General Robert Kennedy, Dr. King's home, offices, and hotel rooms were all bugged. Tape recordings and photographs of King's extramarital involvement with women were distributed to white supremacists such as Senator Strom Thurmond (Loewen, 1995). At one point, a tape recording of Dr. King engaged in sex with another woman was sent to his wife, Coretta Scott King, with a note suggesting that King kill himself. It was also sent to the office of King's organization, the Southern Christian Leadership Conference (SCLC). "The FBI tried to sabotage receptions in King's honor when he traveled to Europe to claim the Nobel Peace Prize. Hoover called King 'the most notorious liar in the country' and tried to prove the SCLC was infested with communists" (p. 225). While gathering this information and passing it on to the media and white supremacist, and other organizations, the FBI refused to pass on to King information they had gathered concerning threats to his life.

As the above sections illustrate, neither local nor federal law enforcement agencies provided adequate police protection to African Americans and whites who struggled for the full extension of U.S. citizenship to African Americans. They also failed to protect African Americans during this time period from the frequent acts of white terrorist violence, which was orchestrated to preserve white racial supremacy. In the next section, we explore the concern of underpolicing in its most modern form—the failure of the police to provide adequate protection to African American crime victims.

Crime Defined by Place and Perpetrator

While working as a deputy sheriff, I was told by a police officer in a major city in South Carolina that while records personnel were cleaning out their files and disposing of old police reports they came across an Incident Report on a murder that had occurred in the 1930s. According to the officer, the entire contents of the murder report and investigation stated: "Nigger A stabbed and killed Nigger B." This report illustrated the low degree of importance that police placed on the lives of African Americans. It is difficult for many whites to imagine how inadequate, or simply nonexistent, police protection and service was for people of color in the United States. Such non-enforcement has had—and continues to have—a devastating effect on the psyche, families, and communities of African Americans. The failure to provide adequate law enforcement devalues the lives of African Americans and is a form of discrimination equally as serious as overly harsh law enforcement.

During the Great Migration of African Americans to northern cities in the first half of the twentieth century, Blacks were required by law and by custom to live in the "worst" areas of the cities to which they moved. These areas were frequently referred to as "red-light" districts because police allowed large-scale prostitution, alcohol violations, drug use, gambling, and other vice crimes to flourish (Hawkins & Thomas, 1991). Similar forms of underpolicing occurred in southern cities. It was common practice in Atlanta to draw "liquor limits" within which whiskey could be sold. In the *Atlanta News*, the Chief of the Atlanta Police Department, John W. Ball, argued that it was important that a few "negro dives" be left open to operate because the police used them to "corral criminals" (Watts, 1992b, p. 916). Applications for renewal of licenses often bore the signature of the chief or of other policemen asking that the petition be granted because these businesses were convenient places to round up suspects. One such application in Atlanta, by Henry Beatie in 1901, stated that he would be of service to the police in "apprehending numerous criminals that sometimes frequent places of amusement of colored people" (p. 916).

Police protection is a form of white social control of African Americans (Hawkins & Thomas, 1991). Non-protection has had the effect of "controlling the black community by undermining the stability of the black family and community life" (p. 76). Segregation of housing forced African Americans to make their homes and raise their children in environments where crime was allowed to flourish. Many whites believed that African Americans had looser morals when, in fact, the police had a standard policy of permitting levels of crime and vice in African American communities not tolerated in white communities. Thus, African-American children were more likely than white children to be raised in an environment characterized by vice and violence. The lives and property of law-abiding, hard-working African-American citizens were devalued, families were disrupted by vice and crime, and legitimate employment opportunities rarely existed in those underpoliced areas. The disproportionate tolerance of vice crime, such as gambling, after hours drinking, prostitution, and narcotics trafficking, in communities largely populated by the poor and by racial minorities, harms these communities:

"First, it *breeds disrespect for the law and the police.* . . . Second, underenforcement of the law *exposes law-abiding citizens in minority communities to criminal activity.* Prostitution and drug dealing are often accompanied by secondary crimes such as shootings and robberies" (Walker, 1999, p. 221).

Walker (1999) identifies four different systems of justice that existed based on the "racial components of the offender/victim relationship" (p. 221). First, those crimes committed by whites against African Americans were rarely prosecuted. Second, the crimes committed by whites against other whites were treated as "normal" crimes. Third, crimes by Blacks against whites produced the harshest criminal justice response. Finally, crimes by African Americans against African Americans were typically ignored. A southern police chief in 1920 stated the situation much more crudely: "We have three classes of homicide. . . . If a nigger kills a white man, that's murder. If a white man kills a nigger, that's justifiable homicide. If a nigger kills another nigger, that's one less nigger" (Friedman, 1993, p. 375).

The 1968 President's Commission on Civil Disorders found that underenforcement remained a critical problem in ghetto neighborhoods (Harris & Wicker, 1988). The commission concluded that ghetto neighborhoods received inadequate police protection, and the police held people to much lower standards of proper conduct in African-American communities than in white ones. The police tolerated drug addiction, prostitution, and street violence at levels not tolerated elsewhere. In addition, the police simply did not treat the concerns of African-American victims as seriously as they did requests for help from white Americans. African-American citizens frequently complained that when they called for the police, they typically came very slowly or not at all. "When they do come, [they] arrive with many more men and cars than are necessary . . . brandishing guns and adding to the confusion" (p. 308). Part of the problem of inadequate police protection appeared to stem from the assignment of police personnel. The commission found that police departments, rather than sending their best officers to ghetto areas with the highest crime rates and calls for service, frequently sent their least competent officers. The commission found that "The slum police precinct is like the slum school. It gets, with few exceptions, the worst in the system" (1988).

I observed similar assignment criteria when I worked in a sheriff's department in the early 1980s. Deputies assigned to work in a district that was almost exclusively African American and poor fell into three categories: the two African American deputies, the rookie deputies, or those deputies who were being punished. This basic assignment procedure made the value placed by the sheriff's department on providing adequate and equal law enforcement to this area abundantly apparent to the deputies themselves. The dual system of justice may not be visible to most white Americans, but it is blatantly obvious to African Americans. They can personally see the nature of police responsiveness in white neighborhoods in contrast to the lack of police responsiveness in economically depressed Black neighborhoods.

This historical legacy of underpolicing in African-American communities continues to be a serious concern. African Americans frequently accuse the police of providing too little protection for their neighborhoods (Walker, 1999). They argue that an insufficient number of officers are assigned, they do not respond quickly enough to calls, and they do not take crimes against African Americans seriously. In certain situations, African Americans receive less law enforcement than whites. A significant variable is the race of the victim. When the complainant is a person of color, the police are less likely to take concerns seriously; they are more likely to lack empathy. "Victimization data consistently reveal that African Americans and Hispanics are more likely than whites to fall victim to household and personal crime. The racial differences are particularly pronounced for crimes of violence, especially murder and robbery" (Walker et al., 2000, p. 287).

Police actions such as arrest, use of deadly force, and verbal abuse reflect broader patterns of social and economic inequality. That is, the inequities in police service reflect both racial and economic discrimination. Reiman (1998) argued that, because of the racist nature of our society, racial and ethnic minorities are disproportionately represented in poverty and, therefore, are most seriously harmed by a criminal justice system that fails to adequately protect its citizens from street crime as well as corporate crime.

Underpolicing in Milwaukee

An example of a contemporary incident that typifies underpolicing in minority communities is the Dahmer-Sinthasomphone case in Milwaukee, Wisconsin, which was heavily publicized in 1991 and 1992. Elements of this case and related events make it particularly significant for our concerns. The case illustrated that Milwaukee police were not providing adequate and equal protection for racial minorities, members of the gay community, and those who are victims of domestic violence. In fact, public discourse in the months following the Dahmer-Sinthasomphone case centered on the issue of underpolicing. Underpolicing overshadowed the Jeffrey Dahmer story itself, which was that of a vicious and grotesque serial killer responsible for murder, necrophilia, dismemberment, and even cannibalism. Serial killers are an aberration for which the creation of criminal justice policy will likely have little consequence. Members of the communities for whom the Dahmer-Sinthasomphone case represented the more pertinent issue of underpolicing united in a movement to change policy within the Milwaukee Police Department in order to force it to better meet the needs of all of its residents (Barlow, Barlow, & Stojkovic, 1994).

A review of newspaper reports on the Dahmer-Sinthasomphone case provided this summary.

> News reports that police officers had (1) been called to a scene involving
> Dahmer (who is white) and one of his victims (a young Laotian boy) in
> May 1991, (2) determined that what they were dealing with was a domes-
> tic situation between homosexual lovers, (3) returned the naked, bleeding
> and incoherent Konerak Sinthasomphone to the custody of Jeffrey Dah-
> mer, who killed him later that evening, and (4) ignored repeated attempts
> by Glenda Cleveland, her daughter and her niece (women of color) to
> convince police that the Asian male was a child, ushered in a period of
> intense concern about relations between police and minorities. (pp. 1–2)

If the police had arrested Dahmer that evening, Konerak Sinthasomphone
and [six] other men might not have been murdered by him.

Three major issues surrounding underpolicing emerged from this trag-
edy. The first issue involved the failure of the police to provide adequate protection in communities of color. Many African-American and other racial
minorities in Milwaukee claimed that police would have been much more
thorough in their investigation of this incident had Konerak Sinthasomphone
been white or had Jeffrey Dahmer not been white. "In a public forum on the
primarily African-American north side, a great deal of hostility and bitterness
was expressed, as citizens complained about slow police response time,
police harassment and police indifference to the community" (Barlow et al.,
1994, pp. 146–147).

A related issue was that the concerns of the African-American women
on the scene were not given the same credibility as that of the white male, Jeffrey Dahmer. Glenda Cleveland struggled desperately and continuously to
convince the officers that Konerak Sinthasomphone was not an adult. So
strong was her belief that Sinthasomphone was underage and in need of protection that she made several calls to the police station to plead for their
attention to the situation. The police interpreted Ms. Cleveland's behavior as
a nuisance and even threatened her with arrest if she did not cease her
attempts. According to Walker et al. (2000), the failure to take seriously the
complaints of African Americans or to have sympathy for victims of color are
prime examples of underpolicing.

Underpolicing was also evident in the explanations of the white Milwaukee officers for their actions. They essentially stated that so many "strange"
things occur in that neighborhood that it was impossible for them to see this
particular incident as significantly different from all the others. This statement implies that racial minorities, particularly African Americans, are prone
to violence, vice, and crime and that it is reasonable that a different standard
of police action is provided in their communities (Barlow et al., 1994; Walker
et al., 2000). No statement better reflects the police view of ghettoes as irrevo-
cably crime ridden than the frequent remark to crime victims—"Don't call us,
call a moving van" (Mayor's Citizen Commission on Police-Community
Relations," 1991).

The second major issue to emerge from the Dahmer-Sinthasomphone
case involves the treatment of homosexuals by police. Many representatives of

the Gay community suggested that the police handling of this incident reflected their historical failure to provide adequate and equal protection to homosexual men and women. Gays and their advocates argued that the police would have been more diligent in their investigation had they not characterized Dahmer and Sinthasomphone as a homosexual couple involved in a "lovers' quarrel" (Barlow et al., 1994). Further, even though police indeed referred to the relationship between Dahmer and Sinthasomphone in those terms, it seems more likely that this comment was made tongue in cheek and that they presumed Konerak Sinthasomphone to be a male prostitute and Dahmer his customer. Whether the officers viewed the relationship as a domestic conflict between gay partners or as a prostitution situation gone sour, they acted in a manner that suggested that it was not worth their time to investigate fully.

Gay spokespersons stated that the Milwaukee police have a history of being homophobic and not taking crimes against homosexuals seriously, particularly hate crimes against homosexuals. According to the testimony of citizens appearing before the commission investigating police-community relations, victims of gay bashing frequently perceived that police blamed the victim and did not aggressively seek out the perpetrators of those crimes. This concern exemplifies the sorts of complaints that triggered the movement to force police to become more aggressive in their enforcement against bias or hate crimes (crimes committed against a person because of that person's race, ethnicity, religion, or sexual orientation). During the decade prior to the Dahmer case, hate crimes had begun to get both scholarly and law enforcement attention. This change was largely due to the greater empowerment of racial, ethnic, and religious minorities, as well as homosexuals, through political protest and the political process.

A final contemporary complaint about underpolicing highlighted by the Dahmer-Sinthasomphone case involved the failure of police to adequately protect victims of domestic violence. Various advocates in the area of domestic violence suggested that this incident reflected the historical failure of police to treat domestic violence as seriously as violence between strangers. Women from all segments of society have expressed frustration in reference to the failure of police to protect them from the crime of domestic violence.

This concern has been particularly acute in African-American communities. As described in chapter 1, I witnessed such underpolicing firsthand as a deputy sheriff. Research indicates that 50 to 60 percent of all spouses (primarily women) have been victims of abuse, and 18.6 percent of all homicides are perpetrated by family members. Women's groups have accused the police of failing to protect victims of domestic violence. Many departments responded by adopting policies that mandate arrest in domestic violence situations (Walker, 1999). The growing political power of women and their movement into police work has had a significant impact on reversing the trend of underpolicing domestic violence; however, concerns still exist that discrimination in domestic violence cases may be taking place at stages in the criminal justice process other than law enforcement.

What is also informative about the Dahmer-Sinthasomphone incident is the response of many white male police officers to the news stories of the case and related events. White police officers frequently expressed that allegations of inadequate or unequal police service in minority communities were unfounded. Some claimed that police attention to people of color in their communities was actually greater than in other neighborhoods and that the people in these communities were frequently uncooperative and unsupportive of police efforts to enforce the law. White male police officers frequently expressed anger at being identified as the problem, suggesting that the problem of police-community relations was to be found in the "community" itself, rather than in the police. During the aftermath of this incident police officers and their spouses held several rallies and argued that they were the true victims in this case. Barlow et al. (1994) described a typical response to this incident by a supporter of the police:

> In a public forum held on Milwaukee's south side, where a large number of working class whites live, along with a small Hispanic population, a police officer's wife drew a huge round of applause when she questioned how police officers were to respond to "lovers' quarrels" between homosexuals and stated that police should not be expected to deal with such "trivial matters." (p. 143)

Even as police and their supporters denied that they failed to provide adequate and equal protection to Gays and Blacks, they referred to their problems as trivial.

Conclusion

Underpolicing in communities of color, particularly poor communities, is a reality. People who lack significant power, due to their numbers and/or to a long history of social and economic discrimination, have much more difficulty encouraging the police to provide them with the same level of service enjoyed by more powerful citizens.

> Clearly, Native Americans, Asian Americans, African Americans, and Hispanic Americans historically have been in positions of less wealth; therefore, . . . they have less law and less access to law, and have been and currently are abused by the law. The inequalities accruing to minorities under our system of law and justice not only are present in the contemporary operation of our legal system, but have existed since its origin. (Mann, 1993, p. 115)

As we will see in chapter 4, the same people who have experienced less protection under the law have endured extreme oppression and violence at the hands of the police on the other end of the scale.

Notes

[1] It should be noted here that throughout most of the nation only men possessed the right to vote. It was not until 1920 with the ratification of the 19th Amendment to the U.S. Constitution that women were guaranteed the right to participate in the political process throughout the entire United States. Of course, in the 1920s women of color had to confront the same racism that men of color faced in actually exercising this civil right. It was not until the passage of the Voting Rights Act of 1965 that all U.S. citizens, regardless of race, sex, or religion, were fully enfranchised in this country.

[2] We begin to use the term African American here because at least at this point participation in the political process was possible, the right to vote and to hold political office having been secured.

[3] One of the first riots occurred in 1900 in New York City and had many similarities to the New York City Draft riots of 1863. The confrontation grew out of competition for jobs between the Irish and African Americans.

[4] In Greensboro, North Carolina a number of African American students from the local historically black college, North Carolina A&T, protested racial discrimination at the local Woolworth's lunch counter. The stores would not serve Black people at the counter, so they marched into the store as a group and sat at the counter, refusing to leave until they were served. The store refused to serve them and they were arrested by the Greensboro Police Department. They returned and continued to occupy the seats and disrupt service until the Woolworth's store agreed to integrate the lunch counter.

4 Overpolicing

All immigrants to the United States have faced some form of discrimination. However, white European immigrants almost always arrived with a sense of hope, toiling through the hard times with the realistic expectation that they would be able to improve their condition. Africans came to this country in bondage. Thus, for Blacks in the United States, discrimination was vastly more pervasive and perpetual. A racist social structure has characterized the United States since its inception. Within this structure, African slaves and later African Americans have been systematically and intentionally relegated to the very bottom of the social stratification system (Katz, 1995).

The police have played a crucial role in maintaining this white supremacy: "White racial dominance over blacks in America from the establishment of black slavery in the seventeenth century to the establishment and consolidation of black ghettos in the late nineteenth and throughout the twentieth centuries depended upon white systems of policing" (Hawkins & Thomas, 1991, p. 66). People of African descent in the United States have never simply accepted slavery, second-class citizenship, and economic inequality. The physical coercion of the police has been essential to maintaining the racist social order.

Fear of Rebellion

To maintain a political and economic system in the United States based on forced labor, legal safeguards were instituted to protect the social structure from rebellion (Hawkins & Thomas, 1991). The threat of slave rebellion was much too serious for the control of slaves to be left solely in the hands of the slaveowners. Therefore, in the 1660s, strict "slave codes" were created to regulate the activities of slaves, particularly in the regions with dense slave populations (Katz, 1995).

In Florida, the slave codes made it illegal for seven male slaves to travel on any public road without a white person present (Friedman, 1993). Most importantly, the laws "permitted any white to punish a slave who stepped out of line" (p. 86). In fact, whites were obligated to apprehend and punish slaves who violated these codes. "This socially-sanctioned granting of large-scale policing rights over blacks obviously reinforced the pathology of white racism as the meanest and most vile white found himself endowed with the power to exercise or abuse his power as he saw fit" (Hawkins & Thomas, 1991, p. 68).

This legally sanctioned relationship of power had a tremendous impact as the predecessor of white policing in the United States.

In chapter 2, we discussed the evolution of policing in the preindustrial era from slave patrols whose express purpose was to prevent slaves from congregating, to repress attacks on the social order, and to catch runaway slaves. Hawkins and Thomas (1991) argued that whites found the free movement of slaves especially disturbing and instituted a series of restrictions eventually requiring written passes for almost all movement of slaves not on the plantations of their owners. The "perception of unpoliced blacks would become an obsession of whites for centuries" (p. 68).

Free Blacks in the Southern States

The criminal law "tended to lump together all blacks, slave and free" (Friedman, 1993, p. 90). Whites were particularly afraid of the influence that free Blacks might have on slaves and, therefore, made associations and interaction between them illegal. One popular method for regulating the activities and movements of free Blacks was the establishment of an extensive system of registration (Hawkins & Thomas, 1991). Free Blacks were required to carry "freedom papers," which were frequently checked by municipal police and slave patrols. The police carefully investigated any Blacks who were new arrivals to their jurisdiction.

> In 1838 the constable of Raleigh was required to check the entire city and its suburbs no less than two Sundays a month and search any suspect house as a preventive measure against strange blacks moving into town. Virtually all southern cities had restrictions on blacks holding night meetings, in addition to curfew laws. (p. 70)

Blacks were not permitted to move freely, participate in politics, carry a gun, or testify against whites. It was a crime for a person who was Black to use any provoking language or menacing gesture toward a person who was white. The police aggressively enforced these laws and punished transgressors, usually with corporal punishment or by forcing free Blacks back into slavery.

The Black Codes

The criminal justice institutions and police patrols that remained following the Civil War initially changed very little. Although the Thirteenth Amendment abolished slavery in 1865, southern states attempted to maintain white supremacy by politically, economically, and socially reducing Blacks to a state of semi-slavery (Mann, 1993; Walker, 1980). In 1866, immediately following the war, the southern state legislatures passed the Black Codes. These new laws were nearly identical to the slave codes, often simply substituting the word "black" wherever the word "slave" had appeared (Katz, 1995).

In some cases the law required special licenses for Blacks to work in any job other than servant or farmer (Katz, 1995). In all southern states, Blacks were prohibited from owning guns or city property; they could not testify in court. It was a crime for Blacks to be "impudent" or to insult a white person (p. 233). Apprenticeship laws allowed whites to force Black children into repressive and often brutal apprenticeships when their parents were deemed unable to support them (Williams & Murphy, 1990).

Another common practice was to arrest freed slaves who did not have written proof of employment for the following year and then send them back to the plantation to work off their sentence in the fields from which they had just been set "free." The following excerpt described this practice:

> Prisoners were soon rented out (their former masters getting first choice) to work off their sentences and fines through labor. Members of the Seventy-fourth United States Colored Infantry were arrested the day after their discharge from the army because they did not have employment certificates. . . . Now, noted one Southerner, "the white community as a whole controls the Blacks as a group." (Katz, 1995, p. 233)

Adamson (1983) argued that the convict lease system was instituted in the South largely as an alternative form of race control and as a new method of maintaining what was essentially a slave economy. The convict lease system resembled slavery "in the political and economic functions it performed, of course, but also in its organization, terminology, and relationship to the wider society" (p. 558). The freedom of Blacks was viewed as both a political and economic threat. The convict lease system was also applied to sharecroppers who attempted to leave their fields for better opportunities and to vagrants, debtors, and petty thieves. It often took years to work off the fine for a county misdemeanor.

The release of thousands of slaves was both psychologically and economically devastating to white people. Freed slaves were released into an extremely hostile environment, and they met resistance to their every attempt to adjust, assimilate, or simply survive. This utter destitution was reason enough for white people to fear them. "To whites in the postbellum South the policeman stood as the first line of defense against blacks. It was his responsibility to break up the black gambling and vice dens, to clear the streets of vagrants, to catch Negro lawbreakers, and on occasion to keep black voters in check" (Rabinowitz, 1992, p. 594). In both the North and the South after the war, white police officers arrested Blacks in far greater numbers than whites, often for misdemeanors such as vagrancy, petty larceny, and disorderly conduct.

Regulation of the Poor

The change to industrial policing in northern cities brought an elaborate and comprehensive criminal justice system designed to regulate the poor working class and to maintain order. Recent immigrants were typically perceived as the greatest potential threat to the social order; they received the brunt of police surveillance and repression. Over time most immigrants gained greater political and economic power, in some instances through the development of powerful political machines. Each of the European immigrant groups eventually escaped the ghetto and its characteristic police oppression. African Americans, however, became permanent residents of the ghetto and constant targets of police violence and repression.

Free African Americans in the Northern States

Even in the northern states, overpolicing of African Americans was commonplace (Hawkins & Thomas, 1991). The rights of northern African Americans were only slightly less restricted than those of freed Blacks in the South. For example, Blacks were often not allowed to vote or testify in court. Indeed, in some "free states," they were not allowed to hold real estate, make contracts, or maintain lawsuits. Ironically, while the Jacksonian Reform Movement of the 1830s greatly extended suffrage by removing the restriction of property ownership for white voters, increased restrictions were placed on the right-to-vote for African Americans (Katz, 1995).

Northern police were not unaffected by slavery. At times they also played a role in its enforcement. In 1850 the Federal Fugitive Slave Law was passed that made it a crime to help a slave escape (Katz, 1995). As evidenced by the following excerpt from a poster in Boston, local law enforcement agents as well as U.S. Marshals aggressively enforced this law.

> CAUTION!! COLORED PEOPLE of Boston, One & All, you are hereby respectfully cautioned and advised, to avoid conversing with the Watchmen and Police Officers of Boston, For since the recent order of the Mayor & Alderman, they are empowered to act as KIDNAPPERS and SLAVE CATCHERS, and have already been actually employed in kidnapping, catching, and keeping slaves . . . April 24, 1851. (Katz, 1995, p. 185)

After emancipation, northern cities became even more fearful of the potential social disorder that could be caused by the massive influx of thousands of freed slaves. People of African descent, whether in slavery, escaping from slavery, or freed were all generally classified as a dangerous class, requiring special police scrutiny and discipline. The police ruled with a heavy hand. Industrial-era police departments were granted great discretion and autonomy so that they could use whatever force was necessary to protect "respectable people" from the so-called "dangerous classes" (Miller, 1977, p. 141).

Ironically, white fears of disorder and crime by Blacks became a self-fulfilling prophecy (Hawkins & Thomas, 1991). As ex-slaves migrated en masse to cities, they were systematically relegated to the worst jobs and housing, frequently alongside "red light" districts littered with crime and vice. Forced to remain in conditions of oppression, poverty, and racism, "many fell prey to the hardships and drifted into a life of crime and vice. Others turned on themselves, fighting and killing as the only way to vent their frustrations" (p. 73). Rather than taking responsibility for creation of the conditions in which such violence and despair is bred, whites generally attributed this pathology to the innate character of Africans.

Racist views about Blacks provided the rationale for heavy-handed and brutal policing. White police officers arrested Blacks at a higher rate than whites (Hawkins & Thomas, 1991). Although the official legal status of Blacks was transformed with the abolition of slavery, their treatment by police and the courts changed very little. Differential treatment based on race was well established within the U.S. system of criminal justice (Walker, 1980). In the North, discriminatory policing typically took the form of discretionary decision-making resulting in unequal treatment based on race. In the South, discrimination was written directly into the laws establishing different punishments and codes of behavior based on race.

Civil Rights Act of 1866

Largely in response to the Black Codes, Congress passed the Civil Rights Act of 1866. The law designated persons of all races who were born in the United States to be national citizens with specific rights (Williams & Murphy, 1990). Republicans in the North felt that the Civil War had been fought for nothing if the same powerful land-owning gentry in the South continued to exercise political and economic control, forcing Blacks into a new form of slavery (Loewen, 1995). In 1868, the Republicans in Congress solidified the Civil Rights Act with the 14th Amendment to the U.S. Constitution, granting citizenship to all those born in the United States. In 1870, Congress passed the 15th Amendment which gave all male citizens the right to vote regardless of race.

Recognizing that these new laws could not be enforced in the South without government troops, a period of military occupation began. As discussed in chapter 3, this decade was known as Radical Reconstruction. Loewen (1995) identified this period as perhaps the most progressive time in U.S. history with regard to race, as the U.S. government used its military and political strength to ensure the rights of African Americans. As federal troops provided protection, African Americans were able to exercise their right to vote and to hold political office both in the South and the North. For the first time in U.S. history, the legal system was made accessible to African Americans throughout the country.

As noted in the previous chapter, white vigilantism developed in opposition to the empowerment of African Americans. It was typical for riots to erupt as Black police attempted to arrest white suspects. News accounts during this period attest to the great controversy surrounding "whether or not blacks should be appointed to police forces, what constituted the legitimate use of force against suspected black lawbreakers, and to what extent police authority was recognized and accepted by blacks" (Rabinowitz, 1992, p. 593). Radical Reconstruction dissolved during the 1870s, and many of the few hard-won advances toward racial justice disappeared.

Decline of Patronage

In some northern cities, African Americans had begun to gain a small degree of political leverage and representation on the police force. As city officials and the political machines sought the Black vote, they extended some benefits. However, the system of political patronage was dismantled just as African Americans had started to gain some privileges of membership. Although the modern era of policing led to reforms that brought the white majority substantial improvement in their police service, racial minorities did not share in this experience.

Industrial police departments had gained legitimacy through their political connections. Modern police forces relied on the law to legitimize their operation. As we have seen, laws are not free from bias. Layer upon layer of racism was embedded within the law. That legacy legitimized racist actions by the police, even though other laws specifically prohibited different standards of conduct and differential enforcement based on race.

Police Harassment and Brutality

When Radical Reconstruction came to an end in the South, the "criminal justice system was one of the major instruments of white supremacy" (Walker, 1980, p. 119). One way that the police maintained white supremacy was through the brutal and discriminatory practices toward Blacks. One early source documenting Black anger toward police is the *Weekly Defiance*, Atlanta's African American newspaper. As early as 1881, the paper noted numerous cases of police harassment and brutality. An Atlanta Police Commissioner was reported to have urged his officers to "kill every damned nigger you have a row with" (Platt et al., 1982, p. 26). The *Weekly Defiance* stated: "We have lived in Atlanta twenty-seven years, and have heard the lash sounded from the cabins of the slaves, poured on by their masters; we have never seen a meaner set of low down cut throats, scrapes and murders than the city of Atlanta has to protect the peace" (Watts, 1992b, p. 915).

This heavy-handed law enforcement was supported by the mainstream media. The *Atlanta Constitution* stated that "A Negro with a bundle on his shoulders at the dead hour of night is always an object of suspicion to a policeman" (Rabinowitz, 1992, p. 599). In 1903, the *Atlanta Constitution* also "called for a stiffer enforcement of the vagrancy law, aimed at 'idle shiftless negroes—for the majority of the crimes punished in the city court are committed by this class'" (Watts, 1992b, p. 914). As a result of these prejudices and the desire to control the Black population, African Americans were frequently arrested for mere "suspicion." Selling an item at too low a price or possessing property such as a "handsome gold watch" was enough to result in time behind bars (Rabinowitz, 1992, p. 599).

Going to jail in the South, particularly for African Americans, was not a minor event. Being sentenced to prisons and jail often meant working on the "chain gang," which was practically a death sentence. The chain gang was an integral part of the preservation of white supremacy and the exercise of racial domination. African Americans deemed "unmanageable" were arrested and convicted on the slightest pretext and then leased out to private individuals and companies. As described in the following excerpt, fortunes were made through the brutal exploitation of convict labor. At the same time, this tortuous and inhumane process was designed to eradicate any will to resist domination:

> In the turpentine camps and mining camps, on levees and railroad con-
> struction projects, manhood was worked and whipped out of them. With
> chains welded to their bodies, waist deep sometimes in mud and slime,
> convicts toiled day in and day out. Their quarters were unbelievably
> filthy. Vermin, investigators reported, crawled over their clothes and bod-
> ies. (Bennett, 1993, p. 273)

Sir George Campbell, a contemporary observer of the chain gang system, was told explicitly that "chain gangs were often used as schools for undisciplined blacks who had grown up since slavery—as schools, in short, for servility" (Bennett, 1993, p. 273).

During the first half of the twentieth century, millions of African Americans left the rural South to escape Jim Crow laws and to search for better jobs in the industrial areas of the North and West (Walker, 1990). As discussed in previous chapters, the conditions they encountered changed very little. Through the practice of differential enforcement and sentencing, the police, along with the court system, played a key role in the preservation of the racist social order.

Differential Enforcement

Although modern police invoke the rhetoric of fairness and equality, a dual system of policing emerged that created extreme differences in the enforcement of the law. The following excerpt illustrates how racism and social prejudices are ingrained in the psyche of the modern police officer and white society in general. Differential enforcement occurs nearly unconsciously:

> As is well known, the preferred targets of special police concern are eth-
> nic and racial minorities, the poor living in urban slums, and young peo-
> ple in general. . . . In fact, this kind of reasoning was basic to the very
> creation of the police; for it was not assumed initially that the police
> would enforce laws in the broad sense, but that they would concentrate
> on the control of individual and collective tendencies toward transgres-
> sion and disorder issuing from what were referred to as the "dangerous
> classes." What was once a frankly admitted bias is, however, generally
> disavowed in our times. That is, in and of itself, the fact that someone is
> young, poor, and dark-complexioned is not supposed to mean anything
> whatsoever to the police officer. Statistically considered, he might be said
> to be more likely to run afoul of the law, but individually, all things being
> equal, his chances of being left alone *are supposed* to be the same as those
> of someone who is middle-aged, well-to-do, and fair-skinned. In fact,
> however, exactly the opposite is the case. All things being equal, the
> young-poor-black and the old-rich-white doing the very same things
> under the same circumstances will almost certainly not receive the same

kind of treatment from policemen. In fact, it is almost inconceivable that the two characters could ever appear or do something in ways that would mean the same thing to a policeman. Nor is the policeman merely expressing personal or institutional prejudice by according the two characters differential treatment. Public expectations insidiously instruct him to reckon with these "factors." (Bittner, 1990, pp. 98–99)

In reading the above excerpt, it is important to note that Bittner used the generic term "public" when, in actuality, he is referring to a very specific segment of the public—the white middle to upper class. The clear point, however, is that although the police did not create the racist and economic discrimination which produced the Black ghetto, their oppressive actions in the ghetto, which are either implicitly or explicitly condoned by white society, have led to a dual system of policing that amplifies these social cleavages.

The behavior of the police in Black communities was completely foreign to the personal experiences of whites. To African Americans, the white urban police officer came to symbolize racist oppression. Their personal experiences commonly included seeing Blacks beaten or even killed with impunity. White people, on the other hand, saw the police as protectors of their communities (Hawkins & Thomas, 1991). This divided reality of policing creates radically different impressions.

In every major city where blacks lived in large enough numbers to be noticed and feared by whites, the white police-force was allowed and often encouraged to keep "the niggers in their place." In large cities the white police presence conveyed totally different racial meanings to the black and white communities. To the white community, white police in black communities provided the first line of defense against "the black hordes." To the black community, white policemen represented nothing less than a hostile occupation army. Young blacks, especially males, grew up hating and distrusting the white police presence in their communities. While at the same time, many young white males grew up dreaming of donning the blue uniform and going forth into black communities to test their mettle. In short, much of the white policing in black communities was little more than another form of white social control which had evolved over the centuries in response to whites' racial phobias of black people. (p. 65)

The modern police officer emerged as the thin blue line—not against crime, but between Blacks and whites. White police officers aggressively enforced both formal and informal racial and economic segregation. Though the police did not create U.S. racism, their activities contribute to the magnitude of the gulf between the groups (Bittner, 1990).

According to Walker (1990), the abuses by police officers against African Americans became so serious that they "spurred a revolution in due process of law that reshaped the entire criminal justice system" (p. 238). Numerous efforts by various organizations, particularly the American Civil Liberties Union (ACLU) and the National Association for the Advancement of Colored People (NAACP), eventually exposed the extreme injustices faced by racial/ethnic minorities and the poor. The U.S. Supreme Court addressed these inequities during the 1960s.

Many accounts indicate that white police in the ghetto were very slow to respond to calls for assistance. When they did arrive, they responded with brutality. The St. Louis Civil Liberties Committee, which sought to defend African Americans who were victims of police abuse, found that the victims were very reluctant to press charges because of fear of police reprisals (Walker, 1990). One African-American man stated that the police told him that they would shoot him and claim that he was robbing a store if he "swore out an affidavit against them" (Walker, 1990, p. 164). Widespread illegal detentions were a regular police practice. A published report in 1959, *Secret Detentions by the Chicago Police*, revealed that the police frequently detained suspects in jail for days without filing charges. For the majority of white citizens this world was virtually unseen. The primary victims of this hidden pattern of abuse were racial and ethnic minorities and the poor.

The ghetto rebellions of the 1960s exposed the hypocrisy of the professional model of policing that claimed the legitimate right of the police to exercise force in the fair and impartial enforcement of the law. Despite the rhetoric of neutrality, the police routinely exercised extreme racial and economic discrimination. Statements such as that of Cleveland's police chief, Richard Wagner, who insisted that the Ohio legislature retain the death penalty "to keep the Negro in line" (Katz, 1995, p. 475), underscore the official sanctioning of discriminatory enforcement. According to Walker (1980), "Blacks in the northern ghetto increasingly saw the virtually all-white police department as an army of occupation" (p. 222). African Americans reached a boiling point and struck back with a series of empowerment strategies. The myth of equal enforcement began to crumble as a series of legal challenges, scholarly research, and violent rebellion exposed the reality of a dual system of justice in the United States.

Violent confrontations between police and racial/ethnic minority citizens showed no signs of waning despite increased awareness of police brutality. Police killings of citizens increased substantially in the 1960s, with 57 percent of all such killings committed against male minorities (Balkan et al., 1980). Although African Americans made up only about 10 percent of the U.S. population, they accounted for 51 percent of those killed by the police between 1960 and 1968 (Platt et al., 1982). The shooting of Blacks by police was without question the most explosive issue in police community relations, and such shootings frequently sparked major uprisings in the Black ghetto. The everyday Black experience with police brutality was both psychologically and physically oppressive.

Bayley and Mendelsohn (1969) studied police minority relations in the Denver area in the late 1960s. They concluded that the police are a visible intrusion in the everyday lives of people of color, out of proportion to their involvement in the lives of whites. In addition to illustrating greater solicited and unsolicited interaction among Blacks and Latinos, these interactions were characterized by high levels of "mistreatment, harassment, and brutality" (p. 122).

Georges-Abeyie (1991) described the overpolicing of U.S. urban ghettoes as "our hidden Petit Apartheid" (p. ix). He provided an example of a typical police-minority interaction. "Ride arounds" are a regular form of brutality and control in which white police officers place a young person of color into the back of the patrol car and then circle the housing project as they beat him. They then dump the victim onto the street where they picked him up, never charging him with a crime. When the victims of such violence attempt to file complaints, they usually face charges of resisting arrest or assaulting an officer (Walker, 1990). The following is a personal account of an early experience with housing project police in the ghetto by an Afro-Caribbean college professor:

> We were taken to the bowels of a thirteen story building, marched into a celled holding area and told to hold onto the bars while three grinning pink-faced officers in blue retrieved what appeared to us to be small oars. . . . Once the paddles were retrieved the 'fun' commenced; a ten to fifteen minute beating by three men in blue. The blows, like Rodney King's, landed primarily on our legs, calves, thighs, buttocks, and the flat of our backs. We saw stars and berated hatred. Had the officers not had guns we would have turned on them in a murderous rage. Instead, we were beaten to the ground, shrouded in our silence and their racial taunts and laughter. (Georges-Abeyie, 1991, p. viii)

The majority of white Americans have difficulty even imagining experiences like these occurring in the United States. It is not surprising that members of the white middle class, whether they are criminal justice college students or members of a jury, have a hard time accepting this reality. Such incidents are far removed from their personal experiences and therefore do not exist in their vision of possibilities. It is easier to deny or ignore this reality than to accept and confront the existence of these everyday brutal injustices.

An example of this denial can be found in the brief existence of Citizen Complaint Review Boards (CCRB) in New York and Philadelphia (Walker, 1990). In the mid-1960s, Philadelphia created a review board that included a majority of civilian appointees. New York soon followed the model after members of the African American community demanded a more aggressive response to police brutality. According to Walker (1990), "the police union forced a referendum regarding the CCRB. . . . In a bitter, racially-polarized election the voters abolished the review board by a two-to-one margin" (p. 274). A year later the model review board in Philadelphia was dismantled. Through such actions, white voters closed their eyes to police brutality and essentially unleashed the police on citizens residing in the ghetto.

The 1968 Report of the National Advisory Commission on Civil Disorders (The Kerner Report) found that physical abuse was only one of the sources of tension between police and African Americans. African Americans experienced numerous forms of harassment and intimidation in their interactions with police. Professor Albert Reiss, an experienced police ethnographer, provided the following testimony to the Commission:

> In predominately Negro precincts, over three-fourths of the white policemen expressed prejudice or highly prejudiced attitudes towards Negroes. Only one percent of the officers expressed attitudes which could be described as sympathetic towards Negroes. Indeed, close to one-half of all the police officers in predominately Negro high crime areas showed extreme prejudice against Negroes. What do I mean by extreme racial prejudice? I mean that they described Negroes in terms that are not people terms. They described them in terms of the animal kingdom. (Harris & Wicker, 1988, p. 306)

The Commission also heard testimony that the police regularly harassed interracial couples and frequently stopped African Americans on foot or in cars for no apparent reason. In addition, African Americans were subject to "contemptuous and degrading verbal abuse" (Harris & Wicker, 1988, p. 303). Ghetto youths were specifically targeted by police for dispersal of social gatherings and indiscriminate stops and searches. "As one Commission witness said, these [degrading incidents] strip the Negro of the one thing that he may have left—his dignity, 'the question of being a man'" (p. 303).

In chapter 3, we discussed the targeting of the Black Panther Party (an organization of African Americans formed to resist racist and economic discrimination through self-help and self-empowerment) by the FBI. According to Silvergate (1974), members of the Black Panthers were victims of police harassment through illegal stops, frisks, and searches. They were frequently arrested under vague statutes and were "shot by policemen who later charged that the Panthers opened fire on a small army of policemen who came with peaceful, lawful intentions" (p. 141).

Police Response to Other Minorities

The Black Panthers were not the only political or activist organization to experience such police harassment, and African Americans were not the only racial minority to suffer from overpolicing during this time period. Inspired by the success of African Americans in their struggle for civil rights, Native Americans also engaged in a struggle for their rights. In 1964 when the state government closed the Nisqually River to Indian fishermen, the Indians protested with "fish-ins" in defiance of the court order. In response, police officers "raided Indian fishing groups, destroyed boats, slashed nets, manhandled people, arrested seven Indians" (Zinn, 1980, p. 516). The following excerpt describes an incident in 1970 in which 150 U.S. Marshals physically removed sixty Pit Indians who refused to leave a piece of land that they claimed as theirs:

> The marshals began swinging their riot sticks, and blood started flowing. [Darryl B.] Wilson grabbed one marshal's club, was thrown down, manacled, and while lying face down on the ground was struck behind the head several times. A sixty-six-year-old man was beaten to unconscious-

ness. A white reporter was arrested, his wife beaten. They were all thrown into trucks and taken away, charged with assaulting state and federal officers and cutting trees—but not with trespassing, which might have brought into question the ownership of land. (p. 520)

The most well-known Native American activist organization was the American Indian Movement (AIM), which also experienced repression at the hands of the police. According to Platt et al. (1982), the FBI infiltrated this organization with undercover agents and incited its members to participate in illegal acts so that they could move in and arrest them. In 1973, approximately three hundred Oglala Sioux, many of them members of the American Indian Movement, entered Wounded Knee, South Dakota and declared it "liberated territory" (Zinn, 1980, p. 524). Within hours more than two hundred FBI agents, federal marshals, state police, local police, and even tribal police surrounded the village. Armed with armored vehicles, automatic rifles, machine guns, grenade launchers, and gas shells, the "law" enforcers soon began firing. As the siege continued, food supplies became scarce, and many who attempted to deliver food, clothing, and medical supplies to the Indians were arrested and the "contraband" seized. In one incident three planes dropped 1,200 pounds of food, "but as people scrambled to gather it up, a government helicopter appeared overhead and fired down on them while groundfire came from all sides. Frank Clearwater, an Indian man lying on a cot inside a church, was hit by a bullet. When his wife accompanied him to a hospital, she was arrested and jailed" (p. 524). After several months of more gun battles and deaths, a negotiated peace was finally reached.

Latinos have also experienced overpolicing in their communities. According to Mirandé (1987), "[p]olice abuse of Hispanics increased at a dramatic rate during the 1970s and reached a peak in 1976–1977 when in Texas alone sixteen Hispanics died while in police custody" (p. 180). The Community Relations Division of the U.S. Justice Department concluded a study of police-minority relations in 1980. This report described "an undeclared war between minorities and police" (p. 187). As Mirandé observed, the white majority appears to condone or ignore such abuses, as evidenced by the case in 1977 in which three Houston police officers were given a one-year prison sentence after being convicted of the murder of Chicano Vietnam War veteran, José Campos Torres. In another case, a police officer, Darrell Cain, stopped twelve-year-old Santo Rodriguez to question him about a service station robbery. Officer Cain interrogated the boy while playing "Russian Roulette." Santo Rodriguez was killed when Officer Cain placed the loaded .357-magnum revolver to Rodriguez's head and pulled the trigger. The police officer was convicted and sentenced to five years in prison for the murder of this 12-year-old boy.

Mirandé (1987) also observed that the *Sacramento Bee* and the *Stockon Record* newspapers reported that it was a common practice for United States Border Patrol officers to chase undocumented workers into local rivers and watch them drown. When news reporters asked Western Regional Commissioner Harold Ezell why border patrol officers did not carry ropes and life rings to help prevent the drownings, he responded that such equipment "would only encourage them to run into the water, thinking they'll be saved if they get into trouble" (p. 181).

Rodney King

The 1991 videotaped beating of Rodney King demonstrated to the world, specifically the white world, that overpolicing in the ghetto continues to inflict physical violence on the bodies of African Americans and other racial minorities. This incident did not shock African Americans in the same way that it did white Americans (Minerbrook, 1992). Many white Americans were horrified because they had so long neglected or ignored the black ghetto, as well as the dangerous interactions that continue to occur between the police and African-American males. Two white criminologists, attempting to articulate a white perspective, wrote "*We watched in horror* as King was repeatedly shot with a stungun and beaten severely (he suffered broken ribs, a broken ankle, a fractured skull and possible brain damage) while he lay helplessly on the ground" (Lynch & Patterson, 1991, pp. 1–2, *emphasis added*). This incident was far too familiar to the everyday residents of the Black ghettos of the United States. Although Los Angeles Police Chief Daryl Gates immediately described the incident as an aberration, the Christopher Commission found:

> [B]etween 1987 and 1990, 4,400 misconduct complaints were filed against the LAPD. Of these, 41 percent were filed by blacks, who make up only 13 percent of the population. In 1989 Los Angeles paid out $9.1 million to settle lawsuits alleging police misconduct. In 1990 that figure had risen to $11.3 million for suits alleging excessive force, wrongful deaths, false arrests, negligence, misconduct, and civil rights violations. (Skolnick & Fyfe, 1993, p. 3)

The commission concluded that a significant number of LAPD officers use excessive force against the public repeatedly; the written guidelines of the Department regarding force are regularly ignored; and the failure to control the officers is a management issue that is at the heart of the problem.

The commonality of such events is expressed in the statement by Rodney King himself that he fled the police because he was scared that they would hurt or even kill him. Most white people find it difficult to believe such a statement because it is outside their frame of reference. However, most Blacks understand his concern completely. The following excerpt was written by Jean Carey Bond, the mother of two children who attended Ivy League colleges, in response to a *New York Times* editorial in 1994 that claimed that the only Black people who had something to fear from the police were criminals:

> Don't tell any African American mother in this nation that the only Black men who have something to fear from the police are those who have committed crimes. When my son, who is in his 20s, was a teenager

attending the Dalton School, he was standing one night at the bus stop at Madison Avenue and 89th Street after leaving a school event. Suddenly, a police car screeched to a halt in front of him, its doors flew open and four white cops jumped out with guns drawn. They threw him up against the wall, patted him down and grilled him, a gun at his head all the while. Fortunately for my son, he didn't flinch; then, along came a white class-mate who, peering through the small crowd that had gathered, saw my son and identified him to the cops. It seems a mugging had occurred in the area and, according to the cops, my son fit the description of the per-petrator—meaning my son is Black. On another occasion, my son was in a taxi that was turning onto our block in Washington Heights late one night when he made the mistake of making eye contact with a white cop in a patrol car that had pulled up beside the taxi. The cops stopped the cab, yanked both my son and the cabby out and frisked them with guns drawn. Given the chronic nature of police misconduct, either of these encounters could just as easily as not ended in my entirely law-abiding son's death. (Katz, 1995, p. 611)

Institutionalized Racism

Our discussion of overpolicing of minority communities cannot be lim-ited to police brutality or even overt racism. In the aftermath of the Civil Rights Movement, the issue has become much too complex for such a sim-plistic approach. Although the fear of physical police violence continues to be a serious concern in African American communities, the most pervasive threat to these communities is from the less blatantly violent forms of overpo-licing resulting from institutionalized racism. The term "institutionalized rac-ism" refers to attempts to justify racial and ethnic disparities as the result of allegedly racially neutral factors, such as prior criminal record, employment status, demeanor, etc. (Walker et al., 2000).

Throughout the 1980s and 1990s, the politicization of race and crime and the war on drugs have converged to produce a criminal justice system in the United States that is generating frightening and debilitating racist effects (Miller, 1996). African Americans continue to be stopped, frisked, arrested, shot and killed, and victimized by excessive physical force at the hands of the police at a rate that far exceeds the experience of whites in the United States (Walker et al., 2000). Both the bigotry of individual officers and groups of officers and the more pervasive effects of institutionalized racism contribute to this reality.

One reason for the frequency of abuses by the police toward Blacks is the exaggerated police presence in economically depressed areas populated pri-marily by people of color. The police have a far more visible role and a greater degree of personal contact in such areas. Police departments routinely assign more patrol officers to the areas where they anticipate having higher levels of street crime and violence (Walker et al., 2000). According to Johnson (1992) the Black ghetto is a central concern of modern police depart-ments because of the police perception that this area is where the crime is located. Johnson further noted that the people living in these neighborhoods must endure a relatively high level of police surveillance and intervention into their daily lives, because "[f]rom the front seat of a moving patrol car, street life in a typical Negro ghetto is perceived as an uninterrupted sequence of suspicious scenes" (p. 392).

Probable Cause Masks the Reality of Profiling

Police suspicion of African Americans, particularly young Black men, is not limited to the ghetto. While conducting cultural diversity training with white police officers from suburban departments in the proximity of a large Midwestern city, we discussed stop and frisk detentions. One of the officers spoke up, saying "a black man in 'my' neighborhood is probable cause for a stop." Police officers are taught that reasonable suspicion is sufficient to justify a stop of a "suspicious" person, to ask them to explain their action(s), and to frisk for a weapon. The police officer in the training class used the words "probable cause." The officers proclaimed that their actions were not based on racism, but rather on years of professional police experience. One officer explained, "We know who is committing the crimes in our neighborhoods. They are coming in from the city into our neighborhoods, committing robberies, burglaries, and selling drugs." When asked if they included the race of the suspect in establishing their probable cause for the stop or arrest, the officers took great pride in explaining that they did not—and proceeded to articulate all around the issue without ever mentioning race. These officers unwittingly illustrated the process through which racism becomes institutionalized. Through such techniques as "profiling" offenders based on racially discriminatory arrest statistics, or conducting business as usual while replacing race with other words or phrases such as "inner city youth" or "looking suspiciously out of place," discussion of race becomes the more technical debate over probable cause.

Some criminal justice scholars have gone to great lengths to argue that race is not a significant factor in arrest decision-making (see Wilbanks, 1987, *The Myth of the Racist Criminal Justice System*). However, Walker et al. (2000) conducted a review of the available research on race and arrests which revealed that, even when all relevant factors are controlled, evidence of discrimination on the basis of race persists. The discrepancy is partially explained by the lack of economic opportunity that produces "criminogenic" conditions in certain areas. This leads to higher participation in crime by Blacks, which in turn results in higher arrest rates. Much of this is a consequence of the broader pattern of societal racism. Police actions "amplify" these attitudes. Stereotyping of suspects on the basis of race leads to (1) higher rates of stopping and questioning Blacks, (2) arresting Blacks on the basis of less stringent legal standards, and (3) shooting and killing Blacks at a disproportionate rate. Jerome Skolnick refers to a "visual shorthand" for suspects: "a disposition to stereotype is an integral part of the policeman's world" (Walker, 1999, p. 227).

Using Arrests to Resolve Problems

According to Johnson (1992), the police descend upon the ghetto and upon African Americans in general with a law enforcement mentality that focuses excessively on the use of arrests as the strategy for resolving problems. Thus, much of the resentment against police in African-American communities is due to the formal intrusion of the police into situations that are only marginally criminal and that are handled informally in white middle class suburbs.

> Police patrol is so heavy and so indiscriminate that it is actively resented and normatively resisted by most blacks. Being stopped or dispersed by police without obvious basis is a routine part of life in the black community, especially for adolescent males. While searching for imaginary trouble, police help to create the real thing. By the same token, when the police encounter real trouble in the ghetto, they often escalate it. The family disturbance, that classic occasion for police intervention in ghetto life, is often inflamed rather than cooled off by police arrival on the scene. (pp. 393–394)

Johnson (1992) further noted that such actions result in an extraordinarily high level of arrests among African Americans, with some studies estimating the probability of a Black male being arrested in his lifetime approaching 90 percent. Not only do these arrests devastate individuals, they have the potential to crush entire communities. The vast majority of those arrested and most of those going to prison and jail under these circumstances are charged with minor discretionary charges or victimless crimes (Irwin & Austin, 1997). The result of the criminalization of such a large proportion of young Black men in African-American communities is widespread social and economic devastation. Miller's (1996) analysis of available statistics and research evidence concludes that the police, as well as other components of the criminal justice system, have become even more aggressive in their struggle to solve complex social problems and human conflicts through criminalization.

Irwin and Austin (1997) note that, as the United States has become entangled in a political one-upmanship in which nearly every politician attempts to prove that they are tougher on crime than their opponent, the nation has been engaged in an unprecedented "imprisonment binge." The United States has achieved the second highest national incarceration rate in the world, just behind Russia, and the highest rate in its own history. In addition, this imprisonment binge has been accompanied by large increases in other forms of correctional supervision, such as probation, parole, and jail. The massive wave of humanity under these various forms of criminal justice control is disproportionately comprised of young, uneducated, unemployed or underemployed Black and Latino males. Politicians have embraced the politics of fear and have adopted simplistic, "get-tough" bumper-sticker policy initiatives to inspire voter interest and to deflect the public's attention from other more controversial issues (Irwin & Austin, 1997).

An increasingly frightened public inflamed by politicians and the media, applies pressure on the police to produce measurable results in their fight against crime (Miller, 1996). For practical reasons, police have tended to take the path of least resistance in their effort to demonstrate that they are doing something about crime and violence. For example, the police have become more and more likely to invoke laws for minor offenses and consensual crimes in order to increase their arrest statistics. Miller observed that the increases in crime statistics that have been reported in the last 20 years are more a result of draconian police practices than real increases in criminal activity. This path of least resistance, along with long-held beliefs that poor people and minorities are more likely to be involved in criminal activity, results in significantly higher numbers of African-American and Latino males being arrested and prosecuted for a variety of offenses, most of which are neither serious nor violent. Targeting the poor and least powerful for increased enforcement allows the police to be less stringent about legal standards and procedures. Such defendants do not have the resources with which to fight back legally.

In an ethnographic study of the Rapid Deployment Unit in the Washington, D.C. Metropolitan Police Department, Chambliss (1994) illustrated how the political obsession with urban street crime and the "war on drugs" is being played out in the streets of our major cities. The Rapid Deployment Unit (RDU) is a product of the riots of the 1960s. The "War on Drugs" has replaced riots as the inner-city crisis. In an area of the city where 40 percent of the Black population lives below the poverty line, the RDU patrols the urban ghetto primarily in search of drug violations. This unit is extraordinarily proactive. Members were frequently observed trampling the civil rights of, and violently threatening African Americans who had committed minor offenses or no offenses at all. Approximately one-third of its arrests came from proactive undercover drug sales, and half of the arrests of this special unit were from vehicular stops with improperly used or no probable cause.

Kraska and Kappeler (1997) provided compelling evidence that the ethnographic observations made by Chambliss (1994) may reflect a national trend in the use of paramilitary police units (PPU). Kraska and Kappeler discovered that municipal police agencies, as well as state and federal agencies, frequently develop special militarized units that patrol in full armor. Common weapons include semi-automatic and automatic shotguns, M16s, Heckler and Koch MP5 submachine guns, and sniper rifles. These weapons are often loaded with powerful scopes, night-vision equipment, and silencers. The units are also armed with percussion grenades, CS and OC gas grenades, shotgun-launched bean-bag systems, battering rams, hydraulic door-jamb spreaders, and C4 explosives. PPUs frequently patrol in two to four officer cars and in some cases urban assault vehicles and vans. Similar to the initial creation of the RDU team, these units are often paraded as emergency teams designed to deal with barricaded subjects and hostage situations.

However, also similar to the RDU, Kraska and Kappeler (1997) discovered that the new emergency appears to be the war on drugs, for these units are used primarily for high-risk warrant work. "The drug war of the late

1980s and 1990s required the servicing of an unprecedented number of search warrants and a lesser number of arrest warrants" (p. 7). These warrants almost exclusively involve "no-knock entries." The police obtain a search warrant based on a tip from a neighbor or some other informant. In some departments, they do not even wait for the warrant if they feel that evidence may be lost. The paramilitary police unit then descends upon the home with all its military might. When these units are not conducting such searches, they frequently engage in saturation patrols, often under the guise of "Community Policing" or fixing "broken windows" (see chapter 2). As observed by Chambliss (1994), these search warrant raids and saturation patrols are highly concentrated in inner-city areas that are heavily populated by racial minorities. These units do not patrol white middle-class suburbia.

All three researchers attributed this new form of policing to the pressures of the drug war. Chambliss (1994) explained that the "war on drugs" launched in the 1980s under the Reagan Administration and continued by the administrations of Bush and Clinton, and the related panic over urban street crime, have placed a tremendous amount of pressure on the police to make arrests, particularly drug arrests. Sadly similar to the measurement of the Vietnam War by body counts, success in the drug war is measured by counting drug arrests. This strategy has pushed the police to concentrate on numbers of arrests rather than on the quality of their arrests. Going for the easy arrest has meant arresting the poor and the least powerful, contributing to high rates of arrest among young urban racial minorities.

The racist effect of the war on drugs can be seen in the fact that 90 percent of all offenders sentenced to prison for possession of drugs are Black or Latino. The following excerpt reveals some of the devastating effects of this particular brand of overpolicing in communities of color:

> The intensive surveillance of black neighborhoods and the pattern of surveillance in white neighborhoods has the general consequence of institutionalizing racism by defining the problem of crime generally, and drug use in particular, as a problem of young black men. It further ghettoizes the African American community and destroys any possibility for normal family and community relations. Young African American and Latino men are defined as a criminal group, arrested for minor offenses over and over again, and given criminal records which justify long prison sentences. (Chambliss, 1994, p. 183)

Institutionalizing racist law enforcement practices in this manner has the effect of further obscuring the racism by redefining the reality of crime so that such practices appear neutral and logical.

Conclusion

The obscured racism embedded in overpolicing gives it frightening power. Overt racism can be seen and addressed head on. Confronting racism which is shrouded in legal and seemingly neutral practices is more difficult.

African Americans are more likely to be stopped, questioned, searched, and arrested than white Americans. They are also more likely to be shot and killed or victimized by excessive physical force at the hands of the police than whites (Walker et al., 2000). The lifetime risk for an African American male to be arrested hovers around 80 percent to 90 percent (Miller, 1996). A study of the country's 56 largest cities showed that a nonwhite male was 3½ times more likely to have a felony arrest than a white male, and 51 percent of all nonwhite males could anticipate being arrested for a felony at some time during their lives.

All races in the United States use illicit drugs in relative proportion to their percentages in the population. Yet African Americans are 18 times more likely to be arrested for a drug offense than whites (Miller, 1996). While African Americans make up only 12 percent of the nation's population and 13% of those who use illicit drugs, they accounted for over half of the annual state and federal prison admissions in the 1990s. The proportional representation of Blacks in U.S. prisons has increased steadily during the twentieth century. Racial disparity in imprisonment is growing, not shrinking. Almost one in every three African American men between 20 and 29 years of age is in prison, jail, probation, or parole on any given day (Irwin & Austin, 1997). Only one in fifteen white men in the same age group are under criminal justice control. "Sixty years ago, less than one-fourth of prison admissions were nonwhite. Today, nearly three-fourths are nonwhite" (p. 4). The overpolicing of communities of color is one of the most devastating problems facing the United States in the 1990s.

5 Police-Community Relations Programs

The history of policing in the United States is marked by racial injustice and interracial conflict. While people of color and some whites have struggled to achieve greater social justice in criminal justice, official efforts have been much less vigorous. As we have seen, strikes and riots to protest unacceptable conditions received no guarantee of civil rights from the police. When discriminatory law enforcement contributed to the outbreak of violence, the police compounded their complicity by ignoring violent attacks by whites on Blacks. They arrested African Americans who fought back and frequently participated in the riots themselves. "Despite overwhelming evidence of police racism, nothing was done to improve police-community relations in the aftermath of the riots" (Walker, 1980, p. 165).

The failure of public officials to take corrective action after the Springfield, Illinois race riot of 1908 led to the formation of the National Association for the Advancement of Colored People (NAACP). Throughout most of its history, this organization has engaged in a tenacious struggle to improve race relations and racial justice, particularly in relation to police. Ironically, police leadership ignored the issue of blatant police misconduct at a time when they were launching their national campaign to "professionalize" the police in order to put an end to police corruption, inefficiency, and brutality. For the next twenty years, efforts to improve race relations in the United States were primarily carried out by private organizations.

Critical Events Converge

In chapter 3 we raised the issue of the hypocrisy of asking Black soldiers to defend freedom and democracy on foreign soil while they were denied those privileges in their own country. "Thoughtful whites had been painfully aware of the contradiction in opposing Nazi racial philosophy with racially segregated military units" (Harris & Wicker, 1944, p. 224). To convince the public to support World War II, the U.S. leadership understood the necessity of defining the war effort in terms of good and evil. It could not tolerate confusion and complications that might make people question the value of the effort. The enemy was evil. Our allies were good. Fascism and dictatorship were evil. Everything that came from these evil nations was also evil—even their racist propaganda. It was critical for the U.S. that all citizens be united to fight a common foe and to achieve a noble purpose.

The U.S. military commissioned Frank Capra, the famous movie director, to produce propaganda war movies. The new lieutenant colonel filmed an emotional presentation of the historical wartime service by Blacks in U.S. history in an effort to motivate African-American support for the war and to improve race relations between the segregated troops. The skillfully crafted movie, "The Negro Soldier," made no reference to slavery, Jim Crow laws, or even the Civil War; it attempted to inspire African-American support for the war by attacking the racist ideology of Adolf Hitler.

The United States leadership could not ignore the serious contradictions presented by U.S. racism. African-American, Japanese-American, Latino-American, and Native-American soldiers returned to racial segregation and discrimination in the United States after risking their bodies and lives to free other countries. The race riots of 1943 were prominently featured in national magazines. The riots gave the enemy ammunition to expose the hypocrisy of United States rhetoric. Fear that the Germans and the Japanese would exploit racial discontent to weaken the U.S. war effort promoted the establishment of numerous state and local human relations commissions. Many religious, business, and political leaders joined the effort to promote racial harmony (Walker, 1990, p. 163).

> The specter of Nazi racism forced increasing numbers of white Americans to confront the reality of racism at home. The war effort itself, with its egalitarian rhetoric, accelerated the change in attitudes. . . . The growing commitment to racial equality proved to be a precipitant to the police-community relations movement. (Walker, 1992a, pp. 816–817)

Investigations of the riots of 1943 identified numerous examples of police incompetence and misconduct. Many of the race-relations efforts focused on the police, specifically the relationship between the police and African Americans.The actions of the police were just as deplorable in the 1940s as they were in the riots two decades earlier. "They had been guilty of discriminatory conduct before the riot and excessive violence toward blacks during disturbances, and it was believed that police actions had helped to escalate rather than defuse racial conflict" (Walker, 1980, p. 197). White America was frightened by the growing racial violence, especially as African Americans began to fight back, and demanded that police improve their effectiveness in preventing race riots. While most police agencies continued to respond with the traditional hardliner's call for more money, personnel, and equipment to control riots, a few pioneers in the area of police-community relations took a different route and attempted to develop strategies to prevent racial violence.

Innovative Responses to Challenging Situations

In 1944, the International City Management Association (ICMA) published the first manual for race-relations training entitled *The Police and Minority Groups*. The authors of this training manual were Joseph Weckler, a staff member of the American Council on Race Relations, and Theo E. Hall, the chief of police in Wilmette, Illinois. Explaining the need for improving police-minority relations, Weckler and Hall (1944) wrote the following:

> The Detroit riots of 1943 cost over a million irreplaceable man-hours of war production. Such breakdowns in civil peace lead directly to unnecessary losses of American lives on distant fronts. The effect of such a riot on home-front morale and national unity is as bad as the loss of a major battle. Such disorders likewise undermine our influence with millions of our nonwhite Allies and neutrals and give our enemies material for effective propaganda against us among many nations. (p. 1)

In the preface to the police training manual, the Executive Director of the International City Management Association, Clarence E. Ridley, described the perspective of the progressive municipal leadership:

> Municipal officials have a definite responsibility to prevent such outbreaks and to help improve relations between the various racial, national, and religious groups which are found in most cities. They have a particular responsibility to protect the legally prescribed civil rights of all people in the community regardless of race, religion, or national origin. This task of maintaining civil rights and public order places a heavy and complex burden upon police departments during periods of tension. The chief hope for police success in handling intergroup relationship lies in the field of prevention. It is impossible to handle a riot "successfully." Deaths and injuries, extensive property destruction and severe damage to public morale are virtually inevitable in any large-scale disorder. (Weckler & Hall, 1944, p. iii)

Other professional organizations prepared training manuals and participated in some of the race relations training for police officers. The National Conference of Christians and Jews became one of the leading advocates for improving police-community relations and sponsored an annual conference at Michigan State University. Academics became involved in the process. Joseph D. Lohman, a University of Chicago sociologist, conducted race-relations training for the Chicago Park District Police and published his materials in a widely used training text. The most vigorous support for police-community and race-relations programs was found in the state of California, where Governor Earl Warren (future Chief Justice of the Supreme Court) enthusiastically supported these programs.

The following excerpt from the report of the California Governor's Peace Officers Committee (chaired by Attorney General Robert W. Kenny) illustrated the perspective of social activists on the crucial role played by the police in the struggle to achieve racial harmony:

> The police play a vitally important role in race relations. No agency of government can be more effective in furthering good race relations, and in preventing riots, than the police. *Police can prevent race riots.* Not only can they prevent such riots from occurring, but, should they occur, intelligent police methods can minimize their consequences. At the same time, lax police policies contribute to race riots and antiquated methods of coping with riots can greatly aggravate their consequences. (Weckler & Hall, 1944, p. 1)

Thoughtful police leadership and well-constructed police policy on how to handle individuals from various minority groups were seen as critical for the maintenance of social order.

In their training manual, Weckler and Hall (1944) did not just criticize police actions, they also cited several examples of how sound police leadership can reduce the severity of racial tension and violence. They discussed police actions in Washington, D.C. in 1943. Police administrators met with the African-American demonstrators, attempted to calm concerned whites, and provided heavy security with direct orders to maintain neutrality and to protect the demonstrators. The police administrator actually marched at the head of the procession.

It is interesting to note that nearly fifty years later the police chief of Reno, Nevada followed a similar strategy to avert violence in his city after the first acquittal verdict in the Rodney King beating case. Chief Kirkland met with concerned citizens, helped them plan their protest march, and walked hand-in-hand with demonstrators at the front of their group. The most revealing facet of police-minority relations in the 1990s is not Chief Kirkland's actions, but the failure of so many other chiefs to do the same thing—or even to have enough awareness of their communities' concerns to be prepared for such protests. The learning that takes place in police crises appears not to be cumulative. Each crisis is observed and analyzed as if it were unprecedented. The police appear to learn by trial and error, committing the same errors over and over again.

Two other examples provided by Weckler and Hall (1944) were in Houston and Passaic (New Jersey). In Houston, police administrators met with a bi-racial group of civic leaders and announced a commitment to a peaceful demonstration. They promised to enforce the law against everyone. In Passaic, police administrators developed an interracial committee to serve as a community liaison and strongly encouraged community input on reducing racial friction. Special attention was given to racial tension in the schools. The police took the lead, working with school personnel and parents to mediate conflict. The message was clear. With sound police management and sincere community interaction, the police can have a significant impact on race relations and on racial violence in particular. The problem, of course, was to convince other police leadership and the rank-and-file of the value of such efforts.[1]

Although certain key police administrators took an active role in promoting progressive programs, the vast majority did not support this progressive agenda. One of the leading advocates for improving police-community relations, particularly with racial minorities, was the chief of the Milwaukee Police Department, Joseph Kluchesky. Kluchesky introduced race-relations training in Milwaukee in 1944, constructed a manual for the training that many departments used or adapted, and he served as a consultant and instructor for race relations to several mid-size departments. Although Kluchesky was invited to speak to the IACP in 1945 at their convention on "the race problem," he found little support for his perspective. Not only did the vast majority of the police chiefs believe that it was not the task of the police to improve race relations, they denied the existence of racism in their departments. The general consensus of the members of the IACP was that the task for police in reference to civil disorders and racial tension was to improve "communications to facilitate the swift mobilization of federal troops when necessary and the development of special riot equipment and training" (Walker, 1992a, p. 820).

One of the most interesting aspects of the race-relations programs developed for police officers in the 1940s was their similarity to programs developed in the 1960s and the cultural diversity training and community policing initiatives that emerged in the 1990s. A three-pronged strategy was initiated which included: (1) race-relations training for the rank-and-file police officers; (2) the development of formal contacts with Black leaders along with the hiring of additional African-American police officers; and (3) establishing guidelines for handling civil disorders (Walker, 1992a).

Weckler and Hall's (1944) manual encouraged police administrators to utilize the press to publicize the actions of minority officers. The publicity would boost minority officer morale and enhance public respect and trust, particularly among racial minority groups. The authors also suggested that police departments raise the educational requirements for police officers and hire more minority police officers, particularly African Americans and Mexican Americans. Weckler and Hall further suggested that the police be more cooperative with the press by sharing with newspapers the facts in their possession that might reduce press sensationalism and dispel inflammatory rumors. The manual encouraged the police to work with other agencies, such as schools and playgrounds, other public agencies, semi-public and private agencies (i.e., the urban league, NAACP, YMCA), and other police agencies in an integrated prevention program designed to reduce racial violence.

Race-Relations Training

The most central element of the reform program of the 1940s was the race-relations training for police officers. The primary thrust of the training was to appeal to the officers' sense of professionalism. Joseph D. Lohman stated that "The police officer must bring under control his personal sentiments and prejudices and subordinate them in a truly professional spirit" (Walker, 1992a, p. 823). In other words, professional officers should act without partiality, bias, or malice. An officer's ability to control emotions is a sign of professionalism.

The manual urged a very practical approach that would establish a pattern of behavior that would benefit citizens and help avoid escalation of events to crisis proportion:

> The question of neighborhood policing involves primarily the problem of protecting law-abiding citizens in slum areas against the neighborhood hoodlum and criminal element of their own group. . . . These people should be given the best possible police protection, not only out of police pride in doing their job, but because such people are the backbone of the neighborhood on whom the police and the whole community will have to depend for intelligent local leadership in times of critical tension between racial, national, or religious groups. (Weckler & Hall, 1944, p. 12)

Weckler and Hall (1944) called for a long-term, ongoing training program with brief emergency training courses. The long-term training should contain a no-discrimination policy, clearly stating that all trainees be given equal treatment. Second, the training should incorporate a thorough understanding of civil rights laws—directing the police officer to safeguard these rights for all citizens and to limit police authority. Third, the training must focus on preventive policing, emphasizing how rumors and unanswered complaints escalate racial tension.

Finally, Weckler and Hall felt that it was essential to include vital background information. This should be taught by the regular training staff and members of the minority groups in the community. This part of the training was designed to accomplish three specific goals. The first goal was to provide officers with facts about racial similarities and differences, emphasizing that no group has biological or racial tendencies toward crime. Secondly, the training was designed to explain the role of social and economic conditions on the perspectives of racial, national, and religious groups. Thirdly, the background information block of training was supposed to demonstrate the important contributions of minority group members to U.S. life and culture.

By the 1950s, most of the voices calling for police relations programs were drowned out by the more conservative hard-line approach. Race-relations programs for police officers faded away in the few departments that had adopted them. Most of these training programs throughout the country "were brief and short-lived, a hasty response to the immediate civil disorder. Moreover, most were initiated by groups other than the police departments" (Walker, 1992a, p. 823). Often training programs lasted only 2 or 3 hours or included less than twenty officers from the entire force. As massive displays of racial violence declined, the crisis waned and the enthusiasm and commitment to race-relations programs faded. When urban racial violence erupted again in the 1960s, police administrators committed the same errors and "rediscovered" the same strategies.

Revisited Concepts

The crisis experienced in U.S. cities in the 1960s sparked a revival of interest in police-community relations. Police departments began to scramble for solutions and strategies. Once again the police were criticized for contributing to racial violence through their indifference to the pain and suffering of racial minorities and through their racially discriminatory enforcement practices. It became clear that the lack of support for police among racial minorities was a serious hindrance to the ability of police to maintain social order. Thus, for the very practical purpose of order maintenance, the police began to develop programs designed to improve relations with citizens and, more generally, to improve their public image.

As the civil rights movement grew more militant in the 1960s, activists came into direct conflict with the police (Walker, 1999). The strategies of sit-ins, demonstrations, and marches put the police officer responsible for enforcing racist laws squarely in opposition to African Americans attempting to assert their rights. Between 1964 and 1967, tensions between the police and Blacks exploded in the numerous urban riots discussed in chapter 2. "Riots by minorities in cities of the United States made the police a public issue. . . . The riots have succeeded in dramatizing the quality of relations between police and minorities—primarily Negroes—as perceived by minorities" (Bayley & Mendelsohn, 1969, p. 172).

In chapter 2 we mentioned the finding of *The 1968 Report of the National Advisory Commission on Civil Disorders* that police practices were the number one grievance identified by communities. The Report emphasized that *the police were not merely a "spark" factor.* The police:

> symbolize white power, white racism and white repression. And the fact is that many police do reflect and express these white attitudes. The atmosphere of hostility and cynicism is reinforced by a widespread belief among Negroes in the existence of police brutality and in a "double standard" of justice and protection—one for Negroes and one for whites. (Harris & Wicker, 1988, p. 11)

As symbols of white power and racism, police were often the target of retaliatory strikes by frustrated, oppressed people of color in the United States. However, this was not a new symbolism that emerged in the 1960s. Police in the United States had played a key role in maintaining the racist social order throughout their history, and racial minorities were thoroughly conscious of this history. White people, on the other hand, have been able to close their eyes to police oppression and racial discrimination. What made the 1960s unique was that it became increasingly difficult for White America to deny racist inequality and the brutality of policing the ghetto.

As in the 1940s, the hypocrisy was exposed to the world at a particularly sensitive time. As the United States proclaimed itself the world defender of freedom and democracy at the height of the Cold War and in the war in Vietnam, television cameras broadcast images of African Americans being beaten by police, sprayed with fire hoses, and assaulted by attack dogs. Blacks sought to attend decent schools, to live without fear of white violence, to obtain adequate employment, and most of all to vote. Criticism of Communist countries for denying people the right of self-determination was juxtaposed with race riots and demonstrations that revealed the stark reality that many U.S. citizens were denied this basic right.

The police were in the trenches of this civil war, fighting the battle to preserve a racist governmental system. They were the most visible symbol of continued violent racial oppression in the United States. Numerous large-scale structural reforms were recommended by *The Kerner Report* and other social commentators of the time. However, when reforms were initiated, the police were the primary focus. In the following excerpt the authors of *The Kerner Report* explained why the police received so much attention:

> And yet, precisely because the policeman in the ghetto is a symbol—precisely because he symbolizes so much—it is of critical importance that the police and society take every possible step to allay grievances that flow from a sense of injustice and increased tension and turmoil.

In this work, the police bear a major responsibility for making needed changes. In the first instance, they have the prime responsibility for safeguarding the minimum goal of any civilized society—security of life and property. To do so, they are given society's maximum power—discretion in the use of force. Second, it is axiomatic that effective law enforcement requires the support of the community. Such support will not be present when a substantial segment of the community feels threatened by the police and regards the police as an occupying force (Harris & Wicker, 1988, pp. 300–301).

As pressure came down on police agencies to improve their public image—and to prevent race riots rather than just contain them—the most common response was the establishment of *police-community relations programs* (Walker, 1999). These programs involved the police, or at least their designated representative, in community programs designed to soften their image, to educate the public on the police perspective, and to open lines of communication between the police and the general public. For example, police-community relations units were established with carefully selected officers who would speak at community centers and schools. In some cases these officers appeared on children's radio or television programs as "Officer Friendly" or "Deputy Bob." Other programs included the establishment of "ride alongs" (clearly distinct from the "ride arounds" discussed in chapter 4) where citizens were invited to ride in police cars as they patrolled; competitive sports events between the police and African-American citizens; and summer camps for ghetto children (Walker, 1980). The mission was to introduce the citizen to the police perspective, not to allow citizens to monitor or judge police behavior.

Some projects that were implemented, such as the establishment of neighborhood storefront officers, reversed the trend toward centralization of the police that characterized modern policing. An important dimension of this type of initiative was to give the general public more direct access to police officers. The more radical of these programs established "community control," or "putting the police in each neighborhood under the control of elected boards of commissioners" (Walker, 1980, p. 227). Community control initiatives eventually failed because of resistance by police. A study by Bayley and Mendelsohn (1969) noted that the police "are impatient with the uninformed comments of outsiders who have no experience of life on the streets or in the ghetto" (p. 194). Police administrators are very resistant to any "outside" review of their activities, particularly by those groups with a long history of hostility toward police.

Officer Attitudes

A common response in the 1960s to growing concerns about hostilities between the police and racial minorities was the creation of training programs, usually targeting rank-and-file police officers. Bayley and Mendelsohn's (1969) study indicated that, although the racial attitudes of police officers reflected those held by the majority of people in society, police officers were slightly more prejudiced than the rest of society. Bayley and Mendelsohn also reported that most police officers rejected claims by minority groups that the police treated them unfairly or improperly. Further, most officers said that they did not believe charges of police brutality made by minority groups. However, these same police officers frequently said they believed that racial minorities require stricter discipline and more control than did white people. Bayley and Mendelsohn (1969) concluded that the officers in the study "understand that minorities have not received a fair deal in American society, but they are nonetheless offended by the militancy, and assertiveness, of them" (p. 150).

Relations between police and racial minorities were loaded with mutual misunderstandings, stereotypes, fear, distrust, and anger. The negative, cynical, and frustrated attitudes of police officers were viewed as important contributing factors to the tensions in police race relations; but it was also considered problematic that members of racial minorities were equally cynical and frustrated in their dealings with the police. Bayley and Mendelsohn (1969) explained the dilemma:

> Policemen also feel cynical, and sometimes angry, because they have been placed, despite themselves, in such an insidious position. They are asked to do a job that few people understand, involving, in the case of minority persons, people who are bitter and frustrated. The policeman's ability to reach the roots of the problems is exceedingly limited; yet dominant society expects him to contain unrest and disorder and criticizes him freely if he does it inconsiderately, in haste, or anger. The police officer, in his relations with minority group people, feels terribly put upon. He, like minority people, feels caught in an embittering situation not of his own making—a situation few people in majority society will make the effort or have the patience to try to understand. (p. 197)

It was hoped that, with proper training on the issue of race, police offic-ers could gain a better appreciation of the plight of racial minorities and reduce their feelings of anger, while learning how to interact with minorities in a more effective and less threatening manner. At the same time, it was hoped that such an effort would be seen by racial minorities as a genuine effort to reduce racial discrimination in the police department. Therefore, police-community relations training was reintroduced in the 1960s in order to alter individual police behavior, making it less inflammatory, and to demon-strate to the public that the police were seriously committed to improving race relations through the development of a more responsive and respectful police department.

Convergence of Social Reforms and Social Action

According to Cizon and Smith (1970), the development of techniques for training police officers in the area of community relations became a high pri-ority beginning with the Law Enforcement Assistance Act (LEAA) of 1965. Previous community-relations training or human-relations training efforts had been haphazard, largely concentrating only on police recruits in acad-emy classes, with lectures on anthropology, sociology, African American his-tory, psychology, ethics, and demographics. The only discussions that took place in these training sessions typically consisted of about twenty minutes of questions to the local college professors who were brought in to lecture on the subject. However, with the passage of the Law Enforcement Assistance Act, funding was provided to launch training programs that were much more extensive, intense, and innovative.

Cizon and Smith's (1970) government report, *Some Guidelines for Success-ful Police-Community Relations Training Programs*, is a review of three training programs implemented in 1965 and 1966 in Indiana, Detroit, and Boston. According to this report, much of the renewed interest in community-rela-tions training focused on the challenge to police work in a democratic society resulting from a convergence of social reforms and social action that occurred in the early 1960s. "Recent Supreme Court decisions on police practices, problems of control in civil disturbances, accusations of brutality from minor-ity groups, and public demands for improved professional service have high-lighted the complexity of police work in a democratic society" (p. 1). The challenge was to "maintain a balance between the security of the community and the rights of the individuals" and to "work with the community in the promotion of law and order" (p. 1).

According to the report, the uniqueness of policing in the 1960s was that the urban areas were populated by minority groups of which the police were not a part. Historically, the police had been drawn from the minority groups they policed. Irish and German immigrants, in particular, used the police occupation as a way to assimilate and to advance socially and politically. For racial minorities, this path was rarely an option. Police jobs were often not available to African Americans, Mexican Americans, and Puerto Ricans. Therefore, white police in the ghettoes of the 1960s were in a culture "alien" to them. Police officers typically lacked the ability to communicate effectively with or to understand the people on their beats, leading to what was termed "mutual antagonism." According to Cizon and Smith (1970), "the police are uncertain as to how they can positively promote law and order among people whom they do not understand and who do not understand them" (p. 3).

The impetus for the renewed interest in police-community relations training among police leaders in the 1960s was the practical need for more effective law enforcement. Improving police minority relations was expected to aid the police in their law enforcement function. In a democracy, effective and efficient policing is only possible if the police are seen as a legitimate force by the people being policed. Police-community race relations training was introduced in the 1960s in an attempt to win the consent and support of the racial minorities who lived in the urban ghettos of the United States and had historically not been able to achieve representation on the police force.

The police and much of the public viewed race relations training as subverting law enforcement and succumbing to the demands of racial minorities. The Supreme Court decisions that required police to inform suspects of their rights, provide lawyers to indigent defendants, and require warrants for searches and seizures were seen as "handcuffing" the police. In this same spirit, police-community relations programs came under attack by more conservative elements as a threat to the "professional" status of police. As the crisis of the ghetto revolts declined, the experiment in police-minority relations lost the little support that it had. The human relations approach to urban unrest was abandoned in favor of the more conservative police approach of purchasing more powerful weapons and more sophisticated technology, developing better deployment tactics, and arresting or eliminating leading militant social activists. According to Bayley and Mendelsohn (1969), the police, who are generally more conservative than most of the public, reluctantly endured race-relations training and were quick to accept this more conservative approach.

The police never fully grasped the importance of good police-race relations as a law enforcement strategy:

> Many policemen, and the public in larger measure, have not yet realized that attention to human relations can pay vast dividends in law enforcement and defense of public safety. Many policemen are unable to see beyond the fact that demands are being made upon them by minority groups. They tend to view police reform as concessions to minorities, which implies a loss of face. Similarly from the public, voices are raised charging that any effort to palliate minority hostility causes a consequent, and equivalent, decline in standards of law enforcement. (Bayley & Mendelsohn, 1969, p. 170)

Although most of the larger municipal police departments created police-community relations programs in response to the riots of the 1960s, these programs were generally marginalized within the departments and had little impact on day-to-day police operations (Walker, 1998). Police-community relations programs, including human relations training, were only halfheartedly and haphazardly introduced with police officers showing significant resistance and resentment toward such programs. The authors of *The Kerner Report* noted that "it is clear that these programs have little support among the rank and file officers. . . . On the command level, there is often little interest. Programs are not integrated into the department; units do not receive adequate budgetary support" (Harris & Wicker, 1988, p. 320). These training programs either disappeared or were relegated to some minor public relations activity. By the 1990s, though, simmering racial tensions once again reached a boiling point, and police-community relations resurfaced yet again.

A New Urgency

Beginning in the 1980s, and then exploding in the early 1990s, racial violence again focused attention on the relationship between the police and the community. However, this time training programs were endorsed by both liberal and conservative voices. A combination of critical events led to significant changes in the professional model of policing and a revitalization of human-relations training for police officers. Police departments across the nation began to develop cultural diversity awareness training programs with conspicuous urgency, often in response to grievous incidents in interactions between police and racial, ethnic, and cultural minorities.

We were directly involved with initiatives to institute cultural diversity training in two separate regions of the country. In each of these circumstances, very specific events prompted community leaders to call into question police-minority relations. While the heightened public focus on police-minority relations was precipitated in each instance by specific incidents, community leaders in both areas were careful to emphasize that these incidents were indicative of long-term problems. The circumstances surrounding efforts to develop human relations and cultural sensitivity training in South Carolina beginning at the onset of the 1990s, and in the Milwaukee area in 1991 and 1992, provide a number of insights into the development of such training.

In both South Carolina and Milwaukee, the push for sensitivity training came from grassroots community organizations—not from the police themselves nor from local "experts" or scholars. In the late 1980s, a series of critical incidents between various police agencies in South Carolina and African-American citizens led to a general feeling of heightened tension and hostility. In 1989, a police shooting of a young, African-American man in rural South Carolina prompted the South Carolina Chapter of the National Rainbow Coalition to call for an evaluation of police training in the areas of human relations, racism, crisis intervention, and use of force. In South Carolina there is one central police academy in Columbia, SC where *all* law enforcement officers receive their training in order to be certified police officers in the state. This centralized training strategy made it easier to focus efforts to improve policing in the state through training.

The director of the SCCJA eventually made a conscious and decisive effort to take the lead in addressing this issue for all police agencies in the state. Although initially very suspicious of us and our intent, the fact that he had previously hired me as a Deputy Sheriff while he was the Captain at the local Sheriff's Department eased the conversation. He invited us to observe as much of the training as we would like and asked for a copy of our evaluation. Within a month's time, the Director responded to the concerns of the Rainbow Coalition, as well as other groups that had been putting pressure on law enforcement throughout the state, by creating a Human Relations Curriculum Committee, appointing me as a founding member, to develop human relations training for police officers throughout the state of South Carolina. The mission of the Human Relations Curriculum Committee was to:

> assist the South Carolina Criminal Justice Academy in the development and evaluation of a Human Relations curriculum that will enable South Carolina Law Enforcement to perform its duties so that each citizen is accorded his or her civil and human rights in accordance with the law.

The addition of "human" rights as well as just "civil" rights was a very conscious effort by the committee members to recognize that the law is not always congruent with "justice." The membership of this committee was dominated by African-American police officers, many of whom were pioneers who broke numerous color barriers, including the first African-American South Carolina Highway Patrol officer and the first African-American instructor at the SCCJA. Most of the members had personally experienced racial segregation laws in South Carolina. Public forums were conducted in order to get community input and support for the curriculum development process. In South Carolina, the focus was almost exclusively on relations between the police and African Americans.

The situation in Wisconsin was much more decentralized, with training for police officers taking place in a combination of basic training academies, employer based training institutes, and within technical colleges throughout the state. The Wisconsin Law Enforcement Training and Standards Board, through its staffing arm in the Department of Justice Training and Standards Bureau, sets employment standards for police officers in the state and sets the content for basic recruit training. Beyond setting the content for basic training, they simply act in an advisory capacity and oversee annual training requirements.

Although all police departments came under scrutiny in 1991, the Milwaukee Police Department received the brunt of indictments regarding police treatment of diverse groups within the community. The initial impetus came from incidents related to the Jeffrey Dahmer serial murder case. The Dahmer incidents took place in a predominately African-American neighborhood; most of Dahmer's victims were African-American; and all were gay (or bisexual) men of color. This case, discussed in detail in chapter 3, brought to a boiling point long-standing tensions between the police and Milwaukee's multicultural community (Barlow et al., 1994).

Upon learning of the situation in which police had been in contact with Dahmer and one of his victims, Konerak Sinthasomphone, Police Chief Philip Arreola moved quickly to suspend the three officers, pending an internal investigation. The Milwaukee Police Association (MPA) reacted to the suspensions just as quickly with a poll of its membership and a vote of "no confidence" in Milwaukee's Chief of Police. On August 1st, Chief Arreola released audio tapes of the 911 call which brought the police into contact with Dahmer and Sinthasomphone on May 27th, and the subsequent call from Glenda Cleveland, the African-American woman who persistently asserted her belief that the young Asian male was a child. Once the public heard the tape of Glenda Cleveland pleading with the police on behalf of the young boy on the evening news, or read the tape transcripts in their daily papers, community outrage over insensitivity to the concerns of minorities escalated (Barlow et al., 1994). After the Wisconsin Attorney General's Office announced that no criminal charges would be filed against the three suspended officers, the three officers were fired by Chief Arreola, though one of the firings was suspended because of the officer's relative inexperience as a police officer. After over a year's struggle in the courts, all of the suspensions were reversed and back pay was reimbursed.

On August 6, 1991, faced with a city polarized on the basis of support for or outrage toward the police, Mayor John Norquist appointed a commission to study police community-relations (Barlow et al., 1994). The commission was asked to examine the police department's service to the citizens of Milwaukee, particularly with regard to "responsiveness and sensitivity to diversity within the community, and to make recommendations for improved police-community relations" (Mayor's Citizen Commission, 1991, p. ii). In the months that followed, the Blue Ribbon Commission conducted public forums and sought input from experts in police-community relations. Numerous police support and police protest rallies were held, indicating the high level of community concern on all sides of the controversy. African American and gay rights activists conducted their own independent investigations of police-minority relations; they formed the Black Ribbon and the Lavender Ribbon Commissions, respectively.

The most consistent recommendation that emerged from all these commissions was cultural diversity awareness training for the police. The mayor's commission concluded that "good relationships and effective policing are best fostered by community-oriented policing with appropriate training, in a Department which values both its own diversity and the community's" (Mayor's Citizen Commission, 1991, p. i). In response, the Milwaukee Police Department issued a request for proposals for developing and conducting cultural diversity awareness training, emphasizing that it should integrate the philosophy of community policing (Koleas, 1991).

Other initiatives in the development of such training emerged. As an outreach effort of the Criminal Justice Programs, the University of Wisconsin-Milwaukee implemented cultural diversity training for law enforcement officers. One of the authors (David) developed and instructed the training seminar, largely for the suburban police departments surrounding the city of Milwaukee. The outreach and extension personnel at the University of Wisconsin-Oshkosh and the University of Wisconsin-Green Bay together developed a three-year continuing education series for Northeastern Wisconsin, entitled "Law Enforcement and Corrections in a Multicultural World." One of us (Melissa) was on the steering committee of this effort, and the other (David) assisted in the development and instruction of the seminars. Several incidents of concern were specifically mentioned: charges of racial harassment filed by five University of Wisconsin-Green Bay African-American students against the Green Bay Police Department, the suicide of a Hmong man after being arrested for physically abusing his daughter, and the kidnapping of a child by her family when their demand that their daughter see a shaman before she received medical treatment was rejected. In addition, the Wisconsin Law Enforcement Training and Standards Bureau began to explore avenues for implementing cultural diversity training for law enforcement and corrections statewide.

The triggering event that ignited national interest in the adoption of cultural diversity awareness training for police officers in the early 1990s was the videotaped police beating of Rodney King. The series of events connected to the beating radically challenged policing strategies throughout the country. Police were motivated to demonstrate their sincerity in the area of improving police-minority relations. The impact has been so substantial that many police administrators and experts have referred to the post-Rodney King era of policing. The general historical and social significance of the events linked to Rodney King is discussed by Axelrod and Phillips (1992) in the afterword of their book, *What Every American Should Know About American History: 200 Events That Shaped the Nation*. Axelrod and Phillips speculated that the 201st most important event to shape America was "the brutal beating of Rodney King by four Los Angeles policemen, the incredible not-guilty verdict in the subsequent trial of the policemen, and the extremely violent Los Angeles riot the verdict engendered" (1992, p. 259).

The Christopher Commission (1991), which was appointed to investigate police community relations in Los Angeles, strongly recommended increased efforts in cultural sensitivity training for Los Angeles police officers. Interestingly, events remarkably similar to those in Los Angeles in 1992 had occurred in Miami a little more than a decade earlier. In this incident, police officers beat Arthur McDuffie, an African American, to death. The acquittal of the officers sparked the Liberty City riot, which was "more violent and destructive than any of the American urban disorders of the 1960s" (Skolnick & Fyfe, 1993, p. 182).

Like the Los Angeles riots, the Liberty City riot became the impetus for efforts to improve relations between police and minorities. A central component of these efforts, according to Deputy Director Eduardo Gonzalez of the Metro-Dade Police Department, has been the development of "Humanity and Community Relations" training in the Miami-Dade County area (Gonzalez, 1992). Each successive investigatory commission appears to make the same observations and the same recommendations as those eloquently stated by Dr. Kenneth Clark as he testified before the 1968 Kerner Commission:

> I read that report . . . of the 1919 riot in Chicago, and it is as if I were reading the report of the investigating committee on the Harlem riot of '35, the report of the investigating committee of the Harlem riot of '43, the report of the McCone Commission on the Watts riot.
>
> I must again in candor say to you members of this Commission—it is a kind of Alice in Wonderland—with the same moving picture re-shown over and over again, the same analysis, the same recommendations, and the same inaction. (Harris & Wicker, 1988, p. 483)

The prophetic nature of Clark's statements is quite remarkable when one reviews how the history of police-minority relations has unfolded in the last few decades. In the period between Arthur McDuffie in Miami and Rodney King in Los Angeles, police-minority relations across the nation were characterized by tensions that typically remain just below the surface until something happens to bring them to the forefront of the community—or sometimes to the level of national concern. As the inability or unwillingness of white Americans to take decisive and meaningful action to eliminate racism from all institutions continues after each of these racial crises, one of the least intrusive recommendations, and one which has grown to be at least somewhat acceptable to the majority, is cultural diversity training for police officers.

Untenable Relationships

The movement to develop cultural diversity awareness training for police officers that re-emerged in the early 1990s reflected a recognition among law enforcement administrators and experts that relations between police and racial minorities were becoming untenable. Ron McCarthy, director of the Deadly Force Training Program for the International Association of Chiefs of Police (IACP) and the retired senior supervisor of the LAPD's SWAT unit, recommended Race and Cultural Awareness Training for police officers to combat unreasonable fear of racial minorities and the excessive use of force (Soloman & McCarthy, 1989). Nancy Taylor's (1991) book, *Bias Crime: The Law Enforcement Response*, contains numerous articles by prominent police executives who recommend training as a means of reducing prevalent policing bias crimes.

Another crucial indicator that police executives and experts throughout the nation began to embrace cultural diversity awareness training in the early 1990s was the endorsement of such training by important national police organizations. The Law Enforcement Steering Committee (LESC) is an organization made up of representatives of the Police Executive Research Forum (PERF), the Federal Law Enforcement Officers Association, the Fraternal Order of Police, the International Brotherhood of Police Officers, the Major Cities Chiefs, the National Association of Police Organizations, the National Organization of Black Law Enforcement Executives (NOBLE), the National Troopers Coalition, and the Police Foundation. LESC met in 1992 to discuss public safety and to formulate a series of policy recommendations for improving police community relations and reducing crime. A central recommendation of this committee was that police departments should initiate "cultural bias training" programs "to enable officers to do their jobs better" (PERF, 1992, p. 6).

NOBLE made cultural diversity awareness training for police officers a primary area of focus in 1993 and developed a series of national and regional conferences around the country to showcase "exemplary programs that address the emerging cultural issues facing law enforcement" (NOBLE & PERF, 1993). Every year the national annual NOBLE Conference contains workshops on police race relations and diversity training as a central feature of their programs. The cultural diversity training movement was further institutionalized when the National Law Enforcement Cultural Awareness Association was formed in 1993, complete with a quarterly newsletter that went out to members all across the United States.

Acute awareness of the problems in police-minority relations has resulted in traditionally conservative police executives and organizations supporting the development of cultural diversity awareness training for police officers. Conservative police organizations and government executives have vigorously supported training efforts designed to strengthen conflict resolution and communication skills. Both NOBLE and PERF support human relations or cultural diversity awareness training because it fits well with their support for problem-oriented or community-oriented policing. Their stated concerns include officer safety, liability, and law enforcement effectiveness (Benson, 1992). In other words, the members of these organizations believe that perfecting the human relations and communications skills of police officers will improve police-minority relations by reducing conflict, tension, and subsequent violence. This improvement enhances the safety of police officers and decreases their probability of being sued.

> Each improved interaction with citizens slowly leads to overall improved police-community relations. Further, cross cultural communication skills enhance officer safety. Knowledge, of words, gestures, and labels offensive to particular groups is the first step to communicating and knowing not to imitate that style . . . can contribute to the successful defusing of potential communications. (Shusta et al., 1995, p. 96)

Police chiefs have an obvious interest in insulating themselves from citizen complaints of police brutality, misconduct, and abrasiveness, given the lawsuits that accompany such charges. Police organizations have come to acknowledge that enhanced understanding and sharpened communication skills can protect officers from departmental discipline and civil suits. In addition, police agencies have become concerned about the tension in police-community relations and the declining sense of authority among police officers. Police often express the hope that such training will be a two-way street, in which the public simultaneously learns about the difficulties and hazards of police work. Leaders of law enforcement organizations can see that traditional forms of policing are not successful in reducing crime or making inner-city streets safer. Community- or problem-oriented policing and cultural diversity awareness training are viewed as strategies that can make a difference.

Cultural diversity awareness training has also received significant support from more liberal groups such as the American Civil Liberties Union, the National Rainbow Coalition, gay and lesbian organizations, and grassroots community groups. Like their more conservative counterparts, liberal groups see the training as a component of community policing. Community activists, however, support such training for reasons differing from those of the police leadership, whose primary concerns are legal liability and police effectiveness. Instead, these groups want departments to be more responsive to the diversity in the communities they police. Police brutality, misconduct, and abrasiveness are concerns because of the impact of this behavior on those who are victimized by these acts—not because of lawsuits. The hope is that cultural diversity awareness training will enlighten police officers regarding the concerns of racial and cultural minorities as well as the poor and lead to better treatment of these groups by police officers.

What is particularly interesting about the current incarnation of race and cultural relations training in policing is that it has received such universal support at least among police leadership and leaders of community organizations if not among rank-and-file officers. Some of the training programs developed in response to pressure from grassroots organizations; others were proactive initiatives of criminal justice and government executives. In short, efforts to develop cultural diversity awareness training have enjoyed widespread support from both traditionally more liberal and traditionally more conservative individuals and organizations.

Expectations and Potential Pitfalls

What can be expected from community policing and cultural diversity training for police officers? Is it reasonable to expect fundamental changes in police-community relations to occur as a result of these training programs, or will such programs merely treat the symptoms of a deeper contradiction of policing in the United States? Is the problem of police-minority relations simply a matter of misunderstandings and miscommunication? Is it simply that police officers do not empathize with minority concerns? Or is the problem much more fundamental to the very structure of society in the United States and the role and function of police within that structure?

The content of cultural diversity awareness programs of the 1990s did not change dramatically from that of programs in the 1960s. Many current programs are designed to teach individual officers cross-cultural communication and conflict resolution skills in a relatively short period of time. Most cultural diversity training seminars also provide specific information about particular cultures. Although the cultural information that is presented in more current training programs is still primarily about African Americans, many other groups have stepped up to demand a share of the curriculum (e.g., Latinos, Asians, homosexuals, women) (Barlow & Barlow, 1993, 1994).

Some training programs have stretched the notion of diversity so far as to include promoting better understanding between a multitude of segments in our population, including married and single people, managers and engineers, people with children and those without children. Though basic human relations skills are clearly a component of policing that is both ethical and effective, we must be careful to segment the legacy of the impact of slavery, lynchings, and hundreds of years of inhumane treatment from more incidental slights resulting from a lack of empathy in relatively mundane interpersonal communications. Reducing programs to an awareness that all human interactions are marked by differences of perception fails to grasp the deep divisions that have been wrought in relations between police and African Americans throughout the course of U.S. history.

Some cultural diversity awareness training for rank-and-file police officers reduces issues of racism, homophobia, sexism, and general social intolerance to a behavioral problem of the individual line officer. These training formats focus on the individual officer rather than the larger organization. "Discrimination, mistreatment, and a non-responsive police force are then framed as individual problems of rogue officers and not as a systemic condition. Training sessions are seen as 'the' solution to the problem of agency-wide racism, sexism, and homophobia" (Blakemore, Barlow, & Padgett, 1995, p. 75). This "bad-apple" approach draws attention and energy away from the larger problem of systematic police racism.

Trainers across the country agree that the most effective way to increase the receptivity of police officers to the training is to convince them that it is beneficial in terms of officer safety, liability, and effectiveness (Benson, 1992; Barlow & Barlow, 1994; Shusta et al., 1995). This emphasis can become problematic if police officers embrace the importance of training in cultural diversity only if it helps them to be more successful in manipulating individuals in the course of their interactions (Blakemore, Barlow, & Padgett, 1995). This basic paradox within the mission of cultural diversity awareness training was revealed in a question asked by an officer participating in one of my training sessions. The officer asked me, "How can I stop a Black family [in an automobile] without being viewed as a racist?" When questioned about the purpose of the traffic stop, the officer replied that he had to stop the family because they were Black and this was cause for suspicion in his suburban township. For this officer, the purpose of cultural diversity awareness training was to provide information that would help to mask the racism that was a daily part of his job.

A recurring criticism of cultural diversity training, as well as most other community relations programs, is that they fail to impact the institutional and structural causes of the conditions that they are attempting to change. At best they address symptoms of racism, such as verbal insults, miscommunication, differential treatment by the police, and hostile police community feelings. These reforms do not alter the economic, political, and social power relations that created and continue to sustain racism in the United States. Early in the developmental stages of police-community relations programs, Bayley and Mendelsohn (1969) expressed concerns about the limitations of this approach to resolve the conflict between the police and racial minorities:

> substantial improvements in police-minority relations cannot be expected solely as the result of changes in police policy and behavior. It will be necessary to change their symbolic status as well, and that is a function of a total system of majority-minority relationships. Reform in certain police practices must certainly be undertaken. There are ways in which the police may lessen the hostility they attract. However, in order to make a dent in deeply ingrained habits of mind among minority people, passed on as part of the legacy of minority status, that change must be thorough, visible and permanent . . . it may not be within the power of the police to do much more than palliate the situation, no matter how heroic their efforts to change. In order to produce better police-community relations changes in police behavior must be one part of a program touching all those aspects of human interaction which create minority status. (pp. 141–142)

In other words, although certain police policies and behaviors may aggravate and support racism, the police did not create racism, and police reform cannot eliminate racism. The police are a contributing factor, but they are not the sole, or even the fundamental, source of racism in U.S. society.

Conclusion

In 1968, the Kerner Commission issued a statement that explains the public's polarization in terms of police-community relations.

> Segregation and poverty have created in the racial ghetto a destructive environment totally unknown to most white Americans. What white Americans have never fully understood—but what the Negro can never forget—is that white society is deeply implicated in the ghetto. White institutions created it, white institutions maintain it, and white society condones it. (Harris & Wicker, 1988, p. 2)

Whether they are police officers or everyday citizens, white people are baffled by the lower level of support for police among racial minorities, particularly African Americans. In our various interactions with police officers, young and old, we have often heard them express genuine astonishment at small African-American children expressing distrust or even hatred toward them as police officers. Frequently police officers question why members of racial minorities are so "uncooperative" and "anti-police" when "*we* are there to help them and clean up their neighborhood."

What these white people do not appreciate, and what Black people are unable to forget, is the whole history of racial discrimination and mistreatment at the hands of the police. The police and the entire criminal justice system are deeply implicated in the ghetto—in its formation and in its permanence. In this section we have examined the long history of the underpolicing and overpolicing of people of color that has contributed to the preservation of racial oppression in the United States. The legacy of police oppression and insensitivity to racial minorities, immigrants, and the poor is a contemporary reality with deep historical roots.

We have attempted to expose a world of policing that is unseen by many in this country today. The vast majority of white Americans, particularly those in the middle and upper classes, have never experienced the police as violent, uncaring oppressors. They have no frame of reference for envisioning the police as a serious threat to their lives. They cannot appreciate the claims of racial minorities concerning systematic police discrimination and brutality. The fact is that white Americans and people of color, particularly African Americans, live in two different worlds, separate and vastly unequal. Skolnick and Fyfe (1993) referred to this divide in analyzing the events after the beating of Rodney King.

> America is, culturally speaking, two countries. One is urban, cosmopolitan, and multicultural. It suffers disproportionately from crime, gang violence, poverty, and homelessness. The other is suburban, relatively safe, relatively prosperous, and—most important—unicultural. Like Simi Valley, and the King trial jury, it is predominately white and middle-class. The cops charged with assaulting Rodney King committed their crimes in the first America, but were tried in the second. (p. xi)

In order to understand the conflicts between police and people of color today, it is essential for police researchers, criminal justice students, police officers, as well as all of White America to relinquish their monocultural worldview and to widen their perceptions to include diametrically opposed interpretations.

No one has more eloquently and succinctly captured the fundamental problem of police-community relations in the United States than Black author James Baldwin (1961) in his frequently paraphrased work, "Fifth Avenue, Uptown: a Letter from Harlem." The following excerpt from this piece reflects the power of his message:

> The projects in Harlem are hated. They are hated almost as much as policemen, and this is saying a great deal. And they are hated for the same reason: both reveal, unbearably, the real attitude of the white world, no matter how many liberal speeches are made, no matter how many lofty editorials are written, no matter how many civil rights commissions are set up. . . .
> *The only way to police a ghetto is to be oppressive.* None of the Police Commissioner's men, even with the best will in the world, have any way of understanding the lives led by the people they swagger about in twos and threes controlling. Their very presence is an insult, and it would be, *even if*

they spent their entire day feeding gumdrops to children. They represent the
force of the white world, and the world's real intentions are, simply, for
that world's criminal profit and ease, to keep the black man corralled up
here, in his place. The badge, the gun in the holster, and the swinging club
make vivid what will happen should his rebellion become overt. Rare,
indeed, is the Harlem citizen, from the most circumspect church member
to the most shiftless adolescent, who does not have a long tale to tell of
police incompetence, injustice, or brutality . . .

It is hard, on the other hand, to blame the policeman blank, good-
natured, thoughtless, and insuperably innocent, for being such a perfect
representative of the people he serves. He, too, believes in *good intentions*
and is astounded and offended when they are not taken for the deed. He
has never, himself, done anything for which to be hated—which of us
has?—and yet he is facing, daily and nightly, people who would gladly
see him dead, and he knows it . . .

He moves through Harlem, therefore, like an occupying soldier in a
bitterly hostile country; which is precisely what, and where, he is, and is
the reason why he walks in twos and threes. (*Emphasis added*)

Baldwin identified several key lessons for those who are interested in
improving police-community relations. The most important is that it is not
individual racist actions of a few "bad apple" police officers that tarnish otherwise positive relationships between the police and people of color. The
oppression emanates from a political, economic, and social system that produced both police repression and the ghetto itself.

The U.S. ghetto has been manufactured through a long history of racial
and economic segregation. People perceived as a "problem population" have
been marginalized and ostracized. They are viewed as a problem because of
their potential to disrupt the social order. Spitzer (1976) refers to this group as
"social dynamite," because of their potential to explode into riots or revolution.

Members of the problem population are at the bottom of the social structure and receive the least benefit from the continuation of the status quo.
They are the ones who have the most to gain from a transformation in the
relations of power. This potential for violent rebellion makes them a special
concern of the police as well as the entire criminal justice system.

As demonstrated in Part 1, the fundamental role of the police is to maintain social order. Although ghetto residents may not be able to mount a violent
rebellion on a large enough scale to bring about a revolution, they clearly have
the power to inflict massive property damage and to strike fear into the heart of
White America. Therefore, the people of the ghetto are carefully surveilled and
controlled to prevent significant disruptions in the social order and to make
white people feel more secure. "Ultimately the police must be understood as a
domestic standing army designed primarily to control potential and collective
insurgency, not individual acts of criminality" (Balkan et al., 1980, p. 117).

The deindustrialization of urban America (Hagedorn, 1991) and the
migration of the Black middle class out of poverty-stricken inner-city neighborhoods in the past few decades have contributed to even greater destitution

of urban ghettos. Jobs, stability, and crucial social institutions have been ripped from these areas, leaving people with very little reason to support the social system, much less support the actions of the police officers charged with maintaining order. The problem of police-community relations cannot be resolved through a public relations blitz. Programs that attempt to sell the police as the friend of African Americans have no credibility. Neither better educated and more sensitive police officers, nor the good intentions of police reformers, can change the fact that the police are in the ghetto supporting a racist and discriminatory criminal justice system that helps to maintain a political and economic system based on the same bias. The solution to resolving the problems of police-community relations in the ghetto is not to improve interactions within the ghetto or even to provide opportunities for people to get out of the ghetto. The only solution is the elimination of ghettos from U.S. society.

It is no accident that the majority of the "successful" community relations programs are located in those communities that need it the least. Block watches, Operation ID, D.A.R.E., and other crime prevention programs designed to improve police-community relations usually thrive in those communities largely populated by white, middle-class citizens. These people are already inclined to believe that the police are fair and friendly and, thus, they are receptive to the crime prevention or "Officer Friendly" message. They rarely have personal experience with police corruption, brutality, or discrimination. Most importantly they have a vested interest in the continuation of the methods of social control that benefit them. Racial minorities and poor people do not reap the same benefits from the police and they are unlikely to be swayed by police officers hosting children's television shows, dressing up as robots or crime-fighting dogs, or handing out gumdrops. If we truly wish to improve police community relations, we must transform the social, political, and economic conditions that have produced the attitudes of mistrust in the people trapped in those circumstances.

Notes

[1] Twenty years later, Passaic, New Jersey was the scene of the wrongful arrest and conviction for murder of Rubin "Hurricane" Carter, black middle-weight boxing champion, whose story is the subject of the movie *Lazarus and the Hurricane*. The events surrounding Carter's arrest, conviction, and ultimate vindication (after nearly 20 years of wrongful imprisonment) demonstrate that race relations were less than ideal, despite the optimistic outlook described here.

Part Three
Police and Rebellion

Between Wednesday, April 29, 1992 and Monday, May 5, 1992, the city of Los Angeles exploded as people of color, particularly African Americans and Latinos, rebelled against a racist political economy that had long denied them justice. In some locations the rebellion largely consisted of non-violent demonstrations. However, the most dramatic and powerful events involved beatings, looting, and burning resulting in 5,633 arrests, 51 deaths, and $1 billion in property damage (Petersilia & Abrahamse, 1994). The Los Angeles riot was concentrated within the area known as South Central, but it spread to threaten Hollywood, Koreatown, and even Beverly Hills (Sonenshein, 1994). The riot was triggered by the acquittal of four white police officers who had been videotaped beating Rodney King, an African-American man. The amateur videotape was shown repeatedly on television throughout the world.

As discussed in chapter 3, there is little doubt that the videotaped beating of Rodney King, the first acquittal verdict, and the subsequent riots in South Central Los Angeles, represent the most significant sequence of events concerning police and society in the last twenty-five years. This urban rebellion radically transformed policing in the United States. Police agencies throughout the country struggled to project a positive image and to initiate damage control. The post-Rodney King era of policing is marked by a sense of urgency to embrace the rhetoric of community policing and cultural diversity awareness.

Attempting to understand the meaning of the 1992 uprising in South Central Los Angeles is a critical step toward understanding police-community relations—in particular, police relations with people of color in the United States. Placing an event into historical context means identifying those characteristics that are distinct from previous incidents, or historically specific to the time period, as well as those characteristics that are reminiscent of or historically consistent with similar previous incidents. The single overriding characteristic that connects all the events reviewed in Part Three is that they involve active resistance against racist oppression.

People struggle against wrongs committed against them with the tools available to them. Wealthy people have access to economic and political power to influence social interactions and to protect their interests. Enfranchised citizens use their voting power or other legitimate forms of political pressure to influence political institutions to enact and enforce policies that preserve their interests. Oppressed people who are consistently denied legitimate access to both economic and political power must either accept their oppression or resist, often through illegal means, in order to secure their interests. It is our contention that the six-day 1992 riot in Los Angeles was precisely such a form of resistance. It was a desperate act by oppressed groups demanding to be heard. The riot was part of larger struggles for justice within a racist and unjust social structure.

Neither African Americans nor other people of color in the United States have passively accepted their exploitation and victimization by White America. A white power elite has long dominated racial minorities with economic, political, and military power, effectively limiting access by African Americans to formal, legitimate avenues to seek redress or even to express their grievances. Throughout the history of the United States, the absolute frustration of economically and politically marginalized groups in the face of these obstacles has led to numerous rebellions in various forms. The nature and extent of these rebellions are shaped by the nature and extent of racism in the United States in a given historical period. The more overt the racism, the easier it is to identify individual or collective acts as resistance to oppression.

When oppression is both brutal and legal, modes of resistance are very limited. For example, when Africans in the United States were reduced to chattel through legalized slavery, sometimes the only means of resistance available was to destroy their own value as slaves by running away, self-mutilation, or suicide.

As oppressed groups gain greater power, it is possible for resistance to become more widespread, organized, and sophisticated. As African Americans gained legal rights, they used this new access to the legal system to fight many of their battles in the courts. When they gained limited economic power as customers, they utilized the boycott. As a result of legal and political struggles, racial discrimination became illegal, and African Americans were guaranteed the right to vote beginning with the Civil Rights Act of 1965. Unfortunately, the legacy of racism did not end at this point. Rather, with the outlawing of overt racial discrimination, racism in the U.S. became more covert.

In the post-Civil Rights era, racism became more complex and difficult to see. It was masked, driven underground, or hidden in economic discrimination. Furthermore, the interconnectedness of the various dimensions of power in the U.S. (i.e., class, race, gender, and sexual orientation in social, political, and economic relations) renders both oppression and resistance extremely complex to recognize. In an overtly racist society, where racism is formal and legal, acts of resistance are clear and easy to interpret. When racism is hidden and distorted, resistance to the oppressions of racism becomes more difficult to identify. The only critical difference between the 1992 Los Angeles riot and the Nat Turner slave rebellion in the South is the complexity of the oppression and the resistance.

In Los Angeles, as well as in the other struggles that we will review, the specific historical conditions of the events shaped the various forms of resistance. When justice is repeatedly denied in the political sphere, the marketplace, and the courts, struggles for justice are taken up in the streets—sometimes in the form of a riot. The United States of America began this way. As colonists were repeatedly denied effective participation in political, economic, and legal spheres, they went to the streets for justice through actions such as the Boston Massacre. Ultimately, freedom from British rule was won through violent revolution.

The United States government and its various institutions, at the federal, state, and local levels, have historically sought to preserve the current distributions of power and property, and those distributions are often dramatically unequal. Various groups in United States, from labor organizations to racial and ethnic minorities, have at times lacked the political and economic power to secure their rights and their interests, and their efforts to obtain this power have often been judged by the government and/or powerful white Americans to be illegitimate or illegal. Political struggles to transform current power relations have taken many forms, depending to a large extent upon the nature and extent of oppression.

Militant actions by people of color against white structures of power in the United States have not, thus far, been able to match the military might of White America. Those who have engaged in militant struggles have typically faced severe consequences, including the loss of life, liberty, and property. Physical struggles, whether in the form of riots or violent insurrection, are the last-ditch effort of desperate and frustrated people. As in guerilla warfare, African Americans cannot hope to win any major battles because they are always outgunned, but they may win the war. History demonstrates that violent struggles in the streets capture the attention of White America and have led to some social change.

As the primary and most visible instrument of social control, the police have been on the front lines of the power struggle. Because the role of police in our society is to maintain the social order, they are placed in direct opposition to efforts to alter the status quo. When racism was literally written into the law and the U.S. Constitution, it was the duty of the police officer to enforce the law and thus protect and maintain racist power relations. "Riots are the most serious threat against the fulfillment of the fundamental police responsibility to protect life and property. Large scale public disorder is proof of the temporary breakdown of local government" (Weckler & Hall, 1944, p. 12). Thus, when rebellions take place, it is the police who are usually the focus of attention and criticism by White America for failing to secure order.

The oppressed also criticize the police because they are the most potent symbols of white racism in the United States. Despite the fact that each commission to investigate racial inequality in the twentieth century has noted that the police are only the enforcement arm of an entire political and economic system marred by racial inequality, social reforms usually go no further than to attempt to alter the strategies and techniques of the police. While reforms have sometimes included efforts to repair the breach in police legitimacy among those who are policed, they have *always* contained efforts to strengthen the power of the police to suppress insurrections more effectively.

The police are integrally linked with struggles for justice by African Americans and other people of color in this country. The role of police and the nature of struggles for justice place the police and oppressed racial minorities in direct opposition. It is this fundamental opposition that can be interpreted as the crux of conflicts between police and people of color in the United States. Thus, the conflicts can never be fully resolved without eliminating the racism embedded within our social structure. Police reform can only temporarily ameliorate the conflict; it cannot eliminate it. Part 3 explores the history of racial "rebellions" or "struggles for justice" through the exercise of resistance to the racist policies and institutions. Through this analysis we hope to contribute to a better understanding of the events in Los Angeles in 1991–1992 and, more importantly, to better understand the nature of conflicts between police and people of color.

As in much of this book, the focus of our study in Part 3 relies heavily on the experiences of African Americans, not because they are the only racial minority to be exploited in the United States, but because they are one of the most visible. The exploitation and oppression of African Americans are enduring characteristics of the United States, and the rebellions of African Americans against this repression have represented profound challenges to the legitimacy of U.S. democracy. As the 1968 President's Commission on Civil Disorders stated:

> We wish to be clear that in focusing on the Negro, we do not mean to imply any priority of need. It will not do to fight misery in the black ghetto and leave untouched the reality of injustice and deprivation elsewhere in our society. The first priority is order and justice for all Americans.
>
> In speaking of the Negro, we do not speak of "them." We speak of us—for freedoms and opportunities of all Americans are diminished and imperiled when they are denied to some Americans. The tragic waste of human spirit and resources, the unrecoverable loss to the nation which this denial has already caused—and continues to produce—no longer can be ignored or afforded. (Harris & Wicker, 1988, p. 34)

The history of racial rebellions discussed in Part 3 is not African American history, multicultural history, or race history—it is American history.

6 From Slavery to Jim Crow

Africans and Native Americans were kidnapped, forced into servitude, raped, murdered, and subjected to cultural genocide at the hands of white Europeans who set out to conquer the American continents. From the outset of this racist oppression, people of color fought in whatever ways they could to resist, often making themselves a very difficult commodity to be exploited.

Both Africans and Indians in the Americas confronted technologically superior military forces that suppressed resistance and ensured continued racist domination. As the new nation took shape, laws and institutions were established that solidified the institution of slavery. The interests of justice and freedom for people of color were in direct opposition to the government and its enforcement agencies. A thorough review of this historical conflict provides us with greater insight into the continuing struggles of people of color to receive justice in the United States and the role of the police as the primary instrument of domestic social control in relation to these struggles.

Early Struggles against Enslavement

Shortly after Christopher Columbus set foot in the Americas in 1492, the pattern was set for white exploitation and enslavement of people of color. Loewen (1995) described the inception: "Christopher Columbus introduced two phenomena that revolutionized race relations and transformed the modern world: the taking of land, wealth, and labor from indigenous peoples, leading to their near extermination, and the transatlantic slave trade, which created a racial underclass" (p. 50). Columbus and the other foreigners who accompanied him used their military advantage to institute a relationship of domination and exploitation by stealing the goods they wanted, raping the Indian women, and forcing the Indians to work for the profit of the Spaniards. The weapons of the Arawak tribe were no match for the white Europeans who had developed numerous military innovations during the long history of European warfare.

Although they were able to gain physical control over the Arawak Indians, the white Europeans were unable to use them to fulfill their primary goal—finding vast quantities of gold. Therefore, they began another profit-making venture—slavery. According to Loewen (1995), the Spaniards captured 1,500 Arawaks: 500 were selected to be slaves on the island of Haiti, and another 500 were selected to be shipped to Spain as slaves. Although only 200 of those sent to Spain survived, Columbus was undeterred in his effort to initiate a new slave trading route: "In the name of Holy Trinity, we can send from here all the slaves and brazil-wood which could be sold . . . Although they die now, they will not always die. The Negroes and Canary Islanders died at first" (Loewen, 1995, p. 52).

Slavery in the Americas was met with whatever resistance was available to the Native Americans. They were forced to mine for gold, raise Spanish food, and literally carry their captors around. The following eyewitness account by Pedro de Cordoba, in a letter to King Ferdinand in 1517, describes the actions of Indians who simply could not bear this inhumane treatment and resisted in the only way that they could:

> As a result of the sufferings and hard labor they endured, the Indians choose and have chosen suicide. Occasionally a hundred have committed mass suicide. The women exhausted by labor, have shunned conception and childbirth . . . Many, when pregnant, have taken something to abort and have aborted. Others after delivery have killed their children with their own hands, so as not to leave them in such oppressive slavery. (Loewen, 1995, p. 53)

Many American Indians attempted to flee to the mountains, to other islands, or deeper inland, but the Spaniards followed them and continued to abduct them into slavery. It is estimated that Columbus himself was directly responsible for sending approximately 5,000 slaves across the Atlantic Ocean. By 1555, the entire Arawak tribe had been wiped out through disease, the slave trade, or murder. Columbus and his Spanish followers also destroyed entire Indian nations in the Bahamas, Hispaniola, Puerto Rico, and Cuba (Loewen, 1995).

Escape was a constant problem because the Indians were natives to the land in which they were enslaved. This fact, along with the high death rate among Indian slaves, motivated white Europeans to introduce African people into the slave trade of the Americas (Loewen, 1995). The trading of Africans as slaves in the New World was initiated on the island of Haiti in 1505 by Columbus's own son. In 1519, Haiti was also the location of the first large-scale slave rebellion; both Indian and African slaves joined together in a valiant struggle against their bondage for more than a decade before the Spaniards were able to suppress it (Loewen, 1995).

Africans did not give up their liberty easily, and there is evidence of their resistance at every turn—from their kidnapping in Africa, to their grueling trip across the Atlantic, to their forced labor in the Americas. Slave ships were particularly hideous places, filled with absolute despair, fear, disease, torture, starvation, and chained bondage. Often too weak from their inhumane treatment to physically revolt, it was not uncommon for Africans to simply starve themselves to death to deny their abductors any profit or benefit (Katz, 1995). Still, the slave ships were very hazardous duty for their crews because of the constant threat of rebellion. "Through their own efforts slaves successfully revolted more than a hundred times on the high seas" (p. 23). After being shipped across the ocean to a strange and unfamiliar land, Africans continued their struggles for freedom.

The Colonial Period

Slave rebellions occurred frequently throughout the history of slavery in the area now known as the United States. As mentioned in chapter 1, the very first non-native people to set up permanent residence in this country were African slaves. They rebelled against their Spanish oppressors and managed to escape to live with the Indians (Loewen, 1995). Five hundred Spaniards and one hundred slaves set out to build a town at the mouth of the Pee Dee River in present-day South Carolina in the summer of 1526. Only one hundred and fifty of the Spaniards survived the rebellion in November. The surviving Spaniards escaped back to Haiti, and the Africans went to live with American Indians.

The first serious slave conspiracy in Colonial America was discovered in 1663 in Gloucester County, Virginia (Bennett, 1993). The plot never materialized because the group of white indentured servants and African slaves were captured after an indentured servant betrayed them. Betrayal was a constant threat to such planned revolts because freedom was often granted to those who reported a conspiracy (Genovese, 1976). White Europeans who traveled to the New World lived in constant fear of the victims of their oppression, a fear that came to shape the character of the southern United States and continues in various forms to this day (Berry, 1994).

Slave rebellions were not isolated to the southern colonies or states. At times, African and Indian slavery existed along the entire Atlantic Coast. The first British colonies to legalize slavery were Massachusetts and Connecticut (Bennett, 1993). In New England as early as 1638, African slaves from the West Indies were exchanged for Indian slaves from Connecticut (Loewen, 1995). Neither Indians nor Africans submitted willingly to their enslavement. In 1657, Indians and runaway African slaves attacked Hartford, Connecticut and burned several homes (Katz, 1995).

On Long Island a slave revolt resulted in the death of seven whites. In retaliation, whites hanged two Black male slaves and an Indian slave and burned a Black woman alive (Bennett, 1993). In New York City, approximately twenty-five Indian and African slaves united against their captors in 1712. This rebellion was particularly significant because at this time approximately one in four of the residents of New York City were slaves (Loewen, 1995). In 1741, another slave revolt erupted in the colony of New York involving a few whites and about one hundred Africans (Katz, 1995). Thirty-one slaves and five free whites were executed for their participation in the slave revolt and related conspiracy.

Although slave rebellions in the colonies were fairly commonplace under British rule, many whites were hesitant to publicize them for fear that other slaves would be incited to do the same. Speaking about one particular slave revolt in 1774, James Madison said "It is prudent that such attempts should be concealed as well as suppressed" (Katz, 1995, p. 39).

Indians and Africans frequently saw themselves as allies in the struggle against white domination. Particularly in the period before the American Revolution, the slave population consisted of both Africans and American Indians. At the time of the 1712 slave revolt, twenty-five percent of the slaves in New York City were Native Americans. White slaveholders were particularly infuriated by the safe havens provided by Indians for runaway slaves. Tribes such as the Shawnee and the Cherokee sometimes acted as stations on the underground railroad to Canada where escaped African slaves found freedom (Katz, 1995). In other cases, free Africans and those escaping from slavery simply went to live among the Indians. For example, a survey by the United States Army in 1831 recorded 512 Africans living among the Choctaw Indians (Katz, 1995). At one point, whites petitioned the government to take the land away from the Pamunky Indians because so many Africans lived among them that they no longer constituted an Indian tribe (Katz, 1995).

It is difficult to distinguish between slave revolts, attempts to re-capture runaway slaves, and the more traditional wars between Native Americans and white European invaders. As mentioned in chapter 2, treaties signed with Indian tribes before the Civil War had provisions guaranteeing that the Indians would return any runaway slaves back to the colonists. None of these tribes, however, returned a single slave (Katz, 1995).

One of the most threatening slave rebellions occurred in Stono, South Carolina in 1739 (see chapter 2). Although the Stono Revolt failed, its timing was significant. The leaders were from a skilled class of slaves who felt that the system of slavery was particularly weak at this time. The U.S. military was involved in a series of confrontations with tribes in Florida. Spain and England were on the brink of war, and Spain was offering sanctuary for runaway slaves. Thus, there was a window of opportunity for escape and freedom. However, the military power of the local civilian militia was too strong. The most immediate result of this rebellion was an increased fear of future insurrections. This fear led to an increase in repressive laws. Following the American Revolution, slavery became even more institutionalized through the law and more firmly established in practice. Slave revolts in the South grew increasingly more futile and desperate (Genovese, 1976).

The United States of America

Under the Articles of Confederation each state was responsible for its own domestic institutions and social peace. However, as slavery became solidified into our legal system by the U.S. Constitution and the U.S. Supreme Court, the federal government of the United States repeatedly demonstrated its unwillingness to protect the civil rights of African slaves. Slave revolts were treated as treasonous insurrections intent on destroying the entire political economy of the country. In fact, a primary driving force behind the development of a stronger federal government system was to increase the nation's ability to put down rebellions of all kinds (Berry, 1994). When the Constitution designated that slaves were to be counted as three-fifths of a person in the U.S. Census to determine the proper amount of representation for each state, slave owners and slave states gained a significant political benefit. The increased representation ensured the continuation of slavery, particularly in the South. The irony of being counted as a fraction of a person—and the use of those numbers to maintain an oppressive institution—leaves a legacy of resentment and a very clear indication of the imbalance of power.

The Fugitive Slave Act of 1793 compounded the injustice. The large population of Quakers in Pennsylvania struggled to put an end to slavery. As a result, Pennsylvania was one of the few states that welcomed free Blacks and helped slaves to become legally free. Slaveholders in North Carolina were vigorous in their effort to take full advantage of the Fugitive Slave law. They routinely went into the state of Pennsylvania, kidnapped free Blacks, and transported them back to North Carolina to be forced into slavery.

The newly strengthened federal government not only refused to intervene to stop the practice of illegally forcing free American citizens into slavery, it refused to even discuss the issue because of the fear that such debates might encourage insurrection among slaves (Berry, 1994). Thus, the emergence of a central United States government further solidified the institution of racial slavery by consistently denying Blacks—slave or free—access to political and legal remedies. All states were allowed to restrict the freedoms and rights of Africans in any way that they saw fit, and all the states were required by federal law to support the institution of racial slavery by returning runaways and by providing a strong standing army to put down extra-legal efforts to weaken the oppressive regime.

The first major slave insurrection plot to surface within the new nation was organized by Gabriel Prosser. On August 30, 1800 approximately 1,000 Africans assembled outside of Richmond, Virginia to attack and seize the city. Prosser, a literate skilled blacksmith and slave, thought that this moment was a particularly good time for a revolt, because it appeared that the United States and France were on the brink of war. He was also encouraged by the division among whites expressed in the political debate between the Republicans and the Federalists (Genovese, 1976). However, a violent storm and flood washed out bridges and flooded roads making it impossible to carry out military actions, and the group was forced to disband (Berry, 1994). Two house slaves, who remained loyal to their master, betrayed the rebels. Over the next month Prosser and forty slaves were arrested, tried, and executed for their conspiracy to promote insurrections among the slaves. The divisions that had encouraged Prosser were quickly resolved in the face of the revolt.

The federal government dispatched troops to the area to secure order and to maintain the current power relations. As a result of this conspiracy, more stringent controls were placed on both slaves and free Blacks in order to make it more difficult for them to congregate, travel, and arm themselves.

In 1811, the biggest slave revolt in North America erupted in the recently acquired territory of Louisiana. Between 300 and 500 slaves marched to New Orleans with flags and drums in grand military style, organized into companies commanded by officers—although mostly armed only with pikes, hoes and axes (Genovese, 1976). They came into direct conflict with 600 well-armed militia and regular troops who were able to crush the revolt fairly quickly. Eighty-two of the rebelling slaves were killed or executed soon after being captured.

It should be noted that at this time Louisiana was not yet part of the Old South in tradition or structure. It had a large racially mixed population (Berry, 1994). Free Blacks often had the right to bear arms, move about freely, and to own property (even slaves). Ironically, two of the militia units that helped suppress the rebellion were made up of free Blacks. The Black militia, which had been in existence for over 70 years, were well established and sought to demonstrate their loyalty during the rebellion. The distinction between the Louisiana Territory and the Old South made this revolt less of a concern to the white slaveowners of the Old South. The Prosser conspiracy was particularly troublesome because it took place in the heart of the Old South, where paternalism and stability were strongest and where white southerners had long argued that slavery was good for the Africans and that the Africans were happy as slaves (Genovese, 1976).

A second slave revolt took place in the heart of the Old South. It was led by the free and literate African seaman who spoke several languages, Denmark Vessey (Katz, 1995). This time the plan was to attack during the summer of 1822, when whites again appeared to be divided over the issue of slavery as signified by the Congressional debate over the Missouri Compromise (Berry, 1994). Vessey used the debate to convince Blacks that their efforts might meet outside help. Weapons and ammunition were hidden away over a four year period. Nine thousand men were poised to rebel in Charleston, South Carolina. The plan was to escape to Haiti, where a successful slave revolt had temporarily gained that country's independence. Once again, two house slaves revealed the plan to their masters. Vessey and five other leaders were arrested, tried by an all white jury, and hanged. The federal government quickly dispatched troops to the area to suppress any further rebellion. The subsequent investigation led to thirty-five more Blacks being executed and forty-two sent into exile. Four white men were also convicted of participating in the conspiracy; they were tried and sentenced to short prison terms and fined (Berry, 1994). While federal troops stood by to prevent any interference with the executions, the condemned men urged slaves everywhere to revolt until freedom was achieved for all people (Katz, 1995). The trial record was viewed as so inflammatory that it was destroyed because of the fear that it would incite more slave revolts (Zinn, 1980).

The most well-known of all slave revolts in North America was the one led by Nat Turner in 1831, involving approximately 70 slaves (Genovese, 1976). This rebellion took place in Southampton, Virginia and was timed to take advantage of the division between the anti-slavers in the western part of Virginia and the pro-slavers in the rest of the state (Bennett, 1993). Turner began with a small group of Virginia slaves with whom he traveled from plantation to plantation, killing the entire families of slaveholders and recruiting their slaves to join his group (Katz, 1995). Federal troops, artillery, and state militia were organized to crush the revolt, but only after sixty whites had been killed.

The fear produced by this insurrection was so intense that the Virginia legislature argued for two months about putting an end to slavery in their state. However, the decision was eventually made to respond by putting greater controls over Blacks, free and slave (Katz, 1995). For example, the fact that Nat Turner was an educated preacher encouraged the legislature to put stricter regulations upon Black preachers and to be much more aggressive in preventing the education of Africans. One Virginia legislator described the seriousness of the threat of education for Blacks: "We have, as far as possible, closed every avenue by which light might enter their minds. If you could extinguish the capacity to see the light, our work would be completed; they would be on a level with the beasts of the field, and we should be safe!" (p. 109).

Barriers to Revolt

The best opportunity for successful revolt, albeit minimal, was in the early stages of establishing European settlements in the New World. As these communities became stronger, the system of slavery became more entrenched in the law, the economy, and social practice. Thus, the potential for a successful revolution was for all practical purposes nonexistent. Only on board slave ships did any successful rebellions occur (Bennett, 1993). The country was filled with armed whites and, as the nineteenth century approached, ratios of whites to Blacks grew in favor of the white community (Genovese, 1976). Although whites in the United States were divided on the issue of slavery, they were quick to unite and mobilize to suppress insurrections. Each failed attempt demonstrated to other slaves that such efforts were suicidal (Genovese, 1976).

Plantations in the Old South averaged only about 20 slaves and half of all slaves worked on small farms rather than plantations. In addition, the Old South slaveholders lived on the residences and frequently interacted with the slaves which created a bond that often had an element of paternalism. Within this system of paternalism, slaves worked hard to secure whatever rights and customs they could to improve their living conditions.

> The slaves understood that the law offered them little or no protection, and in self-defense they turned to two alternatives: to their master, if he was decent, or his neighbors, if he was not; and to their own resources. Their

commitment to a paternalistic system deepened accordingly, but in such a way as to allow them to define rights for themselves. For reasons of their own the slaveholders relied heavily on local custom and tradition; so did the slave who turned this reliance into a weapon. (Genovese, 1976, p. 30)

Slaves used various methods to unofficially negotiate the rules, organization, and expectations of their work. "The actual work rhythm of the slaves, then, had to be hammered out as a compromise between themselves and their masters. The masters held the upper hand, but the slaves set limits as best they could" (Genovese, 1976, p. 303). One such limitation was in the area of working on Sunday. Considerable evidence exists that a merging of custom, white opinion, and slave resistance prevented the plantations from working their field hands on Sunday and holidays, and, in many places, even a full day on Saturday. In fact, if slaveholders desperately needed work done on Sunday, they often asked for volunteers, gave them time off later, or paid them for the labor. In addition, the slaves in the Old South often customarily did not work full days when it rained, at least not out in the elements. When these customs were violated, slaves took great offense and used various techniques to undermine the slaveholders' efforts. "An overseer complained in 1857 that the only way he could have gotten his hands to work in the rain would have been to stand out there himself and watch them every minute" (p. 569). The slaves of the United States fought hard to establish as decent a standard of living as possible. Risking the small gains they had achieved for the almost impossible goal of overthrowing an extremely secure political system was not an attractive alternative for most slaves.

Although early slave revolts failed to bring down the slave economy of the Old South, they did have a small impact on the living conditions of slaves (Genovese, 1976). Although the most immediate effect was an increase in the level of repression on both free and enslaved Africans in terms of restrictions on assembly, education, and ownership of weapons, this was often accompanied by an amelioration of the material conditions of slaves. Efforts were made to improve living conditions to weaken the incentive to revolt. At a minimum, the slave revolts clearly dispelled the myth perpetuated by pro-slavery apologists that Africans freely accepted their condition and were happy as an enslaved people.

Defection

There were alternatives to organized rebellions. The most effective blow that a single person could strike against the system was to escape to freedom. Whenever there was some hope of escape, slaves often attempted this dangerous path; it required a great deal of courage. Slave defection was another argument against the myth that enslaved people were happier and better treated than laborers in the "free world."

Those who attempted to escape faced enormous hardships and obstacles. First, there was the fear of the unknown. Few slaves knew where to go for safety, and slaveholders did everything they could to keep this information from the slaves. Abolitionist publications and activities in the South were illegal, and the laws were vigorously enforced both formally and informally. Slaves were intentionally fed misinformation about what they could expect from potential safe havens, in order to produce fear and distrust of those who promised freedom. Southern whites also worked hard to reduce the number of safe havens available to slaves and to extend the distances between those areas of refuge and the plantations. Second, most slaves lacked the important knowledge of how to get where they wanted to go. The slaveowners passed laws to prevent the education of slaves, which prevented them from acquiring the basic skills of navigation and geography necessary to travel long distances (Genovese, 1976). Slaves who worked near water were often forbidden to learn how to swim (Katz, 1995). Most slaves rarely ever ventured more than a few miles from their plantation, so the terrain was unknown. Third, the land was often very harsh, and the distances were long. Runaway slaves slept in the rain, traveled through dense woods or swamps, and had to locate food without being caught.

Slaves faced a very hostile and vigilant nation armed with laws that sanctioned chasing, catching, punishing, and returning runaways (Genovese, 1976). As we discussed earlier, slave patrols were created with the primary purpose of catching and preventing runaways. In fact, all whites had the power to catch and punish slaves. Some poor whites earned a living as specialized slave catchers, often using fierce hounds to track runaways. These ferocious hounds were known to bite, tear, mutilate, and sometimes kill those that they captured. The odds of surviving all these hardships were slim. Eighty percent of those who escaped were men between the ages of 16 and 35. The punishment for running away was so extreme that the attempts by slaves to run away indicates the strength of the desire to rebel against their oppression (Zinn, 1980, p. 34).

Any defection was a serious problem for the slaveowners, producing both an economic drain and political irritation. Georgia State Supreme Court Judge Lumpkin claimed that by 1855 the South had lost 60,000 slaves to the northern states alone. These runaways were a continuous reminder to the world that the slave economy of the South was inhumane and unjust. Many runaway slaves, such as Frederick Douglass and Harriet Tubman, continued their struggle against this tyrannical system by speaking about the horrors of slavery and helping others escape to freedom. In a desperate attempt to justify this system of oppression, one southern physician suggested that the high number of runaways was not due to the repressive nature of the system, but rather to a disease called Drapetomania, which he defined as the compulsion to run away from home (Genovese, 1976).

The odds of accomplishing a permanent escape were not favorable. Many slaves used temporary absence as a form of resistance. Sometimes slaves ran off to hide in the woods when they were going to receive a whipping or some other harsh punishment in order to give their masters an opportunity to calm down. Some ran to other slaveowners, hoping for mediation on their behalf. Still others ran away in groups to hide in the woods as a form of labor strike and to win concessions to certain demands that they had. One thing is clear: the slaves manipulated whatever power that they could squeak out of the system to make their conditions as livable as possible. This strategy of temporarily running away in order to avoid punishment or work was not viewed as a serious problem, because it was not a threat to the slave economy or to white domination. *Permanently* escaping or defecting to escape enslavement altogether, however, was seen as a serious revolutionary challenge to the political economy of white domination.

Significance of Boundaries

A critical weapon in the struggle against defection in the Old South was the creation of physical barriers to freedom. For the slave states, the construction of such a barrier meant extending the distance between their regime and the "free world." When possible the slave states attempted to eliminate the safe havens through such laws as the Fugitive Slave Act or by struggling against the establishment of free territories near their borders. One of the factors that contributed to the United States engaging in the War of 1812 was the desire to extend the buffer zone between white settlements and Indian Country where slaves could find freedom (Loewen, 1995).

War of 1812   Ironically, many free Blacks fought and died in defense of the United States during the War of 1812 (Bennett, 1993). At least one in six of the sailors in the United States Navy were African (Katz, 1995). Within the naval ranks led by Matthew Perry and Isaac Chauncey, a substantial number of African sailors fought against the British in the battles of the upper lakes. The most notable conflict in which they participated was the Battle of Lake Erie. When Commodore Chauncey responded to Captain Perry's initial concerns about being given so many African sailors, he stated "I have nearly fifty blacks on board this ship, and many of them are among the best men" (p. 63). After winning the Battle of Lake Erie, Captain Perry admitted that "his African American sailors were among the bravest men on his ship" (p. 63).

In the South, Andrew Jackson successfully used two battalions of 400 Black volunteers in his victory at the Battle of New Orleans. Andrew Jackson was so pleased with the loyalty and heroic actions of his African troops that he issued the following proclamation to them at New Orleans on December 18, 1814:

> TO THE MEN OF COLOR—Soldiers! From the shores of Mobile I collected you to arms; I invited you to share the perils and to divide the glory of your white countrymen. I expected much from you, for I was not uninformed of those qualities which must render you so formidable to an invading foe. I knew that you could endure hunger and thirst and all the hardships of war. I knew that you loved the land of your nativity, and that like ourselves, you had to defend all that is most dear to you. But you sur-

> passed my hopes. I have found in you, united to these qualities, that
> noble enthusiasm which impels to great deeds. (Bennett, 1993, p. 454)

Andrew Jackson's admiration and respect for the dignity of the descendants of Africa was short-lived. Two years later he ordered the attack on a
Seminole fort on the Apalachicola River in Florida "precisely because it har-
bored hundreds of runaway slaves, thus initiating the First Seminole War"
(Loewen, 1995, p. 144). At the conclusion of the War of 1812, the United
States took the Spanish territory of Florida, even though Spain had been an
ally of the United States in the war. The problem for white slaveowners was
that, like the rest of Spanish territory, Florida was free territory. Of particular
concern to the white slaveholders were the tribes that provided a beacon of
hope for runaway slaves (Genovese, 1976). Slaveowners believed that it was
critical to eliminate this great temptation to their slaves.

The Seminole Wars   The Seminoles were a triracial community consisting of "Creek Indians, remnants of smaller tribes, runaway slaves, and whites
who preferred to live in Indian society." In fact, the name Seminole is derived
from the Spanish word *cimarron*, which means "runaway slave" (Loewen,
1995, p. 144). In Jamaica, the term became "maroons." Beginning in the
colonial period fugitive slaves from the Carolinas sought sanctuary in Spanish Florida. "This refuge for runaways was a provocation as well as a threat
to southern slave interests" (Berry, 1994, p. 28). After the American Revolution, southern states were quick to ratify the U.S. Constitution of 1789 largely
because they hoped that the Fugitive Slave clause would help them retrieve
their runaway slaves. General Anthony Wayne of Georgia wrote that his
state faced "ruin and depopulation" as a result of the "depredations of the
Indians . . . [and] the insidious protection afforded by the Spanish to our runaway Negroes" (p. 31).

The reluctance of the federal government to invade Spanish territory
with armed troops incited the Georgia government to send its own state militia to retrieve runaway slaves twice. Both times their efforts were prevented by
the Creeks and Seminoles (Berry, 1994). The second invasion occurred in the
fall of 1812 when Spain was an ally of the U.S. against the British. During the
war, the British had built a fort on the Apalachicola River, and free Africans
and Seminoles later occupied it. Over a year after the war had ended, General Andrew Jackson issued the order to attack.

> I have little doubt of the fact, that this fort has been established by some
> villains for the purpose of rapine and plunder, and it ought to be blown
> up, regardless of the ground on which it stands; and if your mind shall
> have formed the same conclusion, destroy it and return the stolen
> Negroes and property to their rightful owners. (Katz, 1995, p. 89)

This fort, which was in Spanish territory, contained approximately one
hundred men and two hundred women and children, 270 of which were
killed in the assault. The few survivors were given to Georgian slaveowners

who claimed that they were their property because they were descendants of slaves they used to own (Berry, 1994). The Seminoles retaliated with an attack on a U.S. gunboat on the Apalachicola River. The U.S. government then launched a full-scale invasion of 4,000 troops led by General Andrew Jackson, who reported that he was able to kill approximately half of the estimated 2,800 "exiles" (p. 34). Jackson continued to move through Florida. Rebellions in Latin America required the attention of Spain, which ceded Florida to the United States in 1819. Now the U.S. government could use the Fugitive Slave Act of 1793 to justify the invasion and prosecution of Seminole communities to capture fugitive slaves.

In 1825, John Quincy Adams' presidential administration declared that all Blacks living in Florida were runaway slaves subject to the Fugitive Slave Act, unless they had papers stating their free status or an Indian was able to prove in court that the African was his slave (Berry, 1994). When slaveholders moved into Florida in great numbers claiming ownership of Africans living among the Seminoles, intense friction developed between the whites and the Indians. In order to reduce this friction, President Andrew Jackson decided to include the Seminoles in the Indian Removal Act of 1830 that forced them to move their entire tribe out of Florida and west of the Mississippi River. To avoid the violent attacks of white society and to protect members of their tribe from slavery, the Seminoles retreated into the Everglades and prepared for war. Whites were not interested in obtaining the land of the Everglades, which was useless for farming, but they were very interested in eliminating any territory that bordered their society but was not under their control.

The Second Seminole War was ignited when an Indian agent took the Seminole Chief Osceola's African wife into custody and consigned her back into slavery (Berry, 1994). Chief Osceola led the Seminoles on a series of raids throughout Florida. General Winfield Scott was given command of the troops in Florida and became engaged in a long and costly war with the Seminoles, with little success (Berry, 1994). These battles have great historical significance when one considers that the Second Seminole War was the "longest and costliest war the United States ever fought against Indians" (Loewen, 1995, p. 144). The seven-year war eventually cost the United States $20 million and the death of 1,500 troops. The presidential administration was heavily criticized by the anti-Jacksonians, the Whigs, and the Federal Party for the failure of this expensive war effort, but the idea that "the nation must expand into Florida and make it safe for slavery was not questioned" (Berry, 1994, p. 42).

It could be argued that these wars constituted the largest and most successful slave rebellion in North America (Loewen, 1995). General Thomas Jessup stated that "This, you may be assured, is a Negro, not an Indian war" (Katz, 1995, p. 80). Hundreds of Africans fought alongside Indians in a struggle to resist the removal of the Indians to Oklahoma and the return of Africans to slavery (Loewen, 1995). Although the Indians eventually were forced to give up their struggle to stay in Florida, many Africans were able to win their freedom and traveled with the tribe to Oklahoma.

This freedom was not won easily. The United States Army secured a surrender from the Indians on March 6, 1837. The war broke out again when southern slaveholders refused to allow the Africans to migrate with the tribe, and Chief Osceola was imprisoned by General Jessup while under a flag of truce (Berry, 1994). These events triggered ongoing armed conflict that lasted for at least another five years. Although hundreds of Africans living free in Florida were caught and forced into slavery, hundreds also traveled west to live with the Seminole tribe in its forced relocation. For these people, the rebellion was a limited success, in that they remained "free"—albeit in an area designated by whites, at a distance sufficiently removed that there would be no temptation to those who remained enslaved.

The Seminole Wars illustrate several important insights into the psyche of White America and into the power of people of color in their struggles for justice. The Seminole Wars verified that "if even one little enclave of Indians and blacks remained unmolested, it posed a threat to the institution of slavery" (Berry, 1994, p. 52). The efforts by individual slaves to defect to other states, territories, and countries had enough of an impact on the institution of slavery for state and federal government agencies to engage in risky and expensive armed conflict to curb defections. The wars demonstrated the great lengths to which the United States federal government was willing to go in order to preserve white supremacy and the slavery of Africans. The ability and willingness of white Americans to come together in their oppression of people of color rendered both organized armed confrontation and running away ineffective. Thereafter, different methods of resistance were employed in the struggle against the institution of slavery.

Political Struggles

Free Blacks in the northern colonies and states used the basic rights of citizenship to initiate political reform. They "held protest meetings, petitioned the local government and state legislature about their grievances, and engaged in a number of activities to challenge the racial status quo and to improve the circumstances of their lives" (Dulaney, 1996, p. 4).

The first legal protest by Blacks was as early as 1644, when eleven Africans in New Netherlands (later named New York) petitioned for their freedom. At the time the petitioners were considered indentured servants. Because they had been promised freedom and had served nearly 18 years, the Council of New Netherlands granted their petition (Bennett, 1993). It is important to emphasize that indentured servitude was not based solely on race. It was not a lifetime sentence, and the descendants of indentured servants were considered free.

In 1773, numerous slaves in the Massachusetts Colony petitioned for their freedom, and eight were eventually successful during the Revolutionary War. The first recorded petition by Blacks to the federal government to end slavery was in 1797. The U.S. Congress refused to accept it. A second petition from free Blacks in Philadelphia was presented to Congress in 1800 (Bennett, 1993). The northern states slowly began the process of outlawing slavery within their borders, beginning with Vermont in 1777 and ending with New York in 1827 (Bennett, 1993). However, the laws of these states, as well as the federal government, continued to recognize the property rights of southern slaveholders over the human rights of enslaved Africans.

Another effort to obtain justice through the political process was the formation of a national Black convention in 1830, which met annually in an attempt to organize the struggle against slavery. In 1838 Charles Lenox Remond became the first African American employed as a lecturer by the anti-slavery movement (Bennett, 1993). A petition was filed in 1878 seeking equal school facilities for Blacks in Boston. Many more Black activists and lecturers would soon follow, including Harriet Tubman, Sojourner Truth, and Frederick Douglass.

In the southern states, the legal struggles to secure some degree of justice were less grandiose. Any political attempt by Blacks to put an end to slavery within the southern states was treated as a treasonous attempt to encourage armed slave revolt. Political efforts such as petitioning the state government were dangerous and futile. "Agitation against repressive laws or abolitionist activities by free African Americans in southern cities was prohibited and would result in imprisonment, whippings, or expulsion from the state. Criminal acts could even result in their enslavement" (Dulaney, 1996, p. 5).

Although early on, particularly in the northern states, some political and legal efforts met with limited success, the weight of the political system was placed squarely behind the racist institution of slavery. Sometimes a few small legal battles were won. However, these exceptions were essentially window dressing that made whites feel as though they were operating within a rational, humane, and just system. Racism and slavery became stronger as they became institutionalized into the legal system. It is interesting to note that free Blacks could vote in North Carolina and Tennessee until 1835, and that they voted illegally in Rapides Parish, Louisiana until the 1850s. Also, Africans could testify against whites in Maryland until the 1800s and in Louisiana until 1852. Even these few exceptional pockets of limited access to the political and legal systems in southern states were eventually wiped away by the 1850s.

A number of legal actions solidified the U.S. legal system's support of white supremacy and the enslavement of Africans. These included the Missouri Compromise, the Fugitive Slave Act of 1850, and the Kansas-Nebraska Act that opened the Northern territory to slavery. Perhaps the most damaging was the 1857 Dred Scott decision, in which the U.S. Supreme Court ruled that "no black could be a U.S. citizen and that black people had no rights in America that white people were bound to respect. . . . The net effect of all this was the *de facto* nationalization of the slave system" (Bennett, 1993, p. 178). Legitimate access to the political or legal process was denied, and massive armed rebellion was seen as suicidal. Only one weapon remained, sabotage.

Sabotage

Our use of the word sabotage means more than just undermining the normal functions of a system in order to bring it down; it also includes actions by the oppressed to relieve some of their misery. African slaves participated in numerous forms of resistance, some of which clearly disrupted the normal functioning of the repressive social order. Others are better understood as efforts to assert rights and freedoms within this repressive order.

The same argument can be made for understanding *political* action. Both terms should be considered from a wide-ranging perspective. All forms of rebellion, from armed confrontation to arson to theft, are political in the sense that they are attempts to be heard and to gain power, albeit a very limited power. Some would limit the concept of political struggle to political campaigns or formal protests, but sabotage is also political. Even the theft of a pig to supplement the poor diet of slaves can be a political act of sabotage.

Sabotage took many forms, from murder to shuffling. Obviously the most violent and dangerous act by a single slave was to murder either the plantation owner or overseer. One of the most common methods that slaves used to murder whites, particularly their owners, was poisoning (Genovese, 1976). The art of poison was well developed by Africans long before they were kidnapped and brought to the American continent. This form of murder was most common early in the slave trade and in the Caribbean. Overseers were most often killed when they were trying to whip or abuse the slave. There were slaves who refused to be whipped and would kill or be killed rather than suffer that form of torture. Not all efforts to confront those who were abusing slaves ended in murder. At times, groups of slaves or the mothers of those being whipped would intercede and attempt to prevent the whipping by force, but not deadly force.

No matter how infrequent or how distant, murders produced an undercurrent of fear. "Murders did not have to occur often: one nearby, perhaps no closer than a neighboring county and perhaps only once in a decade, made a deep impression on masters as well as slaves" (Genovese, 1976, pp. 616–617). With an eye on the long-term objective of preserving the slave system, the southern court systems, in some rare instances, actually acquitted slaves who had murdered their owners or overseers—based on the view that extensive abuse encouraged insurrections. At the same time, however, many whites believed that insurrections were the result of owners being too lenient (Genovese, 1976).

Slaves frequently used less direct methods to undermine the efforts of the first public policing agencies, slave patrols (Genovese, 1976). Facing the potential of abusive and cruel punishments by the patrollers, slaves developed mechanisms to resist them. While some of the efforts to resist involved direct confrontation, most were more preventive and cunning, such as setting up extensive warning systems among the slave cabins or tying ropes and vines across the road to trip horses or knock riders to the ground. The slaves also built trap doors in their cabins to hide slaves without passes from the patrols.

The first line of defense against the slave patrols, as well as against the entire white power structure, was to lie or feign stupidity. "From colonial days to the end of the regime the slaveholders wrung their hands over the slaves' apparently congenital inability to tell the truth" (Genovese, 1976, p. 609). While most slaveowners attributed this common occurrence to a biological defect of Black people (thus supporting their racist notions of white superiority) a few saw lying by slaves as a technique to improve their living conditions. One slaveowner wrote, "[Slave] children learn from their parents to regard white people with fear, and to deceive them. They are always suspicious, and endeavor by their complainings to get some advantage" (p. 609). What made these lies particularly effective was the formal courtesy that slaves portrayed as they misdirected and confused white people.

In her diary, a white woman slaveholder in Georgia demonstrated that not all whites were fooled by this act:

> I generally found that if I wanted a thing done I first had to tell negroes to do it, then show them how, and finally do it myself. Their way of managing not to do it was very ingenious, for they always were perfectly good-tempered and received my order with "Dat's so, missus; just as missus says,' and then somehow or other left the thing undone. (Genovese, 1976, p. 301)

The following observation by a New Yorker traveling through the South illustrated how this deception worked:

> Never, not once, did I get proper directions [from Blacks]. Either I found myself being sent in the wrong direction to the accompaniment of rousing yassuhs, or I found that a chap who had clearly lived in town all his life and whose manners were impeccable somehow did not know where Main Street was. (Genovese, 1976, p. 117)

Similar to other oppressed or defeated people, the slaves came to regard lying as an art form in which they took great pride (Genovese, 1976). The art of lying was taught early to slave children as an important tool in the struggle against white oppression. An essential part of this lying often involved pretending to be ignorant and incompetent, which played directly into racist stereotypes but also insulated slaves from punishment by helping them mask their sabotage.

Other forms of slave resistance were specifically designed both to prevent the social and economic system of slavery from being profitable and to achieve some control over the working and living conditions of the slaves themselves. Some of these methods fit the traditional definition of sabotage— arson, killing livestock, destroying crops, and tool breaking.

Arson was a major problem during the time of slavery in the United States, particularly in the North, as slaves were struggling to gain their freedom. The use of arson by slaves to intimidate whites into granting them freedom was recognized as a tactic forced by circumstances. For example, in 1723 the governor of Massachusetts issued a proclamation stating that African people were intentionally setting fires in an act of desperation over their condition (Bennett, 1993). Slaves were accused of setting dozens of fires in Boston in just one week of that year (Katz, 1995).

Arson was a particularly effective form of sabotage because it required no great skill or money, and it caused significant damage. Precisely because of the covert nature of arson, it is difficult to determine how much arson by slaves actually took place. However, it is clear that a substantial number of southern whites were highly suspicious of slaves' involvement in arson, especially in urban areas (Genovese, 1976). Urban dwellings were much more susceptible to flames than those on the plantation. In addition, African slaves were often bolder and more confrontational in the cities. Partly because of the paternalism of many slaveholders, they were slow to suspect their own slaves. However, at times slaveowners had to face the fact that their slaves were not as loyal, content, and docile as they wanted to believe.

The repercussions from acts of arson were serious; many slaves did not support this level of militancy (Genovese, 1976). Often, the destruction resulted in greater hardship and deprivation for the slaves themselves. When arson was in retaliation for some private offense or injustice, the arsonist usually worked alone. Nonetheless, all the slaves would typically pay a price in some way. For example, slaves often burned the corncrib, the smokehouse, or the ginhouse, each of which meant that the slaves would suffer: "Destruction of food stores meant their own deprivation. Destruction of the cotton threatened the sale of one or more members of the slave community, or worse, bankruptcy and the breakup of the community altogether" (p. 615). Although slaves were usually sympathetic to the grievances that their fellow comrades had, arson received much less support than the other more subtle forms of resistance.

One such method involved taking full advantage of the white racist perspective that Blacks were inherently lazy and ignorant. In this regard, many slaves would work only when they were being watched and even then very slowly and incompetently, often breaking tools or hurting the livestock. In their rationalizations for slavery, many whites insisted upon the inferiority of African people, stating that they had to be enslaved and taught to work. The logical extension of that reasoning is that slaves could not be expected to work at the same pace and ability as a white laborer (Genovese, 1976). Slaveholders' diaries and other writings suggest that African slaves developed a nearly universal reputation for being lazy to the point that many planters came to believe that it was in their nature as a race and that the planters and overseers could do little to make them work faster or harder. One southerner is quoted as saying "It takes two white men . . . to make a black man work" (p. 299).

When African slaves engaged in behavior such as shuffling, working slowly, and acting stupid, they contributed to the racist stereotypes that whites used to justify their position. However, there were few alternatives to relieve a back-breaking, psychologically damaging system. It was therefore logical to feed the stereotypes in order to endure the inhumane hardship of enslavement.

The stereotype of Blacks as lazy and incompetent was built on a foundation of centuries of ruling-class European attitudes toward poor laborers. "When slaveholders insisted that blacks would work only long enough to provide for elementary needs and occasional debauchery, they were associating themselves with a theory generally held by English manufacturers, not to mention the clergy, about the laboring poor" (Genovese, 1976, p. 298). Many people who traveled to the South repeatedly compared the poor working habits of the African slaves to those of Irish, and to a lesser extent Italian immigrants (Genovese, 1976). Stereotypes of the poor and oppressed as lazy and stupid appear to have arisen in part from the behaviors of the oppressed and from the general attitude of superiority held by oppressors.

Slaves would frequently kill or maim livestock, which also slowed the pace of work—both by eliminating this important tool and/or by convincing the overseers that pushing the slave to work too hard could result in a loss of livestock. If an overseer was too demanding, slaves would often collectively slow down their pace and endure the whippings.

Other strategies included allowing crops to become ruined and breaking equipment. The following quote from the editor of the *Planters' Banner*, Daniel Dennett of Louisiana, illustrates the frustration of slave owners at the enormous difficulty they faced in efficiently exploiting their African slave labor:

> On a plantation they can neither hoe, nor ditch, chop wood, nor perform any kind of labor with a white man's skill. They break and destroy more farming utensils, ruin more carts, break more gates, spoil more cattle and horses, and commit more waste than five times the number of white laborers do. They are under instruction relative to labor from their childhood, and still when they are grey headed they are the same heedless botches; the negro traits predominate over all artificial training. (Genovese, 1976, p. 300)

Possibly the most costly and common form of sabotage was theft. Slaves became so accustomed to stealing from their owners that whites came to believe it was in the nature of Africans to steal (Genovese, 1976). Their favorite target was a hog, which they butchered and roasted to be shared in a big celebration. The following excerpt illustrated how serious a problem stealing by slaves became for plantation owners:

> In colonial days Robert Carter even complained that universal stealing by slaves rendered Virginia's plantations unprofitable. Hog stealing reached such proportions that in 1748 Virginia decreed the death penalty for a third offense. George Washington solemnly declared some years later that for every two bottles of wine he drank, thievish slaves enjoyed five. In South Carolina on the eve of the Revolution a plantation manager reported a wave of cattle thefts to his employer and added, "This kind of work prevails so much in your neighborhood that I fear few of your Creatures will be left by the year's end." (Genovese, 1976, p. 599)

This practice continued into the nineteenth century and slaves were known to steal crops, livestock, alcoholic beverages, or just about anything else that was available on the plantations in order to supplement their diets and to improve their general living conditions. These actions became so commonplace that they had an economic impact on the functioning of the plantations. Near the end of slavery in the Old South, a particularly insightful slaveholder, Adele Petigru Allston, came to understand the theft by her slaves very astutely, when she told her son that "The conduct of the negroes in robbing our house, store room, meat house, etc. and refusing to restore anything shows you they *think it right* to steal from us, to spoil us, as the Israelites did the Egyptians" (Genovese, 1976, p. 602).

One specific action that the planters did take to combat theft was their strong support for "Christianizing" their slaves. The slaveholders brought preachers (primarily white) to the slave quarters on Sundays and held Sunday school classes for the slaves in order to instill in them a sense of morality that would encourage them not only to stop stealing, but to accept their servitude as suffering in this world in anticipation of the hereafter (Genovese, 1976). The slaves, however, often co-opted the teachings of Christianity to fit their particular plight. Most slaves appear to have adapted Christianity to their living conditions, including such adjustments as marriage vows that were to last until death or until their partner was sold.

The slaves' sense of morality clearly distinguished between stealing from their masters and stealing from each other. Stealing from other slaves was considered to be a very serious and sinful transgression within the slave quarters; however, taking from their masters was not viewed as a sin at all. Their logic was that if they were property of their masters and took other property from their masters and consumed it, then they did not take anything from their masters; they only transformed the property into another form. It was seen as no different than taking corn from the corncrib to feed the master's chickens or hogs. At other times they rationalized their stealing as providing themselves with the proper meal that they deserved. As noted in the lyrics to a slave song, they also put theft in perspective of the theft of their people by white slaveholders:

> Negro cannot walk without corn in his pocket,
> It is to steal chickens.
> Mulatto cannot walk without rope in his pocket,
> It is to steal horses.
> White man cannot walk without money in his pocket,
> It is to steal girls. (Genovese, 1976, pp. 605–606)

Slaves took great pride and satisfaction in their thefts from the various plantations. Not only did such theft take skill and daring, many slaves remarked that they enjoyed "outwitting Ole Massa" (Genovese, 1976, p. 606). The slaves not only enjoyed the sporting element of stealing from the plantations, they took enjoyment from striking back at those who had enslaved and mistreated them (Genovese, 1976).

Though not direct attacks on the institution of slavery, these acts of resistance were important strategies for undermining the effectiveness of slavery in economic terms. They also provide information important to understanding race relations throughout the history of the United States. Whites were so unaware of the world populated by Blacks that they could not see what was occurring directly in front of them. Many acts of rebellion are intentionally disguised to avoid punishment or are masked by cultural differences. Whites frequently misunderstood and misinterpreted the actions of slaves, often to their own physical and psychological detriment. Learning to listen to the songs of the oppressed, seeking the voices and meanings that are usually silenced and ignored, and seeing acts of rebellions for what they are is a necessary first step in interpreting the actions of those who rebel. The government and its legitimate apparatuses of repression, including the slave patrols and the police, have a long and cruel history of racist oppression. These agencies went to extreme lengths, including the invasion of sovereign nations and the violations of treaties, in order to create and maintain a racist institution of slavery and the general oppression of people of color.

Conclusion

Understanding whose job it was to enforce human bondage is a sobering recognition. Yet it is only through coming to terms with this fundamental historical reality that we can make sense of the rest of the story. When we read about police officers who took part in white terrorist assaults on Blacks trying to exercise their newly won rights to vote after the Civil War (chapter 3), it is difficult to comprehend that behavior. Yet, when we recognize that the very first municipal police in the United States were slave patrols, we glimpse the seeds of destruction inherent in the system. Certainly, these realities go a long way toward helping us to understand the early African American rebellions and confrontations with the police, as the hope ignited by Reconstruction collided head-on with the despair of exercising political freedom only at peril of life and limb. When Jim Crow demolished the Black political power promised by Reconstruction, the police were again on the front line of enforcement of the racist legal order. In chapter 7, we continue to explore the role of the police in protecting the racist legal structure as we examine African American rebellion in the early twentieth century.

7 Agitation vs. Accommodation

As the nation entered the twentieth century, African Americans found themselves imprisoned in an extremely precarious world, where there did not seem to be a clear path to freedom and justice. Indeed, the governor of Mississippi defiantly announced to a cheering crowd, "How is the white man going to control the government? ... If it is necessary every Negro in the state will be lynched; it will be done to maintain white supremacy" (Katz, 1995, p. 350). Individuals and organizations grappled with conflicting strategies: whether to endure suffering in silence and seek relative success within separate worlds, or risk everything by rebelling against the powerful system of white domination (Bennett, 1993). By far the most prominent African-American leader at the turn of the century, Booker T. Washington, clearly advocated the former (Bennett, 1993).

Conciliation

Booker T. Washington was an advisor to U.S. presidents and powerful white industrialists on issues of race. He lectured to African Americans on self-help and self-improvement, while promoting a position of conciliation and racial submission (Bennett, 1993). Washington exercised a great deal of power in obtaining and administrating funds, jobs, education, and other opportunities for both African Americans and whites. He acquired this power largely through accommodation, as he taught Blacks to accept and obey the Jim Crow laws, to forget about politics, and to accept the friendship of southern whites (Bennett, 1993; Katz, 1995). Washington essentially advocated an acceptance of segregation in exchange for better educational opportunities, primarily vocational training. In several states, African Americans established their own towns to avoid persecution and to find success without white interference (Katz, 1995). Washington was the first president of the Tuskegee Institution in Alabama, where he taught his students "the importance of self-reliance, hard work, saving, and learning a trade" (p. 322). Even on the rare occasions when he condemned lynchings, Washington often blamed them at least partly on the lack of education of the victims. He discouraged whites from such actions, not on moral grounds but on the basis of their own economic self-interest (Bennett, 1993).

147

Opposing Voices

Although Booker T. Washington was the dominant African-American leader for at least twenty years, two African-American men worked to replace his politics of acceptance with politics of agitation (Bennett, 1993). William Monroe Trotter and W.E.B. Du Bois fought to destroy Washington's influence and to motivate African Americans to aggressively attack segregation, disenfranchisement, and racial injustice (Bennett, 1993).

Trotter was a Harvard-educated New Englander, who established a paper in Boston called the *Guardian* to launch a series of editorials attacking Booker T. Washington and his policies of accommodation (Bennett, 1993). Du Bois was also Harvard educated and from New England. He left his academic career when he realized that speaking the truth and attacking Washington's policies on moral and logical grounds were not enough without creating the force behind words to make whites accept racial equality and justice. Du Bois' book of essays, *The Souls of Black Folks*, published in 1903, criticized Washington's call for thrift, patience, and industrial training for African Americans. Du Bois claimed that Blacks had a right to advance themselves socially, politically, and economically and a duty to resist white tyranny.

African Americans were divided into two bitterly opposing camps (Bennett, 1993). Those who followed Washington opposed what they saw as endless agitation and demands for equality which would only bring more violence and make living conditions worse for African Americans. Those who followed Du Bois felt that Washington's faith in the goodness of white leadership to guide their future was misplaced. They organized a conference in Niagara Falls, Ontario (hotels on the New York side of Niagara Falls would not accept the Black conference attendees as guests) to initiate organized political struggle for the suffrage of Black people, the improvement of educational facilities for African Americans, and the racial integration of public facilities (Bennett, 1993).

The following statement announced their view of the role of law and the police in the preservation of white supremacy in America:

> We want the laws enforced against rich as well as poor; against capitalists as well as laborers; against white as well as black. We are not more lawless than the white race, we are more often arrested, convicted and mobbed. We want justice even for criminals and outlaws. We want the Constitution of the country enforced. We want Congress to take charge of the Congressional elections. We want the Fourteenth Amendment carried out to the letter and every state disfranchised in Congress which attempts to disfranchise its rightful voters. We want the Fifteenth Amendment enforced and no state allowed to base its franchise simply on color. . . . These are some of the chief things we want. How shall we get them? By voting where we may vote; by persistent, unceasing agitation; by hammering at the truth; by sacrifice and work. (Bennett, 1993, pp. 333–334)

The people in the Niagara organization hammered away at the racial barriers by filing petitions and lawsuits and speaking out against racial injustice and discrimination. They later merged with the founding members of the NAACP (Bennett, 1993).

The extreme legal and illegal racist oppression in the United States made Washington's argument for accommodation extremely compelling to many who simply wanted to survive this period. However, many other African Americans came to believe that accommodation only led to more brutality. In many situations, Blacks found themselves compelled to fight back to prevent being slaughtered in white terrorist attacks.

Rebellion in the Streets

The Atlanta Massacre of 1906 effectively marked the end of Booker T. Washington's dominating influence over the majority of African Americans in the South (Bennett, 1993). African Americans were attacked by white mobs accompanied by local police. As Black men and women sought to defend themselves, the state militia disarmed them, allowing many to be killed (Bennett, 1993). Walter White, an African American who later became an undercover investigator for the NAACP because of his light skin and blond hair, saw the Atlanta riot firsthand as a thirteen-year-old boy (Katz, 1995). He described his feelings as a white mob approached his home, which he was poised to defend with a rifle handed to him by his father:

> I knew who I was. A Negro, a human being with an invisible pigmentation which marked me as a person to be hunted, hanged, abused, discriminated against, kept in poverty and ignorance, in order that those whose skin was white would have readily at hand a proof of their superiority, a proof patent and inclusive, accessible to the moron and idiot as well as to the wise man and the genius. No matter how low a white man fell, he could always hold fast to the smug conviction that he was superior to two-thirds of the world's population, for those two-thirds were not white. (p. 340)

Just before the mob reached his family's house, a group of his father's friends who had barricaded themselves in a nearby building began to shoot at the mob. After a couple of volleys, the mob dispersed; their house and their lives were saved (Katz, 1995).

The race riot in 1908 in Springfield, Illinois limited the influence of Washington's policy of accommodation in the North. Disappointed that the local sheriff had secretly moved a Black rape suspect to another jail, a white mob launched a general attack on all Black citizens—whipping and lynching them (Berry, 1994). After a thorough investigation and trial of three people, only one white woman "who had inflamed the crowd to mob violence in the name of the defense of white womanhood and who expressed pride in her own complicity in a number of the homicides" (Berry, 1994, p. 106) was found guilty. Ironically, the white woman who had alleged the rape later confessed that her attacker was a white man whom she refused to identify.

The horrors of this race riot within sight of Abraham Lincoln's grave inspired a group of white liberals to organize with Black militants, such as Ida B. Wells-Barnett, Du Bois, and Trotter, to form the National Association for the Advancement of Colored People (NAACP) (Bennett, 1993).

The Great Migration of two million African Americans from their southern rural homes to large northern cities to escape Jim Crow laws was a form of emancipation by migration. The movement heightened Black militancy: "Under the impact of industrialization and urbanization, the black psyche changed" (Bennett, 1993, p. 345). The Black press took a leadership role in inspiring, organizing, and informing African Americans. The tone became more militant, and African-American agitators began to find the policies of the National Urban League (formed in 1910 by supporters of Washington's policy of conciliation) and even the NAACP too passive.

Eighteen of the thirty-three major interracial riots in the United States during the first half of the twentieth century took place between 1915 and 1919 (Rudwick, 1972). The most serious was in East St. Louis, Illinois in 1917. The first riot (May 28th) was triggered by a rumor that a white man had been killed by a Black robber. For several days, large white mobs began to roam through the city beating any Blacks they happened to encounter. The police responded to this riot primarily by disarming African-American citizens. Racial disturbances continued through June. Blacks were repeatedly arrested and disarmed, while white mobs encountered, at most, verbal encouragement to stop their violent assaults. Nighttime driveby shootings by whites into the homes of African Americans were commonplace. In some situations, African Americans fought back. These events were exaggerated by the white press, who ignored the initial assaults by whites and played a critical role in inciting fear of armed Blacks on a violent rampage (Rudwick, 1972).

On the first of July a group of Blacks, who had armed themselves for protection, fired upon a car that they thought was filled with armed white men preparing to attack them (Berry, 1994). It was later discovered that this vehicle was a police car; five officers were shot and one killed. The patrol car was publicly displayed to incite white citizens to retaliate (Berry, 1994). The newspaper accounts made the incident sound like a cold-blooded, unprovoked, and planned assassination of the police officers. As discussed in chapter 3, a number of African Americans were killed and thousands were forced to flee their homes—while the police and National Guard displayed either callous indifference or participated in the mayhem. The slaughter triggered a NAACP march of ten thousand people down Fifth Avenue in New York City, protesting "segregation, discrimination, disenfranchisement, and 'the host of evils' forced on black Americans" (Bennett, 1993, p. 349). The march was in silence but an excerpt from their leaflet stated:

> We march because we deem it a crime to be silent in the face of such barbaric acts. We march because we are thoroughly opposed to Jim Crow cars, segregation, discrimination, disfranchisement, lynching, and the host of evils that are forced upon us. It is time that the spirit of Christ

should be manifested in the making and execution of laws. (Katz, 1995, pp. 365–366)

In 1917, a very different kind of race riot occurred in Houston, Texas. This time the riot was clearly a rebellion by African Americans against racist oppression, particularly oppression by the Houston Police Department (Bennett, 1993). As discussed in chapter 3, the African-American soldiers of the 24th Infantry repeatedly faced insulting jeers from the townspeople and assaults from the local police and white citizens. When a Black military police officer insisted that a Black woman, arrested by two white officers for drunk and disorderly conduct, be released into his custody, the white police struck him, arrested him, and placed him in jail. Later that night another Black military police officer attempted to file a report on the incident, and asked the same white police officers a few questions. One of the white police officers informed the military police officers that he did not answer questions from Blacks and struck the officer with the butt of his gun. As the Black military police officer was being taken to jail, he attempted to escape and was shot by the police (Berry, 1994). As rumors spread about white police beating Black soldiers, about one hundred Black soldiers stole arms and ammunition and marched into town to punish the white police. On their way to town, they encountered a group of white police officers and shot two of them. The soldiers then raided the city of Houston and engaged in a deadly conflict with white citizens and police that resulted in the deaths of two African Americans and eleven to seventeen whites (Katz, 1995; Bennett, 1993). Eighteen African-American soldiers were hanged for their participation in this riot and forty-four were given life imprisonment (Katz, 1995).

Nearly half of the race riots of 1919 occurred in northern or border states (Tuttle, 1970). Most of these episodes of racial violence in 1919 began with white terrorist attacks on African-American citizens. As the 1920s approached, many African Americans joined Black separatist Marcus Garvey in what has been described as "the nation's first African American mass movement" (Katz, 1995, p. 373). Garvey, who was born in Jamaica and came to the U.S. during World War I, inspired thousands of Blacks who had always been told they were inferior to be proud of their racial identity. Fifty thousand African Americans followed him in a Harlem parade in 1920. Garvey's message of Black Power was so threatening to white supremacy that J. Edgar Hoover had agents follow him for years. In 1925, Garvey was jailed for mail fraud in a case that helped Hoover reach his position as head of the FBI (Katz, 1995).

Economic Rebellion

One of the responses by African Americans to the economic depression of the 1930s was to become more politically active and organized. For example, the NAACP was able to successfully orchestrate enough political pressure to have a Supreme Court nominee rejected by the Senate because he once opposed Black suffrage (Bennett, 1993). In addition, a political shift in the Black vote occurred as scores of African Americans shifted their allegiance away from the Republican Party because of the failure of the Hoover administration to take action to deal with the devastation of the Great Depression. African Americans turned to the Democratic Party and the Roosevelt campaign which supported a number of social reforms and immediate economic relief.

Blacks also stepped up their protest activity, particularly their "Buying Power." African Americans organized picketing, massive demonstrations, and boycotts to pressure various businesses to hire Black workers, particularly those businesses serving primarily Black customers (Bennett, 1993). The successful "Don't Buy Where You Can't Work" program spread from Chicago to New York, Cleveland, Los Angeles, and a host of other cities (Bennett, 1993, p. 529). At the same time, African Americans organized and activated national organizations to struggle for "economic, political, and cultural democracy" (p. 361).

The Great Depression and the large number of unemployed Blacks spurred the emergence of additional separatist movements. The 49th State Movement petitioned the federal government for a part of Texas to be designated as a new all-Black state. The Nation of Islam was established by Elijah Muhammad, calling for a total separation of the races. What was particularly important about this time period in the history of rebellions by African Americans in the United States was the merging of political and economic suffrage. In other words, African Americans combined their economic power as consumers and their political power as voters to struggle for racial equality and to weaken racial discrimination.

The NAACP organized a legal campaign that took their struggle to the courts, where they finally achieved some successes in revitalizing the civil rights of African Americans. They were able to obtain several favorable Supreme Court decisions. First, the Supreme Court banned the use of the "grandfather clause" to prevent African Americans from voting. Further, the court made residential segregation a violation of civil rights. The Supreme Court also overturned jury trials that occurred in "an atmosphere of mob pressure" (Bennett, 1993, p. 363). A new legal strategy was devised to undermine Jim Crow laws by making it prohibitively expensive to maintain separate but equal facilities in graduate schools. For instance, during the period of racial segregation an African American passed all the requirements to gain admission to the University of South Carolina Law School. In order to prevent integration, the state of South Carolina created an entire law school and law library for this one student at the historically Black South Carolina State College.

Arguably the first modern urban rebellion against discrimination and poverty occurred in Harlem in 1935. African Americans attacked the business district of Harlem, destroying property worth $2 million (Bennett, 1993). New York Mayor Fiorello La Guardia formed a commission to investigate the riot. The Commission produced a report that was never officially released to the public; however, the Black weekly paper, *Amsterdam News*, obtained a copy (Fogelson & Rubenstein, 1969). The spark for the riot was the false rumor that an African-American boy who was caught stealing a pocketknife was beaten to death by white store managers and the police.

The spark was fanned by police insensitivity and nonresponsiveness toward the crowd concerned about the incident. The police officer simply pushed the group out the door of the store, stating that the incident was none of their business. Black distrust and hostility toward the police were important factors throughout the entire disturbance. One concerned citizen asked the police officer, "Can't you tell us what happened?" and the officer responded with "If you know what's good for you, you better get on home." The urban rebellion that erupted was "spontaneous and unpremeditated" (p. 12).

A series of confrontations erupted as African Americans and some whites organized to investigate and discuss the situation, and police moved in to arrest and disperse the groups. Two white speakers in particular were arrested, taken to jail, beaten, and denied access to their lawyers or even food for twenty-four hours. Based on statements made by the arresting officers, the officers appeared to be enraged that these two white men were on the side of Black people (Fogelson & Rubenstein, 1969). Crowds of African-American residents then began to move through the streets, smashing windows and looting shops. Probably no more than one thousand people participated in the riot. The rioters never organized into one group or concentrated on one particular area.

The emphasis on property attacks over personal ones distinguished this from previous riots. The initial attacks were largely focused on stores owned by white Jewish merchants, who "while exploiting Negroes, denied them an opportunity to work" (Fogelson & Rubenstein, 1969, p. 11). As the rioting progressed, many stores owned by African Americans were destroyed as well. The Commission believed that the destruction of property and the looting had a much deeper meaning to the residents than theft for profit: "People seized property when there was no possible use which it would serve. They acted as if there was a chance to seize what rightfully belonged to them but had long been withheld" (p. 13).

The Commission emphasized that many of the police handled the riot admirably, but that the actions of many other police were derogatory, threatening, and racist. One particularly appalling incident involved the shooting of a sixteen-year-old boy, Lloyd Hobbs. On his way back from a movie theater, Hobbs saw a crowd on 129th street and walked over to see what was happening. A police car with two officers in it drove up, and a police officer got out and approached the crowd with his revolver in his hand. The crowd immediately began to run away from the officers, but Lloyd Hobbs cut across the street in a different direction from the crowd. Witnesses stated that, without warning, the officer shot and killed the boy. Although the officer claimed that Hobbs was a fleeing looter, many discrepancies and an altered police report cast serious doubt on the officer's statements (Fogelson & Rubenstein, 1969).

The report notes that many white people claimed after the riot that those who were involved in the rioting and looting were essentially criminals and "hoodlums" (Fogelson & Rubenstein, 1969, p. 16). The noteworthy element of this claim is that it diverts the cause of the riot from the frustrations experienced by the Harlem residents. It tries to suggest that the riot was the result of "bad" people who simply wanted an excuse to destroy property, or to hurt people. These claims helped whites and their businesses and government agencies deny any responsibility. The Commission concluded that:

> While it seems indisputable that the criminal element took advantage of the disorder, it seems equally true from the testimony of observers that many youngsters who could not be classed as criminals joined in the looting crowds in a spirit of pure adventure. Even some grown-up men and women who had probably never committed a criminal act before, but had suffered years of privation, seized the opportunity to express their resentment against discrimination in employment and the exclusive rights to property. (Fogelson & Rubenstein, 1969, p. 16)

Harlem residents expressed their grievances during public hearings before the Commission. Racial discrimination and poverty combined to produce a lack of employment opportunities and low salaries, chronic unemployment, overcrowded and deteriorated housing, inadequate health care agencies, poor educational and recreational facilities, and exclusion from certain school programs. However, according to the Commission's report, "Nothing revealed more strikingly the deep-seated resentments of the citizens of Harlem against exploitation and racial discrimination than their attitude toward the police" (Fogelson & Rubenstein, 1969, p. 113).

Thus, the police were more than just the spark that ignited this smoldering powder keg of resentment and frustration. Police-citizen interactions were repeatedly cited during the public hearings as degrading and oppressive. The various community problems discussed above contributed to an environment in which street crime thrived. However, even those residents who were sympathetic to the special burden that such crime-rich environments place on the police stated that "the police of Harlem show too little regard for human rights and constantly violate their fundamental rights as citizens" (Fogelson & Rubenstein, 1969, p. 106). During the public hearings even police officers themselves testified that they routinely entered the homes of African Americans without warrants and searched them at will. The Commission cited the following event as representative of common police behavior in Harlem. The police searched the home of an African-American man, arrested him, and jailed him for two days without probable cause or a warrant. They acted solely on the basis of an anonymous phone caller who stated that this man was wanted for murder in Philadelphia and that he had weapons in his house. It was later determined that not only was this man innocent of the murder, the murder had not even taken place. This story was completely verified by the police department's own records. Witnesses described case after case that reflected similar police behavior. The police repeatedly admitted to these practices but justified them on the basis of trying to catch people involved in gambling in the "numbers racket."

The police also appeared to be especially concerned about friendly or supportive interactions between the races. One occasion was described at the public hearings involving a man police thought was white with an African-American woman. The man was arrested and taken to the station because he was walking with this woman and was not released until he could prove that he also was African American (Fogelson & Rubenstein, 1969). The testimony given by whites who were arrested during the Harlem riot provide further evidence of such police behavior, because they stated "that the police attempted to impress upon them by words and acts of brutality that whites were not to associate with 'the black bastards in Harlem'." These incidents are particularly revealing in that they show that the racism of the police extends beyond denying African Americans basic civil rights—to the point of acting as self-appointed regulators of acceptable behavior. It is impossible for officers who act this way to be perceived as anything but racist and oppressive.

The Harlem residents' feeling of complete helplessness against oppressive, unjust, and racist police aggression was identified by the Commission as the major cause of their hostility toward legal authority, including the police, the criminal justice system, and political officials. One incident that caused substantial concern in the community just six days before the riot involved the beating of a man by two police officers and a white civilian, in front of hundreds of witnesses, for being a "smart nigger" (Fogelson & Rubenstein, 1969, p. 117). The man was falsely charged with striking an officer and he lost his left eye as a result of the beating. Eventually the doctor at the local hospital in Harlem confessed that he gave the police officer a false medical report to support the officer's claim that the man struck him.

Another illustrative incident occurred a few days after the Harlem riot. A very drunk African-American man struck a police officer with a "slight blow" when he was being arrested for disorderly conduct. Officer Labutinaki struck the staggering man with such a hard blow that the suspect fractured his skull on the sidewalk and died within one hour. Less than one year earlier this same officer shot and killed a sixteen-year-old Puerto Rican boy as he ran away after being surprised in a burglary (Fogelson & Rubenstein, 1969). The Commission found that the police department made no effort to discipline or to regulate the behavior of officers when they violated the rights of African Americans. If any response occurred, it was typically to justify the actions of the miscreant officers. This practice, of course, intensified the disrespect and antagonism of the residents toward police in Harlem.

The residents of Harlem understood that the invasion of their rights by the police was not just because of their race. Being Black *and* poor rendered them defenseless from such assaults. Although the Commission stated that they believed that there were many police officers who operated in Harlem in a humane and respectful manner, in general the police appeared completely comfortable violating the rights of African Americans. As a result, Blacks were not free to associate socially with white people, to be secure in their homes from illegal searches, to enjoy due process of law before being incarcerated, or to live without constant fear of brutal attacks by the police. Furthermore, police officers who engaged in such activity appeared to be immune from departmental discipline or prosecution (Fogelson & Rubenstein, 1969). The Commission concluded that "these attacks by the police upon the security of the homes and the persons of the citizens are doing more than anything else to create a disrespect for authority and to bring about mass resistance to the injustices suffered by the community" (p. 128).

The Commission feared that the citizens of Harlem, encouraged by this spontaneous rebellion, were beginning to realize the power in their numbers and that the solution was mass action. The Commission stated that it was "clearly the responsibility of the police to act in such a way as to win the confidence of the citizens of Harlem and to prove themselves the guardians of the rights and safety of the community rather than its enemies and oppressors" (Fogelson & Rubenstein, 1969, p. 121). The Commission made five general recommendations in reference to the problem of crime and the police in Harlem. First, the Commission recommended that police officers should be instructed not to interfere with associations between Blacks and whites and that such interference would lead to departmental discipline. Second, the police should fully enforce vice laws in Harlem, and should close any place of business that does not admit African Americans. Third, a special community advisory board should be established to improve and simplify the complaint process. Fourth, police officers who violate the law should be subject to departmental discipline and referred to the District Attorney for criminal prosecution where warranted. Fifth, the police department should develop mechanisms for communicating with the public in order to reduce the problem of rumors (Fogelson & Rubenstein, 1969). It is interesting to note that the Commission made no recommendation to hire African-American officers to police Harlem. The police and city officials who refused to make public the report of this Commission chose instead simply to place more police in Harlem as a demonstration of force. Harlem exploded again less than eight years later.

New Leaders Emerge

A. Philip Randolph, who served on Mayor La Guardia's commission to investigate the Harlem riot of 1935, emerged as one of the most influential African-American leaders of the mid-twentieth century. Randolph epitomized Black America's nonviolent agitation for social justice in the 1940s. He went to jail in 1918 for speaking out against the United States' involvement in World War I. He also organized African-American railroad porters into the Brotherhood of Sleeping Car Porters, which he later headed when the union won official recognition by the Pullman Company after a very difficult strike (Bennett, 1993).

Although whites gained solid employment in the war industry due to the arms buildup prior to the U.S. entry into World War II, the unemployment rate for Black workers remained at depression levels. Some plants openly advertised for all workers except "Germans, Italians, and Negroes" (Bennett, 1993, p. 365). As discussed in previous chapters, the hypocrisy of engaging in war against Germany and Japan because of their fascist and racist policies while African Americans suffered discrimination in the United States created serious ideological contradictions that U.S. political leaders wanted to resolve (Bennett, 1993). A flurry of petitions, demonstrations, and protests by African Americans, the NAACP, and the National Urban League made sure that this contradiction did not fade into the background to be ignored (Bennett, 1993). Langston Hughes captured the feeling of frustration experienced by African Americans about the contradiction of sacrificing, fighting, and dying for democratic freedom and racial equality abroad while it was being denied to them at home:

> Looky here, America
> What you done done—
> Let things drift
> Until the riots come
>
> Now your policemen
> Let the mobs run free.
> I reckon you don't care
> Nothing about me.
>
> You tell me that hitler
> Is a might bad man.
> I guess he took lessons
> From the ku klux klan. . . .
>
> Yet you say we're fighting
> For democracy
> Then why don't democracy
> Include me?
>
> I ask you this question
> Cause I want to know
> How long I got to fight
> BOTH HITLER—AND JIM CROW.

On May 1, 1941 Randolph became so incensed at the failure of the United States government to cease its racist policies in the military during World War II that he called for African Americans to march in protest on Washington, D.C. Randolph had once stated that "the Administration will never give the Negro justice until they see masses—ten, twenty, fifty thousand Negroes on the White House lawn" (Katz, 1995, p. 402). When Randolph announced that one hundred thousand African Americans were going to descend upon Washington, D.C. in a march "to demand jobs in war industries and equality in the armed forces" (Bennett, 1993, p. 365), there was immense political pressure because the demonstration would be disastrous to the propaganda effort. Many white liberals opposed the march as poor politics and attempted to discourage Randolph. On June 18, 1941, President Roosevelt and his cabinet had a personal meeting with Randolph to convince him to stop the march. Randolph said that the only way to prevent the march was for the federal government to take immediate action. Just seven days after this meeting, on June 25, 1941, the potential international embarrassment moved President Roosevelt to issue Executive Order 8802, "which banned discrimination in war industries and apprenticeship programs" (Bennett, 1993, pp. 366–367). In addition, a Fair Employment Practices Committee, which included two African Americans, was created to oversee the execution of this order. The Attorney General also created a Civil Rights Section in the Criminal Division of the Justice Department, so that these violations would receive more attention. Although the federal government's efforts to enforce this order were very weak, the concept of achieving gains through collective efforts was firmly established.

The summer of 1943 brought the most serious race riots since the summer of 1919 (Bennett, 1993). As discussed in chapter 3, a large number of African Americans had moved to Detroit, Michigan, resulting in fierce competition over housing and public areas. Although it was clear to everyone that racial tensions were high and the number of incidents were increasing, the local government officials did nothing to try to ward off trouble. On an especially hot day in June, African Americans and whites sought relief in large numbers at Belle Isle; but as rumors of riot spread through the city, the police began to prevent people from traveling to Belle Isle. Whites responded by physically attacking African Americans found outside their neighborhoods, while African Americans destroyed and looted white-owned businesses. The rioting and looting went on for two days. Then groups of whites "attempted to invade" Black communities, while police officers continuously exchanged gunfire with African Americans on the ghetto fringes. The violence continued to increase until the riot covered three-fourths of the city and more than a hundred fires burned out of control (Capeci, 1977). Eventually a large contingent of U.S. military police and an entire infantry division had to be utilized to subdue the rioters. The riot resulted in thirty-four deaths; of the twenty-three African-American deaths, fifteen were at the hands of the police; no whites were killed by the police (Berry, 1994). More than seven hundred people were injured (Capeci, 1977). Nineteen hundred people were arrested, three-fourths of whom were African American (Berry, 1994).

The Black press and many African-American leaders followed the Detroit riot with both a call to action for African Americans and a warning to white Americans. African-American newspapers published pictures of white mobs beating Black citizens, which they described as "German anti-Semitic tactics" (Capeci, 1977, p. 70). Many newspaper editors encouraged Blacks to fight back and not to be slaughtered or beaten like animals. For example, the editor of the *Amsterdam News* wrote, "It's far . . . better to die fighting as a man than to perish like a caged animal."

African-American leaders such as Councilman Adam Clayton Powell, Jr. directly warned Mayor La Guardia that a similar race riot could easily occur in New York. Of particular concern for Powell were charges that, just as in Detroit, the New York police department refused to discipline white officers for brutality against African-American citizens and they had a close association with "hoodlums and Ku Klux Klanners" (Capeci, 1977, p. 71). Mayor La Guardia took these warnings very seriously. After conducting several fact-finding missions, he sought to head off troubles by responding quickly to racial incidents. He made radio broadcasts calling for solidarity and tolerance and even sent a Black and one white member of the city police department to Detroit to learn how to handle such a riot. Mayor La Guardia took steps to address some of the concerns of African Americans, such as hiring more African-American police officers, but most of these actions had no substantial effect on ghetto conditions.

Only six weeks after the Detroit riot, a second major race riot occurred in Harlem, resulting in six deaths, several hundred injuries, and approximately two million dollars in property damage in just twelve hours (Capeci, 1977). The riot was ignited by a shooting incident at about 7:00 P.M. on August 1st, in which a white police officer shot an African-American soldier on leave from the Army's 703rd Military Police Battalion in Jersey City. The white police officer stated that he shot the soldier after he interfered with the arrest of a Black woman, struck the officer, and then attempted to run away. The soldier stated that he protested when the white police officer pushed the woman. In response, the officer threw his nightstick at the soldier, which the soldier caught. The soldier stated that, when he hesitated in giving the nightstick back to the officer, the police officer drew his revolver and shot him. Rumors began to circulate in Harlem that a Black soldier had been shot and killed when he sought to protect his mother from the police.

Groups of African-American residents gathered outside the 28th precinct headquarters. At one point the number accumulated to about 3,000 people (Capeci, 1977). The riot began around 10:30 P.M., as individuals and groups began to break the windows of various businesses. The vandalism which followed was described by many observers as an afterthought. "Thousands of blacks swarmed into the streets, attacking policemen, pulling fire alarms, smashing windows, and looting stores" (Berry, 1994, pp. 132–133). The "air filled with screams and laughter" as the chaos lasted until around 9:00 A.M. (p. 101). Of the six people who were killed, all were African American, as were most of the injured. More than 550 Blacks were arrested.

Having learned from the Detroit riot and having carefully elicited advice from African-American leaders, the mayor acted quickly: "The mayor immediately cut off all traffic to the area, walked the streets with black leaders, kept all policemen on duty, and made a radio speech explaining the incident. Six truckloads of military police were sent by the army to clear out all military personnel so they would not be involved. By the next day, everything was under control" (Berry, 1994, p. 133). The mayor saturated the area with police and fire fighters, isolated the community from outside traffic, and strove to dispel the rumors (Capeci, 1977). Although six African Americans died, and four hundred Blacks and forty police officers were injured, the clash between Black and white citizens never reached the intensity of the riot in Detroit. No groups of white terrorists assaulted Blacks. Nor were whites who walked through the ghetto attacked (Berry, 1994).

The primary targets of African-American aggression were white police officers and white-owned businesses in the ghetto that had refused to employ Blacks. Black-owned businesses or those that had "colored" written on the windows were spared (Berry, 1994). Also, the rioters did not attack institutions that provided social services, such as libraries, schools, or hospitals. "Establishments that were believed to sell inferior goods and charge exorbitant prices seem to have been singled out for attack" (Capeci, 1977, p. 178).

In the aftermath of the riot, La Guardia was careful in how he characterized the incident, so as not to inflame more racial tension. In addition, he moved to ensure that adequate health care and food was made available to the residents of Harlem. The next evening, "1,500 volunteers, most of whom were black, along with 6,000 city and military police, air raid wardens, and City Patrol units secured the riot area, while 8,000 New York state guardsmen, including a black regiment, were on 'stand-by' in several metropolitan armories" (p. 104).

Law enforcement officials were under strict orders to show restraint, which was largely absent in the Detroit riot. For example, as opposed to Detroit, looters were only fired upon if they threatened the officers with bodily harm or resisted arrest (Capeci, 1977). "The police department's efficiency and restraint were largely due to La Guardia's early preparations, which were based on the advice of black leaders and police officials who had observed the Detroit riot" (p. 116). The plan was to have police carefully supervised, to arrest looters when possible, to use force only when necessary, to avoid the use of tear gas, and to shoot only as a last resort. Mayor La Guardia's quick, decisive, calm, non-accusatory, biracial, and multi-dimensional approach to securing order in Harlem in 1943 proved to be extremely effective and should have been an important lesson to future mayors who would experience even more serious urban rebellions a little over 20 years later. Councilman Adam Clayton Powell, Jr., who had pressured the mayor to make changes in New York in order to prevent such a riot, described the mayor's actions as "wise and effective" (p. 116).

The United States emerged from World War II as a dominant world power, claiming to be the leader of the "free" and "democratic" world. The contradiction of racial apartheid in the land of the free cried out for resolution. Many of the same African-American veterans who had faced death to restore democracy in Europe were denied the right to vote at home. For example, shortly after World War II, one hundred African-American war veterans marched to the courthouse in Birmingham, Alabama to register to vote, but they were turned away by white officials (Katz, 1995). Internationally, one of the most embarrassing moments for the United States was in 1947 when the NAACP petitioned the United Nations with "An Appeal to the World," asking the U.N. to intervene on "behalf of a suffering and persecuted minority" within the domestic borders of the United States (Bennett, 1993, p. 369).

Courtroom Justice

Led largely by Thurgood Marshall, then the director of the NAACP Legal Defense and Education Fund, a number of successes were achieved in the courtroom during the 1940s and 1950s. The primary thrust of the NAACP was to break down the racial barriers to a quality education for African Americans, first at the graduate level and then all the way down to elementary education (Bennett, 1993). In 1948, President Truman ordered the United States armed forces to end racial segregation and to provide equal treatment and opportunity regardless of race (Bennett, 1993). In the face of A. Philip Randolph's threat to organize more and larger mass demonstrations, Truman created the President's Committee on Civil Rights in 1951 to determine where and how to improve the government to safeguard people's civil rights (Berry, 1994). Finally, in 1954, in response to the persuasive arguments of Thurgood Marshall, the Supreme Court in *Brown v. Board of Education* finally struck down the "separate but equal" standard that had allowed racial segregation and the Jim Crow laws to flourish. One year later the U.S. Supreme Court ordered that all school districts must desegregate "with all deliberate speed" (Katz, 1995, p. 441). It soon became clear that these courtroom successes did not end the struggle, but they did give African Americans hope that re-energized the spirit of rebellion against oppression.

Direct Action and the Mean Streets

Although the gains made by African Americans in the courts and in politics were highly significant, changes in law did not automatically result in changes in practice. Many Blacks felt that the war against racial injustice could only be won in the streets. Some African-American leaders, such as Martin Luther King, Jr., came to believe that the power to win the war would come from organized, nonviolent, direct action through a national passive resistance movement (Bennett, 1993). As discussed in Part Two, African Americans engaged in numerous direct action campaigns in the late 1950s. For other leaders, the violence encountered from whites trying to deny basic civil rights was too intolerable to be answered peacefully.

With the failure of the U.S. Supreme Court rulings to produce significant social change, many African-American activists became convinced that the only answer was physical confrontation in the streets. Ten years after the *Brown* decision, only 1.06 percent of African-American schoolchildren in the South were in classes with whites and more than 75 percent of the southern schools remained segregated (Katz, 1995; Zinn, 1990). An assistant to Martin Luther King, Jr., Wyatt Tee Walker, described the dilemma when he said, "We've got to have a crisis to bargain with. To take a moderate approach hoping to get white help, doesn't work. . . . You've got to have a crisis" (Bennett, 1993, p. 388). In greater and greater numbers African Americans organized demonstrations against racism. In particular, the refusal of whites to allow African Americans to register to vote led directly to physical confrontations with the police and government officials (Bennett, 1993). For example, the Southern Christian Leadership Conference (SCLC) began a campaign for jobs and freedom in Birmingham, Alabama (Berry, 1994). Many southern police forces responded with brute force. Not only was this police brutality illustrated with pictures in national magazines, the violence was brought for the first time into the living rooms of white Americans through the use of television (Bennett, 1993; Berry, 1994).

The Pressure Intensifies

In 1963 a dramatic surge in the rebellion of African Americans took place, which led to direct and violent confrontations with local governments. The following excerpt describes this intensifying wave of discontent:

> It was a year of water hoses and high-powered rifles, of struggles in the streets and screams in the night, of homemade bombs and gasoline torches, of snarling dogs and widows in black . . . blacks hurled themselves in larger and larger numbers against the unyielding bars of the cage of caste. They surged through the streets in waves of indignation. . . . In scores of cities, North and South, there were riots and near riots, and small wars were fought in Cambridge (Md.), Danville (Va.), Savannah and Birmingham. There were all told, more than ten thousand racial demonstrations (sit-ins, lie-ins, sleep-ins, pray-ins, stall-ins) in this year, and more than five thousand black Americans were arrested for political activities. (Bennett, 1993, p. 386–387)

Thousands of African Americans revolted, devastating a nine-block area in Birmingham, after the house of Martin Luther King, Jr.'s brother and the movement headquarters were bombed (Bennett, 1993). In Danville, Virginia and Savannah, Georgia, Black demonstrators were attacked by white police officers with submachine guns, bayonets, armored cars, tear gas, and concussion grenades. In Cambridge, Maryland efforts to desegregate public facilities led to what Major George E. Davidson of the state police reported as "shooting all over the city—almost on the scale of warfare" (Bennett, 1993, pp. 400–401). Groups of Blacks and whites moved through the night of June 11th stalking and shooting each other, and white terrorists drove through the Black community shooting out of their cars as the residents returned fire. Local and state governments failed to enforce the law and were often themselves implicated in these unlawful acts.

The largest and most well-known protest against racism in the United States was the March on Washington on August 23, 1963 by two hundred and fifty thousand Americans, who called for the immediate passage of a Civil Rights Bill and the enfranchisement of African-American citizens (Bennett, 1993). As glorious as this march was, the hope and jubilance that it invigorated quickly faded just a few days later when four African-American girls were murdered in the bombing of a church in Birmingham and two more youths were killed later that day, one by a police officer (Bennett, 1993). According to Katz (1995, p. 471), this "white backlash would take a heavy toll in lives and crushed hopes, and it would spark a new movement that aimed to use power rather than argument and nonviolent persuasion to attain its goals."

Conclusion

The twentieth century began with the most powerful leading voice of African Americans speaking in favor of accommodation, conciliation, and acceptance of the caste system in the United States, but by the 1930s this position was largely displaced by a clear strategy of agitation, protest, and rebellion. Even Booker T. Washington conceded shortly before his death that segregation and accommodation had not helped African Americans achieve the economic success and political freedoms that he had anticipated (Katz, 1995). The agitation strategies that emerged included political protests, demonstrations, logical and moral arguments, and legal action in the courts. As these activities achieved some success, particularly in the 1940s, they often reduced the likelihood of more violent or physical rebellions. African Americans were invigorated in their struggle for justice both by a few successes in the courts and among various businesses, and by the power that they were able to unleash when they physically struck back in large numbers. The merging of this energy and spirit with the desire among U.S. government officials to present an image of the United States as defender of freedom and democracy during World War II contributed to the initial successes of the modern civil rights movement.

8 Modern Urban Rebellions

Despite the history of rebellions outlined in chapters 6 and 7, White America seemed to be taken completely by surprise by the dramatic ghetto explosions of the 1960s. Urban rebellions are often described simplistically as acts of frustration, meaningless acts by a criminal element, or instigated by outside agitators. Such explanations deny the rationality and humanity of ghetto residents; in addition they distract from more meaningful analysis of these rebellions. The remarkable similarities among modern urban rebellions defy simplistic interpretations. The urban rebellions of the 1960s were preceded by a combination of hope and despair among African-American citizens, which was caused by continuous blocked opportunities and unfulfilled expectations.

Investigative commissions have found that each of the rebellions involved the police in some way, the common thread being that they were seen as a symbol and as an instrument of white repression (Capeci, 1977). According to Walker (1999, p. 34), "tensions between the police and the black community exploded in a nationwide wave of riots between 1964 and 1968. Almost all were sparked by an incident involving the police." Bennett (1988, p. 412) described the essential characteristics of these rebellions when he wrote that they "began with a minor police incident and expanded into assaults on white symbols of authority (police and firemen) and control (white-owned stores)."

The targets of attack by African Americans were primarily the police and white-owned stores, particularly those seen as the most exploitative. The participants consistently expressed satisfaction with their activities and viewed them as purposeful and justifiable protests (Capeci, 1977). Even the exclamations made by rioters, such as "Burn, Baby, Burn," "Get Whitey," or "Black Power," revealed an intent to rebel against a system of white domination (Bowen & Masotti, 1968, p. 15).

Motivations for Riots as Protests

Historically, major race riots in the United States have occurred in clusters, such as those following World War I, during World War II, and in the mid to late 1960s (Capeci, 1977). Each of these historical moments was preceded by intensified interracial competition for jobs, housing, and public facilities, which, in turn, was preceded by massive migrations and changes in

165

the demographic makeup of cities. African Americans who migrated north embraced a sense of hope for a better life, but often ran into direct conflict with new forms of racial discrimination and segregation. Also, many African Americans became disillusioned by the glacial pace of civil rights and economic development in Black communities (Berry, 1994). "Civil rights bills emphasized voting, but voting was not a solution to racism or poverty" (Zinn, 1990, p. 450). Related frustrations included the tepid response of the federal government in relation to the murder of civil rights workers and the failure to receive justice through the legal system. As some African Americans came to reject the idea of relying on the goodness of whites to relieve Black suffering, frustration resulted in violence.

A major part of the Black nationalist movement involved self-protection, mainly because the underpolicing policies of the white police and the white criminal justice system provided African Americans with no protection. In 1959, Robert F. Williams, then director of the Monroe, North Carolina branch of the NAACP, asserted that African Americans "should respond violently when attacked by whites, since justice could not be expected in the local court systems" (Berry, 1994, p. 167). In the early 1960s, Malcolm X emphasized the need for Blacks to take aggressive action. Later in the decade, the Black Panther Party gained notoriety for their message of self-reliance and armed self-protection. Clearly, many African Americans viewed violent resistance and protest as an alternative strategy to achieve social justice.

The motivation, purpose, and meaning of urban rebellions for Blacks is evident if one reads the reflections written after the events. For example, after the Harlem riot of 1964, Langston Hughes wrote an article in the *New York Post* that explored some of the post-riot thinking of African Americans who remembered the Harlem riots of 1935 and 1943:

> White folks respect us more when they find out we mean business. When they only listen to our speeches or read our writing—if they ever do—they think we are just blowing off steam. But when rioters smash the plate glass window of their stores, they know the steam has some force behind it. Then they say, "Those Negroes are mad! What do they want?" And for a little while they will try to give you a little of what you want. (Katz, 1995, p. 464)

In other passages, Langston Hughes puts it in more practical terms when he quotes African-American citizens saying that, after the riots, the white businesses began to hire African Americans, the city began to hire more African-American police officers, and patrol cars containing one Black and one white cop became more commonplace. Another observation was that "The riot of 1943 almost ended *public* police brutality on the streets in Harlem" (Katz, 1995, p. 465). That is, the police no longer felt comfortable using excessive force in broad daylight and in full view of the public; they felt compelled to administer their brutality more discretely. The meaning here is unmistakable—direct violent action, and only direct violent action, makes people listen to the demands of African Americans.

The two dimensions of African-American struggle most visible to White America in the post-World War II era were the modern civil rights movement and the urban riots of the 1960s. While often viewed as profoundly distinct, the differences were largely superficial. Martin Luther King, Jr. once said that "A riot . . . is the language of the unheard" (Minerbrook, 1992). The following excerpt describes the political nature of the ghetto revolts:

> The ghetto revolts have to be regarded as primordial political acts challenging the hegemony of local institutions of social control and conventional definitions of property rights. They were a manifestation of a movement without leadership, a movement that spread from city to city throughout the urban North as ghetto blacks saw their brothers in other cities were able to take over the streets, and become the focus of political attention. (Rossi, 1973, p. 14)

The civil rights movement focused primarily on the overt racial discrimination and segregation in the South. Initially, the key differences between the struggles for social justice in the South and in the North were that African Americans in the Deep South feared a massive, organized, violent response from white citizens and authorities.

> It seemed clear that the nonviolence of the southern movement, perhaps tactically necessary in the southern atmosphere, and effective because it could be used to appeal to national opinion against the segregationist South, was not enough to deal with the entrenched problems of poverty in the black ghetto. (Zinn, 1990, p. 451)

In 1963, the unemployment rate for African Americans was 12.1 percent, as opposed to 4.8 percent for whites. One-half of the Black population lived below the poverty line, as compared to one-fifth of the white population (Zinn, 1990). Whether or not the ghetto revolts were organized, at a minimum they forced local politicians and the police to respond (Rossi, 1973). The following excerpt, written in 1969, describes the political and practical impact that these rebellions had on local institutions:

> Ten years ago, these institutions (and the police, who have been affected differently) could operate pretty much unchecked by any countervailing power in the ghetto. Today, both their excesses and their inadequacies have run up against an increasingly militant black population, many of whom support violence as a means of redress. The evidence suggests that unless these institutions are transformed, the black community will make it increasingly difficult for them to function at all. (Boesel et al., 1973, pp. 58–59)

Violent and destructive rebellions made it impossible for local institutions to ignore the Black ghetto. A number of social activists utilized the threat of violence illustrated by the riots to advance the civil rights movement.

The Watts Riot

The most destructive riot in the United States since the Detroit riot of 1943 occurred in August of 1965 in an area of the city of Los Angeles called Watts (Harris & Wicker, 1988). Los Angeles was viewed by many as a modern, enlightened and relatively progressive urban area. A large number of African Americans had migrated into Los Angeles in search for a better life. The Black population increased from 75,000 in 1940 to 650,000 in 1965. Although many tried to dismiss the riot as the action of a few criminals or outside agitators, surveys indicated that at least 30,000 and possibly as many as 80,000 people participated in this urban uprising (Rossi, 1973; Fogelson, 1969). The commercial district was heavily looted and entire blocks were set on fire. More than six hundred buildings were damaged; two hundred were totally destroyed. On the worst night of rioting as many as one hundred companies of firefighters were engaged in putting out fires, as rioters drove firefighters and ambulances away from the area with stones and gunfire. The riot eventually covered 46.5 square miles and resulted in the deaths of thirty-four people, over one thousand injuries, and $40 million in property damage.

The McCone Commission was established by the Governor of California to investigate events surrounding the riot. This commission reported that between August 11 and August 17 of 1965, African Americans took their grievances to the streets. "They looted stores, set fires, beat up white passersby whom they hauled from stopped cars, many of which were turned upside down and burned, exchanged shots with law enforcement officers, and stoned and shot at firemen" (McCone Commission, 1965, p. 1).

> Pawnshops, hardware stores and war surplus houses were raided, stripped of guns and set on fire. The streets were barricaded with bus benches, and pitched battles were fought with policemen. Some policemen were mobbed and had to club their way to safety. Taunting rebels tried to pull other police out of their squad cars; still others were lured into traps with false reports and ambushed. Surging through the streets, clashing with police, setting fires, stoning firemen, attacking, scattering, regrouping, passing the word, clutching to rumors, shouting, screaming, crying, the insurgents were transformed by the fire of battle into an awesome power. Eyewitnesses reported the "carnival gaiety" among participants, who exchanged two- and three-finger salutes and shouted slogans: "Burn, Baby, Burn." (Bennett, 1993, p. 419)

The injuries included 90 police officers, 136 firefighters, 10 members of the national guard, 23 persons from other government agencies, and 773 civilians. Of the 34 killed, one was a firefighter who died when a burning wall fell on him, one was a deputy sheriff, and one was a Long Beach police officer who was accidentally shot by a fellow officer (McCone Commission, 1965). Twenty-six of the deaths were ruled to be justifiable homicides by police officers and members of the National Guard; all of the victims were African-American citizens. In addition to the 934 LAPD officers and the 719 Los

Angeles County deputies, 13,900 guardsmen were called out to suppress the rioting. Nearly four thousand people were arrested, including over five hundred who were under eighteen years of age. The vast majority of those arrested had only minor criminal records or none at all (McCone Commission, 1965). Although the primary area affected by this riot was South Central Los Angeles, rioting also occurred in San Diego for three days. Minor disorders took place in Pasadena, Pacoima, Long Beach, and the San Pedro-Wilmington area. The riot "terrified the entire county and its 6,000,000 citizens" (McCone Commission, 1965, p. 2).

The Spark

On August 11, 1965, a white California Highway Patrolman was told by a passing African-American motorist about a reckless driver. The officer gave chase and pulled the car over. The driver was a 21-year-old African American, Marquett Frye. His brother, Ronald Frye, age 22, was a passenger. Marquett Frye failed a sobriety test, and the officer told him he was under arrest. The officer then called for his motorcycle partner, a tow truck, and a car to transport Marquett Frye to jail.

The stop was near Watts and only a few blocks from the driver's house. Because it was a hot evening, a number of residents were outside. The crowd of onlookers grew from around 25 to 50 to between 250 and 300 persons within about 15 minutes. At about this time, Marquett's mother came to the scene and began to scold Marquett for drinking. After some arguing, the scene erupted into a fight between the officers and the three Frye family members, in which one of the officers hit Marquett Frye in the head with his nightstick, and all three Fryes were arrested. When backup officers arrived, they reported that the crowd consisted of more than 1,000 people (McCone Commission, 1965).

The McCone Commission (1965) accepted the police officers' version of the incident. It concluded that "the arrest of the Fryes was handled efficiently and expeditiously" and that all actions taken by the officers were "in accordance with the practices of other law enforcement agencies" (p. 1). Although the officers chose to go directly into a hostile crowd to arrest a man and a woman characterized as inciting violence, the Commission concluded that it found "no basis for criticizing the judgement of the officers on the scene" (p. 12). The last police car to leave the scene was stoned by the crowd, which then broke into groups rather than dispersing. Some began stoning automobiles; others dragged white people from their cars and beat them.

As rumors and accusations spread around the city, many African Americans and whites attempted to restore order, but the rioting continued in various forms for six days. On the second day, a group of community leaders suggested that the police department withdraw the white police officers from the area and replace them with African-American officers in civilian clothes and unmarked cars. Despite the successful use of somewhat similar methods by La Guardia in the Harlem Riot of 1943, the Deputy Chief of Police dismissed this suggestion as an untested method, and the McCone Commission supported his decision. One explanation for this bias was that the McCone Commission was dominated by relatively conservative middle-class white males. McCone himself was an industrialist and former director of the CIA. The only two African-American members of the Commission were a municipal judge and a Presbyterian pastor (Fogelson, 1969). The Commission concluded that there was no evidence of a master plan or a single group of agitators that caused this riot. However, the members did state that the general lawlessness around the country in the summer of 1964 was an important factor.

Placing the Blame

When the McCone Commission Report elaborated on what were viewed as the causes of the riot, it focused on deficiencies of African Americans as persons, rather than on the conditions of the ghetto. It went to great lengths to argue that although South Central was not an "urban gem," it was definitely not a "slum" (p. 75). When the Commission referred to the problem of unemployment, it identified the problem as a lack of skills among African Americans in the ghetto. The social conditions such as racism, lack of school funding, and business decision-making that created these deficiencies and failed to produce jobs in the ghetto were ignored. The deficiencies of a society in which a large segment of the population was prevented from sharing in the tremendous post-World War II economic boom were not noted. Rather, the McCone Commission identified the following three fundamental causes:

1. Not enough jobs to go around, and within this scarcity not nearly enough that the untrained Negro could fill.

2. Not enough schooling designed to meet the special needs of the disadvantaged Negro child, whose environment from infancy onward places him under a serious handicap.

3. A resentment, even hatred, of the police as the symbol of authority. (p. 2)

The McCone Commission described African Americans as being "totally unprepared to meet the conditions of modern city life" (p. 3). Even when the McCone Commission pointed to police-community relations as the third cause, it identified only the resentment of African-American citizens, not specific police practices. The resentment was described as hatred of "authority" in general, not *white* authority. The McCone Commission stated that the riot was not a "race riot," but rather an "explosion—a formless, quite senseless, all but hopeless violent protest—engaged in by a few but bringing great distress to all" (pp. 4–5).

The McCone Commission went to great lengths to strip the Watts uprising of all meaning and rationality. Despite this denial, the McCone Commission unwittingly substantiated the view that urban rebellions arise from a collision of hope and despair. "To those who have come with high hopes and great expectations and see the success of others so close at hand, failure brings a special measure of frustration and disillusionment" (p. 4).

Police-Community Relations

African-American citizens who testified before the McCone Commission made numerous charges of police brutality. Throughout the report, the Commission articulated unwavering support for the police department, the chief of police, and police department policies, even as it noted that "one witness after another has recounted instances in which, in their opinion, the police have used excessive force or have been disrespectful and abusive in their language or manner" (p. 27). The Commission's desire to justify any excessive force by police is evident in their careful recounting that "on the other hand" the police provided example after example of how the resistance of African-American citizens required "more than normal action by the police" (p. 28). The McCone Commission went on to stress the importance of not allowing accusations of brutality to weaken the police, who represent the "thin thread" between us and "chaos" (p. 28). When a witness from the American Civil Liberties Union identified a number of cases of police brutality, McCone stated that "as CIA director he learned that in all the recent American riots and overseas insurrections the issue of police brutality was raised in order to destroy effective law enforcement" (Fogelson, 1969, p. 120).

The McCone Commission argued that the solution to the problems of riots is for the police to gain a better understanding of the Black community and for African Americans to understand the extent to which police provide them with "security" (p. 29). They essentially identified police-community relations as a problem of attitudes and misunderstandings. The recommendations included the need for more "non-punitive contacts" between the police and citizens, particularly African-American youth, to reduce these misunderstandings and to convince Black youth of the "value of the police" to them (p. 35). The McCone Commission also recommended more intensive in-service "human relations training programs" for police officers. Finally, the report recommended that more African Americans and Mexican Americans be placed on the police force.

Allegations of Consumer Exploitation

The report noted that complaints of consumer exploitation included being charged higher prices for lower quality goods in the Black community as opposed to prices and goods in surrounding white communities, being sold spoiled meat and produce or day-old bread, and being charged higher interest rates for furniture and clothing. Citizens also complained about the lack of affordable transportation for poor people in the community, so that they would have the option to shop elsewhere. Claims of racial discrimination in the practices of insurance companies and institutional lenders were also noted. Although the Commission rejected allegations of racial discrimination, it was forced to admit that many businesses were very exploitative of poor people. As James Baldwin (1961) had noted, "anyone who has ever struggled with poverty knows how extremely expensive it is to be poor" (p. 62). The

McCone Commission (1965), however, refused to acknowledge consumer exploitation as a reasonable explanation for the rioting.

Many of those who testified before the McCone Commission suggested that a pattern of destruction by the rioters reflected a motive of retribution toward exploitative merchants. The McCone Commission rejected this assertion because many businesses with good reputations were also destroyed. The Commission ignored the likelihood of unintended consequences in situations of uncontrolled burning, as well as its own evidence that many Black-owned businesses were spared. Fogelson (1969) noted that, "with few exceptions, they looted and burned only white-owned stores which charged outrageous prices, sold inferior goods, and applied extortionate credit arrangements" (p. 129). The McCone Commission (1965) even appeared to ignore its own report, in which it had been noted "with interest that no residences were deliberately burned, that damage to schools, libraries, churches and public buildings was minimal, and that certain types of business establishments, notably service stations and automobile dealers, were for the most part unharmed" (p. 24). Not only were many Black-owned businesses spared, but so were some white-owned businesses that had a reputation for providing reasonable credit for African-American residents of Watts (Rustin, 1969). The places that were most likely to be burned or looted were food markets, liquor stores, furniture stores, clothing stores, department stores, and pawn shops. Reading the report, it appears as though Commission members were adamantly opposed to certain specific interpretations of events and consistently ignored evidence that refuted their foregone conclusions. Perhaps Commission members feared giving the rioters too much credibility because such an interpretation might encourage future riots. The fact that they mentioned the riots in the summer of 1964 as a contributing factor supports that possibility.

The McCone Commission offered a number of recommendations. First, it recommended that more employment and training opportunities be made available to residents in South Central Los Angeles. Second, in the area of education it called for more preschool education, intensive instruction in small classes, and remedial courses. With regard to law enforcement, the recommendations included greater emphasis on crime prevention and improved mechanisms for handling citizen complaints and strengthening community relationships. Because the Commission did not accept the seriousness of the complaints by African Americans and the American Civil Liberties Union concerning police misconduct in the ghetto, there was no recommendation that the police take steps to reduce racial discrimination, harassment, or brutality by police—or to provide better police protection to the ghetto area. The report further pointed out that changes should not focus just on African Americans, because the Mexican-American population was growing rapidly and was also a disadvantaged group. The McCone Commission's biased perspective was further demonstrated by the following statement that ghetto conditions are at least partly self-inflicted: "unless the disadvantaged are resolved to help themselves, whatever else is done by others is bound to fail" (p. 7).

A statement by one African-American youth following the Watts riot provides more understanding of the meaning and causes of this disorder than the entire 101-page McCone Report: "We won . . . We won because we made the whole world pay attention to us. The police chief never came here before; the mayor always stayed uptown. We made them come" (Rustin, 1969, p. 150). Although the McCone Commission labored hard to deny rationality, purpose, or meaning in the Watts riot of 1965, the people of Watts knew its meaning and many African Americans had tried to explain it to the McCone Commission. The Watts riot was clearly a rebellion against white racism as it is manifested in police misconduct, economic inequality, and consumer exploitation. According to Bennett (1993), underneath the riot "there was a wild kind of order that made Watts a major insurrection comparable in its day and time to Nat Turner's historic attack 134 years before" (p. 420).

Summer of 1967

The summer of 1967 was unique in terms of the number and magnitude of large scale modern urban rebellions that took place. During this brief time period, 164 disorders were recorded in nearly 150 different cities, leaving 82 dead, 3,400 injured, and 18,800 arrested (Harris & Wicker, 1988; Katz, 1995). Eight of the disorders were considered major riots, and thirty-three were classified as serious disturbances. In some cases, the disturbances occurred in primarily African-American neighborhoods; in other cases, they were in Puerto Rican neighborhoods. President Johnson responded by establishing a National Advisory Commission on Civil Disorders (The Kerner Commission) to investigate these riots and to answer the following three questions: "What happened? Why did it happen? What can be done to prevent it from happening again and again?" (Harris & Wicker, 1988, p. 32). In a radical departure from the McCone Commission, President Johnson set the tone for the Kerner Commission in an Address to the Nation on July 27, 1967:

> The only genuine, long-range solution for what has happened lies in an attack—mounted at every level—upon the conditions that breed despair and violence. All of us know what those conditions are: ignorance, discrimination, slums, poverty, disease, not enough jobs. We should attack these conditions—not because we are frightened by conflict, but because we are fired by conscience. (Harris & Wicker, 1988, p. xxvii)

This commission was not going to be another whitewash. It found meaning and purpose in the riots and attempted to translate them for white society. The Kerner report did not paint an optimistic vision for the future of race relations, as its basic conclusion was that: "[o]ur nation is moving toward two societies, one black, one white—separate and unequal" (Harris & Wicker, 1988, p. 1). The Kerner Commission warned that discrimination and segregation were threatening the future of America and that if we continued on the current course of racial polarization, we were endangering basic democratic values of equality, democracy, and justice. It warned that segregation and poverty had created in the racial ghetto a destructive environment totally unknown to most white Americans. The report was presented almost as an ultimatum to White America to seriously address the issue of racism and poverty in the United States—an ultimatum that has yet to be met, as evidenced by the Los Angeles riot of 1992.

What Happened?

Although the Kerner Report stated that the unfolding of the various riots was complex and in some ways irregular, it identified a number of remarkable similarities in the patterns of disorder. We will list only a few here. First, African-American rioters primarily attacked local "symbols" of White America and the property of white Americans within the Black neighborhoods, rather than attacking white people themselves. A related finding was that the overwhelming majority of persons killed or injured during the riots were African Americans. The riots generally began with rock throwing and the breaking of windows, which then led to looting of the merchandise inside. Although the riots were each seemingly ignited by a particular incident, they were actually the result of an increasingly disturbed social atmosphere created by a series of tension-heightening incidents. The particular "triggering" incident was just the incident that brought the community to a breaking point. About half of the prior incidents and about half of the "breaking point" incidents involved confrontations with police (Harris & Wicker, 1988).

Another very telling characteristic that the riots had in common was that the typical rioter was a young, life-long resident of the city, somewhat better educated than non-participating African Americans, and underemployed or employed in a menial job. In addition, the Kerner Report stated the typical rioter "was proud of his race, extremely hostile to both whites and middle-class Negroes and, although informed about politics, highly distrustful of the political system" (Harris & Wicker, 1988, p. 7). The critical message in this profile of the typical rioter is that the riot was not provoked by outside agitators, nor could it be dismissed as the actions of the criminal element in the neighborhoods, nor even the most poor or most ignorant. The riots were not irrational, meaningless, criminal acts.

A survey of Denver residents following the summer of 1967 found that African Americans and those who were "Spanish-named" claimed that the primary cause of the ghetto riots was "discrimination and unequal treatment" (Bayley & Mendelsohn, 1969, p. 140). Police brutality and harassment was identified as the second most important factor among African Americans and fifth most important among the Spanish-named (Bayley & Mendelsohn, 1969). To those who were most likely to either be involved in the riot or to personally know people who were involved, the intent and meaning of the riots was obvious—the cause was the system of racial oppression and discrimination.

In contrast, in the same survey, whites said the primary cause of the riots was "outside agitators, Communists, and troublemakers" and that the *"least* important reason was police brutality and harassment" (Bayley & Mendelsohn, 1969, p. 141). The great disparity between the perspectives of whites and people of color on the "reality and effects of police activity" provides evidence that "in respect to the police, minority and majority people live in completely different worlds" (Bayley & Mendelsohn, 1969, p. 141). In a different survey police officers attributed the cause of ghetto riots to the faults of African Americans, such as "disrespect for law, crime, broken families, etc." (Boesel et al., 1973, p. 57). In addition, more than three-fourths of the police officers surveyed claimed that the riots were the immediate result of agitators and criminals. In opposition to these claims by white citizens and the police, the Kerner Commission found no conspiracy behind the urban disorders of the summer of 1967. According to the Kerner Report, "the rioters appeared to be seeking fuller participation in the social order and the material benefits enjoyed by the majority of American citizens" (Harris & Wicker, 1988, p. 7).

Why Did it Happen?

People living in the riot areas expressed numerous grievances to the Kerner Commission, many of which had to do with the social and economic conditions of the ghetto. The most consistent and most serious of all the grievances, though, were "police practices" (Harris & Wicker, 1988, p. 144). Among the complaints were concerns about overpolicing, such as physical and verbal abuse by the police, lack of police respect for Black citizens, and the failure of police departments to construct adequate channels for complaints. Citizens were also very concerned about the lack of police protection in their communities—underpolicing. In addition, citizens were angered by racial discrimination in the employment and promotion of police officers. Finally, the Kerner Commission found that the typical police department response to complaints in the aftermath of disturbances was to train and equip police with more sophisticated weapons, rather than to address the citizens" concerns. Furthermore, because there was little change in the social and economic conditions in the riot areas, racial polarization only increased (Harris & Wicker, 1988).

Based on the investigation conducted by the National Advisory Commission on Civil Disorders, the primary cause of the explosive atmosphere that produced the rebellions during the summer of 1967 was white racism (Harris & Wicker, 1988). The racist attitude and behavior of white Americans toward Black Americans were said to be directly responsible for the creation of the urban ghetto, along with its volatile characteristics. Pervasive racial discrimination and segregation in employment, education, and housing had deprived most African Americans of the substantial economic progress made by white Americans since World War II. The massive migration of African Americans from the rural South to the major cities in the United States, combined with large-scale white flight from those urban centers, resulted in a concentration of impoverished Blacks and a serious lack of resources to meet their needs. The Kerner Commission stated that racial and economic segregation produced the Black ghetto where the absence of opportunities resulted in crime, drug addiction, welfare dependency, and deep feelings of bitterness and resentment. The frustration of the unattainable American Dream (flaunted daily in the media), the unfulfilled promises of civil rights, and white terrorism directed against nonviolent protests further created a feeling of powerlessness in which violence became the most readily available method of political expression. The alienation and hostility expressed by many African Americans toward the institutions of law and government created a climate in which there was little alternative to violence (Harris & Wicker, 1988).

The police were constructed within a racist political and economic system and have frequently been called upon to enforce racist laws and policies. According to Lohman (1968),

> the uniformed police, by the nature of their mission to maintain order and secure the established institutional arrangements . . . appear as the most visible and tangible representatives of an intransigent social order which insurgent groups seek to transform through their demand for equal opportunity and equal treatment. (p. 361)

The police are one of the most important instruments of the repression of racial minorities in this country. During the public hearings, the residents of the communities where the riots occurred presented viewpoints of the police as symbols of white power, white racism, and white repression (Harris & Wicker, 1988). Even if the police had behaved in a professional and legal manner, the logic of "policing" impoverished communities characterized by poor health and sanitation, substandard housing, and economic exploitation to maintain such conditions would be viewed as repressive and racist. But the police did *not* behave professionally and legally.

Following the summer of 1967, Burton Levy (1968) wrote an essay on the role that the police played in contributing to the riots and on the potential for reform. In it, he critiqued an analysis of police-minority relations he had written three years earlier. At that time, he had suggested that the fundamental rift between the police and the Black community was caused by misunderstandings. Levy had attributed the negative attitudes toward African Americans held by individual police officers to the stereotypes and prejudices found throughout society. He also believed that the negative attitudes of Blacks toward the police were produced by a few bad apples on the police force and the history of southern police in the United States. He had advocated a dialogue between the police and members of the Black community to clear up these misunderstandings. In 1968, however, he concluded that no matter how well the police packaged and marketed their department, "over the long run, it is difficult to sell a bad product—or to sell the product to people who are severely depressed socially and economically" (p. 352).

After more intensive study of the police throughout the country and after reviewing a series of other studies on the police and statements made by the police themselves, Levy came to the conclusion that the fundamental problem was "a police system that recruits a significant number of bigots, reinforces the bigotry through the department's value system and socialization with older officers, and then takes the worst of the officers and puts them on duty in the ghetto, where the opportunity to act out the prejudice is always available" (p. 348). He further concluded that the potential for real reform of police practices was greatly hindered by the fact that the vast majority of white Americans refused to believe the claims of Blacks concerning police abuses. As long as the white community remained politically dominant and refused to accept that the "problem is one of a set of values and attitudes and a pattern of anti-black behavior, socialized within and reinforced by the police system," real reform of the police was unlikely (p. 356). Without fundamental reform, police-community relations programs were simply a sham.

What to Do?

The Kerner Report made a number of recommendations for preventing future riots, many of which addressed the need to eliminate racial and economic discrimination and segregation (Harris & Wicker, 1988). We will focus primarily on their recommendations for the police. To address concerns of overpolicing, the Commission recommended that a review be conducted to ensure proper police conduct and to eliminate abrasive police practices. To address concerns of underpolicing, the Commission recommended that ghetto residents receive more police protection and that the dual standard of law enforcement for white and Black communities be eliminated. Third, the Commission suggested that effective mechanisms be put in place to address grievances; these mechanisms would help the police be more responsive and accountable to the communities they policed (Harris & Wicker, 1988). Fourth, the Commission recommended that police administrators develop clear policy guidelines to help officers in the proper use of discretion. The fifth recommendation was the development of innovative programs to achieve greater community support. Finally, the Kerner Commission called upon cities to eliminate racial discrimination in the recruiting and promoting of African-American police officers and, specifically, the hiring of more African-American police officers (Harris & Wicker, 1988).

The Assassination of Martin Luther King, Jr.

The last series of ghetto revolts in the 1960s occurred in reaction to the assassination of Dr. Martin Luther King, Jr. on April 4, 1968. When the most prominent Black nonviolent social activist in U.S. history was murdered by a white man, the frustration, disillusionment, and anger of many young African Americans simply could not be contained (Rossi, 1973). "[B]lack communities exploded, one after another, like firecrackers on a string" (Bennett, 1993, p. 432).

> Within hours of the murder, many ghettos erupted. In 172 cities, people
> took to the streets to loot and destroy. By the time a simple mule cart had
> carried Dr. King's body to its final resting place, 32 black people had
> died, 3,500 had been injured, and 27,000 had been arrested. President
> Johnson ordered 4,000 troops to Baltimore, 5,000 to Chicago, and 11,000
> to Washington, D.C. (Katz, 1995, p. 477)

For the first time, there were "planned strategic acts of violence" by African Americans, involving ambushes or sniper fire against white police officers (Berry, 1994, p. 180). For example, three police officers were ambushed
and killed by African-American snipers in Cleveland, while in New York
City two police officers were shot while waiting for a traffic light, two more
were shot while sitting in a parked patrol car, and two were injured when
their communications truck was firebombed.

Black leaders within various "Black Power" and Black nationalist groups
encouraged a militant stance, calling for African Americans to react to violence
with violence. "The cry of 'Black Power' was born of anger and despair. It was
a response to unfulfilled promises and to white violence" (Katz, 1995, p. 477).

White people and government officials were particularly frightened by
the Black Panthers. Soon after the Watts riot, Panthers began to arm themselves. Their Chairman, Bobby Seale, proclaimed, "Armed ghetto
citizens . . . will stop police brutality on the streets" (Katz, 1995, p. 480).
Malcolm X, who was perhaps the most inspirational of the Black Power leaders, made the following statement in late 1964:

> You'll get freedom by letting your enemy know that you'll do anything to
> get your freedom; then you'll get it. It's the only way you'll get it. When
> you get that kind of attitude, they'll label you as a "crazy Negro," or
> they'll call you a "crazy nigger"—they don't say Negro. Or they'll call
> you an extremist or a subversive, or seditious, or a red or a radical. But
> when you stay radical long enough and get enough people to be like you,
> you'll get your freedom. (Zinn, 1990, pp. 452–453)

Many Black Power or Black Nationalist leaders rejected the traditional goals
of integration. Rather, they stressed "black pride, black dignity and black self-
determination (Bennett, 1993, p. 423).

Significant gains were made in civil rights. "As a direct result of the direct
action of the sixties, black Americans made their biggest gains since slavery,
eliminating legal barriers and scoring so many firsts that the phrase 'the first
Negro' lost its meaning" (Bennett, 1993, p. 432). President Johnson
appointed the first African-American cabinet member; Thurgood Marshall
became the first African-American Supreme Court Justice; Sidney Poitier
received the Academy Award; and James Baldwin was honored for his novels
and essays. In addition to these individual achievements, African Americans
on average were making their greatest gains since Reconstruction in terms of
income, health, education, employment, and voter participation.

Rippling Effects of the Civil Rights Movement

One of the more interesting developments of the civil rights movement is that its effects spilled over into so many other groups, communities, and peoples, as it "extended the boundaries of freedom for white women, white students, and poor people of all races and creeds" (p. 433). Many Black leaders, including Dr. Martin Luther King, Jr., Bobby Seale, and Mohammed Ali, spoke out vigorously against the Vietnam war and encouraged people to refuse the draft (Katz, 1995). Many leaders described the war as a form of racist imperialism and were angered by the disproportionate number of racial minorities and poor people sent to Vietnam.

On August 20, 1970, a Chicano Anti-War Moratorium was issued, urging Chicanos to refuse military service and to fight for justice at home. A major concern was that Mexican Americans were overrepresented among the combat troops in Vietnam, as well as among those killed or wounded. An estimated twenty percent of the casualties were Chicano (Mirandé, 1987). A large number of Chicanos in East Los Angeles organized a rally in support of the August 20th moratorium. As the result of a number of conflicts, tensions between Mexican Americans in Los Angeles and the police had reached the boiling point. The Sheriff's department claimed that at some point in the rally, the participants began throwing rocks at the police. The police decided to disperse the crowd by marching through them. "Tear gas was freely used and crowds were attacked viciously and indiscriminately. Hundreds of civilians, many of them women, children, and elderly persons, were injured. The exact number is unknown but more than four hundred persons were arrested" (p. 178).

The following excerpt from *La Raza*, an East Los Angeles community newspaper described the "riot" as follows:

> They [the Los Angeles Sheriff deputies] indiscriminately fired tear gas capsules into unaware crowds of Chicanos who were sitting on the grass. Shoes, purses and lost children on the field stood as symbols of the inhumanity expressed by the deputies. . . . Men were kicked, struck in the chest and stomach and brutally beaten over the head. They were dragged unconsciously to awaiting police cars. Our people rallied time after time and pushed the perros back with stones and fists but sticks, stones and fists cannot stand against guns, clubs, and tear gas missiles. (Mirandé, 1987, p. 179)

A second substantial riot in East Los Angeles broke out again on January 31, 1971. The actions of the Mexican Americans, this time, were largely directed at white businesses which they felt were exploiting and mistreating them (Mirandé, 1987). In contrast to previous conflicts between Chicanos and Anglos in Los Angeles, this one was largely a "commodity riot" (p. 18), with very little interpersonal violence. The primary focus was on destroying and looting white businesses. Most of the personal violence was directly between the Chicano people and the police. Thirty-five persons were shot, and hundreds were injured in a single day.

The Prisoners' Rights Movement

In the late 1960s and early 1970s, the spirit of the modern urban rebellion appeared to have rippled into U.S. prisons. A number of inmates were casualties of the urban rebellions; many became political teachers and leaders helping inmates organize to demand their rights as prisoners. From 1969 to 1970 there were thirty-nine major prison disturbances (Walker, 1980). Prison riots became even worse in 1971 after inmate George Jackson was shot in the back by a correctional officer, while allegedly trying to escape. Jackson had become a revolutionary writer while serving his tenth year for committing a robbery of seventy dollars (Zinn, 1990). Many prisoners believed that he was assassinated by the government in order to suppress his revolutionary potential. Prison rebellions erupted throughout the country shortly after Jackson's death, including places such as San Jose, Dallas, Boston, San Antonio, and Bridgeton, New Jersey. The most influential riot occurred at Attica. Forty correctional officers were taken hostage, while the inmates took over four prison yards. After five days, on the order of Governor Rockefeller of New York, correctional officers, the police, and the National Guard stormed the prison with a hail of bullets from automatic rifles, carbines, and submachine guns. Thirty-one prisoners and nine of the hostages were killed, all by the bullets from officials who rushed the prison.

The American Indian Movement

Native Americans in this country also became more militant in their struggles for freedom and justice during the 1960s (Matthiessen, 1991). The energy and hope of young Indian students led to the formation of the National Indian Youth Council as Native Americans began the process of re-establishing their roots with their tribal elders. Their goal was to resolve their own social problems, such as high rates of disease, alcoholism, malnutrition, infant mortality, unemployment, suicide, substandard housing, poverty, and racial discrimination (Nabokov, 1992).

The actions of the Indian students to reject the strict supervision and control of the federal government, inspired two Ojibwa inmates in the Stillwater State Prison in Minnesota, who began to educate themselves and their fellow Indian inmates on the history and culture of the Native people (Matthiessen, 1991). These two Ojibwa Indians, Clyde Bellecourt and Eddie Benton Banai, were particularly concerned about racial discrimination against Indians in the criminal justice system. When released in 1964, they began to organize "city Indian" people in the "red ghetto," to increase their opportunities to enjoy their rights as citizens of the United States. In 1968, Bellecourt and Banai joined with several other Native Americans to establish the American Indian Movement (AIM), as a militant organization designed to fight for the civil rights of Indians. AIM members in cities throughout the midwest "borrowed tactics from black militants" (Nabokov, 1992, p. 360). For example, much like the Black Panther Party, they focused on jobs, housing, and education; they also established street patrols to "protect Indians from police abuse and violence, filming arrests and advising those taken into custody that they did not have to plead guilty, they were entitled to an attorney and a jury trial" (Matthiessen, 1991, p. 36). AIM joined with other Indian groups to protest such injustices as the termination of Indian tribes and reservations, the denial of fishing rights guaranteed in U.S. treaties, and the racial discrimination and poverty experienced by Native Americans in the cities and on reservations.

Native Americans were involved in a number of high-profile protests, particularly in the late 1960s and early 1970s. In a largely symbolic gesture, various Indians occupied the island of Alcatraz from November 1969 to June 1971, claiming it as Indian territory (Matthiessen, 1991). In 1970, Leonard Peltier led a group of Indians to take over the abandoned Fort Lawton outside Seattle. AIM also staged a symbolic camp at Mount Rushmore and a National Day of Mourning at Plymouth Rock to protest their mistreatment by the U.S. government. In February 1973 Leonard Peltier and other AIM members took the side of tribal elders at the Pine Ridge Reservation who had been denied participation in the tribal government (Nabokov, 1992). Well-armed members of AIM seized the town of Wounded Knee and posed for the media as they occupied the community church and general store. The area was surrounded by an army of law enforcement personnel and gunfire was exchanged. Like the Black Panther Party, AIM was, for all practical purposes, dismantled by the federal government and other law enforcement agencies as they moved to intimidate, infiltrate, and provoke its members into crimes so that they could be prosecuted and imprisoned. Leonard Peltier has been a prisoner since 1977 for the murder of two FBI agents at the Pine Ridge Reservation in South Dakota. He has been the subject of numerous protests, books, a report on *60 Minutes*, and even a feature film calling into question the government's actions in relation to Native American political protest.

The Miami Riot of 1980

The Miami riot of 1980 looked in many respects like the ghetto riots of the 1960s (Porter & Dunn, 1984). First, the riots took place in an area known as Liberty City, which was an urban ghetto created by economic and racial discrimination and segregation. When Miami was first being constructed as a city, African Americans were forced to live in a place called "Colored Town," later named Overtown. In the 1920s, when Colored Town became unbearably overcrowded, Liberty City was established as a second African-American section. African Americans were not allowed to own property or operate businesses outside of these designated areas.

These communities were well known for the lack of social services, extremely high mortality and disease rates, high levels of crime, and substandard housing (Porter & Dunn, 1984). As one of the growing sunbelt communities, Miami was enjoying a period of prosperity which the people in Liberty City did not share. Liberty City's high rates of unemployment and underemployment were juxtaposed with the wealth and prosperity of Miami's dominant majority.

The Miami riot was triggered by an incident involving the police. According to the police, Arthur McDuffie (a 33-year-old, divorced, Black insurance agent and father of two small children) failed to bring his motorcycle to a stop at a red light. Police further reported that McDuffie "popped a wheelie" and "gave the finger" to a nearby police car and then raced away (Porter & Dunn, 1984, p. 33). The pursuit of McDuffie lasted eight minutes and involved more than a dozen patrol cars. After McDuffie came to a stop, an officer attempted to pull him off of the motorcycle when McDuffie "turned around and, with his right fist, swung at and grazed the officer" (p. 33). As more units arrived on the scene, McDuffie was beaten by between six and twelve officers until he laid motionless on the ground, "his head split open and his brain swelling uncontrollably. He died four days later" (p. 34). Immediately after the beating, the police officers involved began to damage the motorcycle with their nightsticks and even ran it over with a patrol car. They then reported that McDuffie's injuries were the result of him losing control of his motorcycle and crashing. Their coverup, however, was not successful. Based on the initial investigation, the Internal Review Section investigators determined that McDuffie was beaten to death by heavy eighteen-inch metal flashlights. At that point, the case was turned over to the state attorney's office. All of the officers involved were white.

On December 28, 1979, State's Attorney Janet Reno announced that four of the officers involved had been "charged with manslaughter and tampering with evidence" (Porter & Dunn, 1984, p. 36). The police sergeant in charge was charged with "tampering with evidence and leading the coverup" (p. 36). The charges against one of the police officers were increased to second-degree murder when two other officers involved testified that McDuffie was handcuffed when the fatal blows to his head were struck. Before the trial started, another of the four officers charged was given immunity to testify for the state.

The trial was transferred to Tampa where defense attorneys effectively used their peremptory challenges to eliminate all potential Black jurors (Porter & Dunn, 1984). The officers who were given immunity all described how they attempted to coverup the beating by damaging the motorcycle and falsifying police reports. After a four-week trial, the jury deliberated for only two hours and forty-five minutes and found all of the defendants not guilty of all charges (Porter & Dunn, 1984).

Although many people in Miami, both white and Black, were "shocked" by the verdict, for African Americans, the results of the trial "represented the truest, most damning test of the entire legal system—the system they had so often been counseled was their best hope for achieving equal treatment in American society" (Porter & Dunn, 1984, pp. 47–48). To African Americans in Miami, neither the fatal beating nor the verdict were isolated events. Rather, they were connected to a long history of racial segregation, discrimination, and violence inflicted upon them by white citizens and the police. The not-guilty verdicts at the McDuffie murder trial confirmed what African Americans already knew: there was no justice in the criminal justice system for African Americans.

This perspective was expressed by many African-American citizens in the aftermath of the verdict. Shortly after the verdict was announced, several African Americans spoke on a Black radio station to express their anger. One stated, "It's a crying shame, that all-white jury turning those white officers loose. How long can we continue to take this nonsense? When are we going to raise up and be heard?" (Porter & Dunn, 1984, p. 49). A Black woman expressed the frustration of having no legitimate access to justice when she asked, "Where can we go? What can we do?" (p. 49).

The riot began as groups of Blacks began to throw rocks and bottles. White people who attempted to drive through Black neighborhoods were particular targets. All types of businesses were destroyed through looting and arson. Although only one of the 102 stores that were burned down completely was Black-owned, just about any business that had merchandise worth taking was eventually looted before the three days of rioting came to an end. When the riot spread to an attack on the Metro Justice Building, it became obvious that local police could not handle the situation. The National Guard was called in to help restore order.

A simple report of the damage resulting from the riots—18 dead, $80 million in property damage and 1,100 arrests—sounds very similar to the riots of the 1960s. But the Miami riot of 1980 had one very dramatic difference. The riots of the 1960s were largely property riots, in which stores and buildings were the major targets of burning and looting. Also, the majority of those who died in the earlier riots were African Americans, frequently killed by white police officers and members of the National Guard. Out of the 101 victims of the Watts, Newark, and Detroit riots, "only two or three were white people killed intentionally by black rioters" (Porter & Dunn, 1984, p. xiii). The Miami riot involved much more violence directed specifically at white people (seven were killed, as was another victim whose light skin color probably made him a target):

> What was shocking about Miami was the intensity of the rage directed by blacks toward white people: men, women and children dragged from their cars and beaten to death, stoned to death, stabbed with screwdrivers, run over with automobiles; hundreds more attacked in the street and seriously injured . . . attacking and killing white people was the main object of the riot. (Porter & Dunn, 1984, p. xiii)

Several examples of this new form of violence appeared in the first night of rioting. Two white brothers driving down 62nd Street were showered with rocks until they wrecked the car, severely injuring a small girl who was Black. A crowd of young Black men dragged the two brothers out of their car and beat them with their fists, feet, rocks, bottles, and pieces of concrete. One man was killed after he was shot several times, run over by a car, and stabbed with a screwdriver. The other miraculously survived. A white girl who was in the back seat of the car snuck out and ran across the Liberty Square Housing Project, where several African Americans helped her get a cab to leave the area (Porter & Dunn, 1984). At least one young Black man on the scene called the police for assistance, but they said that they did not have enough personnel to respond to or to contain the violence. About an hour later, three more white men were beaten and stoned on almost the same spot; all three died. A fifty-five-year-old white woman's car was stopped by a shower of rocks and her window was broken. Black rioters poured gasoline on her and on the car and set her on fire. An African-American bystander managed to drag her out of the car and transport her to the hospital, where she died. A light-skinned man from Guyana was beaten so badly that a friend could only identify him by his boots and his distinctive hair.

> The real significance of Miami, then, seems to be that it was the first time in modern history when blacks crossed those certain bounds and limits that governed their conduct in civil disorders of the past. . . . Miami . . . represents the first time that antiwhite rage built up among blacks to the extent that they were no longer satisfied with attacking images, but needed to go after the real objects of their hatred . . . the lesson is that keeping blacks in a position of economic and social isolation and of political disenfranchisement and where they feel deprived of basic human justice can be allowed to continue only at greater and greater peril to the health, safety, and peace of mind of every member of American society. (Porter & Dunn, 1984, p. 178)

Conclusion

When conditions remain unchanged, racial tensions smolder until the next spark ignites the flames of violence. The Kerner Commission Report identified the pattern of disorder that characterizes the modern urban rebellion—a pattern that has remarkable similarities to rebellions throughout history. The failure of White America to make the changes necessary to eliminate the frustration that finds no outlet except violence has created a climate in which the pattern repeats consistently.

9 Rebellion in Los Angeles, 1992

In the eyes of participants, the Los Angeles riot of 1992 was a political rebellion against racial discrimination, economic exploitation, and social injustice. It contained elements that marked each of the rebellions discussed previously (Harlem '35, '43, and '64, Watts '65, Detroit '67, Newark '67, and Miami '80). First, the police were the spark that ignited the riot, but they were also much more than *just* a spark. A second and related characteristic was that the residents of South Central Los Angeles, where the uprising occurred, felt that they received no justice through the political process—and particularly no justice from the criminal justice system. Third, the participants' frustrations were intensified by an amalgam of hope and despair arising out of unfulfilled expectations and blocked opportunities. Fourth, the participants were from the community; they were not criminals or outside agitators as characterized by many whites. The purposiveness of the rebellion was evidenced by the fact that the violence was specifically directed toward businesses viewed as exploitative and against various symbols of white oppression, including the police. Fifth, the destruction of property included looting and burning, often with an element of excitement and satisfaction. Sixth, the rebellion was preceded by a series of racial conflicts, often resulting from interracial competition for jobs, housing, or public facilities. Finally, the rebellion in Los Angeles forced political officials and government agencies to pay attention to the voices of the oppressed.

The Role of The Police

The spark that lit the fuse—which burned until the verdict ignited the explosion in South Central Los Angeles—was the videotaped beating of Rodney King by several Los Angeles police officers. On March 4, 1991, a videotape filmed by George Holliday was shown for the first of many times on televisions across the nation. The Christopher Commission, appointed after the public release of the videotape, described its mission as follows:

> The videotaped beating of Rodney G. King by three uniformed officers of the Los Angeles Police Department, in the presence of a sergeant and with a large group of other officers standing by, galvanized public

185

demand for evaluation and reform of police procedures involving the use of force. In the wake of the incident and the resulting widespread outcry, the Independent Commission on the Los Angeles Police Department was created. The Commission sought to examine all aspects of law enforcement structure in Los Angeles that might cause or contribute to the problem of excessive force. (Christopher Commission, 1991, p. vii)

The public's reaction to the graphic evidence of brutality was strikingly uniform: "We watched in horror as King was repeatedly shot with a stungun and beaten severely while he lay helpless on the ground" (Lynch & Patterson, 1991, p. 1). President George Bush referred to the videotape as "sickening." African-American criminologist Georges-Abeyie (1991) provided insight into where opinion diverged: "On Monday morning, March 4, 1991, nonblack America awoke to a nightmare all too real and familiar to America's black and Hispanic citizens; the spectacle of a nonwhite male being brutalized by the police" (p. vii). While white, middle-class Americans have a difficult time reconciling their images of their "friends in blue" with the images on the videotape, African Americans and other people of color in the United States easily identify with the behavior captured on tape. They have either experienced such behavior firsthand or have heard of similar police behavior through their family members, friends, and neighbors. The images on the videotape were not "shocking"; they were confirmation of personal experiences.

For four days before and four days after the videotape was released, the *Los Angeles Times* conducted a survey of Los Angeles residents on their perceptions about police brutality in their city (Christopher Commission, 1991). Four days before the release of the videotape, nearly 63 percent of the respondents stated that police brutality among the Los Angeles Police Department (LAPD) was common. The same question was asked again just four days after the tape was released, and the results had not changed very much. Sixty-eight percent of all respondents (59% of whites, 87% of African-Americans, and 80% of Latinos) stated that "incidents of LAPD brutality were either 'very common' or 'fairly common'" (p. 16). Although a majority of both groups reported a negative opinion of the police in Los Angeles, the differences in percentages were substantial. The history and conditions explored in this book should make it easy to understand why African Americans and other people of color would perceive the police as more brutal than they are perceived by whites.

As race and crime have become blurred in the eyes of many whites, simply being a Black man has come to symbolize predatory violence. Building on a long history of whites fearing Black victims of White oppression, the fear of crime has led many whites to deeply fear Black men; to assuage the fear, they have demanded more aggressive law enforcement and get-tough-on-crime strategies. Many African Americans felt that the all-white jury acquitted the officers because "they were *not revolted* by the police beating. . . . This jury, in fact, fully approved the police conduct. This is the message black people heard" (Minerbrook, 1992, p. 36).

The verdict intensified the polarization of the races. Many whites accepted that justice was served. One of the jurors justified the acquittal by stating that not much damage was done, yet King had "eleven skull fractures, a broken cheek bone, a fractured eye socket, a broken ankle, missing teeth, kidney damage, external burns and permanent brain damage" (Kappeler et al., 1998, p. 132). The fears of African Americans were substantiated: "The police are not their friends" and "equal justice does not exist" (Minerbrook, 1992, p. 36). White people and Black people in the United States saw the same videotape, heard the same explanations, heard about the same verdict, and watched the same riot, but they experienced and interpreted these events from very different perspectives.

The Christopher Commission (1991) provided the following description of events based on their investigation of the incident. California Highway Patrol Officers Melanie Singer and Timothy Singer were passed by King in his Hyundai, which they said was traveling between 110 and 115 miles per hour. They turned on their lights and siren and pursued King's vehicle. King initially failed to stop for the officers and, during the pursuit, he ran through a stop sign and a red traffic light. LAPD Officers Laurence Powell and Timothy Wind joined the pursuit, along with a Los Angeles Unified School District Police squad car that was in the area. Eventually, King stopped at a red light. When it turned green, he drove slowly through the intersection, pulled his car over to the side of the road, and stopped. Twenty-three police officers responded to the scene. Four LAPD officers (Sgt. Koon and Officers Powell, Briseno, and Wind) were directly involved in the use of force. Before the videotaping began, Sergeant Koon shot King twice with a Taser electric stun gun. On the video, Rodney King was struck with fifty-six baton blows and six kicks. Among the officers on the scene, there was one African-American male, one African-American female, four Latino males, two white females, and fifteen white males. Ten of the officers were field training officers, responsible for on-the-job training for new police officers. Following the beating, Rodney King was arrested for evading arrest and held for four days. He was released by prosecutors because of "insufficient evidence to prosecute him" (p. 8).

Both George Holliday, who videotaped the beating of Rodney King, and Rodney King's brother, Paul King, attempted to report the apparent police abuse. The police did not take a written complaint and no effort was made to investigate the incident until the videotape was aired on the television news. Shortly thereafter, investigations were initiated by the Federal Bureau of Investigations, the Los Angeles District Attorney's Office and the Los Angeles Police Commission. The four police officers who actually conducted the beating were indicted. Officer Wind was fired because he was still a probationary employee. The two California Highway Patrol Officers, Timothy and Melanie Singer, received written reprimands for not reporting excessive force in sufficient detail. Their sergeant was suspended for ten days for delaying the report to his lieutenant, and the lieutenant was demoted to sergeant for failing to initiate an investigation into the incident (Christopher Commission, 1991). Even though Mayor Tom Bradley said he was "shocked and outraged" by the video, and LAPD Chief Gates said that the video was "shocking," not one of the seventeen Los Angeles Police Department officers who were at the scene but did nothing to protect the life of Rodney King were charged with anything (Christopher Commission, 1991).

Several computer and radio transmissions made by the officers after the beating were retrieved by the Christopher Commission. These transmissions demonstrated the racist and callous attitudes of the police officers. The computer messages are official Departmental communications, typed into Mobile Digital Terminals (MDT) that are in the patrol cars. The messages are subject to observation by the field supervisor and are retained for subsequent audit. Shortly before the pursuit of Rodney King, the patrol unit operated by Officers Powell and Wind sent a transmission referring to a domestic dispute between an African-American couple, which they described as "right out of 'Gorillas in the Mist'" (Christopher Commission, 1991, p. 14). When Sergeant Koon first reported the use of force on Rodney King, he stated the following to the Watch Commander's desk at Foothill Station: "You just had a big time use of force . . . tased and beat the suspect of CHP pursuit, Big Time" (p. 14). The station responded to the report by writing, "Oh well . . . I'm sure the lizard didn't deserve it . . . HAHA I'll let them know OK" (p. 14). When the LAPD dispatcher (P.D.) requested an ambulance from the Los Angeles Fire Department (F.D.) to provide medical treatment to the beaten Rodney King, the conversation was recorded as follows:

> P.D.: . . .Foothill & Osborne. In the valley dude (F.D. dispatcher laughs) and like he got beat up.
> F.D: (laugh) wait (laugh).
> P.D.: We are on the scene.
> F.D.: Hold, hold on, give me the address again.
> P.D.: Foothill & Osborne, he pissed us off, so I guess he needs an ambulance now.
> F.D.: Oh, Osborne. Little attitude adjustment?
> P.D.: Yeah, we had to chase him.
> F.D.: OH!
> P.D.: CHP and us, I think that kind of irritated us a little.
> F.D.: Why would you want to do that for?
> P.D.: (laughter) should know better than run, they are going to pay a price when they do that.
> F.D.: What type of incident would you say this is.
> P.D.: It's a . . . it's a . . . battery, he got beat up." (pp. 14–15)

This verbal exchange reveals the motivation for the beating. The officers were angered that their authority was challenged when Rodney King attempted to run away from them, and they wanted to teach him a lesson. Approximately fifteen minutes after the beating was officially reported to the station by Sergeant Koon, the unit occupied by Officers Powell and Wind sent the message "oops" to some foot patrol officers (Christopher Commission, 1991, p. 15). After the foot patrol unit responded "Oops, what?," Powell and Wind's unit wrote, "I haven't beaten anyone this bad in a long time" (p. 15). The foot patrol unit responded, "Oh, not again . . . why for you do that . . . I thought you agreed to chill out for a while. What did he do?" (p. 15). Powell and Wind then wrote, "I think he was dusted . . . broken bones later after the pursuit" (p. 15). The nurses at the hospital where King was taken initially to be treated for his injuries stated that the officers with King "openly joked and bragged about the number of times King had been hit" (p. 15).

More Than Just a Spark

Following the airing of the videotape, LAPD Chief Gates referred to the incident as an "aberration" (Christopher Commission, 1991, p. 11). However, from the data it appeared that the only aberration was that this particular case of brutality was videotaped. Several key characteristics of the incident suggested that it was not an aberration. More than twenty uniformed police officers stood around and watched the beating, did nothing to prevent it, and did not report it. Second, the comments made on the MDT and over the radio indicated that this beating was not the first or even the second by the officers involved. Third, there appeared to be no fear among the police officers involved that they would be turned in. They beat Rodney King in front of many witnesses, announced their actions on the MDT knowing it was monitored by supervisors, and joked about their brutality in front of civilians. Even more dramatic, however, was the pattern of police use of excessive force during the five years prior to the incident.

The Christopher Commission (1991) reviewed the files of 83 cases of alleged excessive or improper force by the LAPD officers from 1986 to 1990, resulting in more than a $15,000 settlement or judgment against the department. The findings revealed "a significant number of officers in the LAPD who repetitively use excessive force against the public and persistently ignore written guidelines of the Department regarding force" (p. iv). Although the majority of the cases involved "clear and often egregious misconduct resulting in serious injury or death to victims," the discipline of the officers was frequently "light or nonexistent" (p. 55). The taxpayers of the city, however, were severely penalized. The city paid more than $20 million in judgments, settlements, and jury verdicts in over 300 lawsuits against LAPD officers between 1986 and 1990 for the use of excessive force alone. The most common type of excessive force was physical beating, with nearly 25 percent involving a pursuit, and 42 percent occurring after the suspect was subdued or in custody. Taxpayers suffered the only punishment; the guilty officers continued to police the streets.

Most of the information gathered for the Christopher Commission report came directly from the department's own records. A number of LAPD officers, supervisors, and administrators confirmed the statistical findings with personal experience. In his testimony before the Christopher Commission (1991), former Assistant Police Chief Jesse Brewer testified, "We know who the bad guys are. Reputations become well known, especially to the sergeants and then of course to lieutenants and the captains in the areas. . . . But I don't see anyone bring these people up. . . ." (p. ix). In addition, a large number of current and former LAPD police officers testified that "a significant number of officers tended to use force excessively, that these problems were well known in their divisions, that the Department's efforts to control these problem officers were inadequate, and that their supervisors were not held accountable for excessive use of force by officers in their command" (p. ix).

During the investigation, the Christopher Commission also found hundreds of recorded MDT transmissions between officers demonstrating the callous attitudes of a substantial number of officers regarding the use of force. Officers wrote messages about beating suspects, being eager to be involved in a shooting, and enjoying pursuits—sometimes as an opportunity to inflict violence on a suspect. The following are examples of a few of the transmissions.

> "Capture him, beat him and treat him like dirt . . ."
> "Sounds like a job for the dynamic duo . . . after I beat him what do I book him for and do I have to do a use of force [report]"
>
> "Wakeup . . . the susp on our perimeter got caught, but he got beat by a BB bat"
> "Tell [an officer] to use a baton next time."
>
> "We prond him out of his jaguar . . ."
> "He is crying like a baby."
> "Did you educate him."
> "Take 1 handcuff off and slap him around."
>
> "Well dont seatbelt him in and slam on the brakes a couple of times on the way to the sta . . ."
>
> "They give me a stick, they give me a gun they pay me 50G's to have some fun."
>
> "I shoulda shoot 'em huh, I missed another chance dammmmmm."
> "I am getting soft." (pp. 49–53)

Remember that all of these messages could be monitored by the officers' supervisors. The officers sent these over an official communication device, knowing that they were being monitored by their supervisors and recorded for potential future audits. The inaction of the police administration tacitly condoned these actions.

The MDT transmissions provided the Christopher Commission with evidence of widespread racism among the LAPD. Among the MDT transmissions by police officers were messages that described African Americans with references to animals and that used "mock African-American language," often in connection with acts of violence. For example, the unit that received the "Gorillas in the Mist" message from Officers Powell and Wind responded with "hahaha ... let me guess who be the parties" (Christopher Commission, 1991, p. 71). The following are a few other examples.

> "Sounds like monkey slapping time."
> "Oh always dear ... what's happening ... we're out huntin wabbits"
> "Actually, muslim wabbits."
> "Just over here on this arson/homicide ... be careful one of those rabbits don't bite you."
> "Yeah I know ... Huntin wabbits is dangerous."
>
> "Wees be reedy n about 5"
> "Wees also bees hungry."
>
> "Don't be flirting with all ur cholo girlfriends."
>
> "Okay people ... pls ... don't transfer me any orientals ... I had two already."
>
> "Don't cry Buckwheat, or is it Willie Lunch Meat."

Again, these racist statements were typed on an official communication system, where they were recorded and held for review by supervisors. According to the Christopher Commission (1991), "Other officers took no steps to prevent this behavior; supervisors made little effort to discipline it or to review the messages" (p. 73). What was particularly disturbing was that many of these messages actually came from the supervising units themselves. Just as officers stood by and watched Rodney King be severely beaten, they stood by and watched these racist comments and actions, doing nothing to stop them.

The role model for such behavior was the Chief of Police, Darryl Gates. His quotations in the media often included racist, sexist, anti-Semitic, and heterosexist remarks. For example, he referred to a female news reporter as an "Aryan broad," and he claimed that the Soviet Union sent "Jewish spies" to Los Angeles to disrupt the Olympics (Kappeler et al., 1998, p. 136). On an episode of *60 Minutes* on "Gay Cops," Gates stated that he liked hiring lesbians because of their "upper-body strength" (p. 136). When Chief Gates was questioned about why he did not have more Hispanic police officers in the LAPD, he claimed that they were "lazy" (p. 151). When questioned about the disproportionate number of African Americans killed by the infamous LAPD choke hold, he explained that the veins and arteries of African Americans "do not open up as fast as they do on *normal* people" (p. 136).

Numerous instances and types of excessive force, particularly toward racial minorities, were described in testimony before the commission. "Witnesses repeatedly told of LAPD officers verbally harassing minorities, detaining African-American and Latino men who fit certain generalized descriptors of suspects, employing unnecessarily invasive or humiliating tactics in minority neighborhoods and using excessive force" (Christopher Commission, 1991, p. xii). Police discourtesy and harassment toward minority citizens was reported to be so frequent that a Catholic priest made the following statement: "I don't feel I could find a single person who couldn't tell you a story of police abuse, humiliation, or degradation at the hands of the [local] Police Division—not a single one" (p. 75).

A common form of harassment in South Central Los Angeles was the routine and unjustified use of the "prone-out" position, particularly with African Americans and Latinos. The prone-out position is a control technique in which the suspects are told to kneel down and then lie flat on their stomachs with their arms spread out from their sides or behind their backs. This technique is taught in police academies to be used on felony stops or when officers have reason to believe that they are in danger of being attacked by the suspect. The Christopher Commission (1991) heard numerous accounts from citizens that the police frequently used this technique with African-American and Latino males on ordinary traffic stops and in situations that did not pose any threat to the officer or involve a felony. Even the police officers themselves testified that the "use of the prone-out position in African-American and Latino communities was 'pretty routine'" (p. 76).

As part of the aggressive style of the LAPD, African-American and Latino males were routinely stopped, apparently without probable cause or reasonable suspicion. The following MDT transmission reveals the racism involved in these stops:

> "U can c the color of the interior of the veh . . ."
> "Ya stop cars with blk interior."
> "Bees they naugahyde."
> "Negrohide."
> "Self tanning no doubt."

According to the Christopher Commission (1991), these police actions made many racial minorities feel that certain parts of Los Angeles were closed to them. The threat of being detained, searched, humiliated, or even beaten or arrested effectively removed the possibility of venturing into these areas. The practices of police brutality, harassment, and discrimination, which the leadership of the LAPD appeared to dismiss as the "aggressive style" of the department, created a substantial amount of resentment and hostility among those who were targeted by the police: young African-American and Latino males. The everyday life experiences of African Americans and Latinos in Los Angeles made the Rodney King beating just another example of "routine police work" in their community.

Seeking Justice

The second element in common with other urban rebellions was that the 1992 Los Angeles riot was a form of political protest that resulted from the inability of the people involved to receive justice through the legitimate political process. The police activities described above sent a clear message to African Americans and Latinos that they could not expect justice from the criminal justice system. Testimony before the Christopher Commission (1991) recounted numerous attempts by people of color to follow formal, legal processes to protest mistreatment and discrimination by the police. These attempts invariably failed, leaving the citizens frustrated by their inability to redress their grievances, to obtain any changes in police procedures, or even to have officers disciplined. "No area of police operations received more adverse comment during the Commission's public hearings than the Department's handling of complaints against LAPD officers, particularly allegations involving the use of excessive force" (Christopher Commission, 1991, p. xix). The public's frustration with, and suspicion of, this process was warranted. There were 2,152 allegations of excessive force by LAPD police officers from 1986 to 1990; only forty-two of them were sustained (Christopher Commission, 1991).

Many people of color (especially in Los Angeles) viewed the trial of the officers accused of beating Rodney King as a test—a measuring rod of their ability to receive justice. As in the case of the Miami riot of 1980, the initial excessive force by police did not immediately set off rebellion. Rather, the community waited to see if justice would finally be obtained through the legal process. "The black community hoped that the legal system would exact punishment. When it did not, they responded" (Berry, 1994, p. 231). The videotape appeared to be irrefutable evidence of racist police brutality. The acquittal verdicts were a cold slap in the face to those who had hoped that this time White America would finally recognize the reality of a brutal system.

Hope And Despair

The third common element with other rebellions was the combination of hope and despair created by unfulfilled expectations and blocked opportunities. The expectations of many people of color had been enhanced by a number of events. The successful passage of civil rights laws over twenty-five years earlier had outlawed discrimination on the basis of race. Federal, state, and local initiatives had been launched to institute greater access to opportunities through various affirmative action programs. It appeared to many that Los Angeles was a model of progress in terms of race relations in that it "had a black mayor, an inter-racial city council, and a reputation as a multicultural 'melting pot'" (p. 2).

In the years following the civil rights movement, many doors had opened to racial minorities who occupied the middle class, but those living in poverty in the inner city had far less opportunity. In Los Angeles, as in most major urban centers in the United States, the economic restructuring of the 1980s did not benefit those at the bottom. This economic restructuring was largely characterized by the movement of manufacturing jobs out of cities and into the suburbs or overseas, leaving the ghettos even less revenues for improving health, education, and social services. The problems of poverty, chronic unemployment, crime, broken families, teen pregnancies, violence, and despair mounted. "Per capita income in South Central was less than half that of Los Angeles county as a whole, and poverty and unemployment were more than double" (Tierney, 1994, p. 160). As the Anglo Westside of Los

Angeles County experienced a strong economic boom with the influx of foreign and aggressive economic development, and as Los Angeles "portrayed itself as the new financial and cultural capital of the Pacific Rim," South Central festered in underdevelopment (p. 160). This tremendous economic inequality produced a class of people who lacked the economic and political power to change their condition. Nonetheless, the hope that things might change still existed.

The fact that the police officers who beat Rodney King were being prosecuted raised hopes that enough progress had been made to achieve some degree of justice. Hope began to fade, however, as the trial progressed, particularly when the venue was changed to Simi Valley. Racial and ethnic minorities are consistently underrepresented on juries due to the selection process. The probability of this underrepresentation was heightened when the trial was moved from where the beating took place to where many white police officers had moved to escape the inner-city (Fukurai et al., 1994). Although every area of the country had been bombarded with showings of the videotape, the defendants' concern about pre-trial publicity in the county of Los Angeles was the basis for the judge's decision to change the venue of the trial to Ventura County. While Los Angeles County was 40.8 percent white, Ventura Country was 65.9 percent white. The demographic makeup of Ventura County made it highly unlikely that the jury would be racially diverse. It should also be noted that the new venue for the trial was a largely middle- to upper-class community, indicating limited direct exposure either to police in action or to urban racial minorities.

The city of Simi Valley where the Superior Court of Ventura County was located was a "pro-police and conservative community" (Fukurai et al., 1994). It was not surprising that the final jury included three persons who were relatives of police officers, one who had served in the Navy as a Shore Patrol officer, and one who had served as a military police officer in the Air Force. The jury consisted of six white men and four white women, one Hispanic woman, and one Asian woman. All the jurors were married with children; eleven owned their own homes. On the questionnaires administered by the judge during the jury selection process, all of the jurors stated that they "had positive opinions of police in general and the role of police officers" (p. 86). African-American Judge LaDoris Cordell, of the Santa Clara County Superior Court, summed up the situation when she stated that "this was a jury well attuned to the defendants, while politically and demographically a world apart from the victim" (p. 87). This fact was not lost on the people of South Central Los Angeles, who began to view the whole trial as just another sham.

The rising expectations for justice among people of color were crushed when the jury failed to find the officers guilty. Even Mayor Tom Bradley announced that "today the system failed us" (Fukurai et al., 1994, p. 74). At the highest level of government, on the other hand, President Bush stated that "The court system has worked" (p. 74). It was precisely the contradiction between the belief that things had finally changed and the painful evidence to the contrary that angered and frustrated so many. The acquittal produced feelings of despair among the people of South Central:

> To African-Americans more than any other group, the verdict was the straw that broke the camel's back, rather than an exception to the rule of justice. A long stream of police misconduct toward Blacks of all social classes built a wave of resentment; the jury decision seemed to endorse all the times that police officers stopped, insulted or injured African-Americans. And beyond the police issue was the economic decline of South Central Los Angeles. Abandoned by industries, banks, and insurance companies, bereft of stores and shops, and feeling cut off from city hall, many in the area felt a powerful alienation from the system. (Sonenshein, 1994, p. 63)

Meaning And Purpose

The fourth characteristic common to urban rebellions is the dismissal of meaning and purpose by many whites. Dismissing the significance of a riot by reducing it to the actions of individual criminals allows those in power to blame the victims of their oppression rather than to take responsibility for the oppression that caused the uprising. An example of this phenomenon was provided by the following interpretation of the Los Angeles rebellion by President Bush:

> What we saw last night and the night before in Los Angeles was not about civil rights. It's not about the great cause of equality that all Americans must uphold. It's not a message of protest. It's been the brutality of a mob pure and simple. And let me assure you I will use whatever force is necessary to restore order. (Berry, 1994, p. 233)

At a later date President Bush utilized the riot for political purposes, when he attributed the problems of the inner city that contributed to civil unrest to the Great Society programs initiated by Democrats under President Lyndon Johnson (Berry, 1994).

Although polls showed that most whites agreed with African Americans that the acquittal verdict was wrong, fewer whites could understand the riot as a response to that verdict (Berry, 1994). As in previous urban rebellions, many whites suggested that the riot was the work of outsiders who took the opportunity to cause trouble, or they blamed criminals looking for an excuse to steal and destroy property. One of the jurors who voted for the officers' acquittals stated: "These people would have rioted anyway" (Minerbrook, 1992, p. 36). Interestingly, however, "the unrest started in the relatively stable, comparatively well-off Hyde Park neighborhood. The area around the intersection of Florence and Normandie, which became notorious for the Reginald Denny beating, was a similar neighborhood" (Tierney, 1994, p. 150). As in previous rebellions, frustrations concerning racial discrimination and the denial of justice transcended economic class.

Mainstream media at first reported that the riot was the work of outsiders and criminals: "After a spasm of anger over the King verdicts, it became clear that a good deal of the violence in Los Angeles came from gang-bangers seeking to capitalize on the unrest" (Duffy et al., 1992, p. 21). The reporters followed this statement with the conclusion that "perhaps 1 in 5 rioters was from the immediate area; most were outsiders who had poured in for the easy pickings from broken shop windows" (p. 22). Later, though, these reporters inadvertently provided evidence that rendered the "outsider" or "criminal" explanations problematic. Not only did they state that "much of the damage was caused by people living near the ruined stores," they also observed that violence was not confined to South Central Los Angeles when they stated that "cities from Atlanta to Seattle suffered racial skirmishes last week in the wake of the King verdict" (p. 23).

If these civil disturbances were taking place in cities throughout the country, who were the "outsiders"? The anger and frustration felt by African Americans spread across classes, regions, and political perspectives. In addition, the cities that avoided collective violence were not without criminals; exits from the interstates were not closed. They were cities where political officials provided an avenue through which the people felt their voices of protests could be heard (Clark, 1992). For example, police chiefs in Miami, San Diego, Boston, and Chicago quickly and publicly announced their shock and dismay about the verdicts. Some met with community leaders, opened telephone hotlines, and even participated in formal protest marches (Clark, 1992). As described in chapter 5, Police Chief Kirkland of Reno, Nevada joined, in uniform, a group of over 600 people, in a march to protest the verdict and he spoke to the community at a rally (Marquis, 1992). In addition, these police chiefs worked diligently to contain rumors and to ensure open communication between the department and community leaders.

Social researchers joined political officials and the media in denials of the political nature of the Los Angeles uprising. Morrison and Lowry (1994) argued that for several reasons attempts to claim that the riot represented a political struggle oversimplified and misrepresented the situation in Los Angeles. First, the targets of violence were not white people, except those who accidentally wandered into the middle of the fray. Rather, they were "retail establishments, ranging from neighborhood convenience stores to discount houses and supermarkets" (p. 19). Second, the people who were most directly harmed by these attacks were not white, but Korean shopkeepers. Finally, they pointed out that over half of those who were arrested were Hispanic, not African American. Morrison and Lowry summarized the major causes of the riot as "territorially based on ethnic tensions" and "an abundance of young men with time on their hands" (p. 39). The primary recommendation made by these researchers for preventing the devastation of future riots was to initiate "competently organized police action" (p. 43). Their interpretation of events relied on a very limited definition of "political." They identified one incident as the only legitimate form of political protest among the events in Los Angeles:

> The only focused political protest of the day occurred in front of police headquarters (Parker Center), demanding Chief Darryl Gates's resignation. About 6 P.M., several hundred demonstrators carrying signs gathered at Parker Center, over four miles northeast of the disturbances in South Central. Many of the demonstrators were white; signs identified representatives of the Progressive Labor Party and the Revolutionary Community Party. (p. 22)

Their definition of "political protest" is linked to carrying signs, political affiliations, and organized demonstrations, which would dismiss the political purpose of almost all of the rebellions discussed thus far in this book. Tierney (1994) has noted, however, that not *everyone* in the riot participated for *political* reasons. The fact that not all of the actions are directly "grievance-related" or "protest-oriented" does not in itself eliminate the political nature of collective action. An event may be political for some participants and not for others.

Petersilia and Abrahamse (1994) determined that approximately 51 percent of those arrested during the riots were Latino, while only 36 percent were classified as Black. The largest single category of arrestees was Latino men between the ages of 18 and 24. As noted above Morrison and Lowry (1994) cited this fact as evidence against the political nature of the riots. They argued that the Hispanic population did not have the same grievances as African Americans, because they were "not ethnically linked to Rodney King" (p. 39). However, African Americans were not the only racial group in Los Angeles at the time of the riot to be angry and frustrated by the high levels of poverty, segregation, economic inequality, and injustice in the criminal justice system. Mexican Americans had repeatedly been victims of white terrorist violence and police harassment in Los Angeles. Rodney King could easily symbolize the injustices endured at the hands of the police. One need not be Black to be outraged by the jury verdict.

> The riot was much more than a protest by blacks against an injustice to a fellow black. Such an interpretation would vastly oversimplify and misrepresent the unrest. The heavy involvement of Latinos suggested that they too used this opportunity to vent their frustrations. Testimony reported by the Webster Commission showed that both Latinos and blacks in Los Angeles feel powerless to change their position and have lost faith in the leaders and institutions of the community. (Petersilia & Abrahamse, 1994, p. 145)

The grievances among Blacks and Latinos, particularly regarding the police and those they believed were exploiting them, were very similar. The diversity among rioters demonstrated this fact.

Korean merchants in urban Los Angeles replaced white Jewish merchants of the 1960s as symbols of economic and racist exploitation (Tierney, 1994; Freer, 1994). Many African Americans and Latinos living in South Central Los Angeles believed that the Korean immigrant, despite being a racial minority, did not face the same barriers. They observed Korean immigrants purchasing businesses in the ghetto, while living outside the ghetto.

They watched Korean merchants make money from African Americans and Latinos in the ghetto without providing employment opportunities or reinvesting in the community (Bobo et al., 1994). They felt exploited by Korean merchants through high prices, shoddy merchandise, and high interest rates on credit and complained about being treated with disrespect and suspicion.

Looting and Burning

The destruction of property through looting and burning, often with an element of excitement and satisfaction, is another common element of urban rebellions. Petersilia and Abrahamse's (1994) analysis of arrestees showed that only 10 percent were charged with a violent crime. In contrast, 35 percent were charged with property crimes, and 42 percent were charged with civil disobedience or curfew violations. The assaults on property were not random.

Tierney (1994) noted that the looting targets were property determined to be "deserving of community retaliation or expropriation" (p. 151). "Businesses were overwhelmingly targeted" as opposed to churches, community institutions, and homes (p. 151). The businesses most frequently attacked were retail stores, particularly those "whose owners were easily identified as non-community residents" (p. 152). Nearly 34 percent of all the businesses attacked were Korean owned, while another 8.7 percent were owned by other Asian nationalities. Although Koreans constituted only 2 percent of the city's population, they were more likely to own businesses in South Central and adjacent downtown areas than whites.

The burning and looting frenzy was reminiscent of the arson and theft that characterized the rebellions under slavery. These activities provide both an opportunity to improve the rioter's living conditions and a chance to obtain some retribution against those viewed as responsible for exploiting or oppressing them.

> Reasons for the looting likely included not only anger over the verdict and resentment of Korean shopowners and business owners in general, but also the desire for consumer items, basic food and clothing needs, and fear that the supply of goods would run out or that stores wouldn't reopen. (Tierney, 1994, p. 163)

The excitement and jubilation of many of the looters can be compared to the enjoyment experienced by slaves when they roasted a pig stolen from a plantation house. Genovese (1976) quoted a slave who expressed this sensation: "Roast pig is a wonderful delicacy, especially when stolen" (p. 599).

Racial Conflict

The sixth element of the Los Angeles riot, characteristic of other urban rebellions, was that it was preceded by a series of racial conflicts, although these conflicts were more complex than those previously recorded. Like many large U.S. cities, the ethnic diversity of Los Angeles was clearly more complicated than just white and Black. Los Angeles was experiencing radical demographic changes that led to a number of inter-ethnic conflicts as people competed for limited resources, jobs, and housing (Baldassare, 1994). The African-American population during the 1980s had grown by less than one percent, and the Anglo population decreased by 8.5 percent. The Hispanic population increased by 62 percent and the Asian population increased by 110 percent. The African-American residents who remained in the South Central area were primarily the very poor, since those who achieved middle-class status frequently moved to more affluent or suburban areas. According to Baldassare (1994), "inter-ethnic hostilities in inner-city areas emerged as the poor urban blacks found themselves surrounded, and in some instances displaced, by large numbers of newly arrived foreign immigrants." Most of the recent Hispanic immigrants from Mexico and Central America were also poor and undereducated—and in direct competition for the same jobs as the poor Blacks.

While Blacks resented Latino immigrants for competing with them for jobs and pushing wages down, Latino immigrants were frustrated by their own difficulties in having a shot at the American Dream (Tierney, 1994). Latinos who participated in the riot were primarily recent immigrants from Central America, rather than members of the more stable Mexican American community (Sonenshein, 1994).

In contrast, Asian immigrants, particularly those from Korea, arrived with capital, higher education, and more entrepreneurial skills. Language and cultural barriers made it difficult for Korean immigrants to work in the professional careers for which they had been trained (Freer, 1994). One opportunity that was available to them was to invest in small businesses in economically depressed areas such as South Central Los Angeles. These businesses required relatively moderate capital investment and were relatively inexpensive to operate. The downside was they were labor intensive, had a low profit margin, and were located in the inner city where there was a high crime rate and very little cash for purchases. As a result, such businesses typically have low inventories, poor selection, and high prices—creating difficulties for customers facing chronic unemployment and persistent poverty in their daily lives. The situation was "exacerbated by cultural differences and misunderstanding" (p. 176). While these business opportunities may not have been ideal for Korean Americans, they were well beyond the reach of most people of color living in South Central. In addition, Asian Americans were frequently held up as the "model minority" whenever people of color attempted to expose institutional racism, discrimination, and exploitation—increasing the resentment and heightening tensions.

The competition for limited resources had already boiled over in a number of inter-ethnic conflicts prior to the Los Angeles rebellion. One case received a great deal of media attention. In March 1991, a Korean store owner shot and killed a thirteen-year-old African-American girl "in a dispute over a container of orange juice" (Freer, 1994, p. 188). In response to the incident African Americans in Los Angeles organized a boycott of Korean grocery stores. When a "white judge ruled that the Korean grocer would not have to serve jail time for the killing," the feelings of frustration intensified. African Americans experienced yet another example of the lack of justice in the white-dominated criminal justice system (Baldassare, 1994, p. 5). The interracial tensions became even worse in June of 1991 when another shooting of an African American by a Korean merchant was ruled as justifiable homicide by the police (Freer, 1994).

Korean Americans were angered by the organized boycotts, and they were frustrated about what they viewed as a lack of attention given to the killing of Korean merchants (Freer, 1994). During the riot in 1992, armed battles broke out as Korean merchants attempted to protect their businesses, assuming that they would not receive protection from the police (Baldassare, 1994; Petersilia & Abrahamse, 1994). The Los Angeles riot

> involved clashes among a range of groups, including blacks and whites; blacks and Asians; Latinos and blacks; and Latinos and Asians. In a broader sense, the unrest constituted a collective attack by minority group members both on Anglos and on minority business proprietors. (Tierney, 1994, p. 155)

Each of the different minority groups in this struggle felt that neither the police nor the courts would provide them with safety or justice. They believed that it was necessary to take matters into their own hands.

Being Heard

The rebellion in South Central forced white people in Los Angeles and throughout the United States to hear the voices of oppressed people in urban communities. It prompted the attention of political officials and other government agencies, especially at the local level. Both whites and people of color engaged in discussions surrounding the issues of race, economics, and government services. "The riot focused public attention on the grievances of the poor black community, including police brutality, homelessness, joblessness, violence, drugs, lack of education, and economic opportunity" (Berry, 1994, p. 232).

The criminal justice system and, more particularly, the police were the institutions most profoundly impacted by the events in Los Angeles. The videotaped beating of Rodney King and the Los Angeles riots constitute watershed events in police history in the United States. In the words of a Kansas City police officer, "Police work has been forever changed into two phases—before Rodney King and after Rodney King" (Witkin et al., 1992, p. 31). The most significant impact on police has been the push to create at least the appearance of police departments that are more responsive to all facets of our multicultural society. Kansas City Police Chief Steven Bishop stated that "the predicate for change in the 1990s is the Rodney King incident. . . . People want a more active role in saying how they want to be policed'" (Witkin et al., 1992, p. 27). Barry and Cronkhite (1992) argued that the "post-King era" of policing was the time "to renew emphasis on ethics and to promote the community-oriented policing philosophy" (p. 8). They stated that the police must respond to the scrutiny placed upon them by the videotaped beating of Rodney King by becoming more responsive to the community through the adoption of a client orientation.

As we discussed in Part Two of this book, such efforts, often referred to as community relations programs, were initiated as early as the 1940s following a series of race riots. Police-community relations received serious and widespread attention among police executives and political officials following the disturbances of the 1960s. Numerous programs, including race relations training, ride-alongs, and crime prevention units were initiated throughout the United States in an effort to obtain greater community support for police, particularly among racial minorities. In the 1980s, a movement was already underway to move away from many of the elements of the professional model of policing toward a more responsive police force through community-oriented and/or problem-oriented policing. The videotaped beating of Rodney King and the subsequent riots in Los Angeles had the effect of shifting this movement into high gear.

Such police reforms are often presented in textbooks and the media as the inspiration of various police chiefs or public officials. In fact, police departments have most often been forced into various public relations efforts, including community relations programs and cultural diversity awareness training. The police did not freely choose to become more client-oriented; they responded to pressure from communities. Police agencies did not freely decide to open their doors to racial minorities and women; they were forced to become more representative of the population they police. Though the police are often portrayed as the thin blue line protecting the law-abiding citizens from dangerous predators, it has often been citizens who need protection from the police. The Los Angeles rebellion was an exercise of power by those at the bottom of the political and economic system. Ultimately, the power exerted by rioters did influence the police, if not the political and economic system as a whole. One important change locally was the replacement of Chief Gates with African-American Police Chief Willie Williams, a strong proponent of community policing. In connection with both the adoption of community policing and because of the concerns about police-minority relations, many police institutions and academies made changes in how they recruit and train their police officers. Communication skills, service-orientations, race relations, community relations, and cultural diversity awareness training have all become much more prominent in both the recruitment and training processes.

Conclusion

The major question that remains, however, is whether these changes are substantial enough to improve police-community relations, and whether they will be accompanied by social changes that alter the conditions that have produced problems between the police and people of color. Even in Los Angeles, reforms have already been curtailed. Although community policing has not been abandoned, Police Chief Willie Williams' employment contract was not renewed. The Los Angeles Police Commission said that although Williams was extremely successful in building a connection between himself and the community, he had not been successful at obtaining the support and loyalty of the police officers. This development was predictable given the shift in the political climate which occurred after the impact of the Los Angeles riot dissipated.

The long-term impact of the rebellion in Los Angeles was not the hoped-for progressive reforms, but rather a conservative reaction largely led by white moderates, as reflected in the mayoral election of 1993. The twenty-year-old liberal, multicultural coalition that had been established under Mayor Bradley was soundly defeated as the conservative Republican financier Richard Riordan defeated liberal council member Michael Woo for the office of mayor of Los Angeles (Sonenshein, 1994). The more aggressive and hardcore approach of Mayor Riordan was reflected in his political campaign slogan, "Tough enough to turn L.A. around" (p. 67). Still, the new conservative mayoral administration vowed to continue to develop relationships with various minority groups and to encourage police reform. Will the long-term effects be similar to previous urban rebellions? Will the words "the same analysis, the same recommendations, and the same inaction" (Harris & Wicker, 1988, p. 29) apply once again?

The path to social peace and racial harmony begins with listening to marginalized voices and trying to understand and appreciate their perspective.

> The resort to insurrection in the United States, especially when more than merely a violent outburst against vicious local conditions, provides a yardstick with which to measure the smoldering resentment of an enslaved people. (Genovese, 1976, p. 591)

Understanding the smoldering resentment that led African slaves to resort to insurrection can be a key to understanding the smoldering resentment of people of color that erupted in Los Angeles in 1992.

Throughout much of the history of the United States, the U.S. Constitution was interpreted to maintain white supremacy. The police and the entire criminal justice system, sometimes backed by the U.S. military, have provided the coercive force necessary to require racial minorities to submit to racial discrimination and segregation. "It is no wonder that many African Americans long regarded law and order as an instrument for their repression" (Berry, 1994, p. 241). Efforts to resist racist laws or to rebel against the racist government placed those who did resist in direct conflict with the police. The police were both a symbol and an instrument of white oppression. The history of the police and the history of race relations in the United States are integrally linked. Neither can be understood without reference to the other.

The modern urban rebellion as a form of resistance is linked to the formation of the ghetto, a direct result of racial segregation, discrimination, and exploitation. These areas are characterized by inadequate and substandard housing, poor social and government services (including the police), and high levels of unemployment, underemployment, and poverty. Because the police constitute the primary arm of the government charged with social control in the ghetto, they are implicated in many ways when the ghetto explodes.

Part Four
Marginalized
Police Officers

Thus far, we have argued in this book that we cannot fully understand the relationship between the police and society without incorporating the experiences and perspectives of all members of our diverse society. We have focused primarily on those members of society, particularly African Americans, whose voices have most frequently been ignored or marginalized by society's white majority. By seeking insight from those whose lives are most affected by police but whose experiences are most likely to be excluded from traditional analyses, we hope to add an important dimension to our understanding of police and society. In Part Four, we turn our attention to the other side of the relationship—the police.

While conducting research on the role of the media in police-community relations in Milwaukee, the authors were reminded that just as it is wrong to conceptualize "the community" as a single entity, it is also misleading to think of the police as having one voice or perspective. We discovered multiple perspectives and interpretations of events among the police; the most notable divisions occurred along racial lines. Distinct—and often diametrically opposed—viewpoints were presented by the chief of police, police supervisors, the white male rank and file, police union members, African-American police officers, and Latino police officers. Although we were examining perspectives on a highly politically charged incident involving issues of gay rights, domestic violence, gender, race, and class, voices of women police officers and gay and lesbian police officers were remarkably silent (Barlow et al., 1994).

As we have emphasized throughout this examination of police and society, explanations are incomplete if they are monocultural. Part Four explores the diversity among police by focusing on the personal experiences and social issues surrounding marginalized police officers. Inclusion on police forces has been a dominant political and social mission of people of color, women, and gays and lesbians seeking social justice through a more responsive police force. Just as it is misleading to study police and society without incorporating a multiplicity of perspectives from society, to study the police without fully incorporating the unique experiences and perspectives of marginalized police officers is also incomplete and distorted. In Part Four, we focus primarily on those members of the police force whose voices are frequently missing. As in the earlier chapters of the book, our historical analysis focuses heavily on police officers of color, particularly African Americans. However, we also explore issues specific to Native American tribal police officers, women police officers, and gay and lesbian police officers. These choices are partly based on the particular insights offered by these groups and partly based on the availability of information.

Although women and people of color have a rich history of working in various forms and situations within policing agencies, the job of police officer was for many years almost exclusively reserved for white males. Despite the Civil Rights Act of 1964, more than thirty years later over 80 percent of all police officers are white males (Bohm & Haley, 1997). The *recorded* history of gay and lesbian police officers is even shorter than that of women and people of color. The discrimination against gays and lesbians continues to such an extent that only a tiny fraction of police departments have gay and lesbian police officers who feel comfortable in openly expressing their sexual orientation.

The same racism and sexism that produced the policing practices discussed thus far in this book have long oppressed members of certain groups from employment as police officers. Thus, the experiences of women, people of color, and gays and lesbians who become involved in policing provide a useful lens through which we can look even more closely at police and society. The unique position of marginalized police can give us insight into the intersection of cultures and groups. Marginalized police officers are invaluable "cultural contacts." Reviewing their difficulties and successes in bridging the gap between the two worlds in which they live can help us achieve greater understanding of the historical, current, and future role of police in our society.

As we explore the historical experiences of marginalized police, a number of key questions or issues are addressed for each group. First, we examine the struggles for social change and justice reflected in efforts to be represented on local police forces. In our long history as a racist, sexist, and heterosexist society, unjust power relations have been physically preserved by the domestic social control apparatus of the state—the criminal justice system. The police have long operated with the legal power to use coercive force to suppress the social movements that seek to alter these power relationships. Thus, one strategy in the overall struggle to transform a government that has traditionally been non-responsive and often openly oppressive is to infiltrate the most visible instrument of social control—the police. Achieving representation on the police force is one method of facilitating social change at the macro-level by contributing to the empowerment of racial minorities, women, and gays and lesbians. The methods, arguments, and expressed motivations of members of these groups provide insights into the massive civil rights and social justice movements that have occurred in this country's history.

On an individual level, many people of color, women, and gays and lesbians seek to achieve a sense of empowerment in their own lives by becoming police officers. The social change that they seek is the opportunity to work in an occupation that has traditionally excluded them. Initially, their goal is to gain access; the goal also involves survival, which means overcoming the barriers and the resistance of an especially hostile work environment. The individual police officer often strives to become accepted as a regular member of the police department. Finally, just like white male police officers, the individual officer's goal is to develop a career that involves advancement and self-fulfillment.

It is particularly useful to trace the history of select marginalized police and to examine the motivations of the police officers, the unique barriers that they faced, and the conflicts they must resolve in working for an organization whose primary role is to maintain the current unequal and discriminatory power relations. These officers face both the relatively unique external conflict of working in an environment that is hostile toward them and the internal conflict of working as a social control agent whose actions may be detrimental to themselves or to people like them.

The final area which we explore concerns why police departments want to hire women and members of minority groups. In many situations the motivations for hiring "women and minorities" were responses to political pressure; in others, administrators saw an opportunity for more effective policing and/or social control. In a few cases, such as the Native American tribal police, the social control motives are laid bare. We will learn that white males initiated the change in policing strategies clearly as a method of becoming more effective at maintaining control over the Native American population. On the other hand, there is evidence that creating a more diverse police force produces social control agents who are less offensive and violent and more responsive to the criminal victimization of people of color, women, or gays and lesbians.

Police departments have long been a critical battleground in struggles for justice. In most cases, discrimination by police officers continued long after initial entry of marginalized groups into departments through the refusal to grant them full police powers. This situation did not change until departments were bombarded with a series of court rulings that forced them into granting full police powers regardless of race, religion, or gender. Efforts to gain representation and acceptance in this arena expose the essential role of the police in maintaining current power relations. Here, we review historic and current issues surrounding the recruitment, daily work, and social ramifications of marginalized police. We examine the potential for social change through minority empowerment and the potential for social control through enhancement of the effectiveness of an agency created to prevent social change.

10 Native American Police Officers

Introduction

A major shortcoming in the use of force to control people is that it exposes inequalities and angers those who are repressed. Therefore, an important aspect of successful social control is to imbue the methods with legitimacy (Hoare & Smith, 1971). Nowhere is the practice of cloaking oppression in a mantle of legitimacy better exemplified than in the practice of utilizing members of oppressed groups to "police" themselves. Under apartheid, South Africa systematically placed key Black Africans in uniform to maintain order in Black townships. Nazi Germany used concentration camp prisoners to regulate other prisoners. The Kapo was an inmate official in Nazi Germany's concentration camps who possessed the following characteristics:

> (1) he is a member of the inmate population, (2) he acts as an overseer entrusted with command over ethnic peers, (3) he is an extension of the dominant authority, and executes considerable power, but does not make policy, (4) he is rewarded with privileges and promotions, and (5) in order to keep those privileges, he must continuously demonstrate his loyalty to his masters: He is often regarded as a "quisling" by his clientele. (Alex, 1969, p. 19)

Not only do these social control agents serve as a buffer between the oppressed and the oppressors, they are often much more effective in communication, information gathering, and locating insurgents than are members of the oppressing group. The institution of tribal police and African-American police as agents of social control helped to effectively maintain fundamental race and class divisions in the structure of the United States.

Native American Tribal Police

As a racial minority in their own land, Native Americans have a unique experience in relation to the now dominant culture of white European Americans. Numerous attempts have been made by whites in various periods of American history to practice cultural genocide by destroying Native American traditions and distinctiveness. One of the unique social control mechanisms used against Native Americans was the "Indian reservation." As white Europeans sought to conquer the area now known as the United States, the native people of the land, who had already constructed communities, farms, and intricate societies, stood in their way. In a long series of violent struggles and wars, white Europeans destroyed much of the civilization that these native peoples had built.

Throughout much of the nineteenth century (1828–1887), the U.S. Government was actively engaged in a policy of removal and relocation. Native Americans were stripped of their lands and forced to move onto reservations or to live in designated Indian territories. Theoretically, these policies were the result of treaties by tribes with sovereign status who ceded their lands to the government. In reality, the tribes had no options against the military policies of the federal government. (Byrne, 1996).

The Occupying Army

In addition to forcing relocation, government authorities refused to let tribes follow their traditional ways. Early efforts to force an Anglo-Saxon judicial system upon the Indians were rooted in an attempt to Christianize, civilize, and assimilate the indigenous populations into white European culture. In 1806, President Thomas Jefferson articulated this grand design in a speech to a delegation of Indians: "When once you have property, you will want laws and magistrates to protect your property and persons . . . You will find that our laws are good for this purpose . . . You will unite yourselves with us . . . form one people with us, and we shall all be Americans" (Washburn, 1971, p. 61). The speech also foreshadowed the government's efforts through allotment to force tribes to embrace the value of private property over their deeply rooted culture of communal life. The process of privatizing the land also meant breaking the Indians' communal monopolistic control over the land within the reservation and creating new opportunities for land acquisition.

The imposition of Western law was another disruptive change on peoples who had been uprooted from their homes. In 1796, punishment was established for Indians who crossed state and territorial lines and committed any of various offenses. Inciting Indians against the United States became a crime in 1800. In the Treaty of Ghent (1814), Congress placed Indian tribes in the United States under federal jurisdiction, and in 1817 Congress established a new system of criminal justice applicable to both Indians and non-Indians within Indian Country. Under federal jurisdiction all offenders were to receive the same punishment. The only exceptions were offenses involving Indians against another Indian. Amendments placed Anglo-Saxon federal judges and marshals in charge of enforcing federal law on Indian reservations.

The military, as the primary enforcer of law and order, was incapable of protecting the Indians on the reservation. The frontier was almost impossible to police, given the vast expanse of territory and small population. The common themes in the history of racial minorities in the United States with regard to underpolicing and overpolicing applied to life on reservations. Indians had to endure being victimized by outlaws; conversely, if an Indian were arrested by the federal marshals, they were thrust into a foreign criminal justice system that left them lost and confused. They were frequently transported to courts hundreds of miles away and expected to mount a defense in a language and culture they did not understand (Hagan, 1966).

Until the last quarter of the nineteenth century, Indian reservations were largely regulated by federal troops.

> In 1824 the federal government established a Bureau of Indian Affairs in the War Department, a clear sign of the official attitude in Indian-federal relations: hostile. Although in 1849 the Bureau of Indian Affairs was transferred to the Department of the Interior, Indians had few contacts with white Americans that were not hostile. (Garbarino & Sasso, 1994, p. 434)

In 1849, a shift in public opinion was taking place, at least in Washington and on the East Coast, toward peace and away from militaristic solutions. As the Indian wars became more distant to those in the East, sympathy toward Indians grew, as did the desire to assimilate them into the "American" way of life (Hagan, 1966). Washburn (1971) identified another reason for this shift in focus—land acquisition. As sovereign nations, the tribes retained valuable land that the new nation wanted. As tribe members became assimilated landowners, this land could be opened for settlement and exploited. In other words, shifting the social control apparatus from military occupation of a nation to civilian law enforcement allowed the land in Indian Country to be annexed into the United States and made it accessible to white citizens.

Although the Bureau of Indian Affairs was removed from the direct official control of the War Department in 1849, for all practical purposes the military remained the primary enforcer of law and order on the reservation (Hagan, 1966). In 1862 the Homestead Act opened up Indian land in Kansas and Nebraska to white homesteaders. White Europeans wanted to restrain Native Americans and not allow them to move about freely, fearing a threat to both life and property.

> The reservations became prison camps, federal soldiers seeing to it that Indians stayed in their allotted areas. The government established reservation schools and boarding schools in an attempt to Anglicize Indian children. Agents were put in charge of the reservations, and though many of them were genuinely sympathetic toward the tribes, they could do little, for they did not set policy.

With no mode of enforcement other than the military available to the Indian agents, they were often puppets of the local federal troops. The War Department was not pleased with the loss of the Bureau of Indian Affairs and continued to lobby for its return. Opposition to the military's supervision of Indian Affairs, however, became more intense following the end of the Civil War. The general public was war-weary, and the military was downsizing rapidly. As the last of the Indian Wars were underway in the West, the people of the United States were forming a "revulsion against the seemingly endless bloodletting on the Plains" (Hagan, 1966, p. 1).

An investigation by a Congressional committee in 1865 concluded that Indians were on the road to extinction. This investigation led to an 1867 commission to eliminate Plains warfare in three ways: (1) concentrating the Indian populations within reservations, (2) extending the federal government's control over Indians on reservations, and (3) utilizing missionaries and teachers to assist in the civilization of Indians. In 1868, the Peace Commission met in Chicago and presented the president and Congress with a set of resolutions to feed, clothe, and protect Indians living on reservations (Washburn, 1971).

The Society of Friends was a major player in the new policy. The Quakers wanted to "civilize" American Indians and envisioned self-government as the key to civilization and eventual assimilation. They convinced President Grant's administration to seek recommendations from church groups for appointments to Indian service. In addition, the Civilian Board of Indian Affairs was established to advise the government and to exercise joint control with the Secretary of the Interior to administer funds. Eventually the desire to maintain control over the Indian population led to the creation of tribal police.

The Formation of Tribal Police

While different tribes had different approaches to achieving justice, the Western Plains Indians primarily struggled to obtain greater autonomy and sovereignty for their tribes. Attempts to assimilate or adopt white European customs frequently caused serious divisions within the tribe. As compared to other minority communities, the idea of using tribal members to "police" other tribal members under the laws of white people was generally not an acceptable idea of racial and social justice. Thus, in contrast to other marginalized police, the formation of tribal police cannot be seen as a community strategy by Native Americans to facilitate social change. The motivation to create or hire Native American tribal police, therefore, cannot be attributed to an effort to appease a minority group or to respond to their demands for greater representation. A key motivation for most white authorities in this instance was clearly to develop a more effective mechanism of control.

Minorities Policing Minorities as a Strategy of Social Control

While on a campaign to apprehend a "hostile" band of Apaches in the Arizona Indian Territory, a cavalry officer stated that using standard tactics there was "like chasing deer with a brass band" (Roberts, 1992, p. 58). Recognition of the inefficiency of traditional techniques of investigation, travel, and conflict in Indian territory led the U.S. Army to employ Native Americans as scouts. "The Army's success in pacifying most of [the Apache] depended on enlisting warriors from one band to track and fight against those of another" (p. 52).

This observation is a good foundation for attempting to understand the strategic use of tribal police specifically and persons of color as police in general.

If social control agents are not part of the culture they are attempting to suppress, they typically lack understanding of the people, their language, customs, and values. Communication is hindered, and agents of social control cannot anticipate people's actions or predict their movements. This misunderstanding leads to inaccurate information, poor cooperation, confusion, frustration, and ultimately unnecessary violence and the use of force (Soloman & McCarthy, 1989). That force is typically crude and awkward because the agents of control are ignorant with regard to the people they are policing.

Many military leaders believed that all Indians were enemies and that the use of them as scouts was placing too much faith in their abilities and loyalties. The same concern arose in the use of tribal police. We will see that one of the greatest fears expressed about the use of racial minority police officers, particularly African Americans, was the concept of placing guns in their hands. Typically, as soon as the "hostile" Indians were subdued and imprisoned, Indian scouts were stripped of their uniforms and guns, and forced to live on the same reservations as those they helped to subdue. Many whites believed that allowing Indians to be armed and to be accepted as soldiers gave them too much power. Possibly even more important, it gave them a sense of self-esteem and equality that could lead to efforts to break the chains of racial segregation, repression, and exploitation. These fears were similar to those toward African-American soldiers who served in World War I and World War II.

The Origin and Success of Tribal Police

The development of tribal police served two purposes. The first goal was to secure peace on the reservation by settling disputes, enforcing federal regulations, tracking and capturing fugitives, and making sure that tribes stayed on the reservation. The tribal police were the eyes and ears of the Indian agents responsible for the maintenance of the reservation. The other goal was to expel white intruders who cut timber, gathered nuts, fished, hunted, stole horses, and grazed cattle on Native American land (Hagan, 1966).

The goal of maintaining order on the reservation was clearly reflected in the early efforts to appoint tribal members to "police" the reservation. In 1874, Indian Agent John P. Clum came to the San Carlos Indian Agency in the Arizona Territory to administer the Apache reservations. He was placed in charge of a rough, mountainous area about the size of Connecticut. The reservation was in a state of disorder, with continual rebellion and violence. The military had a continual presence and had controlled the former agents. Clum transformed this situation by advocating self-government. He appointed a handful of Apaches to serve as social control agents, or "tribal police," and hired a white man, Clay Beuford, to serve as the Apache Tribal Police Chief (Hagan, 1966).

These newly created tribal police were extremely successful. Clum's records suggested that in approximately two years he and his small group of tribal police (never more than twenty-five) captured or killed 159 "renegades," including Geronimo and his fifty followers. Clum reported that "our little squad of Indian Police [has] done more effective scouting . . . than General Kautz has done with all his troops and four companies of Indian Scouts" (p. 37). When General August V. Kautz complained to the secretary of the Interior about Clum, the Secretary sent an inspector to investigate. The inspector "alleged that Clum had been subjected to 'persistent and bitter opposition from military authorities,' but, 'by the aid of his Indian Police force accomplished far more than [Kautz] with his two regiments of regulation soldiers to assist'" (p. 38).

The phenomenal success of the San Carlos Tribal Police led to the virtual elimination of the military presence on the reservation in three months (Hagan, 1966). Their continual success staved off repeated efforts by the U.S. Cavalry to discredit Clum and to move back in. During the 1870s, tribal police were established on reservations for the Pawnee, Klamoth, Madoc, Navajo, Apache, Blackfeet, Chippewa, and Sioux. The creation of Indian police forces was officially authorized in 1878. By 1880 two-thirds of the Indian reservation agencies had Indian police.

The second goal for establishing tribal police was to "civilize" the Indians by undermining the power of tribal chiefs and weakening traditional lines of self-government (Hagan, 1966). As the two cultures clashed, Native Americans were forced to conform to Western, Anglo standards of conduct. Tribal police were often used to curtail recreational activities (such as horse stealing and gambling) that were viewed as criminal by the dominant white culture. They were also responsible for suppressing their own tribal religion by opposing the influence of medicine men, confronting witches, and stopping unwanted activities such as the old "heathen" dances (e.g., the Sundance and the Scalpdance). In addition, tribal police were instructed to force children to attend Indian boarding schools (Washburn, 1971).

These activities were difficult, both morally and physically, for the tribal police. Enforcing white preferences broke long-held traditions and turned family members and friends into enemies. The police actions often directly conflicted with their religious beliefs. The extremely high mortality rate of those children who attended the Indian boarding schools, combined with the numerous violent confrontations associated with forcing the children to attend, made that duty particularly challenging. The schools were notorious for beating the Indian language and culture out of the children (Hagan, 1966). "By 1871 . . . the key to dealing with Indians was to be vigorous repression of things Indian, both law and day-to-day administration of reservations, so as to undercut traditional patterns of leadership, social control, and religion" (Lurie, 1980, p. 23). Many tribal police officers resigned because they could not reconcile the duties with their religious beliefs or the harm to their children.

Self-determination vs. Social Control

One may question why Native Americans chose to become tribal police. Why would they be willing to endure such hardships and danger, only to help in the continuing brutal repression of their own people? Why were the tribal police so loyal to Indian Agents who represented a regime that had enslaved their people and continued to discriminate even against the tribal police officer? Why would these racial minority police officers be active participants in their own exploitation?

Motivations of Individual Tribal Police Officers

Some members of the tribal police likely saw their actions as ultimately benefitting Native American people by helping to remove the military from their reservations, by reducing the magnitude of violence in the social control process, by bringing a certain amount of self-determination to the tribe, or by pushing Native Americans to accept the inevitable process of assimilation. Despite numerous shoot-outs and controversial enforcement policies, the actions of the tribal police did help to prevent massacres. As a result, the use of military force declined (Hagan, 1966). There was also merit in viewing autonomous policing as central to self-government.

The primary motivations, however, were probably self-interest— *personal* empowerment and self-determination. First, those who were recruited to become members of the tribal police were very carefully selected. The Indian agents sought Indians who were highly skilled trackers and warriors, disciplined, and already on the road to assimilation. The agents frequently selected warriors who were not in positions of leadership within the tribe, but who were ambitious. The tribal police were one way that these lower-level warriors could achieve greater power and property. Agents were careful to select representatives from each clan within the tribe. In addition to broadening the overall knowledge among the police of the entire tribe, it made the police appear to be truly representative (Hagan, 1966). In general, the agents selected those tribal members who were considered progressives—those who displayed a willingness to adapt to the ways of the whites. The more traditional or conservative members, those who resisted assimilation, were rejected (Washburn, 1971).

The second important motivation for Native Americans to join the tribal police was to restore their lost sense of manhood (Washburn, 1971). After being defeated and forced to live as farmers or welfare recipients on reservations, Plains Indian warriors lost their traditional path to wealth, glory, and power. More important, without weapons, permission to hunt, the ability to engage enemies, or the ability to steal horses, many warriors felt that their manhood had been taken from them. Being on the police force was attractive to a number of Native American warriors:

> Prestige and power, the right to bear arms among fellow warriors
> deprived of their arms, the privilege of wearing formal uniforms express-
> ing that authority, and the frequent scouting and teaching missions
> against renegades, gave back to the Indian something he thought he had
> lost forever. (Washburn, 1971, p. 171)

In other words, tribal police officers could envision themselves as the last of
the warriors.

The Erosion of Self-Determination

The tribal police and tribal courts are often presented as an example of
self-government on reservations. However, when tribal organizations strayed
too far from white European dogma, they confronted concerted efforts to
assert white supremacy and control. The purpose of the tribal police and
courts was to maintain order on the reservation by weakening both armed
and peaceful organized resistance among the Indians (Washburn, 1971). It
was a method for white Americans to impose their will on the tribes:

> The origin of Indian police and Indian courts derives not, as might be
> thought, from an attempt to allow or give a measure of self-government
> to the Indians. The reverse is true. Indian police and courts were created
> in large measure for the purpose of controlling the Indian and breaking
> up tribal leadership and tribal government. (Washburn, 1971:168)

Although the establishment of tribal police was authorized in 1878, no
specific provisions were made for the trial and punishment of offenders until
1883, with the creation of the formal Courts of Indian Offenses by Secretary
of the Interior, H. M. Teller. He wanted "to eradicate 'certain of the old hea-
thenish dances; such as the Sundance, scalp-dance, & C.' as well as to attack
the institution of polygamy, the power of medicine men, and other Indian
customs" (Washburn, 1971, pp. 169–170). It is significant that these judges
were not elected in a democratic process by the people they were supposed to
serve. The tribal judges were appointed by and served at the pleasure of the
Indian agent. Although they might be Native Americans, the judges were
usually selected because of their efforts to physically, intellectually, and spiri-
tually separate themselves from Native American culture. In other words,
particular Indians were selected as judges and police officers because of their
willingness to adopt white values, customs, and legal procedures.

Ex Parte Crow Dog The lack of real commitment to permitting true
self-government by Native American tribal nations was reflected in the passage of the Major Crimes Act of 1885, a reaction to the U.S. Supreme Court
decision in *Ex Parte Crow Dog* (109 U.S. 556, 1883). On August 5, 1881, on
the Rosebud Reservation in the territory of Dakota, a Brule Sioux chief was
killed by a Sioux Indian named Crow Dog (Snyder-Joy, 1996). Chief Spotted
Tail was popular among the white Indian agents, the white local community
members, and the white military leadership because he was considered "pro-

gressive" and accommodating. He was not nearly as popular among his fellow Sioux, particularly the more traditionalist chiefs. "Spotted Tail had been a pliant and peaceful chief who acted as a buffer between the United States and the more aggressive Sioux leaders, such as Red Cloud, Sitting Bull, and Crazy Horse" (Deloria & Lytle, 1983, p. 168)."

Spotted Tail was well rewarded by the federal government for his pro-U.S. government position and peace counseling. Many of the other chiefs were resentful of the favoritism, special privileges, power to select tribal police officers, and two-story house that the federal government had given Chief Spotted Tail. Captain Crow Dog of the Tribal Police became the leader of the rival faction that wanted to challenge Spotted Tail's authority (Hagan, 1966). When Spotted Tail began to take up with the other chiefs' wives, Crow Dog resigned from the tribal police force and shot and killed Spotted Tail at point-blank range (Deloria & Lytle, 1983).

Like other communal societies, the Sioux believed social equilibrium was the ultimate goal in resolving transgressions. Western jurisprudence, with its emphasis on retribution, was alien to the Sioux. Interactions between whites and Indians in which each party tried to resolve transgressions against the other through their traditional ways were almost always interpreted as shockingly barbaric (Deloria & Lytle, 1983). Historically, whites misinterpreted the role of the Indian chief as similar to that of European rulers, such as kings. For example, Europeans continuously sought out "the" chief of a particular Indian tribe to make agreements and treaties for the entire tribe. Although the members of a tribe may have shared a common language and ancestry, they were often very fragmented and organized under clans and representative chiefs. This situation was especially true among nomadic tribes. Chiefs acted primarily as mediators of conflict, striving to maintain social cohesion and equilibrium. The chief sought to create satisfaction among all parties rather than to establish guilt or innocence. It was not uncommon for chiefs to pay restitution to an injured party from their own property in order to keep peace.

In keeping with this tradition, the families of Crow Dog and Spotted Tail met in order to resolve the murder of Spotted Tail. Spotted Tail's relatives eagerly accepted the proposed compensation offered by Crow Dog's family for the purpose of preventing a continuing feud. When the white public and the federal government officials who had befriended Spotted Tail discovered that Crow Dog was not going to be executed and that he was not even going to appear before the tribal court, protests erupted and the federal government arrested Crow Dog. Crow Dog was tried, convicted, and sentenced to hang in the federal territorial court in Deadwood, Dakota Territory. To the shock of many, the federal marshall agreed to release Crow Dog so that he could settle his affairs at home. Although many people wagered that Crow Dog would never return, he struggled through a snowstorm to arrive at the appointed time to face his sentence. He became a hero in the eyes of the public. Newspapers and attorneys volunteered to take a writ of habeas corpus to the U.S. Supreme Court, and eventually Congress even voted to pay his legal expenses. The Supreme Court ruled that Congress had clearly established tribal jurisdiction over crimes involving an Indian against another Indian while in Indian Country. Crow Dog was granted his writ and released (Deloria & Lytle, 1983).

Although the white public may have been relieved that this "noble and honorable savage" was released, they continued to view the failure of the tribal justice system to execute Crow Dog as a sign that Indian justice was savage and primitive, and in need of greater efforts to Christianize and civilize the justice process. Public pressure on Congress led to the Major Crimes Act of 1885 (Deloria & Lytle, 1983). Without consulting Indian opinion, Congress transferred jurisdiction to the federal government for seven major crimes (murder, manslaughter, rape, assault with the intent to kill, arson, burglary, and larceny) when committed by an Indian in Indian country. The reservations in Oklahoma that held the Five Civilized Tribes (Cherokee, Choctaw, Creek, Chickasaw, and Seminole) were exempt because their tribal justice system had already developed an Anglo-American system of government by the 1860s. The "Seven Major Crimes Act of 1885 . . . illustrated the persistent congressional efforts to eliminate by legislation the legal distinctions between the Indian and the non-Indian population in the United States" (Washburn, 1971, p. 173).

Land Acquisition   The desire to remove Indians from special legal status was further advanced in 1887. Self-proclaimed "friends" of the Indians, such as Massachusetts Senator Henry Dawes, agreed that private property was the key to "civilizing" the Indians and ultimately assimilating them into White America. (Recall the comments by Thomas Jefferson earlier in the chapter.) "Private property [federal officials] believed, had mystical magical qualities about it that led people directly to a 'civilized' state" (Deloria & Lytle, 1983, p. 9). The expressed feeling was that teaching the Indian the value of private property and individualism was an essential step toward assimilation.

A convergence of ideologies occurred as the "enemies" of the Indians also supported this act. White land grabbers sought to acquire cheap land from the Indians by thrusting them into the world of competition and individualism (Washburn, 1971). The idea was that once the land could be placed into the hands of individual Indians, instead of the tribal collective, certain isolated, poverty-stricken Indians could be encouraged to sell their plots for minimal amounts. This result was exactly what occurred on the Menominee Indian Reservation when it was terminated in 1961 (Lurie, 1980). The plan was to achieve final assimilation by eliminating the legal tribal status of the Indians and to disperse the ex-tribal members from rural to urban areas. An essential part of this plan was to destroy communal ownership and to gain control over land and property. Menominee Enterprises, Inc., which was established to administer the previously communal property, "entered into a contract with a land developer to create artificial lakes and sell vacation home sites" to whites. When the Menominees won back their tribal status in 1973 after a long struggle, the plots of land that had been sold were lost. However, the newly established Menominee Tribal Government has aggressively sought to purchase back these lands whenever they become available. The only people who did not benefit from the Dawes Severalty Act of 1887 were the Indians (Washburn, 1971).

The Dawes Act was the result of a massive drive toward "severalty" or "allotment" (Washburn, 1971). This act was an effort to destroy the tribal customs of communal ownership of land. It empowered the president to take segments of reservation land away from the tribes and give it to individual tribe members (Deloria & Lytle, 1983). Those who received allotments would be given preference for tribal police appointments (Hagan, 1966). Twenty-five years after initially receiving an allotment of land, the title to the land was given to the respective Indian, free of restrictions against sale. Once an Indian received title, U.S. citizenship was granted and the Indian was placed under the civil and criminal jurisdiction of the state or territory. However, the Burk Act passed in 1906 accelerated the allotment process, allowing many of the allotments of land to be sold to whites without delay. "Surplus land" that was not allotted to tribal members was sold directly to whites by the federal government. The effects of this program were devastating to tribal sovereignty, unity, and self-reliance. Tribal landholdings dropped from 138 million acres in 1887 to 48 million in 1934. Twenty million of the remaining 48 million acres "were desert or semiarid and virtually useless for any kind of annual farming ventures" (Hagan, 1966, p. 10).

American Indian Policy: 1887–1998

The federal policy toward Indian affairs between 1878 and 1934 centered on the assimilation of individual Indians, the systematic dismantling of traditional tribal cohesion, and the continued intrusion of the federal government. In 1924, all Indians were granted U.S. citizenship, largely in response to positive publicity that Native Americans received as a result of their dedicated service in World War I. Although they were not then eligible for the draft, "they volunteered in large numbers and compiled a remarkable record of heroism" (p. 25). Many Native Americans were not pleased by the granting of citizenship—seeing it as another attempt to weaken their tribal status and treaty rights (Lurie, 1980).

Another result of this positive wartime publicity was the launching of a major federal investigation of Indian problems conducted by John Collier, the Commissioner of Indian Affairs (Lurie, 1980). The 1928 Meriam Report produced by this investigation process stated that the "economic base of traditional Indian culture had been destroyed by the encroachment of white civilization" (Washburn, 1971, p. 76). The "continuing loss of land as a result of allotment was singled out as a primary cause of Indian despair, demoralization, and poverty" (Lurie, 1980).

Even though federal efforts to weaken tribal sovereignty greatly diminished the size and power of tribal police, small pockets of tribal police remained and played an important role in identifying heirs, making up payrolls, acting as handymen, and assisting other law enforcement agencies as informants and trackers (Hagan, 1966). Tribal courts were hit harder than the police. Many were lost between 1887 and 1934. Most of those that remained merely served to record vital statistics and to hold preliminary hearings for off-reservation courts (Hagan, 1966). Despite federal efforts to destroy communal relationships, degrade chiefs, and eliminate the need for separate tribal governments, many tribes managed to maintain traditional forms of government (Washburn, 1971).

The Indian Reorganization Act of 1934 formally ended the government's policy of allotment. It returned to tribal ownership the surplus Indian lands previously open to sale and acquired additional lands for the reservations. Also known as the Wheeler-Howard Act, it enabled tribes to organize for the common welfare and to adopt federally approved constitutions and bylaws (Washburn, 1971). Traditional Native Americans criticized these newly formed tribal governments because the constitutions were based on Anglo-American culture and values.

The federal government officially recognizes more than 320 Native American tribal governments in the continental United States. Each of these tribes has the "legal authority to create its own police force to maintain order within its tribal territory" (Bartollas & Hahn, 1999, p. 326). State governments, for the most part, do not have jurisdiction over matters involving Indian tribes or Indian people in Indian country unless there is a federal statute granting them jurisdiction (French, 1982). The federal government retained jurisdiction over non-Indians who committed crimes against other non-Indians. The U.S. Supreme Court case *Oliphant v. Suquamish* (435 U.S. 1978) ruled that tribal courts did not have criminal jurisdiction to try non-Indians without specific congressional authorization (Wachtel, 1982). As a matter of fact, "no offenses over which Indian tribal courts have jurisdiction carry a penalty of more than six months in jail" (Washburn, 1971, p. 175). Tribal police have limited powers to enforce the law and to maintain order on the reservation.

The legal jurisdiction of tribal police is limited to misdemeanors committed by Native Americans on their reservation, even though officers receive training equal to or greater than that of their white counterparts in similar size departments (Snyder-Joy, 1996). The federal government retains jurisdiction for any major crimes that occur on the reservation. The tribal police do play an important role in resolving criminal cases on reservations. They are usually the ones who discover the crime, conduct the initial interviews, know the personalities and circumstances involved, and provide continued assistance throughout the case. Their recommendations are respected by the federal government (Deloria & Lytle, 1983).

Many Indian reservations have experienced radical economic and political changes since the 1980s primarily due to the large-scale introduction of casino gambling enterprises (Bartollas & Hahn, 1999). This development has produced a massive influx of revenue, as well as the security problems associated with running such a business and serving a large number of outside visitors. Most tribal governments have chosen to greatly enhance the quality, size, and activities of their tribal police forces so that they can handle the necessary security measures without relying on the Bureau of Indian Affairs police officers. Many of the reservations with smaller populations have also chosen to hire a substantial proportion of non-Native American police officers.

The restricted status of tribal police officers, particularly the prohibition against arresting white people, is a serious source of frustration for tribal police officers attempting to enforce the law on Indian reservations, especially with the heavy influx of white people visiting casinos on the reservation. On the Oneida Indian Reservation near Green Bay, Wisconsin, some tribal forces have found methods to reduce the problem. The Oneida Tribal Police convinced the local sheriff's departments to deputize tribal police officers so that they could have full arrest powers (Byrne, 1996). This was no easy achievement. The Oneida had to navigate through complicated politics. A number of lawsuits by local authorities were designed to destroy the use of tribal police on the Oneida Indian Reservation, but the Oneida prevailed. In another example, the members of the Navajo Nation Department of Public Safety and the McKinley County, New Mexico, Sheriff's Department now cross-deputize each other in order to avoid jurisdiction complications ("Navajos," 1998).

Conclusion

The history of tribal police is checkered. Many Native Americans resented the betrayal of their people in helping white Americans impose their system of justice. On the other hand, the tribal police often served as a buffer preventing more brutal repression. Clearly minorities are far more successful in their own communities than outside forces would be. For example, when Brown County (Wisconsin) formed a multi-jurisdictional law enforcement group (MJG Unit) in the 1990s, Tribal Police Chief Danforth made the following statement: "Having a tribal officer on the MJG Unit, I felt, would be beneficial. I knew he'd get in where non-Indian personnel were not able to" (Byrne, 1996, p. 117). If marginalized communities successfully overcome repression, is it a necessary step that members of that community participate in the social control demanded by the majority?

11 African-American Police Officers

The efforts of racially marginalized populations to gain access to the police force are marked by three important elements. First is the long-term struggles for social change and justice within a racially oppressive society. "To the Black community, white policemen represented nothing less than a hostile occupation army" (Hawkins & Thomas, 1991, p. 65), just as the military control of the reservation was greatly resented by Native Americans. Because of concerns about both overpolicing and underpolicing by white social control agents, Native Americans and African Americans have made efforts to remove the occupying armies.

The second element is the desire to gain entry, and eventually full acceptance, into agencies of social control. Many racial and ethnic minorities, including African Americans, have utilized appointments to the position of police officer as an avenue toward assimilation, integration, and economic and social success. It was hoped that joining the profession would reduce their level of exploitation in society.

The third element is the motivations of white authorities for including racial and ethnic minorities in their police forces. A key to understanding these appointments is to view them as a very practical mechanism for improving the effectiveness of the social control agency. The appointments help to secure the legitimacy of the agency of social control both by reducing individual racist interactions between the police and racial/ethnic minorities and by masking or softening the racist effects of an oppressive regime. In some situations, it was necessary to employ minority police to reduce racial tensions and anger in order to maintain social order. In other situations, the right to vote in political elections gave African Americans the power necessary to attract the attention of political officials who wished to remain in office. Minority appointments also strengthen the ability of the policing agency to control or regulate the activities of minority group members, by creating a force that is more attuned to their concerns.

Finally, the motivations for hiring minorities were accompanied by very specific criteria for hiring. Most of the pioneering Black police officers were middle-class, well-educated, and committed to preserving the status quo. That preservation, not a desire for social change, motivated authorities to include minorities in their ranks.

Community Empowerment

The history recounted in this book is evidence of why "African Americans came to believe that only police officers of their own race would provide them the protection of the law, and fair and equitable law enforcement" (Dulaney, 1996, p. 11). During Reconstruction African Americans for the first time gained a certain amount of political power through their newly acquired right to participate in the political process.

The Fulcrum of Political Power

In May 1867, the *New Orleans Tribune*, the first daily African-American newspaper formally established in the United States, expressed concern about the lack of Black police officers. With African Americans obtaining the right to vote under Radical Reconstruction in the southern states, the editors threatened to elect an African-American mayor to appoint African-American police. In response, the Governor of Louisiana began to appoint Blacks to the police force within a few days. In 1870, African Americans occupied 28 percent of the police officer positions in New Orleans. Although no other city appointed as many African-American police officers to their ranks as New Orleans, the pattern was similar in many other southern cities. The presence of African Americans on police forces was deeply resented by many southern whites.

In Raleigh, North Carolina, when the hiring of four African-American police was announced, the *Daily Sentinel* ran the headline, "*The Mongrel Regime!! Negro Police!!*" (Rabinowitz, 1992, p. 595). In Clinton, Mississippi in 1871, a shooting broke out during a confrontation between an African-American police officer and an intoxicated white citizen, resulting in three whites and ten to thirty African Americans being killed (Kuykendall & Burns, 1980). For the next four days, mobs of white men roamed the area, murdering an estimated ten to fifty African-American leaders. As white Democrats lost their absolute control over local politics, white terrorists used violence to attack and intimidate African Americans who attempted to vote or to invoke their rights as citizens. The Reconstruction era was littered with white violence and terrorism often in direct resistance to the exercise of police authority by African Americans (Dulaney, 1996).

During Reconstruction, Republican politicians created a new state police agency which was 40 percent African-American. Although this organization was very active in hunting and arresting fugitives throughout Texas and many individuals and local law enforcement agencies requested their assistance, the agency and its members came under heavy criticism from Democrats and the conservative press. Many whites were furious with this official arming of freed slaves to act as police officers. It was not uncommon for locals to actively resist their enforcement efforts and even to mobilize local law enforcement to arrest state police officers, charging them with illegal searches and arrests. Immediately after the Democrats regained control, they dismantled the state police and reinstituted the Texas Rangers. (Recall the discussion in chapter 2 about Texas Rangers and the capture of runaway slaves.)

"Despite the presence of black police officers, the criminal justice system was still used to regulate blacks' behavior and enforce the racial status quo" (Dulaney, 1996, p. 14). Nonetheless, whites vehemently resisted the presence of African Americans on police forces. Unlike the African-American police of the twentieth century, these Black police officers worked in all areas of the city, patrolled their beats, and performed the same duties as any other police officer. Although they faced tremendous resistance from white southerners, Black officers had full police powers to arrest any citizen who broke the law, and they played a major role in providing some protection for African Americans from white terrorism. In fact, "African-American officers achieved a level of equality and mobility that they would not achieve again anywhere in the nation until the 1960s" (p. 17).

As African Americans escaped from the bonds of slavery or were released from the military following the Civil War, police jobs provided a tremendous—albeit brief—opportunity to achieve a high level of self-determination. These appointments, like other political positions obtained by African Americans during Reconstruction, were only temporary (Rabinowitz, 1992). After Reconstruction, Black police officers were systematically eliminated from almost all the southern police departments. "In department after department, blacks lost their jobs either by dismissal or by being forced to resign" (Williams & Murphy, 1990, p. 9). By 1910, African Americans had disappeared from southern police forces.

As the brief gains were stripped from African Americans in the South, African Americans in the North were beginning to use their right to vote to gain some representation on police departments (Dulaney, 1996). As early as 1861 African Americans were serving as police officers in Washington, D.C. In fact, President U.S. Grant was arrested by a Black police officer for driving a team of horses at a "dangerous pace" (Kuykendall & Burns, 1980). Chicago appointed its first Black police officer in 1872. Both Philadelphia and Cleveland appointed their first African-American police officers in 1881, followed by Columbus, Ohio in 1885 and Detroit in 1890.

African Americans organized their voting power and were able to achieve these appointments through their participation in the political machines that dominated urban politics into the twentieth century. Although these officers were appointed as part of the political patronage system, their numbers never reflected their proportion of the population. At best, they were largely token appointments with limited powers and duties (Dulaney, 1996).

Restricted Success

African Americans who were able to obtain police positions in the nineteenth century due to political patronage were confronted with racism from both inside and outside the department. Initial attempts to appoint African-American police officers almost always met open hostility from white officers and the white public. In a number of northern cities white police officers threatened to strike if Black officers were appointed. In Brooklyn, white officers actually "mutinied" (Dulaney, 1996, p. 21).

A number of strategies were employed to make African-American police officers virtually invisible to the white public. For example, in most cities African-American police were required to patrol in plainclothes so as not to offend white citizens. They were restricted to African-American neighborhoods, and they were forbidden to arrest whites (Dulaney, 1996; Peak, 1997; Williams & Murphy, 1990). If a white person committed a crime in a Black neighborhood, the Black officer usually had to call for a white officer to come to the scene to make the arrest. In Detroit, for example, African-American police officers in the 1940s did not patrol with white police officers, patrolled only Black communities, and were not assigned to the motorcycle squad, the arson squad, or the homicide squad (Hawkins & Thomas, 1991).

Several other precautions were taken to avoid offending white police officers. Between 1890 and 1930 in Chicago, African-American officers worked only with other African-American officers, and they were not allowed to work white neighborhoods. Although strong political patronage resulted in larger numbers of African-American officers than in other cities, there were still quotas so that the positions for which African Americans were hired were designated as Black police officer positions. Therefore, they were not officially competing with white applicants for the same jobs. When a few Black officers finally received promotions, they were restricted to non-command assignments, they were required to abandon their uniforms and work in plainclothes, and they were never allowed to supervise white officers (Dulaney, 1996). "In one instance, black lieutenants were even assigned to walk a beat as patrol officers" (Kuykendall & Burns, 1980, p. 7).

"Reform" Eliminates Limited Gains

Ironically, African Americans were essentially eliminated from almost all police departments in the North as a consequence of police "reform" (Dulaney, 1996). As discussed in earlier chapters, the introduction of civil service and professionalism transformed the police from serving as an instrument of local political machines. The reform movement to modernize, depoliticize, and improve the quality of policing had a devastating impact on the employment of African Americans as police officers. A nationwide movement to dismantle the political machines and to weaken their ability to make appointments for political patronage eliminated the point of entry that had allowed African Americans to make some inroads in gaining representation in police forces. Because they were not yet well established in the profession, as were the Irish, their opportunities vanished with the reforms (Dulaney, 1996). The number of African-American police officers peaked in 1900 at a level of 2.7 percent of the total number of police officers. By 1910, they made up less than 0.1 percent of the police workforce (Williams & Murphy, 1990).

Once the patronage was removed, new qualifications and racially biased civil service testing stopped the flow of Blacks into police work. The "professionalization" of the police force often translated into discriminatory standards. Black applicants often had to obtain outside physicals, eye exams, and other tests, because the departments would reject them for numerous alleged physical deficiencies (Dulaney, 1996). The first African-American New York police officer, after the consolidation of the five boroughs, was Samuel Battle in 1911. He had to get an outside exam after being rejected three times for an alleged heart murmur. After being appointed, white officers did not speak to him for over a year, he could not sleep in the police barracks, and he was subject to abusive language from both white and Black suspects. In 1919, Battle saved a white police officer from a Harlem mob after the officer had shot and killed an African-American citizen. He served for thirty-five years and became the first Black sergeant and the first Black lieutenant of the New York Police Department.

"Despite attempts by reformers to upgrade, professionalize, and reform the police, the color line continued to influence the status of African Americans in northern cities. Black officers were relegated to segregated assignments, quotas, and token roles in urban police departments" (Dulaney, 1996, p. 28). According to a study of the St. Louis Police Department, many African Americans argued that the professionalization process, which led to new standards for the hiring of police officers, systematically excluded many African Americans just as they began to achieve the political muscle to demand appointments (Watts, 1992a). In St. Louis only one of the 68 applicants was hired after the governor promised to hire more African-American police officers in 1920 (Watts, 1992a). A representative of the hiring board explained that "'Most of the colored men whose names have been proposed have jail records, and it is very hard to get a decent colored person on the police force.' He did not mention that 30 percent of the white recruits at that time had prior arrest records" (p. 876).

One exception to this reform effort was in Chicago. Chicago's political machine remained in power well into the twentieth century; therefore, political patronage continued in full force. The national movement toward police professionalization had little impact on the numbers of African-American police in Chicago because politicians needed to secure votes in the African-American community. It was important to those in political office to have at least some African Americans on the police force because "Black citizens often requested that police departments assign only black officers to their communities" (Dulaney, 1996, p. 27).

Overcoming Setbacks

African Americans continued to seek the hiring of more African Americans as police officers. In the 1940s and 1950s, they began to challenge the policies of racial segregation and discrimination that limited both the access of African Americans to the police force and the powers of those who had succeeded. In the Deep South, not a single African American was appointed as a police officer until the 1940s. In a few "border state" cities, where African Americans had the right to vote and were able to exercise some political influence, there were a few Black police officers. However, they were assigned exclusively to Black neighborhoods, they did not wear uniforms, and they could not arrest whites.

In Memphis, Tennessee in 1919, Black politicians attempted to trade Black votes for Black police jobs with the Republican political machines. However, white citizens revolted and the police were removed (Dulaney, 1996). In 1927, the West Tennessee Civic and Political League once again demanded the appointment of Black police officers. The Democratic mayor responded by saying that this demand was "the greatest menace to white supremacy in the city since Reconstruction days" (p. 31).

In contrast, African Americans were eventually successful in Louisville, Kentucky in the 1920s. The struggle began as early as 1885, when a group of African Americans complained to the mayor of the powerful Irish Democratic political machine about police abuse and asked for the appointment of Black police officers. It was not until this machine was broken, with the election of a Republican mayor in 1917, that any real possibility for change existed. In 1923, under intense political and public pressure from African-American citizens, the mayor appointed some plainclothes Black police officers. In 1928 the Black police officers were given uniforms and allowed to patrol the entire city.

The first two Black police officers in St. Louis were hired as part of a political debt that was incurred in wresting control of the state of Missouri from the Republican Party. Despite serious opposition from the members of the police force and other Democratic politicians, Black officers were appointed in 1901. From 1900 to 1920, very few African Americans were on the police force and they were relegated to the inferior status of "Negro Specials," who could only work in Black neighborhoods, in special "colored units," wearing civilian clothes (Watts, 1992a, p. 870). The Republican candidate for governor received support from the powerful African-American Liberty League after he promised to appoint additional "Negro law enforcement officers in uniform" (p. 876). The support helped secure his election, and Black officers in Missouri became uniformed in 1920. However, they were not allowed to arrest whites until the 1930s. "Pressure from black politicians and organizations upon government and police department officials was the fundamental stimulus" (p. 870) to the growth in the number of African-American police officers in the St. Louis Police Department, and in the achievement of full status as a police officer with equal functions, assignments, and duties.

Despite the gains, Black officers remained exclusively in African-American neighborhoods until the 1960s. This segregated assignment was largely based on what the public wanted. While Black citizens requested African-American officers in their communities, "whites simply considered it unacceptable for black officers to exercise authority within white areas, even after the time when it became permissible for black police to arrest whites within black neighborhoods or on the boundaries of black and white areas" (Watts, 1992a, p. 887). The pattern was similar in city after city. African-American citizens struggled to achieve some measure of representation on the force (Dulaney, 1996); repeatedly, those hard-fought efforts met aggressive resistance. The Police Commission in Baltimore, Maryland rejected the demands for Black police officers as a "'humiliation of Anglo Saxon blood' to appoint 'colored policemen' and have them arrest white citizens" (Dulaney, 1996, p. 33).

Atlanta was one of the few cities in the South that did not have any African-American police even during Reconstruction, although many African Americans struggled for representation during and after that time period. After the riot in 1906 when white police officers participated in the murder and arson of Black citizens, a renewed effort was made to appoint some Black officers to obtain "more equitable law enforcement" (Dulaney, 1996, p. 39). In 1946, three hundred African-American veterans of World War II protested in front of city hall, demanding the right to be appointed police officers. Their spokesperson argued that "black men had served their country against Nazi Germany, but now, back home in peacetime, they could not qualify to serve the city of Atlanta as police officers" (p. 41). The real turning point did not take place until 1947 when African Americans won a lawsuit against the state of Georgia, eliminating white-only Democratic primaries (Dulaney, 1996). Armed with access to the political process, African Americans were able to lobby successfully for Black police officers. The Negro Police Committee organized a media blitz and secured numerous endorsements. They gained a hearing that nearly deteriorated into a race riot when whites attempted to block the demonstration. Atlanta Police Chief Herbert Jenkins mediated the conflict by agreeing to hire African-American police officers under very specific and limited conditions. They would not be allowed to exercise any police powers over white people, they would have their own precinct station, and they would not be given civil service status until they had proven to be a success (Dulaney, 1996).

In the 1940s, when some restrictions had been lifted from African-American police officers in the North, the newly appointed African-American police officers in the South had to accept very limited police powers to be appointed at all (Dulaney, 1996). Like the northern African-American police officers of the nineteenth century, they worked exclusively in Black neighborhoods, could not arrest whites, and frequently were not allowed to wear uniforms. Throughout the 1950s, African Americans in most southern cities continued to work specific Black beats, from separate "Negro substations," and/or during the "black watch," usually in the evening (Dulaney, 1996, p. 56). They were also not allowed the same privileges and status as white police officers. They were "second-class or even quasi-law enforcement officers" (p. 52). In 1948, when the first African-American police officer was promoted to sergeant in St. Louis and allowed to command a platoon, it was an all-Black unit called the "Soul Patrol" (p. 50). In most southern cities, however, Blacks were simply ineligible to be promoted above the patrol officer rank (Dulaney, 1996).

The city of Miami has a long history of racial segregation, oppression, and violence. Police had long underpoliced Colored Town (the area of Miami eventually renamed Overtown). They overlooked the white terrorism designed to insure that the residents of Colored Town did not encroach on white neighborhoods or threaten the city's white population. At the same time, police overpoliced the area, frequently using brutality and unnecessary violence to control and punish the Black residents of Colored Town.

As early as 1903, African Americans in the area called for better law enforcement in their community, and specifically for the appointment of Black police officers, whom they anticipated would provide them with better protection from crime and violence while not subjecting them to racist brutality (Dulaney, 1996). Under such conditions, open hostility between Black citizens and the white police officers intensified, and white and Black civic organizations began to demand more effective law enforcement in Colored Town. These demands were ignored until African-American citizens in Miami gained some degree of influence in city politics. In 1944 the local chapter of the Progressive Voters League forced white politicians to respond by appointing the first African American to the police force. Concerns persisted, not only about the activities of white police officers, but white judges as well. A Miami minister stated that "white judges usually treated black-on-black crime as a joke" (p. 57).

In 1950, the city of Miami constructed a "Black" police station to house all its African-American police officers who were assigned to police Colored Town. It also appointed an African-American judge and bailiff responsible for administering a "Black only" court (Dulaney, 1996). Many members of Miami's African-American community viewed the creation of a separate "Negro police station and court" to administer criminal justice in Colored Town as a unique opportunity to exercise at least some level of self-government.

Given the history of white policing and racial terrorism, this particular form of racial segregation was seen as a blessing to many members of the Black community, even if the level of self-government was very limited (Dulaney, 1996). The formation of an entirely separate police force greatly increased the opportunities for a number of African Americans to be appointed as police officers. Even the potential to move beyond the position of uniformed patrol officer increased because they were taken out of direct competition with whites for such positions. "No other city in the South could match the 'opportunities' that the separate police station provided blacks for participation in law enforcement" (p. 59). Even so, the African-American officers were not allowed to join the white Miami chapter of the Police Benevolent Association, so they formed their own Miami Colored Police Benevolent Association, which sued the Miami Police Department in order to force them to allow Black officers to take the sergeant's exam.

Individual African-American police officers faced a number of other forms of discrimination. Although the formation of the Black police station meant that African-American officers could patrol all day instead of just the "Black watch" from 6:00 P.M. to 2:00 A.M., they were still only allowed to police in the Black community. Black officers were not allowed to wear their uniforms to and from work, and their titles and uniforms differed from those of white officers. In addition, these "patrolmen," rather than "policemen," were not given the power to arrest white people (Dulaney, 1996). The separate and unequal status of African-American officers was further illustrated by the fact that they rarely received any training, and they had different hiring standards than white officers.

Although all these conditions initially had been welcomed in contrast to the terrible conditions in the past, by the end of the 1950s they were no longer acceptable. African-American police officers and citizens began to pressure the Miami Police Department to end the official policy of racial segregation and discrimination. Many felt that this second-class citizenship was perpetuating a sense of disrespect for the Black police officer in the Black community. In 1960, the first Black recruit gained entry into the Miami Police Academy, the separate titles were dropped, and African-American police officers were granted the right to arrest whites "with the assistance of white officers" (Dulaney, 1996, p. 61). In 1963, the Black police station and court system were abolished.

As late as 1961, a study by the President's Commission on Law Enforcement and Administration of Justice found that "31 percent of the departments surveyed restricted the right of blacks to make felony arrests; the power of black officers to make misdemeanor arrests was even more limited" (Williams & Murphy, 1990, p. 8). Sullivan (1989, p. 331) described the recollection of a former executive director of the National Organization of Black Law Enforcement Executives, who grew up in a small Louisiana town where Black police officers rode in cars marked "Colored Police" and were allowed only to arrest "colored people." A 1968 *Ebony* magazine study found that twenty-eight departments restricted the arrest powers of Black officers. In addition, they were often denied desired assignments, especially high-profile duties such as honor guards (Sullivan, 1989).

African-American citizens had to "agitate, petition, and argue for nearly half a century to regain representation in law enforcement . . . they believed that *only* police officers of their race would police their communities fairly and diligently" (Dulaney, 1996, p. 45). Success in gaining a few police appointments for Blacks was just the beginning. The next task was to shake the very foundation of American apartheid—the separate but equal doctrine. This legal precedent had to be struck down to put an end to racial segregation and discrimination against Black police officers within the police department.

Individual Empowerment

The most basic reason why African Americans joined police agencies is the same as for any other minority group. As Charleston (South Carolina) Police Chief Reuben Greenberg explains, "Entry into law enforcement has long been a means by which impoverished immigrant groups have attained economic and political power" (Dulaney, 1996, p. ix).

"When a member of either the lower-class ghetto or the economically emerging lower-middle-class ghetto decides on a police career, in most cases it will not be out of a love of service to the people but rather a means to advance economically" (Palmer, 1973, p. 20). In one study, the majority of African-American NYPD officers chose policing as an occupation because of its potential for social mobility (Alex, 1969). A study of African-American recruits with the NYPD in the 1980s indicated that "the choice of police work for socially mobile minorities may parallel the selection of work by ethnic immigrants decades earlier—notably civil service employment—as a lever of social and economic advancement" (Maghan, 1992, p. 11). Police work offered economic rewards, opportunity, and security. In addition, the bureaucratic nature of the job meant that hirings and promotions, as well as pay and benefits, were supposed to be based on civil service regulations requiring nondiscriminatory job practices. In other words, African Americans felt that they would face less racial discrimination in these governmental positions than they would in the private sector.

No group was more successful at improving their economic and political status through employment on police forces than the Irish. Impoverished Irish immigrants were used extensively to police Irish neighborhoods in New York City (Miller, 1977). The Irish eventually dominated many large urban police departments and used these positions as an opportunity to establish themselves financially and politically in the United States.

Although the Irish experienced ethnic discrimination and poverty in the United States, there were key differences between the experiences of the Irish and those of African Americans. First, the Irish gained access to the political process relatively quickly, which allowed them to organize and eventually to control local urban politics in many cities. Second, if being Irish was perceived as disadvantageous, second-generation Irish changed their names, suppressed their accents, and essentially passed as non-Irish, Protestant Europeans. Third, when the Irish first joined police agencies they were frequently sent to Irish neighborhoods, but they had full arrest powers, full status as police officers, and they were rather quickly allowed to police any area of the city. None of these things were true for the African-American pioneers in policing (Dulaney, 1996).

The very first African Americans to act as police officers in the United States did so in the city of New Orleans, shortly after the United States acquired the city. From 1805 to 1820 "free men of color" served on all four of the city's early police organizations. The irony of this achievement was that these police officers were charged with maintaining a racist, slave society. As discussed in chapter 2, one of the primary duties of preindustrial police in the South was to catch runaway slaves and to enforce the Slave Codes. "By accepting the racial status quo and the legal oppression of other blacks, these law enforcement officers became the first African Americans to confront the paradox of policing a society where the color of a person's skin often determined guilt or innocence" (Dulaney, 1996, p. 7).

Why did they agree to serve in this manner? "They were motivated by a combination of self-interest and a sense of service" (Dulaney, 1996, p. 10). In other words, much like the Irish immigrants, they sought to improve their condition in life. "If the duties of citizenship required patrolling, policing, and suppressing 'black' slaves, the 'free persons of color' in New Orleans were willing to assume such tasks in order to improve their own precarious position in a society where skin color usually determined status and condition of servitude" (p. 9). Similar to poor whites who served as slave patrollers throughout the South, free African Americans hoped to carve a position for themselves distinctly elevated from slavery. The unique history of New Orleans (see chapter 6) provided them with some hope that this goal could be achieved. From the early eighteenth century, while under control of the French and the Spanish, Africans and their descendants played a critical role in the colony, and not just as slaves (Dulaney, 1996). Free Blacks often "served as a buffer between whites and the slave population" and many even owned slaves themselves (p. 9). They served in the militia during battles with both English and Native Americans and, as a result, many African slaves earned their freedom. While under Spanish rule, free Blacks fought to suppress slave insurrections during the Cimarron War of 1784. Because of a shortage of women in the colony, a substantial amount of intermarriage took place, and the colony was uniquely interracial. By the time Louisiana was purchased from France by the United States in 1803, "these 'free persons of color' had developed a fairly stable social and economic position in New Orleans and had formed two militia groups" (p. 8).

These free Blacks had reasonably hoped to serve in the same role under United States rule. As slavery became more entrenched and resistance to slavery intensified, white fears about armed Blacks soon erased any possibility of continued militia activities (Dulaney, 1996). "In 1822, the New Orleans council directed the city labor manager to employ only white workers in city jobs" (p. 10). The Black militia units were disbanded, and by 1830 there were no Black officers on the New Orleans police force. As discussed in the previous section, the entry of minority officers into police forces was a series of minor successes followed by major setbacks. Personal empowerment suffered the same sequence of gains followed by losses as community empowerment.

The Common Thread

Minority police have always confronted the problem of working in a social system grounded in racial segregation. Claude Dixon, one of the first

Black officers appointed in Atlanta in 1948, stated that "When we took the oath, all eight of us had to stand up there and say, 'I do solemnly swear as a nigger policeman that I will uphold the segregation laws of the city of Atlanta" (Dulaney, 1996, p. 52). Whether or not this statement was the literal oath of Dixon and his colleagues, the message was clear: Black police officers were to enforce the laws of racial segregation, despite the dire consequences to their people, their families, and themselves. As a result, many African-American citizens came to view the Black police officer as just another part of the system designed to harass and abuse them.

The balancing act by African-American police officers in trying to provide quality law enforcement to the Black community while enforcing racially biased laws produced a number of conflicts. While African-American leaders were demanding the use of African-American police officers in the Black community, a number of Black citizens felt that African-American police were traitors to their race (Dulaney, 1996). For example, one African American in Houston stated that "A Negro [police officer] is nothing but a snitch" (Dulaney, 1996, p. 62).

> It is a paradox . . . for the Negro that in becoming a policeman he has improved his *economic* status, yet he may justly feel that he has lost esteem. He now becomes simply by way of mobility, an open and vulnerable target of hostility, abuse, and derision, accessible to all the contradictory expectations regarding his occupation. (Alex, 1969, p. 21)

Following the 1935 riots in New York, it was noted that "many in the Harlem community feel as much resentment toward Negro police as toward white police, and even toward the Negro police lieutenant, who sometime back was a popular hero and a proud community symbol" (Kuykendall & Burns, 1980, p. 9). Cashmore (1991) noted that during the riots of the 1960s, African-American police and "moderate" African-American leaders were objects of the Black rioters' anger, along with white police, politicians, and merchants. "The entire institution of law enforcement was under attack: not the personnel who staffed it" (p. 90). In other words, they were not just angry with the activities of white racist police officers; they were angry with the institution of policing that served to maintain their status as second-class citizens. An organizational position statement by the Afro-American Patrolmen's League of Chicago (AAPL) recognized this concern in 1967 when it stated, "We will no longer permit ourselves to be relegated to the role of the brutal pawns in a chess game affecting the communities we serve" (Dulaney, 1996, p. 74).

Other African-American police officers did not agree that there was a conflict. The objective of these African-American police officers was to provide police protection to their community. They dismissed accusations of being used by whites to oppress their own people as either fraudulent or misguided. African-American NYPD police officers in the 1960s explained that middle-class African Americans were very supportive of them and viewed them as "a symbol of accomplishment" (Alex, 1969, p. 17). The quotes from Black officers in the 1970s to a news reporter in the following excerpt reflected the perspective of many African-American police officers who rejected the claims that they were race traitors:

> "I don't buy this junk about black policemen being used to spy on the community. Some of these fellows calling everybody brother will rip you off as soon as you turn your back" scoffed one of them. Another, who had been wounded and crippled, affirmed, "I believe in protecting my community from those who represent a threat to it. . . . Everybody knows the crime rate is highest in our neighborhoods. The victims most often are the people who live there." (Watts, 1992a, p. 885)

The Role of Minority Police Organizations

While participating in cultural diversity training, many white police officers asked me why African-American, Latino, and even women police officers have their own separate organizations. They usually asserted that such organizations divide police officers by emphasizing their differences and by seeking preferential treatment. History once again provides the answers. First, white police officers and their police unions initially refused to allow African Americans to join as regular members. "In nearly all cities, the racial proscriptions that limited job opportunities of African-Americans also limited their participation in rank-and-file fraternal and benevolent associations" (Dulaney, 1996, p. 66). Second, African-American police officers found themselves in an isolated environment. They were rejected by their racist white colleagues, and they were often criticized by African Americans for assisting in racial oppression (Cashmore, 1991). If the profession of policing was to provide personal empowerment, minority officers needed to organize with others who shared their unique experiences. Third, white police officers and their organizations were not interested in promoting the same causes and issues as these other officers, such as eliminating discrimination in hiring, promotion and policing, recruiting police officers of color, and building relationships with the community. "To defend and advance their interests as police officers, specifically black officers, they developed organizations to advance their unique interests" (Cashmore, 1991, pp. 95–96). Fourth, white police officers and their organizations not only did not take on these causes, they frequently actively worked to obstruct them.

The white leaders of police reform in the United States "did not address the continuing color line in the profession" (Dulaney, 1996). Thus, African-American police officers organized themselves into a number of associations across the country to struggle for equal rights. These organizations first emerged in the South where racial discrimination was the most pronounced. The first formal African-American police association, the Texas Negro Peace Officers' Association, was initially formed in 1935 in Houston as a social organization for those who shared a common bond. Soon this organization became heavily involved in the struggle to increase the number of African-American police officers in the state of Texas and to improve their status as officers throughout the South.

The second association, the Miami Colored Police Benevolent Association (MCPBA), organized in 1944 after Black officers were rejected from the department's Police Benevolent Association. "The hostile, segregated environment, both public and professional, in which the lower South's two largest African-American police forces worked had forced them to organize." The MCPBA worked to improve the working conditions of Black officers, help train Black officers, and improve police-community relations. In order to obtain the right to be promoted, the MCPBA filed one of the earliest racial discrimination civil rights suits against a police department in 1955. Although conditions in the South were more racist and restrictive than those in the North, African-American associations were formed in the North for very similar reasons.

While African-American police associations in the South were busy struggling simply to obtain full police powers, African-American associations in the North were able to focus more on recruitment, promotions, community relations, and general civil rights issues (Dulaney, 1996). From 1943 to 1949 despite serious opposition (including concerns of African-American leaders who feared legitimizing any type of segregation), African-American police officers in New York worked to form the Guardian Association. The primary mission of the Guardian Association was to "obtain equal treatment for African Americans" both in the department and in the community at large (p. 69). One of their early efforts was to borrow a "hooking" strategy used by Irish and Jewish police officers to reach back and help lower-ranking officers of their group to obtain supervisory positions. They started a mentoring program in the African-American community called the "Dutch Uncle" program that was designed to encourage young people to enter the field of law enforcement.

> Community involvement became the forte of the Guardians . . . they supported community protests against unfair law enforcement, acted as clearing house for complaints against the police, and played a major role in trying to resolve the issues that led to the 1964 race riot in Harlem. Members also served as marshals and security for the 1964 March on Washington. (p. 70)

The Guardian Association established a pattern of emphasizing community issues over concerns within the department which would come to characterize African-American police organizations (Dulaney, 1996). Many of the African-American police organizations that formed in the 1950s and 1960s

> proposed a new standard of professionalism for all police officers . . .
> They felt that a police officer's duty was to serve the community; he or she was first and foremost a public servant accountable to the people of the community . . . The ultimate goal was to have a community-based

police force that existed to serve the people, not simply to deter crime; it should be a public-service agency thoroughly involved in all aspects of the community.

The civil rights movement stimulated a more militant approach among African-American police associations in attacking racist discrimination in the department and in the community. For example, the "Shield Club" in Cleveland was formed in 1946 directly in response to the department's treatment of an African-American officer. When members of the Congress of Racial Equality (CORE) attempted to integrate a dance hall, the private guards hired by the dance hall harassed the CORE members. Officer Coleman attempted to prevent the harassment; the guards shot him and severely beat his partner. The Cleveland Police Department refused to prosecute the white guards who assaulted the officers, and they suspended Officer Coleman for three months without pay. African-American officers formed the Shield Club to support Coleman, and were systematically harassed by their supervisors. They later expanded their activities to include active community service, such as sponsoring underprivileged youth to attend ball games and food drives for needy families.

The Guardians Civil League in Philadelphia (GCL-1956) worked to resolve complaints that the Philadelphia Police Department discriminated against African-American police officers in terms of assignments, promotions, and discipline. The GCL also took a strong public stance against police abuse of African-American citizens. The Afro-American Patrolmen's League in Chicago (AAPL-1967) was even more aggressive in their vision of merging both individual and community empowerment, as they identified their roots as being deeply planted in the Black community. They clearly saw themselves as a critical link in the long struggle against racial oppression. The AAPL openly criticized racism within the Chicago Police Department, other police agencies, and U.S. society in general. In discussing the power of the police department, co-founder of the AAPL, Edward Palmer (1973), argued that "No longer must the power rest in the hands of a few but rather in the hands of the community" (p. 24).

The Officers for Justice Peace Officers in San Francisco (OFJ-1968) was initially formed by one white officer and one Black officer to protest the San Francisco Police Department's policies of setting quotas that established a limited number of Black officers and Black promotions. The OFJ also challenged a number of racist police practices in the community. With the support of these organizations,

A new breed of African-American police officer emerged: one who spoke out against racism in the police department (thus breaking the traditional code of silence among police on such issues) and who adopted the methods, strategies, and tactics of the activists and so-called "black militants" in the African-American community. (Dulaney, 1996, p. 74)

The national civil rights movement had a major impact on the formation of African-American police associations and their involvement in communities. Frequently African-American police officers and their associations had to choose sides in the conflict between African-American demonstrators seeking social change and the police who were responsible for preventing social change. For example, during the riots of the 1960s, police were responsible for riot control, which often "placed black police in the position of restraining and arresting other African Americans who were demonstrating for rights that would benefit the officers themselves" (Dulaney, 1996, p. 73). While other rank-and-file organizations focused their efforts on better working conditions, shorter hours, and better pay, African-American police organizations were forced to confront much broader social issues.

In 1972, the first of five goals listed by the First National Conference of Black Policemen was "to improve the relationship between the black community and the police department" (Dulaney, 1996, p. 79). The organization that emerged from this conference, The National Black Police Association (NBPA), concentrated much of their work on civil rights and other political issues. They also supported new policing strategies, such as team policing, which were precursors to community policing.

The struggle for individual empowerment by African-American police officers continued into the 1980s and 1990s. Racial conflict was evident within departments and between departments and communities of color. For example, in 1983 after a number of questionable arrests and allegations of police beatings of arrestees, racial tension between African Americans and the New York Police Department (NYPD) led the chair of the House Judiciary Committee to ask John Conyers, the chair of the Criminal Justice Subcommittee, to investigate the situation (Katz, 1995). Conyers found rampant *internal* racial conflict in the department. In the words of one African-American police officer, "We can't help the black community . . . because we are still hard-pressed to help ourselves" (p. 585). One of the most disturbing aspects of the investigation was the number of African-American plainclothes officers who had been killed in the line of duty by fellow white police officers who mistook them for lawbreakers.

The threat of violence to African-American undercover police officers from their white counterparts is not isolated to the NYPD. For example, in 1989, Derrick Norfleet, an African-American officer working undercover to purchase crack from a local dealer in Oakland, was intentionally struck by a patrol car driven by a fellow officer (Stewart, 1992). Three white police officers immediately attacked him, beating him with their fists and a flashlight (Stewart, 1992). Although Officer Norfleet was threatened and harassed by his fellow police officers and supervisors for doing so, he sued the Oakland Police Department. He won a $60,000 judgement. The jury ruled that although the beating was acceptable, the one officer went too far in striking Officer Norfleet with his patrol car. Officer Norfleet put the case in larger perspective when he stated, "Even in my case, those guys lied and they brought in outside people to lie . . . I know for a fact that if I hadn't also been a police officer, I wouldn't have had a chance in that courtroom" (Stewart, 1992, p. 59).

In Nashville, Tennessee in 1992, Reginald D. Miller, an African-American police officer, was stopped by a white officer for having an expired license plate on his undercover pickup truck. Officer Miller stated that, upon stopping the truck, he reached down to put the parking brake on and then put both hands on the steering wheel to avoid "spooking" the officers ("Beating," 1992). The arresting officer pulled Miller from the truck and shoved him face down on the ground. The white officer later stated that he saw Miller reaching down for something. Four other officers arrived on the scene as backup, all of them white. One of those officers testified that he "put his knee in Miller's back and grasped his forehead and eye socket to pull his head up and back" (p. 6). Another officer testified that he "kicked Miller in the groin area more than once in what he said was an effort to get the struggling suspect to spread his legs" (p. 6). Fortunately, supervisors in charge of the undercover operation intervened and stopped the white officers from continuing to beat Officer Miller. The Nashville Police Chief stated that, while this incident was "regrettable," it was not as serious as the beating of Rodney King, because it was not a "sustained beating" (p. 6).

In New York one month earlier, a Black undercover New York Transit Police officer, Derwin Pannell, was shot by two white police officers while he was attempting to arrest a suspect. The officers investigating the incident stated that Officer Pannell had apprehended a suspect and was searching the suspect's pocketbook when three other officers arrived on the scene. The two white male officers immediately began shooting at Officer Pannell, firing twenty-one bullets. Officer Pannell was hit twice in his bullet-proof vest and once in his neck. The female officer did not fire her weapon. Transit Police spokesperson, Al O'Leary, stated that "Some minority officers are so convincing in their plainclothes assignments that they could conceivably be mistaken for criminal suspects" ("Friendly," 1992, p. 7). The police chief responded by expanding the training for the undercover police officers to better understand the dangers of undercover work, particularly for racial minorities. The Police Guardian Association organization stated that "the incident illustrates the danger facing Black officers, particularly those in plainclothes" and urged Black police officers to refuse plainclothes assignments.

Such incidents have a devastating effect on the camaraderie between officers, but what is probably most disturbing to African-American citizens is that these events are just the tip of the iceberg. African-American police officers from the Los Angeles Police Department who testified before the Christopher Commission (1991) reported numerous incidents of being stopped while off-duty by white officers "in circumstances not resulting in an arrest or otherwise involving any apparent infraction or illegal activity by the African-American officers" (p. 77). After the Black officers identified themselves as police officers, the white officers frequently responded that the identification could have been stolen and must be checked. An African-American police officer told a *Milwaukee Journal* news reporter about his fellow white officers, "If it wasn't for my badge and gun I'd just be another nigger in the street to them" ("To Keep," 1992).

Racism and racial conflict within police departments remains a serious problem. The vast majority of police agencies continue to underrepresent African Americans in relation to their proportion in the population. This underrepresentation becomes even more dramatic in the higher ranks. Although progress in the employment of African-American and Latino police has been slow and steady, employment discrimination continues to exist, particularly in terms of promotions (Walker et al., 2000). The struggle has largely shifted from gaining access and full police powers to achieving equal opportunities for individual career advancement and exerting influence over police practices. Nothing has had a greater impact on the hiring, promoting, and career advancement of African-American police officers than the election of African-American mayors and the appointment of African-American police chiefs (Dulaney, 1996).

The 1974 election in Detroit of Mayor Coleman Young was a prime example of how African-American political power can transform a police department (Hawkins & Thomas, 1991). A major part of Young's campaign was to reform the Detroit Police Department and to stop the police decoy and surveillance campaign called STRESS, which in thirty months was responsible for hundreds of warrantless police raids and twenty-two civilian deaths, most of them African-Americans. Mayor Young acted quickly to reform the police by disbanding STRESS, appointing a new board of police commissioners, selecting an African-American police chief, and instituting parallel promotions for white and Black officers. In addition, he aggressively recruited African-American police officers through a number of strategies. Through actively searching for potential candidates, advertising in the inner city, implementing an Affirmative Action program, and changing entrance and promotional exams to be less culturally biased, the representation of African Americans on the Detroit Police Department went from 19 percent in 1974 to 47 percent in 1987.

Many of the pioneering African-American police chiefs took on the very controversial task of transforming their white-dominated police departments into multicultural departments reflective of the communities they were policing (Dulaney, 1996). When Hubert Williams was appointed police chief of Newark, New Jersey in 1974 (recall the discussion of the riot in that city in chapter 2), he "enacted innovations and personnel policies to make the department more responsive to and representative of Newark's citizens" (p. 87). Williams established police storefront offices and encouraged police officers to act as community service workers. He also implemented a number of serious crime-fighting programs including police sweeps, roadblocks, and a truancy task force. All of these strategies have become essential components of problem solving and community policing. In addition, Chief Williams "admitted that he used 'color-conscious' policies in promoting and assigning officers" (p. 87). Chief Williams "believed that in a city where the composition of most neighborhoods was more than 50 percent African-American, it was good policy and good management to assign detectives and administrators who reflected the composition of those neighborhoods" (p. 87).

One of the primary objectives of Reginald Eaves, the first African-American police chief in a major southern city, "was to change the composition of the Atlanta police force in order to make it more representative of the city's population" (Dulaney, 1996, p. 90). In four years, the percentage of African Americans on the Atlanta Police Department increased from 23 percent to 35 percent, or proportionate to the city's African-American population (Dulaney, 1996). Although the Atlanta Police Department remained predominately white at every level, Chief Eaves appointed nine police captains and twenty-eight sergeants. Seven of the captains and twenty-one of the sergeants were African Americans.

The National Organization of Black Law Enforcement Executives (NOBLE) was formed in 1976. Black leaders hoped to become a more powerful political force and believed that Black law enforcement executives could have a more effective impact on the criminal justice system through a unified voice. Chief Hubert Williams was unanimously elected as the first president. NOBLE has devoted many of its efforts to a range of issues that directly impact the African-American community, including racism, police use of deadly force, the proliferation of guns, juvenile delinquency, and community policing. African-American police chiefs initiated a number of policing strategies that have become the international standard for community policing.

An important by-product of these efforts was the exponential increase in opportunities for African-American police officers. Nothing secured their individual empowerment of job security and career development more than African-American citizens electing African-American mayors who in turn appointed African-American police chiefs. Chief Reuben Greenberg summarized the relationship as follows:

> The extent of black participation in American policing historically has been closely associated with the presence or absence of African-American political power . . . African Americans are represented in law enforcement agencies because of black influence or control of executive and legislative positions in political entities. (Dulaney, 1996, p. xi)

As a result of these factors, the appointment of an African-American police chief is no longer a rare event (Bartollas & Hahn, 1999). During the 1980s the number of U.S. cities with an African-American police chief increased from around 50 to 130 (Bartollas & Hahn, 1999).

Social Control

Our final section on African-American police explores the motivations of those in power to hire African Americans as police officers. We have traced the repeated efforts of African-American citizens to obtain representation in police departments. We have also reviewed evidence of the opposition of white Americans to the hiring of African Americans as agents of social control. This opposition was adamant, consistent, and often violent. Thus, it was uncommon throughout American history for African Americans to be hired as social control agents. Given extensive efforts to restrict African Americans from these positions, because of the perceived threat to white supremacy and the racist status quo, why did some white police administrators eventually seek to hire African-American police? Why did some whites argue for the recruitment of African-American officers?

Numerous factors have influenced the decision making of white officials regarding the use of African Americans as agents of social control: the level of racism in society, the intensity of African-American resistance to white supremacy, the degree of African-American access to the political process, the effectiveness of white police officers in maintaining social order, and the problem of international embarrassment. It should be noted, however, that white Americans do not speak with one voice on these issues. The hiring of African-American police officers was influenced by local, national, and international factors on political, social, and moral levels.

Throughout the brutal and inhumane history of racism in the United States there have been whites who stood up, protested, struggled, and even took up arms in an attempt to prevent it (Loewen, 1995). Notable white opponents of racism in U.S. history, such as John Adams, Henry David Thoreau, John Brown, Harriet Beecher Stowe, and Abraham Lincoln, defied the racism of their day. Former Confederate General James Longstreet became a Republican following the Civil War because he became "convinced that equality for blacks was morally right" (p. 188). Robert Flournoy was a Mississippi planter who had organized a company of Confederate soldiers until he resigned because of a conflict in his conscience. During the war, he encouraged Black slaves to flee to Union lines, and during Reconstruction he published a newspaper called *Equal Rights*, which argued for the desegregation of the state's public school system.

The motives of some white police leaders to recruit and promote African-American police officers were genuine efforts to achieve social and racial justice. Given the overwhelming evidence that a number of whites throughout most of U.S. history had used any means available to prevent African Americans from achieving equality with whites, it is also probable that the hiring of Blacks as police officers was sometimes an issue of social control. Lessons from the history of Native American tribal police give rise to the expectation that social control was the driving force behind most such appointments. It was a long-standing practice of police administrators to assign members of immigrant groups to their own communities where they could be particularly effective (Watts, 1992a). "Historically immigrants (Irish, Italian, and German) were hired by police departments because they could communicate and operate more effectively than could nonindigenous officers in neighborhoods with immigrants" (Shusta et al., 1995, p. 42). These officers could speak the language of and easily establish a good rapport with members of their communities. They could work in plainclothes and discover criminal acts (Watts, 1992a). Frequently, police departments required residency in the political ward for five years before being hired and continued residency after the hiring (Miller, 1977). We will trace the development of reasons for hiring Black officers so that we have a better understanding of the role of police in society today.

In the preindustrial era, the idea of arming Blacks and giving them the authority to enforce the very racist laws and customs by which they were restricted seemed too much of a contradiction to most whites. In addition, the constant fear of rebellion was intensified by the possibility that Black police or militia would turn their arms against white oppressors. The people of New Orleans, however, initially took a more practical approach. White officials appointed Blacks to the police force and armed them to serve in the militia because they could not find a sufficient number of whites to fill those positions (Dulaney, 1996). If Blacks did not do the job, it would not be done. Second, the Black police officer was doing the dirty and dangerous job of controlling slaves and enforcing racist laws, which freed whites from doing such distasteful work, while providing some protection from direct violent confrontation. Third, the Black police and militia were effective at regulating the activities of Black people, putting down slave rebellions, and protecting New Orleans from foreign invaders (Dulaney, 1996). Eventually national confrontation over the issue of racial slavery overcame this practical use of available labor, and Blacks were removed from this service until Reconstruction and the era of industrial police.

After the Civil War and during Reconstruction, Republicans had a strong self-interest in securing the freed Black man's right to vote. African Americans had every reason to vote Republican—the party of Abraham Lincoln that had opposed slavery and supported the education, political participation, and full citizenship of African Americans, while opposing the Black codes, white terrorism, and white Democrats.

The Republicans were seen as northern invaders by the vast majority of southern whites who consistently voted Democrat. To remain in office, Republican political officials needed the Black vote, and African-American leaders demanded that some Blacks be appointed as police officers in order to provide fair and just policing, as well as to protect them from white terrorists.

> With only a few exceptions, the black police officers who were hired during Reconstruction arrested whites, worked in all areas of the cities where they served, and were instrumental in pacifying some of the postwar violence against black Americans—even though their presence as police officers often provoked that violence. (Dulaney, 1996, p. 17)

In general, white police officers could not be depended upon to enforce the law against whites terrorizing Blacks, nor could they be counted on to physically protect Blacks from assaults. Therefore, the Republicans used African-American soldiers and police officers to protect African Americans from white violence and terrorism while they attempted to exercise their right to vote.

Although politics played an important role in the hiring of African-American police officers under Reconstruction, the use of minorities policing minorities as a more effective system of social control was also on the minds of many Republicans. For example, in 1868 when Raleigh, North Carolina hired its first African-American police officers, the following excerpt was printed in the Republican *Daily Standard*:

> If it is true . . . as obliged in certain quarters that a large portion of the thefts and burglaries are committed by the colored, the colored police-men will have means of information and consequently of bringing the perpetrator to justice, which never would have been extended to the former police. All classes will learn that the laws must be respected and the colored people will not feel that it is an oppression on them or their race when tried and punished by a Republican mayor. (Rabinowitz, 1992, p. 595)

Thus, the social control aspect of minority police was both physical and men-tal. African-American police officers would be more effective at finding crim-inals and their presence would give the police and the law greater legitimacy in the minds of African-American citizens.

A key factor for many of the police chiefs who initiated the hiring of Afri-can-American police officers in the South was the history of success in other cities. The endorsement of Atlanta police chief Herbert Jenkins was instru-mental in preventing a riot at the city council meeting where they voted to hire African-American police. Chief Jenkins argued that African-American police officers in other parts of the South were particularly effective in fight-ing crime in Black communities (Dulaney, 1996). Numerous Black, white, and interracial civic organizations and media outlets reported that Black police officers had been able to reduce homicide rates and vice crimes in Black communities in other southern cities. In the 1940s and 1950s, police chiefs throughout the South justified retaining African Americans on the force because of this impact on reducing crime and maintaining order in their communities. The chief of police in Summerton, South Carolina stated that his African-American officers "were successful in keeping peace in the town's black community, because they 'knew more about their people' than white officers and received 'better cooperation'" (p. 53).

Following the race riots in the 1940s, certain churches and civic groups began to support the idea of hiring more African-American police "because the utilization of blacks as police officers in the black areas would contribute substantially to the reduction of black hostility toward police" (Kuykendall & Burns, 1980, p. 6). A survey conducted in several southern cities in 1952 found that the majority of respondents did not believe that a Black suspect would resist a Black officer to the degree that they would resist a white officer and that "black officers were more effective in obtaining information and in finding wanted persons in black areas" (p. 9). In a 1953 survey of police chiefs in southern cities, the police chiefs credited their Black officers with "reducing crime and delinquency among African Americans, improving understanding and cooperation between Black citizens and the police, and decreasing police indifference about crime among African Americans"

(Dulaney, 1996, p. 53). In 1965, testifying before the McCone Commission about the Watts Riot, a white Los Angeles police officer stated that "most white patrolmen couldn't distinguish between law-abiding and lawless blacks" (Kuykendall & Burns, 1980, p. 9). All of these factors centered on one key motivation for the continuing use of African Americans as police officers, their *effectiveness* at securing social control.

Experts on policing have recommended increased minority employment since the 1940s. Remember that an important recommendation of Weckler and Hall's (1944) publication for the prevention of civil disorders was the hiring of African Americans as police officers.

> Many cities with sizable Negro populations are now seeking to obtain additional Negro policemen because they are often more effective than white policemen in troublesome Negro neighborhoods. A capable Negro officer frequently finds it easier to gain the confidence of the Negro leaders and under some circumstances has less difficulty in making necessary arrests than a white policeman. (p. 7)

Since almost all of the riots of the 1940s were initiated by white terrorists attacking African Americans, the focus on controlling Black people seems misplaced. On the other hand, Weckler and Hall also argued that the success of African-American police officers in controlling their own people could have a positive impact on race relations by producing a more positive image of Blacks in the eyes of the average white citizen.

In the 1960s, largely in response to the growth in the civil rights movement and related lawsuits, many cities throughout the United States hired more African-American police officers and gave them full police powers. Many African-American citizens and political leaders wanted Black cops in their neighborhoods, and they launched a determined program to gain greater representation on police forces across the country (Alex, 1969). They were now much more powerful politically than in earlier eras of U.S. history. Their arguments were well received.

> (1) the Negro policeman has the confidence of the Negro community; (2) he is considered a friend and not an enemy; (3) he is more understanding of the problems of the community because he is a Negro; (4) he acts as a buffer between the "brutal white cop" and the Negro citizen; and (5) the general quality of police work is raised by suppressing the handicap of racial prejudice. (Alex, 1969, p. 14)

"Many departments inaugurated programs to recruit black officers in order to improve the *image* of the police department with black citizens and with white liberals" (Dulaney, 1996, p. 71, *emphasis added*). The elements of community policing were developed in the postmodern era as police departments attempted to meet expectations. The African-American police officer emerged as an important figure in this transformation:

> The image of the police officer was intended to change from a representative of a de-personalized and possibly antagonistic agency to a protector,

friend and neighbor. Using whites in the new role might have seemed too much like old wine in new bottles, but black officers were perfect in neighborhoods where suspicion and mistrust of the police were highest—low-income areas with dense black concentrations. (Cashmore, 1991, p. 97)

In the wake of the urban rebellions of the 1960s and the violent confrontations between police and African Americans, image management became a key strategy for police departments throughout the country.

Police departments needed to transform the old image of themselves as an occupying army to be resisted. They needed to create the right image for the police, because the basis of support for policing our society must come from all citizens. Therefore, police agencies should be representative of the populations they serve. If they are not, they will be unable to respond empathetically to many community concerns. If the community cannot identify with the officers, there is a tendency to believe that law enforcement agencies represent the dominant society and are institutionally designed to preserve the status quo. "Who do we think is fooled when police departments send white 'undercover' cops to black neighborhoods? It's an absurd charade that . . . reinforces the 'occupying army' model of policing to which the black community has grown accustomed" (Muwakkil, 2000).

As we have seen previously, an essential element in being an effective social control agency in a democratic society is to be seen as legitimate in the eyes of those being policed. Following the appointment of an African-American police officer in Harlem in the 1960s, a civil rights leader remarked, "It has made a dramatic difference. It's more difficult for the inhabitants of Harlem to look upon the police as their enemy when he's the same color they are" (Alex, 1969, p. 29). It "is very difficult for minorities who feel discriminated against to view law enforcement as being responsive to their needs, unbiased and generally interested in justice if they do not see members of their group represented on the department's personnel roster" (More & Wegener, 1990, p. 389). The hiring of African Americans as police officers diffused claims of racial bias, whether or not the bias had actually been reduced.

The strategy of employing minorities to police minorities is best understood as a method of creating a more effective social control apparatus. A major shortcoming in the use of force to control people is that it exposes inequalities and angers those who are repressed. Therefore, a useful strategy, from the perspective of those with power in an unequal society, is to legitimize the apparatus of social control (Hoare & Smith, 1971). Nowhere is the practice of cloaking oppression in a mantle of legitimacy better exemplified than in the practice of utilizing members of an oppressed group to police themselves.

The importance of establishing good will and public confidence in the police among urban racial minorities was especially critical following the 1960s urban rebellions. The increased recruitment of African Americans into the police in the late 1960s and early 1970s was an effort by city governments "to create a wider base of community support for the police with the ultimate purpose of avoiding political difficulties and securing peace" (Alex, 1969, p. 24).

As already noted, Black officers would be much more likely to gain cooperation and information from African-American citizens because they could more easily obtain their trust and confidence than a white officer who symbolized centuries of racist oppression and brutality. "Blacks in uniform patrolling the ghettos would be a welcome, if unfamiliar, sight, it was reasoned; less obtrusive than whites, whose reputation for violent approaches made 'policing by consent' impossible" (Cashmore, 1991, p. 97). Blacks could also be sent in plainclothes into white communities, where racist stereotypes among the citizens would make the Black officer nearly invisible as an agent of social control.

Beyond helping to create a more democratic image of police, African Americans played a direct role in controlling the Black population (Cashmore, 1991). An essential part of all policing is gathering intelligence. "Information of strategic value about the population to be managed must be collected on a systematic basis for the control to remain effective" (pp. 98–99). The lack of preparedness of the police in times of urban rebellions in the 1960s, as well as into the 1990s, demonstrated inadequate intelligence-gathering. African-American police were used extensively to infiltrate Black radical groups and to cultivate informants. African-American police officers were used "to counter the threat of some of the more revolutionary groups, particularly those factions espousing illegal, military-type attacks against public property and established authority" (p. 99). Such groups included the Black Panthers and the Black Muslims or Nation of Islam. African-American police officers were used extensively to watch these groups from the inside and to act as major witnesses for the prosecution in trials (Alex, 1969).

The *Kerner Report* (1968) included a number of recommendations to create a police department more closely connected to the citizens being policed.

> Loss of contact between the police officer and the community he serves adversely affects law enforcement. If an officer has never met, does not know, and cannot understand the language and habits of the people in the area he patrols, he cannot do an effective police job. His ability to detect truly suspicious behavior is impaired. He deprives himself of important sources of information. He fails to know those persons with an "equity" in the community—homeowners, small businessmen, professional men, persons who are anxious to support proper law enforcement—and thus sacrifices the contribution they can make to maintaining community order. (Harris & Wicker, 1988, p. 305)

The above passage presents an important component of community policing, while also establishing the justification for hiring police officers of color. The *Kerner Report* recommended that more African-American police be hired precisely because they were more likely to gain access to information that would make them more effective at enforcing the law and maintaining social order in the Black communities. "Negro officers also can increase departmental insight into ghetto problems, and provide information necessary for early anticipation of the tensions and grievances that can lead to disorders" (Harris & Wicker, 1988, p. 315).

The *Kerner Report* also suggested that having white officers and Black officers working together could reduce racial stereotypes and prejudices held by some white officers (Harris & Wicker, 1988). In one study, a number of African-American police officers stated that they often taught white officers how to work more effectively in the African-American community. Others, however, complained that the strategy of using "salt and pepper" teams was simply to have the African-American police officer do all the dirty work for the white officer (Alex, 1969).

Cashmore (1991) argued that the recommendation by the *Kerner Report* to hire more African-American police was a strategy of co-optation.

> Basic ethnic inequalities would remain, of course, but the illusion of mobility and change would be created. A particularly cynical interpretation of this process would hold that Blacks would be attracted into the institutions, then promoted into positions of authority and influence, whereupon their actions would be tantamount to a betrayal.

Alex (1969:29) summarized the strategy as follows:

> The recruitment of Negroes therefore provides city government the means by which it can transform opposition and dangerous criticism of the police into support and compliance. By incorporating individuals from the "enemy's" camp, that is, by opening up a new set of jobs to Negro candidates, it contributes to the viability of the policeman as the guardian of all members of the community. In these terms, it secures peace by means of ensuring acceptance from a hostile group, and also lends legitimacy, hence security, to the police in relation to these groups. (p. 29)

Edward Palmer (1973) described the benefits of hiring African-American police: "The police department realizes that control is more absolute if done by a member of the community being controlled. This member will intuitively be cognizant of the inner workings of the community. As an extra dividend, he will give the illusion of hope" (p. 21). It was a sound tactical device to deflect people's attention away from the fundamental criticism of the unequal structure of law and social control in the United States. Blazing the path for the postmodern era, the idea of putting a "black face" on white oppression had substantial appeal to those in power.

At the same time, though, African Americans gained political power from their recruitment into large police departments in the late 1960s and early 1970s. Under political pressure from civil rights leaders, African-American newspapers, and Black voters, numerous police agencies initiated efforts not only to recruit more African Americans into their departments, but also to place them in higher and more visible command posts (Alex, 1969). The recruitment of African-American police officers was "a realistic adjustment to the growing political power of the Negro community" (p. 31). The growth in the number of African Americans in both the rank and file and in executive police positions was a reflection of that political power. The most dramatic symbol of increased power was the appointment of African-American police executives. The selections of Lee Brown to head the racially troubled Houston Police Department and Willie Williams to lead the post-Rodney King Los Angeles Police Department were evidence that police departments were responding to the concerns of people of color.

Who Influences Whom?

Throughout the history of racial and ethnic relations in the United States, the inclusion of members of oppressed groups in police agencies has had both liberating and repressive effects—reflected in intentions and in outcomes. Historically African Americans have pushed for African-American police, hoping that Black police officers would provide their communities with a higher quality of policing. However, the influence of white society and the homogenizing effects of a white-dominated police subculture have often dashed those hopes.

Many have argued that Black and white police officers generally function in very similar ways. In fact, a study in the mid-1960s found that "one in ten black officers exhibited extreme negative attitudes toward black citizens" and that African-American officers were sometimes more demanding of African-American citizens than their white counterparts (Kuykendall & Burns, 1980, p. 9). This strictness or overreaction on the part of the African-American police officer is often an attempt to "prove to the establishment that he is not 'one of those'" (Palmer, 1973, p. 23).

Through the process of becoming a police officer, the African-American officer is effectively isolated from his community and his roots: "With the gun he follows the white man to become likewise an oppressor. The only difference is that he becomes an accomplice in the oppression of his people" (Palmer, 1973, p. 22). The following statements made by a few Black officers may help to explain why this might be the case:

> "I believe that some black cops are tougher on the black offender . . . These people (criminals) are letting down their own race."
> "Sure black cops are tougher. They have to be."
> "The black cop sometimes feels as though he is not getting the respect due him from the younger blacks he locks up."
> "The black cop must lean on the offender a little harder . . . it's mostly a matter of respect." (Leinin, 1993, pp. 234–235)}

If these statements are to any degree representative, it is easier to understand why African-American police did not radically change police oppression of urban Black communities. While there are valid reasons to continue to increase the number of police officers of color, this activity cannot by itself counter institutionalized racism embedded in policing.

Despite the rhetoric surrounding the appointment of African-American police chiefs, they have not had a substantial impact on making police more accountable to their communities (Cashmore, 1991). While African-American mayors have long sought civilian review boards to oversee police activities, African-American police chiefs such as Lee Brown have opposed them. "Even those who do favour more accountability are constrained by community, political and organizational influences associated with policing policy" (pp. 101–102). For example, Chief Willie Williams was initially hired by a multicultural political coalition in Los Angeles headed by an African-American mayor. His charge was to increase police accountability and build public support and faith in the police (Sonenshein, 1994). Yet, as he began to do that, often in opposition to the wishes of the police union and the white rank-and-file, he was fired by the new administration that placed a higher value on police morale than on the support of racial minorities.

> Naming black police-chiefs and electing black mayors approximates a public-relations exercise . . . There is a great symbolic value in the drama of blacks hauling their way out of slavery, then marching to Montgomery, before exploding onto the streets of Los Angeles and finally entering the corridors of power. But this colossal symbolic value should not be confused with the minuscule actual value it has had for the majority of America's black population, whose material position has remained largely unaffected by the elevation of specific individuals to powerful positions; or, at least, positions that appear to have power. (Cashmore, p. 103)

In other words, placing African Americans into these positions creates the appearance of social justice and racial equality. In reality, these leaders are seriously constrained by structural conditions.

No matter who is in charge or who is carrying out the orders, the police are in the business of maintaining the status quo. The presence of persons of color at the helm of an organization whose fundamental purpose is to preserve the social order does not by itself change that basic purpose. The structural conditions of policing in the United States are characterized by racist, sexist, heterosexist, and economic relations of power. The criminal law is shaped by these relations and the police officer is constrained by the laws. Thus, the ability of police officers, or even police administrators, to make policing a more just and responsive enterprise is limited.

Given the legacy of racism in governmental institutions and bureaucracies, there are reasons to question whether those African Americans who do rise through the ranks to positions of leadership are subject to undue influence by the white power structure. African Americans who are selected to become police officers, or who are viable political candidates, are carefully scrutinized by those in positions of power. Edward Palmer (1973) argued that, whether Black or white, persons interviewing prospective police officers

> will be impregnated with white values to such an extent that any deviation from white standards will be exorcized. . . . What the interviewer

> wants in essence is a strong black back, and a mind that is fairly mallea-
> ble and highly susceptible to brainwashing at the expense of his own
> humanness. (p. 21)

Clearly, the candidate must satisfy those on the oral board that he or she has
the proper attitude and values to be a good police officer. The many hurdles
in the process of becoming a police officer have long been filled with opportunities to eliminate those who do not fit the mold.

Once the right African American is found and becomes a police officer, an
indoctrination process begins to mold them into proper conduct. "We know
from an assortment of police studies that an assimilation process takes place in
which the values, attitudes, and perspectives of a 'police subculture' are generally absorbed as the new recruit gains more experience in the ranks" (Cashmore, 1991, p. 104). Beginning in the academy, through field training, and on
the police force, certain personal characteristics and perspectives are encouraged and rewarded, while others are shunned and lead to isolation or criticism.

Those African Americans who are likely to be rewarded and promoted
by the police agency are those who demonstrate the values, attitudes, and
opinions deemed appropriate by those in control of the police department. If
one takes into account the characteristics of those African Americans who
choose to become and are selected as police officers, the indoctrination process that takes place once one is selected, and the selection process for promotion, chances are that the African-American police administrator will
behave and think much like a white police administrator.

The socialization of African-American police officers was evident in a
study conducted in 1984. The researcher summarized the officers' perceptions of critical issues in policing:

> They feel that their efforts to protect the public from criminal victimiza-
> tion have been all but neutralized by a series of legal decisions and high
> court rulings which favor the offender. They see their authority and
> autonomy over the street criminal slowly eroding in the face of directives
> not aimed at reducing crime, but at reducing the likelihood of police mis-
> conduct and abuse of authority. But most of all, like their white brother
> police officers they feel beset by a public who is at best indifferent toward
> their efforts to reduce criminal victimization and maintain some degree
> of law and order in the black community. (Leinin, 1994, p. 210)

Like their white counterparts, these particular African-American police
officers appear to have fully adopted the rhetoric that police officers are a
beleaguered and misunderstood group and that their mission is "to catch bad
guys." They made statements that suggested that following Supreme Court
rulings and respecting an individual's civil rights was an "option," rather
than a moral and legal mandate. They even stated that they viewed the
"choice" of protecting civil rights or padding their arrest quotas by arresting
all suspected law violators regardless of the evidence as a "dilemma" (p. 211).
These particular African-American police officers appear to define their role

within the narrow confines of crime-fighting, rather than seeking social change or attempting to achieve some sense of racial and community justice. Therefore, "It is unlikely that more blacks in the police-force will make any difference to the material lives of either those locked in the underclass or those striving to escape it" (Cashmore, 1991, p. 106).

The statements by these particular African-American police officers could be a sign that they were being successfully co-opted and socialized into the police subculture to a point that race did not matter. The homogenization process that occurs during the selection, training, and socialization of police officers may have eliminated the social justice advantages to the African-American community of having African-American police officers. Maybe as minority officers become institutionalized, they become identical to the white officers. "No evidence suggests that African American, Hispanic, and white officers behave in significantly different ways" (Walker et al., 2000, p. 111). The research suggests that they fire their weapons, use excessive force, and make arrests with similar patterns and rates.

It is also not clear that achieving representation proportional to the population will have a substantial impact on police-community relations problems. At the time of the videotaped beating of Rodney King and the subsequent riots in South Central, the Los Angeles Police Department (LAPD) had the same proportion of African-American police officers (14%) as were represented in the city's population (Walker et al., 2000). Despite this representation, the Christopher Commission found a "racist climate within the department, with officers making racist comments over the department's computerized message system."

Demographic studies have consistently shown that African Americans who achieve middle-class status often leave the city (Cashmore, 1991). "As the professionals have acquired income and status, they have mimicked 'white flight,' moving away from the inner cities into the suburbs" (p. 105). Such changes in lifestyle and experiences are likely to distance successful African-American police officers and administrators from those African Americans who remain stuck at the bottom. The belief that those who want success badly enough and work hard enough can succeed in America, and its corollary that those left on the bottom are simply not trying hard enough, is held by many middle-class African Americans as well as their white counterparts.

As African Americans become police officers, they move into the lower-middle class and sometimes lose their bond to lower-income African Americans:

> As the emerging lower-middle class black moves away from his lower class birth place, he attempts to remove all vestiges of what he was in a vain attempt to become all white and all right. His people have become "those people." "I can't understand them," and the final economic slur, "I made it," are part of his new lexicon. . . . With his loss will go his desire to serve and help his people. . . . He has also lost some of his sensitivity and compassion. For implicit in the statement, "I made it," is the underly-

ing thought that they "didn't make it," were worthless and under no cir-
cumstance could ever arrive at his present position. (Palmer, 1973, p. 20)

Much like the influences toward a particular "police personality," the influence of becoming part of the middle class is likely to encourage values of stability and conservatism rather than radical social change.

The assumption that because a police officer is African American, he or
she will identify with all African Americans is a mistaken stereotype. Many
white political leaders, police chiefs, private citizens, and even social scientists view African Americans as an "ethnic monolith" with one voice, one
perspective, and a universal bond of mutual understanding (Georges-Abeyie,
1989). The fact is that the so-called "Black community" includes a very
diverse collection of classes, religions, and national origins. "Race does not
equal ethnicity" (p. 38). Among these heterogeneous groups there exist varying levels of social distance and connection with each other. It may be that
the social distance between most African-American police and other segments of the Black population is so wide that little real benefit is gained for
African Americans by having African-American police officers.

Conclusion

The question for future developments in policing is whether the coloriza-
tion of policing in the United States is a substantive change in the enforcement of the law, or is simply cosmetic. We have looked at the struggle by
African Americans for representation. We also looked at the motivations of
individuals to serve as police officers and the motivations of administrators to
hire them. What is the potential for social change through minority empowerment? Is it possible for an agency designed for social control to succeed in
that goal while creating an opportunity for change?

No one has been more critical of the use of Black police to police Black
people as a method of control and oppression than Edward Palmer. He has
referred to "the role of the police in the black community as a direct continuation of the slave overseer" (Palmer, 1973, p. 26). Yet, Palmer also argued
that if properly educated, motivated, and organized, African-American
police officers could be a major impetus for social change in the struggle for
racial justice and equality. He stated that "organized black police represent
power, and organized black police who have black community support represent a real political and economic threat to the white power structure" (p. 27).
The first task for African-American police officers is to work to "stop brutality, harassment, intimidation and murder against the black community" (p.
76) at the hands of the police, black and white.

The white police administration has used the black police against black
people. This is the only serious reason black police are hired . . . But it is
my view, in conclusion, that the black police, properly organized, could
lead one of the strongest and most effective movements for change, while
still being considered within the system.

The use of African Americans as agents of social control and their growth in numbers and power within police departments and urban politics can be seen as more than an effective enhancement of social control.

> To some, this may be nothing more than an insidious form of social control and an effective one at that . . . But it *is* more than a form of control. It is a wondrous spectacle enacted over two-and-a-half decades and designed to celebrate a society once caught on the horns of an American dilemma, but now truly directed towards an egalitarian society in which the "law and authority" Kerner found so vital is stronger than ever. Afro-Americans have the respect they yearned for; many of them have actually worked their ways to positions in which they can dispense respect, not just earn it. It is an example of black Americans being given opportunities and seizing them to assert themselves. It is also an ironic self assertion. (Cashmore, 1991, p. 107)

12 Women Police Officers

The crossing of gender lines in policing involved a number of issues very different from those of crossing racial lines. For example, while the introduction of racial minorities into policing was often seen as a threat to white supremacy, the ability of Black officers to meet the requirements of the job tasks was rarely seen as a threat to the white police officer's self-image. African-American men do not challenge the "quintessential police officer role in the same way women do" (Martin & Jurik, 1996, p. 71). In other words, after finally gaining admittance to the job, African-American males because of stereotypes regarding their strength, dexterity, and general athletic abilities were perceived as enhancing the officer image. While stereotypes about women resulted in positive evaluations for dealing with children or some domestic situations, the idea that a woman could successfully do all the work of a police officer was a threat to masculine notions of police work. If a woman or a gay man could do it, maybe the job was not as difficult or as dangerous as the prevalent stereotype. Male officers' self-image as "real" men and masculine defenders of truth and justice was threatened.

Police Matrons

The initial entry of women into the criminal justice system was in the 1820s. A number of Quaker women volunteered to work as "prison matrons" in newly created correctional institutions for women in the United States. As upper-middle-class women from the American Friends Society began to enter prisons to provide religious and secular training to the female inmates, they were appalled by the conditions in which the inmates were living, and they blamed much of it on the fact that the guards were men (Schulz, 1995). One highly publicized case was that of Rachel Welch, a pregnant female inmate at the Auburn Prison in New York. She was flogged so severely by a male prison official that she died shortly after childbirth (Bartollas & Hahn, 1999). The Quaker women were particularly disturbed by the sexual vulnerability of women inmates to both the male inmates and the male guards.

The massive industrialization, urbanization, and immigration that characterized early nineteenth century life in the United States produced dramatic social upheaval. It also produced vast increases in the number of women among the homeless, the poor, and the unemployed (Feinman, 1994). It is not surprising, therefore, that this period is fraught with "a steady and marked rise in the arrest and incarceration rates of women and girls for prostitution, disorderly conduct, drunkenness, and vagrancy" (Feinman, 1994, p. 91). Following the general theories about crime and institutionalization of that time, women correctional reformers thought that female offenders could be reformed by eliminating the corrupting influence of society, particularly urban society (Barlow et al., 1993; Schulz, 1995). Largely as a result of the lobbying efforts of these middle-class women, female institutions were built in rural areas and staffed completely by women. Although these early efforts led to the formation of new career opportunities for women, the position of prison matron did not radically challenge sexual stereotypes in that it reinforced "women's traditional role as the caregiver to other women" (Schulz, 1995, p. 373). This particular area of employment "was unique because the women stressed the moral basis of their work and the ways their activities differed from those of men" in the criminal justice system (Martin & Jurik, 1996, p. 49).

According to Higgins (1992), the first police matrons in this country were officially appointed by the New York City Police Department in 1845 to handle women and girls in custody. Against much opposition, this appointment was the result of a campaign by the American Female Reform Society of New York City (Walker, 1992b). The strongest opposition came from rank-and-file and senior police officers (Bartollas & Hahn, 1999). The opposition to these appointments focused on the argument that women would be "contaminated" or "demoralized" if they had regular contact with "depraved creatures" (Feinman, 1994, p. 93). Opponents also argued that no "decent, sober, respectable" woman could be found who would want to take on such a task (p. 93).

In 1887, despite the fact that the city of New York was detaining 14,000 women prisoners and housed 42,000 women in overnight shelters, the Men's Prison Association objected to the placement of a police matron in each police station (Bartollas & Hahn, 1999). They objected because of the lack of space for the matron, the violent nature of women prisoners, and the belief that the police matrons would not be able to physically control the women at the stations. The reformers, on the other hand, claimed that there was a need for some "womanly presence" in the police station "to prevent sexual abuse and attacks upon arrested and incarcerated women by policemen and male prisoners and to protect young girls and first time offenders from hardened women criminals" (Feinman, 1994, p. 93). The women being housed in police stations "were almost always poor and frequently intoxicated, two conditions that made them vulnerable to advances by the men responsible for their care" (Schulz, p. 373).

The second successful campaign to obtain police matrons was orchestrated by the Women's Christian Temperance Union of Portland, Maine in 1877. "As early as the 1820s, women had begun to replace clergymen as leaders in the crusade against sexual sin . . . their prime interest centered on eliminating prostitution" (Feinman, 1994, p. 92). By the 1880s, a number of national women's civic and social organizations were actively involved in the struggle to place women in police stations (Higgins, 1992). The Federation of Women's Clubs, the National League of Women Voters, the National Women's Christian Temperance Union, and a number of local associations, clubs, and social agencies organized to bring about numerous social reforms to address the issues of vice and sexual activity outside of marriage (Higgins, 1992; Schulz, 1995).

Many had been active abolitionists before the Civil War and were now turning their attention to other social causes frequently associated with religion, temperance, and immorality (Schulz, 1995). One of these efforts involved the appointment of women to work in prison institutions and in police stations to help save women and children from a life of crime and delinquency. "By the 1880s these women succeeded in creating another new profession for women—police matron" (p. 374). In 1888, Massachusetts and New York passed laws requiring all cities with a population over 20,000 to employ prison matrons to care for female inmates (Horne, 1975). By the turn of the century, most major U.S. cities had adopted the use of police matrons.

Policing Women and Children

The social reform movements in the early part of the century, particularly around World War I, were directed at differences of class and culture (Schulz, 1995). Of particular concern was the perceived immorality and vice among the poor, particularly the recent Irish and Italian immigrants who were predominately Catholic. Many wealthy philanthropists and middle-class reformers initiated a number of campaigns to restrict immigration, to prohibit the sale of various drugs and alcohol, to criminalize gambling and prostitution, and even to arrest and deport socialists (Barlow, 1985). A number of efforts were made by the social reformers to "save" the wretched poor from their own vices. Most of these efforts focused on poor immigrant children who were viewed as unwashed, undisciplined, disorderly, and morally weak (Barlow, 1985).

During World War I poor immigrant women came under intense scrutiny. The mobilization of soldiers meant that a large number of men, mostly young and away from home for the first time, were concentrated in training camps across the country (Feinman, 1994). It was feared that these camps would attract a large number of women and girls seeking these men for "patriotic, romantic, and financial reasons" (p. 95). Zones surrounding these military camps were established by the federal government in which houses of prostitution and the sale of alcohol were prohibited.

Women were hired by the Law Enforcement Division of the Commission on Tramp Camp Activities to operate in a quasi-police capacity within the zones that surrounded the U.S. military training camps. The primary task of these early policewomen was to keep prostitutes away from the camps, locate runaway children and return them to their homes, and regulate the commercial amusements around the camps (Horne, 1975). The women were given full police powers to arrest both women and men, and they patrolled transportation depots, amusement areas, rooming houses, and any other public place where women and girls might congregate and get into trouble (Feinman, 1994).

The prostitutes, and not the men who were their customers, received the legal and moral blame for such behaviors (Schulz, 1995). It was the women who were arrested and the girls who were detained and returned to their homes (Feinman, 1994). The success of the women who policed the military camp areas convinced a number of police departments to hire women for similar purposes. Their activities were concentrated in the area of "juvenile delinquency, female victims of sex offenses, women criminal suspects, abandoned infants, missing persons, vice squads, matron duty, and clerical work" (p. 95). Sometimes women actually went out on limited patrol to watch women, girls, and children in order to prevent crime or protect them from harm. In 1922, the International Association of Chiefs of Police passed a resolution stating that "policewomen were essential to a modern police department" (Horne, 1975, p. 19).

The appointment of policewomen was also an essential part of the movement to closely regulate the morality of poor people, as they were hired specifically to instill a sense of morality, self-discipline, and industry within poor immigrant women and children (Schulz, 1995). Many of the early reformers, particularly Quaker women in the early part of the nineteenth century, sought to rescue women and children who were being abused by a system that was not designed to meet their specific needs. But by the twentieth century, the salvation offered by these "overwhelmingly college-educated, native-born, upper-middle-class women . . . was viewed by their clients as coercive social control. . . . Their presence in poor, immigrant neighborhoods was often unwelcome and unappreciated, as they tried to force their values on others in a maternal, yet coercive manner" (p. 376). The primary contribution to the field of law enforcement by these pioneering policewomen was to "bring under municipal control behavior by women and children that had previously not been viewed as requiring the attention or intervention of the police" (p. 376).

The police matron was initially responsible for providing custodial care for women and children who were housed at the police station. Police administrators soon began utilizing them in a number of other ways (Schulz, 1995). Although responsibilities increased, these duties continued to reflect sexual stereotypes. Women were perceived as better than men at nurturing and communicating with women and children but incapable of enforcement duties. The use of police matrons by police departments expanded to include such

tasks as interviewing accused women and even providing sentencing recommendations like a modern-day probation officer (Schulz, 1995). For example,
Marie Owens became actively involved in assisting detectives and visiting
courts in cases involving women and children (Higgins, 1992; Grennan,
1993). The Chicago Police Department listed Marie Owens on their payroll
as a "patrolman" for thirty years until she retired (Horne, 1975), although she
was probably originally appointed by the Mayor as a way to provide for the
widow of a Chicago police officer. It was not until the twentieth century,
however, that the "policewoman" emerged (Schulz, 1995, p. 374).

The Transformation Begins

The critical factor in transforming police matrons into policewomen was
the authority to enforce the law, even if only within the realm that was specifically designated for their sex. In 1905, Lola Baldwin was given police powers
in the city of Portland, Oregon to be able "to more authoritatively and effectively deal with problems involving girls and young women who were being
threatened by poor social conditions and undesirable influences" (Higgins,
1992, p. 342). Baldwin was originally hired by the Portland Police Department
"to protect women and girls from the miners, lumberjacks, and laborers"
(Feinman, 1994, p. 93) attending the Lewis and Clark Exposition of 1905.
After the fair was over, she was given a permanent position (Walker, 1992b).
She was so successful in performing her duties that the Portland Police
Department established the Department of Public Safety for the Protection of
Young Girls and Women, which she headed. The women working in the
department were called "safety workers" or "operatives" rather than "police."

Alice Stebbins Wells was the first person to be called a "policewoman" in
the United States (Schulz, 1995, p. 374). She was appointed in 1910 by the
Los Angeles Police Department, after the city received a petition with the sig-
natures of 100 influential citizens asking for her appointment (Higgins,
1992). Wells exemplified the concept of the policewoman as a social worker;
she envisioned her role as a woman helping women (Schulz, 1995). The following excerpt described her duties:

> the supervision, and the enforcement of laws concerning dance halls,
> skating rinks, penny arcades, picture shows, and other similar places of
> public recreation . . . the supervision of unwholesome bill-board displays,
> the search for missing persons, and the maintenance of a general infor-
> mation bureau for women seeking advice on matters within the scope of
> the police department. (Higgins, 1992, p. 343)

The profession of policewoman emerged in conjunction with the profession of social worker. Their duties were very similar; both engaged in the
practice of "policing" the moral behavior of young women and parenting
poor immigrant children (Schulz, 1995). In fact, Wells was a social worker
who came to believe that "a woman invested with police powers could be of

more help than if she worked through a private reform or charity agency" (Feinman, 1994, p. 94). Wells spoke extensively throughout the country and the world to promote the role of women in policing (Walker, 1992b; Horne, 1975). Wells even lectured to the International Chiefs of Police and gained their support in the formation of the International Association of Police-women in 1915 (Horne, 1975). Wells became the first president of this organi-zation, which later collapsed when its largest sponsor died in 1932 (Horne, 1975).

These upper-middle-class, educated women did not align themselves with law enforcement officers. They saw themselves as superior to both the poor and immoral women they were "helping" and to the working-class police officer (Schulz, 1995). "They conducted interviews and wrote case his-tories; they went to court and made recommendations regarding sentences based on their case studies," they counseled women and helped them in obtaining clothing, housing, and employment (Feinman, 1994, p. 93). The entry requirements and training for the position of policewoman far exceeded that of the male police officer (Schulz, 1995). The standards often required a high school diploma, some college, and years of experience in social services (Walker, 1992b). Even the very few African-American women who were hired to work specifically with African-American women and children were usually "teachers, social workers, or ministers' wives with status in the com-munity" (Schulz, 1995, p. 375). The offices of policewomen were often located away from the police stations, in an effort to create a "professional, nonthreatening atmosphere" (p. 375). Many of these policewomen were orig-inally social workers who wanted the legal authority to properly "discipline" lower-class clients and to take children into custody, but they did not want to be seen as the female version of a policeman. They did not want to lower themselves to the policeman's level.

Many policewomen viewed the segregation of their gender and duties from those of policemen as the only way to achieve promotions and to have an impact on policy (Schulz, 1995). Separation was an important part of the women's strategy to gain acceptance and to have a significant impact on policing (Martin & Jurik, 1996). They argued for the formation of Women's Bureaus so that they would not be viewed as competing with men. Similar to the special Colored Bureau in Miami or the separate tribal police, police-women demanded Women's Bureaus that would be physically and ideologi-cally separate from the male-dominated police station (Schulz, 1995). They wanted a completely separate bureaucracy where women could be promoted without directly competing with men (Schultz, 1995).

The policewomen's movement was initially assisted by the movement to professionalize the police (Walker, 1992b). One part of the professionalization movement, which faded in the 1930s, was the idea that the police could be an important instrument for broader social reform. An important element of this movement was that crime prevention was an important role for police and that the best way to prevent crime was to stop juveniles from entering a life of crime.

Many social organizations and reformers argued that women were best suited for providing "counsel and guidance to children," and they fulfilled their crime prevention duties "by patrolling, in plain clothes, those places where it was believed that children might come into contact with vice" (p. 853).

The primary weapon in the crime prevention fight was "protective custody." Policewomen would frequently take into custody children who they felt were in morally or physically hazardous situations (Walker, 1992b). Women argued that crime prevention was an integral part of policing, and many progressive police reformers agreed (Martin & Jurik, 1996). The dilemma of this argument was that if the primary task of policing was crime prevention and women were better at this task than men, then "men would assume a second-rate status within police departments" (Martin & Jurik, 1996, p. 50).

The gains made by pioneering policewomen were swept away in the 1930s (Grennan, 1993). The Great Depression caused the loss of many police jobs. The layoffs disproportionately affected policewomen and the Women's Bureaus, as they were often seen as an expensive luxury. Their mission was also curbed significantly in the 1930s as police departments across the United States embraced the image of "crime-fighter," which largely rejected the more social-work oriented duties traditionally performed by policewomen (Schulz, 1995). The crime control model of policing completely overpowered the crime prevention model, as law enforcement leaders such as J. Edgar Hoover promoted the image of police officers as "soldiers in a war against crime" (Martin & Jurik, 1996, p. 51).

With the emphasis placed on the military-style command structure and on "fighting" crime rather than preventing it, women found themselves and their duties becoming more marginalized than ever (Martin & Jurik, 1996). The crime control model "firmly reinforced male, working-class culture and values in police departments and reaffirmed the superiority of the masculine virtue of being able to overcome resistance" (p. 51). Ironically, the peripheral role that women had carved out for themselves so that they would be accepted into policing became their greatest liability (Martin & Jurik, 1996).

Neither police administrators nor policewomen themselves sought the integration of women into the ranks of patrol officers (Schulz, 1995). The women did not ask for the same assignments as male police officers; they did not wear uniforms; and they rarely carried a gun. Policewomen willingly accepted their specialized role in policing, a role they had actively organized to obtain. Despite the fact that women did not directly compete for the same jobs as male police officers, "support from within the police environment was usually unenthusiastic, reluctant, and grudging" (Schulz, 1995, p. 375). The hiring of policewomen was not the invention of white male police executives. Rather, outside forces insisted police departments incorporate women for the responsibilities described earlier. In fact, many of the first policewomen were selected by, and their salaries paid at least in part by, private organizations (Walker, 1992b).

The police establishment and many city officials were opposed to the policewomen's movement. While in some cities, such as Los Angeles, the appointment of the first policewoman encountered little resistance, the struggle took two years in Chicago and eight years in both Cleveland and Boston (Walker, 1992b). Most of the campaigns emphasized the "traditional image of women as the guardian of children and other women" (p. 851). It should also be noted that much of the resistance to women in the workplace, particularly a male-dominated workplace, is based on mythical and class-biased ideals of feminine attributes. The stereotype of women waiting for men to come home from work to an orderly, relaxing environment was irrelevant to working class women's lives (Grennan, 1993). "Women of the lower classes have always worked inside or outside the home," often accomplishing dirty, backbreaking, and dangerous tasks (Grennan, 1993, p. 168).

When the Great Depression ended, the hiring of women police resumed. With the growing public concern about morality and juvenile delinquency following World War II, hirings increased and the assignments offered to women police officers became more diverse (Schulz, 1995). Policewomen were given uniforms copied from the military uniforms worn by women during the war. This presented a problem because the uniforms consisted of skirts, and no holsters were issued to women officers. Since they were trained in the use of firearms and expected to carry them, they usually had to carry their guns in pocketbooks (Schultz, 1995). In the South, there was a shortage of men wanting to go into police work, so many southern departments used women to regulate traffic and to enforce parking regulations (Grennan, 1993). These efforts were so successful that other cities throughout the country began to hire women specifically for traffic control.

The Second Generation of Women Officers

The inclinations of women entering police work after the war were very different from those of their predecessors. They both requested and fought for the expansion of their role (Schulz, 1995). They were usually military veterans who were career-focused and wanted to advance through the ranks. Much like early immigrant and African-American police officers, they were drawn to police work because of the job security and opportunities for advancement in civil service employment. Although women continued to be better educated and held to a higher entry standard than male police officers, they began to reject the social work orientation that had restricted their opportunities within the police department (Schulz, 1995).

Women entering police work in the 1950s were motivated more by self-interest than by "societal benefit" (Schulz, 1995, p. 378). The focus shifted from fighting patriarchy in society to fighting patriarchy within the police department. Women in all sectors of the workforce recognized that gender segregation was hindering their employment opportunities; they began to challenge these barriers.

The emphasis of the "second generation" of women police to be seen as police officers rather than social workers was evident in the revised name of the International Association of Policewomen when it was reestablished in 1956. The name was changed to the International Association of Women Police (IAWP) (Schulz, 1995, p. 378). However, the organization was slower in seeking equal status with male police officers than many members would have preferred. For example, in 1960 Lois Lundell Higgins (president of the IAWP) declared that women would remain in police work as long as they did not attempt to compete with male officers. She urged women to focus on those "peculiarly feminine" talents that had made them a success in policing and not to seek "work that has been and always will be predominately a man's job" (p. 379). Even in the 1970s, IAWP typically selected social work professionals and directors of Women's Bureaus to speak at their annual meetings, rather than women on patrol or in nontraditional assignments. In the 1980s the IAWP finally began to focus more on law enforcement and to incorporate activities at their annual meetings that paralleled those of the male police organizations.

As with African-American police, the most successful challenges by women police to discrimination were through the civil rights movement and the women's movement—and by suing police departments in court (Schulz, 1995). "Part of the impetus for a broader use of women in policing is undoubtedly a result of increased pressures in the society at large as women demand equal job opportunities through the political and legal channels open to them" (Milton, 1972, p. 35). A number of lawsuits were filed throughout the country following the initial thrust by two women police officers in the New York City Police Department. Although it took two years, three court cases, and thirteen judges, in 1963 the New York City Police Department obeyed the court order to allow women to take the sergeant's exam (Schulz, 1995). These types of lawsuits were assisted by federal legislation designed to put an end to unjustified employee discrimination.

In 1963, Congress passed the Equal Pay Act, which prohibited differential pay for equal work (Schulz, 1995). In 1964, Title VII of the Omnibus Civil Rights Law prohibited employee discrimination in the private sector based on sex, race, color, religion, or national origin. Although this law greatly facilitated African Americans obtaining full police status in the major cities of the United States, it did not have the same impact for women. An International Chiefs of Police survey in 1969 found that the quota for women was about one percent of the workforce, that they had higher entrance requirements, that they were rarely allowed to take promotional exams, and that they were assigned to special tasks such as clerical work or working with juveniles and women (Milton, 1972).

Women on Patrol

The "experiment" of putting women police officers on regular patrol was initiated in 1968 by the Indianapolis Police Department (Schulz, 1995).

Officers Blankenship and Coffal became the first policewomen to "strap gun belts to their waists, drive a marked patrol car, and answer general-purpose calls for service on an equal basis with policemen" (p. 380). Whether by design or simply because of poor planning, the experiment was not well conceived. The women officers were removed from their previously restricted duties on one day's notice and placed on patrol together in Car 47 with no training whatsoever for their new assignment. Nonetheless, the event was historic and revolutionary, as policewomen broke the gender barrier and entered the previously male-only world of policing.

It was not until 1972, when Congress passed the Equal Employment Opportunity Act (amending the Civil Rights Act of 1964), that women began to be placed on patrol in cities throughout the country (Schulz, 1995). This legislation made it mandatory for all state and local governments to follow the same guidelines as the federal government regarding employment practices. Race, creed, color, or sex could no longer be used as a condition of employment (Grennan, 1993). This process was further advanced by the 1973 Crime Control Act, under which federal grants from the Law Enforcement Assistance Administration could be withheld if state and local governments maintained discriminatory employment practices (Schulz, 1995).

The hiring of more women, particularly women of color, was eventually seen by many police executives as a way to meet affirmative action goals and to enlarge their pool of applicants (Feinman, 1994). Berkeley Police Chief Bruce Baker stated that the reason he was willing to "experiment" with women in policing was because it would provide his department with "a wider selection of officers, especially minority officers. . . . This is very important since we have had a good deal of difficulty in attracting qualified blacks" (Milton, 1972).

In the 1970s, policewomen sued police departments throughout the country challenging entrance requirements, selection criteria, discriminatory assignments, and promotional procedures (Martin & Jurik, 1996). Many of these lawsuits resulted in court orders or consent decrees that established affirmative action programs. According to a 1997 study by the National Center for Women and Policing, progress in the hiring and promoting of women "has been made only in departments where legal battles to fight discriminatory hiring and promotion practices have resulted in consent decrees or other court orders forcing agencies to increase the numbers of women" ("Rank Objections," 1998, p. 1). Police departments throughout the country were forced to establish hiring requirements and performance evaluations based on "bona fide occupational qualifications"—ones that could be verified as necessary to the successful performance of the job (Grennan, 1993). However, "candidates still tend[ed] to be judged on qualities, standards, or attributes associated with masculinity (e.g., self-confidence and assertiveness)" (Martin & Jurik, 1996, p. 54).

The urban riots of the 1960s and numerous claims of police brutality led many social reformers to emphasize intelligence, emotional stability, and sen-

sitivity, rather than strength and aggressiveness, as the appropriate characteristics for police officers (Martin & Jurik, 1996). The move to place women on
patrol was facilitated by the eventual recognition that police work involved
much more than law enforcement. The 1967 President's Commission on Law
Enforcement had recommended hiring more women police officers because
of the strong criticism of the police in the 1960s and the need for a more "professional" police officer (Milton, 1972). The commission concluded that
"policewomen can be an invaluable asset to modern law enforcement, and
their present role should be broadened" (p. 6).

> More and more progressive police administrators, realizing that the puni-
> tive approach to crime is not effective in the total picture, turn to many
> crime prevention ideas and actions to curtail crime and prevent criminal
> behavior before the law is broken. This will be one of the key areas in
> future usage of policewomen and men, also, as police agencies move from
> the punitive to preventive approach in many areas . . . [The policewoman]
> is the ideal choice to work in crime prevention. (Horne, 1975, p. 3)

Those who promoted the crime prevention model in policing over the
crime control model argued that the hiring of more people of color and
women as police officers would facilitate improved police-community relations (Martin & Jurik, 1996). Most police executives were not enthusiastic
about putting women on patrol. However, those who wanted to lead the way
to a more humanistic or community-oriented style of policing often saw
women as presenting a more positive image of the police department and as
helping the police agency become more dedicated to service and police-community relations (Milton, 1972). Thus, even in the late twentieth century, the
motivation for police executives to hire women was still in part based on sexist stereotypes of women as more nurturing and caring.

The early 1970s marked an explosion of women into areas and duties of
police work from which they had been excluded. Women entered local, state,
and federal agencies of various sizes throughout the United States. The first
women were sworn in as agents with the Secret Service in 1971, the Federal
Bureau of Investigation in 1972, and the Military Police in 1973 (Horne,
1975). Hiring quotas and duty restrictions for women in a number of state
law enforcement agencies were gradually removed. Women began "to be
integrated into the patrol ranks in most major police departments in the
United States" (Grennan, 1993, p. 165)

In 1972, Car 47 in Indianapolis was assigned eight women police officers, so that there would be women on duty twenty-four hours a day, seven
days a week (Horne, 1975). Like many other agencies, however, the transformation in Indianapolis was not complete and still resembled an "experiment." By 1975, only 14 of the 74 policewomen employed by the department
worked on patrol. Most of them, including sergeants, were relegated to secre-
tarial and clerical duties.

Even among many of the agencies that allowed policewomen to go on patrol, quota systems remained in place, designating certain positions as policewomen jobs and limiting the number of women who could be hired. Most agencies did finally lower the hiring standards required for women to that of the same level as men (Horne, 1975). Pennsylvania became the first state police agency to allow women to perform the same duties as male officers (Feinman, 1994). Each of these advances was preceded by an experiment to see if women could do the job. By 1975, numerous police agencies began reporting the successful performance of women officers, even in "dangerous and potentially dangerous situations" (Horne, 1975, p. 24).

Studies were conducted as early as the 1970s to evaluate the "experiment" of assigning women officers to patrol duties. Most "concluded that men and women were equally capable of police patrol work" (Martin & Jurik, 1996, p. 55). Later studies suggested that female officers were less likely to perceive conflict situations as personal confrontations that challenged their abilities as a police officer (Hale & Bennett, 1995). The same research reported that women were less likely to discharge their weapon than their male partners. The researchers found no difference in women's probability of being injured.

Resistance to Women Police

Despite the fact that the effectiveness of women police was demonstrated repeatedly in research studies, many male police officers and police executives resented the full integration of women into the police department (Walker, 1992b; Grennan, 1993; Feinman, 1994). O. W. Wilson's textbook, *Police Administration* (long regarded as the standard on the subject of police management) presented a "blatantly anti-female viewpoint" (Walker, 1992b, p. 856). Although recognizing their potential value in working with juveniles, Wilson expressly stated that women are not qualified to head the juvenile unit, partly because men are "less likely to become irritable and overcritical under emotional stress" (p. 856).

Women faced overt and covert discrimination and hostility from rank-and-file officers as they were slowly integrated into patrol, usually on a token basis (Martin & Jurik, 1996). Many rank-and-file officers opposed assigning women to patrol, arguing that they did not have the physical size and strength to handle the job (Walker, 1999). The arguments were not based on fact, as the research discussed earlier indicated. Studies specifically designed to address the question of job performance consistently reported that women were just as effective as their male counterparts in the performance of their duties (Feinman, 1994). Many of the first women patrol officers were confronted with concerted efforts to make them fail or to leave police work altogether. The resistance faced by these pioneering women on patrol was "blatant, malicious, widespread, organized, and sometimes life-threatening" (Martin & Jurik, 1996, p. 68).

In numerous cases, male officers refused to train women properly, intentionally exposed them to danger, and even refused to provide backup for

women police officers in precarious situations. In other situations, male officers would condescendingly overprotect women officers to a point where they
were not allowed to learn to do the job independently. As a result, women
faced supervisor hostility, which often manifested itself in close and punitive
supervision. In many cities, wives of police officers organized protests against
women becoming patrol officers because they feared that their husbands
would be killed if paired with a woman partner or that women officers would
be a threat sexually (Fletcher, 1995).

Women police officers faced a unique dilemma. If they acted too "feminine," they were viewed as inadequate officers; at the same time, male police
officers resented women behaving like men (Martin & Jurik, 1996). Women
who chose to emphasize their femininity as a way of coping in a male-dominated environment tended to embrace the service aspect of policing. They
accepted a paternalistic bargain—conforming to the gender stereotypes of
"seductress, mother, pet, and helpless maiden in interactions with male officers" (p. 97). Women who chose "to gain acceptance by being more professional, aggressive, loyal, street-oriented, and macho" (p. 97) tended to
identify with the crime control model of policing. These women were often
not viewed as "real women." For example, displays of physical bravado by
women, similar to those expected from male police officers, were interpreted
as either overreacting or overcompensating, or the woman would be catego-
rized as a "dyke" or "bitch" (p. 97).

As women leaned in one direction or the other, divisions and antago-
nisms between women police officers sometimes emerged from resentment of
the others' choices. No matter which coping mechanism they chose, their
small numbers made women police officers highly visible. Thus, any of their
mistakes were exaggerated and attributed to their gender, rather than to their
individual abilities or experiences, as would be the case for male police officers who made mistakes. Those men who accepted and supported women as
police officers frequently faced being ostracized or ridiculed by the other
officers (Martin & Jurik, 1996).

Studies in the late 1980s and early 1990s continued to show that male
police officers and administrators resented women police officers, did not
trust them, and did not want to work with them as partners. While some of
these officers accepted the fact that women were going to remain in police
work, others expressed "their hostility by harassing them in all possible
ways" (Feinman, 1994, p. 105). Because of this lack of trust and male officers' expressed concerns about women in terms of strength and toughness,
women police officers must constantly prove themselves, particularly in reference to their "willingness to use force, to use their guns, and to shoot to kill if
necessary" (p. 105). Similar to the situation experienced by racial minorities,
overt discrimination by sex has been prohibited by law, but other forms of
subtle discrimination continue to slow progress (Schulz, 1995).

Police executives have often expressed the view that "women, for the most
part do not belong on patrol because of their lack of physical strength and their

inability to maintain an imposing presence in the face of challenges to police authority" (Grennan, 1993, p. 164). What is particularly important about this observation is that nothing is more important to the elimination of sexual harassment than a commitment by police leadership not to tolerate it (Gratch, 1995). Administrators must directly issue written policies that prohibit sexually harassing behaviors and these directives must be vigorously enforced. Those who deviate should be disciplined at all levels of the organization.

One of the factors that has greatly restricted promotions for women is that their techniques of conflict resolution do not match the masculine approach of achieving order through intimidation, crime fighting, and arrests. Thus, the devaluing of different styles of policing can lead to poor performance evaluations or perceptions that the person is not a good candidate for promotion (Grennan, 1993). "The literature on work performance clearly supports the proposition that women are as capable as men of performing patrol duties. However, the acceptance and advancement of women on patrol have been impaired by discrimination: subtle, overt, and covert" (Hale & Minniti, 1993, p. 179).

Compared to African Americans, women achieved leadership roles much more slowly. By 1993 only four women had been appointed chief of a major police department (Schulz, 1995). A study by the Police Foundation in 1991 found that only 3 percent of the supervisors in municipal police departments and only 1 percent of the state police supervisors were women. "Consequently, women are not part of the decision-making and control process, and they can do little to change the system" (Hale & Bennett, 1995, p. 49). A 1997 study by the National Center for Women and Policing (NCWP) shows substantial improvement in some of these numbers, but women still do not make up a large enough proportion of the command staff to impact policy. The NCWP study found that women still represent only 11.6 percent of the sworn officers in the United States, but they now possess 8.8 percent of supervisory positions ("Rank Objections," 1998).

Schultz (1995) reported that the promotion of women has been slowed in part because they have been less willing to sacrifice the hours and working conditions that allow them greater access to their family and because they are less likely to receive the choice assignments that most frequently lead to promotion. Although women are entering police work in increasing numbers, high attrition rates keep them at a small proportion of the police force (Hale & Bennett, 1995).

A Hostile Environment

The findings of the Christopher Commission (1991) demonstrated that women police officers continued to face a generally hostile environment at the onset of the 1990s. In the Los Angeles Police Department, 36 percent of white women officers, 34 percent of African-American women officers, and 27 percent of Latina officers interviewed stated that they had encountered gender discrimination. Many of the concerns of women police contained in the report identified continuous intimidation, sexist remarks, testing, verbal expressions of not being wanted, and not being judged based on ability.

> It appears that male officers do not overtly refuse to work with females but rather use subtle tactics such as not talking to them in the car or not providing them with information to help them learn the job. In addition, there were numerous cases described in which male officers deliberately orchestrated a fight, provoking the suspect to see how a female probationer would "handle herself." One male officer indicated "women should be able to handle the testing and not to be so sensitive and think it's harassment." (p. 83)

Two organizations that existed within the Los Angeles Police Department, "White Anglo Saxon Police" and "Men Against Women," demonstrate just how hostile the environment is for women and officers of color (Feinman, 1994, p. 110). While conducting interviews with LAPD officers, the Christopher Commission found that many of the male officers interviewed, regardless of race or rank, were "unaccepting of female officers" (p. 85).

LAPD Field Training Officers made the following remarks to the Christopher Commission:

> We work with many female officers, but only know one who was equal in ability to male officers. Women tend to be smart and good at writing reports, but weak and timid.

> Female police officers don't want to do anything but collect a paycheck.

> A lot of male officers prefer working with men over women. For me, it's a question of body strength. The department needs a more stringent height requirement.

> I know most officers have problems working with female officers and dislike working with them because they believe women don't have the physical stature to do the job.

Imagine being a woman recruit trained by an officer who has such preconceived ideas about women police officers in general.

Everything the female officer does is viewed through this prism of gender bias. Rank-and-file male police officers expressed these opinions:

> Female officers generally cannot back up officers.

> Female officers sometimes exacerbate the situation because they feel they need to assert themselves or escalate the potential for use of force.

If a woman officer decides not to use force when she could have (perhaps because there was a more effective way of handling the situation), her approach would be viewed as timid and would confirm the prejudices. If the female officer used force when it was unnecessary, it would likely be viewed as showing fear, overreacting, or being too emotional. The female patrol officer is in a "double bind." If she behaves as a strong, aggressive partner, she is perceived as a threat to the male partner's ego. If she exhibits more feminine or submissive behaviors, she is perceived as a threat to his safety and well-being. The officer may exhibit the same behavior as a male officer, but it will be interpreted to fit preconceived notions. The road to success is strewn with barriers of such prejudices. As is always the case with stereotypes, preconceived notions must be overcome before performances can be judged on merit alone. If the female officer complains about the double bind, she will be viewed as overly sensitive or emotional.

In addition to direct statements by male police officers describing their attitudes about women police, the Christopher Commission reviewed mobile digital terminal (MDT) transmissions sent from various LAPD police car computer terminals. Male officers repeatedly referred on MDT communications to their female counterparts with condescending or derogatory nicknames. MDT transmissions "revealed a constant stream of sexist comments and remarks with obvious sexual overtones" (p. 88). As we noted earlier, all these transmissions are supposed to be regularly monitored by the police supervisors, which suggests that such language and attitudes were either condoned or at least tolerated by police supervisors.

Even today "women officers must cope with gendered organizational policies and practices, hostile environments, and an occupational culture whose 'cult of masculinity' glamorizes violence and denigrates women" (Martin & Jurik, 1996, p. 49). One of the ways in which "policing remains associated with masculinity" is that "real" police work is defined as fighting crime by courageously subduing criminals with physical force (p. 72). Of course, this myth masks the reality that the vast majority of police work routinely involves restoring order through interpersonal skills rather than through bravado.

Despite abundant evidence to the contrary, most complaints about female officers by male officers concern the inability of women police officers to provide them with adequate physical protection. The real threat of women police officers, however, is to the macho crime fighter image (Martin & Jurik, 1996). If women perform successfully in this supposedly "masculine" occupation, their very presence threatens the male self-image. By doing work that has been traditionally labeled by society as "masculine," male police officers strengthen their gendered identity as men. Relying on a woman for assistance or backup weakens the image. Women police officers challenge the "definition of policing as men's work and police officers as masculine" (Martin & Jurik, 1996, p. 64).

Women are perceived as a threat to the group solidarity of police officers in that they impede traditional male bonding (Martin & Jurik, 1996). In many occupations that are perceived as dangerous, a special kind of bond or group solidarity forms. Traditionally, police work was male dominated and marked by high levels of suspicion of outsiders (Martin & Jurik, 1996). This machismo work culture contributed to a working environment that is frequently characterized by drinking, crude jokes, racism, and expressions of masculinity. The police squadroom has frequently been described as a "men's locker room" in terms of language and practical jokes, which often focus on women's bodies and the heterosexual exploits of the men (Martin & Jurik, 1996). Women cannot possibly participate on equal terms with the men, since they are the primary objects of discussion. Thus, they are never fully integrated into the social network.

Women police officers have to be especially careful in off-duty socializing, not only because these encounters, at least in the past, have had a "stag party" atmosphere, but also because of constant concerns about gossip and because of unique family responsibilities (Martin & Jurik, 1996, p. 70). The restricted socializing has a negative impact on women's career advancement in that it "deprives them of an important source of information and feedback, as well as the opportunity to make contacts, cultivate sponsors, and build alliances that contribute to occupational success" (p. 69). Although some women police officers may be accepted by the male officers on various levels, they can never be fully integrated into this hostile environment. If women are to stay in police work, particularly if their numbers and supervisory roles increase, either they must always be outsiders or this work culture must be transformed.

Interviews with women police officers have revealed that most of them have experienced sexual harassment on the job in the form of sexual propositions and threats, unwanted touching, sexual pranks or jokes, or the expression of anti-woman sentiments by their male counterparts. This harassment is an important source of stress for women police officers (Martin & Jurik, 1996). For African-American women, this stress is compounded by the fact that they are also excluded from full acceptance because of their race. Nonetheless, there are proportionally more women of color entering police work than white women (Feinman, 1994). Like the vast majority of poor women, African-American women have historically "worked in occupations involving physical manual labor and are not put off by this aspect of policing" (p. 108). African-American women have less often faced the problem of being overprotected by condescending males than white women, particularly physically attractive white women. On the other hand, they are more likely to be stereotyped as being sexually aggressive or lazy. African-American males initially tended to be more accepting of women as police officers, but they too usually expressed a preference for working with male partners.

After conducting numerous interviews with a wide cross-section of women police officers, Fletcher (1995, p. xix–xx) captured much of the interpersonal stress for women entering police work in the following passage:

> Policing is a club for men; this club has a strict hierarchy (white males first, then black and other minority males, then white females, black females, and finally, gay males); the club still operates in a culture of socializing and informal contacts impervious to legislation; people who are not wanted in the club may be harassed, ostracized, denied desired assignments, days off, shifts, or promotion; speaking or "grieving" (filing a grievance) about what happens within the club breaks the code and,

thereafter, breaks the officer. This is a club where harassers can get away with virtually anything because no one, male or female, can afford the punishments that follow ratting on a fellow cop. And this is a club where you can get killed if people don't like you.

Despite the generally hostile environment, the women interviewed by Fletcher (1995) reported many of the male police officers were supportive or at least neutral toward the idea of women as police officers. They frequently stated that once they had worked closely with male officers they were almost always able to win them over by demonstrating their skills, courage, and abilities. Whether the good opinion generated from a specific personal experience helps eliminate general stereotypes is another issue. Fletcher found that the boys' club mentality continues to permeate the system, accepting male police officers almost immediately while requiring women police to prove themselves over and over. In addition, the police culture continues to operate in such a way that the "lone jerk, the lone harasser, who can make any male or female officer's life miserable," is still supported or at least overlooked by the other officers (Fletcher, 1995, p. xx).

Conclusion

The potential impact of women police officers in police agencies is predicated on their unique perspective and the hope that new ways of viewing the role of the police will challenge the white male dominated police subculture. The impact has been diluted by the pressure on women police officers to be accepted. They have struggled to blend in, often resulting in behavior that replicates the dominant male perspective. As women moved into traditionally male police roles, they quickly adopted the crime-fighter, law enforcement mentality and behavior (Schulz, 1995).

Many early feminists struggled to demonstrate that women were "equal" to men, and the women currently being promoted to police executive positions usually built their careers on the belief in "gender-neutral" policing (Schulz, 1995, p. 381). Feminist criminologists have argued that legal gender-neutrality almost always means becoming male-like. In other words, as women entered the police force as regular patrol officers, they did not transform policing by merging their ideas, beliefs, and methods with those of the male police officers; rather, the woman police officer more typically attempted to think, believe, and act like a male police officer. While this adjustment was no doubt necessary to gaining acceptance in police departments in the 1970s and 1980s many feminist scholars now argue that women will only have a substantial impact on policing by "accentuating, rather than subordinating, their femininity" (p. 381).

Rather than a gender-neutral strategy, gender diversity should be valued and not shunned. Women who were selected by police agencies for hiring and for promotion were filtered through background investigations and personal interviews that rejected any candidates who "failed to express 'correct' masculine attitudes emphasizing toughness and aggressiveness" (Martin & Jurik, 1996, p. 61). Because of the powerful police socialization process, the integration of women into policing did not produce any radical changes in police strategy or method.

A number of studies comparing women and men police officers have concluded that "women may approach and handle situations differently from men, but men and women obtain the same outcomes" (Grennan, 1993, p. 173). The Christopher Commission (1991) reported that while 13 percent of the police officers in the Los Angeles Police Department were women, no woman was found to be among the 132 officers who were determined to be the worst offenders in shootings, in the use of force, and in personal complaints. Virtually every indicator used by the Commission indicated that female officers were not as likely to use excessive force as the male officer. Almost all of the female officers told the Christopher Commission that women police officers were "more communicative, more skillful at de-escalating potentially violent situations and less confrontational" (p. 84). In fact, the report noted that many officers, both male and female, stated that women police officers were better at averting potential violence because they were less personally challenged by suspects who defied them.

Police executives who wish to transform their police departments to fit a new style of community policing would do well to learn more classically feminine techniques at conflict resolution and communication. Elements of community policing have led to the re-conceptualization of what constitutes "real" police work. The focus on community partnerships, problem-solving, and conflict resolution have demanded that police officers rely more on interpersonal skills than on physical strength or armament to effectively do their job (Martin & Jurik, 1996).

Male police officers have been resistant to this transformation as being too "touchy-feely," demeaning, or feminine, but women police officers appear to have successfully engaged in such styles of policing. Studies comparing the policing styles of men and women found that "policewomen were typically seen as exercising more restraint in using their firearms and in managing family disturbances; as being more sensitive to citizens' needs and using a style of policing more consistent with community oriented policing; as sustaining disciplinary action less frequently; and as using less sick time" (Bartollas & Hahn, 1999, p. 287). Women police officers may well be able to lead the way in developing policing strategies that best reflect the goals and tactics of postmodern police.

13 Gay and Lesbian Police Officers

Gay and lesbian police officers confront a number of the same issues as other marginalized officers who are treated as outsiders by the white, heterosexual, male-dominated police occupational culture. However, the history and many specific issues for gay and lesbian police are unique. Gay male police officers have probably been in policing since its origin, but they could not openly declare that identity. Similarly, lesbian police officers have probably been in police work since the first women entered the force, but again could not openly acknowledge their sexual identity. The resistance to hiring gay and lesbian police officers is partly a result of heterosexist society's general condemnation of homosexuality. As seen in the previous chapter, policing is a heavily "gendered" occupation that is entangled with male police officers' perceptions of their own masculinity, which makes the issues of gay and lesbian police officers even more complicated.

Multiple Challenges

It also means that gay male and lesbian female police officers often face very different challenges. Lesbian officers appear to be more acceptable to the heterosexual male police officer than the gay male police officer, because the former pose no threat to the heterosexual police officer's self-image. The heterosexual male police officer may be able to accept that a lesbian police officer can successfully do the job because of the stereotypes that lesbians are women who are exceptionally masculine. In contrast, male officers interviewed in one study "did not view gay males as being 'masculine' and therefore felt that they could not rely on them for 'backup' in dangerous situations" (Shusta et al., 1995, p. 55).

In interviews with gay and lesbian police officers, Meers (1998) found that a number of lesbian police officers agreed that they have less trouble being accepted than gay men. One lesbian police officer suggested that "there's this bizarre idea that a woman that's a lesbian is somehow one of the guys. A gay officer is more of a threat to the whole macho mystique." In fact, many lesbian officers told Meers that they faced greater obstacles because of their female gender than because of their sexual orientation. In addition, many heterosexual men who are repulsed by the imagery of two men having sex may find the picture of two women having sex erotic or sexually arousing (Leinen, 1993). One gay police officer explained the dilemma to Meers (1998) as follows: "When you talk to straight men, if they think of two men kissing or making love, they get disgusted to the point where they're ready to throw up . . . If it's two women, they think it's a turn-on" (p. 30).

Stereotypes about gay males depict them as not being "real men," as being exceptionally feminine, or physically weak.

> Of all the occupations seemingly antithetical to homosexuality perhaps none is more so than law enforcement, a profession that traditionally symbolizes the essence of manliness. Cops are expected to present an aura of toughness and aggressiveness. They are expected to demonstrate courage, bravery, and confidence. Above all male cops are expected to avoid the appearance of femininity . . . gay men are thought to possess traits (e.g., insecurity, effeminacy, and oversensitivity) that prevent them from carrying out police work and to lack the emotional requirements that cops have come to believe will protect them from the dangers inherent in policing, such as courage, bravery, and loyalty to their fellow officers. (Leinen, 1993, p. xi)

If the gay man can successfully do the job, then it is a serious challenge to the heterosexual male police officer who attempts to define his own sense of manhood by working in a traditionally masculine or "macho" occupation. The stereotypes about gay men obscure the fact that they are as likely to be "masculine" as they are to be "feminine" in the areas that masculinist conceptions of police (such as physical strength and aggressiveness) deem important.

Coming Out

On November 22, 1981, while testifying before a New York City Council committee in favor of a gay rights bill, Sergeant Charles Cochrane became the first police officer to openly announce in a public forum that he was gay "and proud of it" (Leinen, 1993, p. 2). What was particularly courageous about Cochrane's statement was that it was made at a time when such a revelation was sufficient cause, throughout most of the police agencies in the United States, to deny a police candidate employment or even to fire a police officer currently on the job. For example, the Los Angeles Police Department (LAPD) circulated a departmental memorandum in 1975 that "confirmed that homosexuality was an absolute bar to employment" (Christopher Commission, 1991, p. 89). The LAPD did not prohibit such discrimination until May 17, 1991.

The Risks for Employment

At the time of Sergeant Cochrane's revelation, the Atlanta Police Department would not hire a police candidate if their background investigation "indicated homosexuality" (Leinen, 1993, p. 12). In the state of New Jersey until 1989, police officers could be fired simply because they were homosexual. The following statements indicate there were serious consequences even in the 1990s for gay and lesbian police officers who wanted to be honest about their sexuality: "Homosexual police officers are perceived to be the most marginalized of all police minority groups. This marginality is so extreme that in most police departments 'coming out' would likely be a 'kiss of death' to an officer's career in policing" (Bartollas & Hahn, 1999, p. 329). As of 1991 the Chicago Police Department, with a force of 12,000 officers, did not one have one officer who had publicly announced that she or he was gay (Leinen, 1993). Up until 1993, the Dallas Police Department "systematically refused to hire gays under the pretext of the state's penal law, which criminalizes certain homosexual conduct" (p. 11). In 1992, a twenty-year veteran of the Federal Bureau of Investigation was fired when it was discovered that he was gay (Shusta et al., 1995). As of 1993, a full eleven years after Sergeant Cochrane's announcement, "most law enforcement agencies did not knowingly hire or retain homosexuals" (p. 52).

Personal Risks

Sergeant Cochrane's statement also braved the vast majority of police officers who were openly hostile to homosexuals and their imagined lifestyle. A study conducted in the 1960s found that the police ranked homosexuals among "the most disliked categories of people." Another study in 1978 found that 20 percent of the California police officers interviewed stated that they would resign from their police department if it hired homosexuals (Bartollas & Hahn, 1999). When attending the New York City Gay Pride Parades in 1987 and 1988, in which members of the Gay Officers Action League (GOAL) marched, Leinen (1993) observed on-duty police officers react in a variety of ways from "intense contempt to disgust to turning away to just plain curiosity" (p. 43). The responses were easily overheard and seen by closeted and openly gay officers, as well as citizen participants and observers of the parade.

Many of the gay police officers interviewed by Leinen stated that they believed that many of the homophobic attitudes held by heterosexual officers, aside from their concern about AIDS, are primarily based on "the belief that gay sexual relationships were either 'sick,' 'sinful,' or 'immoral'" (p. 117). Immediately following a ceremony in September 1997, in which Anthony Crespo became the first openly gay police officer to receive the NYPD Medal of Valor for heroism, another police officer returned a medal to the president of the Gay Officers Action League (GOAL) which was presented to him by GOAL for his bravery (Meers, 1998). A board member of the officer's union stated that the officer said that "his wife and children felt humiliated" by his receiving the award from a gay police officer association (Meers, 1998, p. 26).

"Nearly all gay and lesbian cops have stories to tell about their own experiences with homophobia. The tales range from playful ribbing to the crassest

kind of harassment imaginable" (Meers, 1998, p. 28). Sometimes the discrimination becomes life-threatening, as claimed by an officer who is taking the
Miami Police Department to court after his fellow officers refused to come to
his assistance when he requested emergency backup on five separate occasions (Meers, 1998).

Some might wonder why gay and lesbian people would choose police
work when it is such a hostile environment. According to interviews conducted by Leinen (1993), motivations for gays to become police officers were
not much different than those for women and persons of color; the reasons
are primarily economic. While a number of reasons were given, the most frequent included the relatively high income, job security, good benefits, pen-
sions, and opportunity for career advancement (Leinen, 1993). Because
policing is a civil service job, it attracts members of racial minority groups,
women, and the poor. People who want to avoid the overt discrimination of
the private sector and who want to achieve some social mobility from the
lower and working classes are particularly attracted to the civil service nature
of police work. For a substantial number of the officers, community service
was also a very important factor, usually in terms of helping to prevent crime.

The Occupational Climate

The Christopher Commission (1991) interviewed a number of gay and lesbian officers who "recounted stories about harassment of suspected homosexual officers and about the daily patter of slurs and jokes concerning 'faggots,'
'dykes,' and 'queers'" (p. 90). Nearly all of the gay and lesbian police officers
and about ten percent of the field training officers who testified before the
Christopher Commission said that 'gay-looking' suspects are regularly subjected to derogatory comments about their presumed sexual orientation (p. 90).
The Commission reported the following examples of Mobile Digital Terminal
(MDT) transmissions that appeared to confirm many of these statements:

> "Just finished writing 4 tickets to some poo buts"

> "Did you check your fruits at the part . . . I hope you watered them . . ."
> "I figured how to get rid of them . . . Im sending in a bunch of naked
> girls, that will scare them away . . ."

> "I'll c u at the County Jail bun-boy . . ."
> "If I was a bun-boy you'd be asking to sleep over my house homo"

> "Houston PD has a new chief—Elizabeth Watson 40 yrs old . . ."
> "I bet that's going over reeeeeaaalll good with the troops dude . . . they
> have some dyke bleeding heart for a mayor . . ."

The fact that such transmissions flow so freely on official channels of communication indicates that the hostile environment for gay and lesbian police
officers in police departments ripples throughout the ranks of supervision and
management.

The investigation of the Los Angeles Police Department by the Christopher Commission (1991) found that not only were many of the individual officers hostile toward homosexuals, the hostility was condoned if not encouraged by the department's administrators. In 1988, a Los Angeles Police Department "background investigator told a Central Division watch commander that he had identified several 'faggots' in his applicant pool and was searching for reasons to disqualify them" (p. 88). The Commission discovered that the "most recent graduating class reported that they were required, as part of the application process, to provide the name of at least one member of the opposite sex with whom they were involved romantically" (p. 90). Until 1991, the psychological exam administered to LAPD applicants included the question, "Are you attracted to members of your own sex?" (p. 90). At a time when other major law enforcement agencies were actively seeking to improve relations with gays and lesbians, LAPD Chief Gates "banned off-duty officers from wearing uniforms at police information booths during street fairs in neighborhoods populated by gays" (Shusta et al., 1995).

Many individual high-ranking police officials also voiced direct opposition to the hiring of gay police officers, often because of the concern that hiring them would undermine the camaraderie and morale of police officers (Leinen, 1993). In direct opposition to Houston's official hiring policies, one deputy chief of the Houston Police Department likened the hiring of two gay men as civilian instructors at the police academy to "thieves, prostitutes, and narcotic addicts teaching classes on their activities" (p. 10).

A lesbian was denied employment with the Dallas Police Department because she admitted during a lie detector test that she had sexual relations with another woman. The police chief stated in 1992 that "police officers can't choose to ignore the laws we don't support. We have to support all the laws, and as long as [sodomy] is against the law, we can't hire someone who acknowledges violating the law" ("Dallas PD," 1992, p. 3). The city of Dallas fought the lawsuit all the way to the Texas State Supreme Court, where the candidate won her case in 1993. When the department was ordered by the court to remove all references to one's sexual orientation from the candidate screening process, one of the City Council members responded by saying that "to accept or condone immoral conduct is reprehensible for any city. . . . This issue is much bigger than homosexuals serving in the Police Department. It's about right and wrong" (p. 6).

Society's Opposition

In addition, to individual police officers and police executives, many police, civic, and religious organizations are also very hostile toward homosexuals, particularly in reference to them becoming police officers. Even the International Association of Chiefs of Police (IACP) argued in the late 1970s and early 1980s that homosexuals were not good choices as candidates for police officers, insinuating that they were not "stable, trustworthy, or morally principled" (Leinen, 1993, p. 8). The *Chief-Leader*, a civil service newspaper, editorialized that the NYPD should continue to discriminate against homosexuals because it should not "publicly recognize immoral behavior" (p. 8). Police union and fraternal organization leaders in some cities have "vociferously opposed hiring gay cops" (p. 8), and New York was no exception. When the NYPD initiated a program to hire gays in 1984, the head of the Patrolman's Benevolent Association (PBA) publicly stated that he was going to fight the program because homosexuals "could not hold the dignity and image of a police officer" (p. 8). Fierce opposition to the recruitment of homosexuals also erupted among the NYPD's religious-fraternal organizations, including the Jewish Shomrin Society, the Irish Emerald Society, and the Catholic Holy Name Society of the NYPD.

Strong opposition to the recruitment of gays was expressed by the leaders of religious groups outside of the NYPD, such as the Representatives of the Archdiocese of New York, the Central Rabbinical Congress and the Knights of Columbus (Leinen, 1993). In speaking out against a law that would forbid discrimination based on sexual orientation, Rabbi Hillel Handler of the Union of Orthodox Rabbis publicly stated that it "attacks the moral foundations of this city" (p. 10). In contrast the police chiefs of the San Diego Police Department and the El Cajon Police Department in California actually severed their departments' longtime relationship with the Boy Scouts of America in its Law Enforcement Explorer Scout program in 1992 because the Boy Scouts banned homosexuals from their organization ("In Rift" 1992). Shortly after being voted "Police Officer of the Year" by the El Cajon Chamber of Commerce, police officer Chuck Merino announced that he was gay. The Boy Scouts removed him as director of the Explorer Post. The national spokesperson for the Boy Scouts of America said, "We have always reflected the expectations of mainstream American families. . . . We don't believe that homosexuals provide a role model that's consistent with these expectations. So we won't allow for the registration of homosexuals as members or as leaders in our organization" (p. 14).

Personal and Community Motivations to Brave Discovery

In various studies, homosexual police officers have expressed considerable stress about the constant fear of being discovered (Bartollas & Hahn, 1999). Most of the gay police officers interviewed by Leinen (1993) feared being exposed and becoming the victim of discrimination and harassment by homophobic police officers and supervisors. They also feared that they would be ostracized by their fellow police officers and that "they could find themselves abandoned when they most needed help (for example, if they called for a backup in a potentially life-and-death situation)" (p. 27). One police officer told Meers (1998) that he did not reveal his sexuality because "I don't want to put myself in the position when one day I'm relying on one of these deputies to back me up and they don't come because I'm gay" (p. 32). Some of the gay and lesbian officers interviewed by Leinen (1993) were more concerned about their families discovering their secret than their co-workers.

Even after Sergeant Cochrane's declaration, the organizing of the Gay Officers Action League (GOAL), the passage of departmental policies forbidding discrimination based on one's sexuality, and the direct recruitment of gays by the NYPD, the overwhelming majority of gay and lesbian police officers choose not to reveal their sexual orientation. Gay men reported that, at times, they took extreme measures to appear particularly masculine or "macho" to deflect suspicion. In other cases, they would create elaborate fictional personal histories or stories about their sexual activities and relationships (Leinen, 1993).

The "totally closeted" gay police officers in the NYPD were largely successful in hiding their sexuality from their heterosexual colleagues and often even from their homosexual ones. Many of these gay police officers had to be very careful as they moved through the gay community as private citizens, because of the fear of being stopped, searched, and identified by the police. They were acutely aware of police tactics in these areas, and they frequently would not carry any police identification. Gay police reported that they were very careful not to take any kind of police action when in these settings, even though there were high levels of victimization by predators who viewed gay people as easy targets to rob or assault. Revealing one's identity as a cop in the gay community was also problematic. There was a danger of being ostracized and an increased risk of one's sexual identity being publicly exposed. The stress from worry about being labeled was very high in both the on- and off-duty worlds.

Given these risks, why do gay and lesbian police officers "come out?" Most gay police officers do not leap from the polar extremes of being closeted to public announcements. The vast majority who do come out do so in incremental stages and do not necessarily progress all the way to being public. Gay police officers can struggle to hide their sexuality, tentatively allow their sexuality to become visible, openly declare their homosexuality, or state it in a public forum if the opportunity arises (Leinen, 1993). Many officers "come out" only tentatively at work. They do not announce their sexuality publicly or directly, but they offer clues or suggestions about being gay. These clues may simply be acts of frustration or they may be provided specifically to lead to exposure in a more gradual fashion. Leinen (1993) believed that these actions were most commonly motivated by "the officer's frustration with and unwillingness to continue living a lie" (p. 72). The gay officer may also confide in a partner or a few co-workers, which once again helps to relieve some of the stress of always having to act like someone they are not. Others reported believing that it is important morally and practically to be open and honest with one's partner and friends. Gay officers carefully choose their confidants—people who are likely be understanding and trustworthy.

The next level in the coming out of a gay police officer involves announcing one's sexuality in a more public forum, particularly throughout the station (Leinen, 1993). Some officers openly present their homosexuality by bringing a same-sex partner to social event or through the wearing of various insignia, such as a rainbow flag or pink triangle, which identifies their membership in a gay police officers' association or their support for gay rights. Others decide to march in the annual Gay Pride Parade with GOAL members to publicly announce their homosexuality. Many of the same motives for the tentative exposure were observed in the situation of full disclosure, such as the desire to "reduce stress and tension associated with having to maintain a constant pretense of heterosexuality" (p. 98).

The motivation for gay police officers to come out was often focused on improving their own personal working conditions and private lives. "The act of coming out for gay and lesbian officers is primarily about being able to be as open about their personal lives as their straight counterparts" (Meers, 1998, p. 32). Some gay police officers come out in an effort to reduce the stress of confronting homophobic remarks. In other words, they hope that once other officers discover their sexual orientation, they will not feel as free to make derogatory comments. One officer revealed that he decided to come out after a friend (one of his fellow officers) said to him, "Look at the faggot. All faggots should die of AIDS." They also anticipate qualifications as a good cop will help reduce negative stereotypes about homosexuals and will help trigger greater acceptance.

Some reasons may be more community-oriented, particularly for those who use a very public forum to announce their sexual orientation. Officers reported the positive impact of coming out on improving the quality of policing received by members of the gay community. Many gay police told Leinen (1993) that they overlooked discrimination or abusive treatment of citizens by homophobic police officers because of their intense fear of being exposed. "Coming out" allowed them to take action in incidents of discrimination against gays. In fact, their open presence on the force sends a warning to other police officers that assaults and verbal attacks against gays may be reported.

However, the intensity of concerns about the consequences of revealing one's identity means that many gays remained closeted. Thus, the potential for quality policing in the gay community is severely restricted. Similarly, the goal of hiring gay police officers to improve the quality of policing in the gay community is not likely to be reached if the officers choose to remain invisible. Some members of GOAL have claimed that "some of the hard-won gains by gays are being watered down by the persistent reluctance of most gay cops to step forward, be counted, and then be *heard*" (p. 15).

The Recruitment of Gay And Lesbian Police

Although many cities continued to reject candidates precisely because they were homosexual, as of 1991 ten police departments in the United States had initiated programs to recruit homosexuals: Seattle; San Francisco; Portland, Oregon; Philadelphia; New York City; Minneapolis; Madison, Wisconsin; Los Angeles; Boston; Atlanta (Leinen, 1993). The Milwaukee Police

Department initiated a recruitment program for gays and lesbians in 1992, however, it did so very quietly (Shusta et al., 1995). Despite concerns about police morale, "researchers reported that urban police departments adopting nondiscrimination statutes and actively recruiting homosexual officers have not reported any drop-off in morale within the organization" (p. 54).

The motivations of the gay community and the incentives of the police departments to recruit gay and lesbian police officers bear a striking resemblance to those that triggered efforts to recruit African-American police officers. The gay community had long experienced both underpolicing and overpolicing, with the police failing to protect them from numerous hate crimes while often subjecting homosexuals to oppressive treatment and harassment (Leinen, 1993). For example, both homosexual and heterosexual officers testified before the Christopher Commission (1991) that LAPD officers were "far more aggressive in enforcing minor infractions against suspected homosexuals than against presumed heterosexuals" (p. 90).

At the same time, many of these officers also stated that many of their fellow officers treated "lightly" calls in which the complainant or victim was a presumed homosexual, particularly if the call involved a domestic dispute between gay men (p. 91). "One gay officer described instances in which he witnessed officers actively dissuade victims of 'gay bashings' from pressing charges against the perpetrators by threatening to arrest the victim and place them in the same cells as the perpetrators" (p. 91). Sometimes the allegations involved excessive use of force against homosexuals, particularly gay men, by the police officers themselves. One police officer stated: "It's easier to thump a faggot than an average Joe. Who cares?" (p. 91). According to another officer, "gay people tend to get beaten more frequently than straight people because 'they love it.'" According to Leinen (1993), "the police, who should have been at the forefront of the fight against bias-related crime directed against homosexuals, often engaged in, or at least condoned, verbal and physical attacks against gays" (p. 7).

In the 1980s, as gay and lesbian people became more organized and more militant in their struggle for better treatment by a heterosexist and homophobic society, many adopted strategies borrowed directly from the civil rights movement (Leinen, 1993). Much like members of the African-American community, members of the gay community made direct appeals to police departments to stop discriminatory police practices. When they did not receive a favorable response, they often took to the streets in protest or went to the courts for legal remedies (Leinen, 1993). Unlike the federal government and national politics, "local police departments are feeling the heat from city councils and progressive mayors to be more responsive to the communities they protect" (Meers, 1998, p. 26).

Members of the gay community organized to demand that the police be reflective of the entire community. In addition to insisting on training programs to sensitize police officers to hate crimes, gay bashing, police harassment, and other police-related problems in the gay community, numerous gay organizations demanded that the police departments directly recruit gay and lesbian police officers (Leinen, 1993). It was hoped that the more diverse police departments would take the complaints of gays and lesbians more seriously and that officers would not harass, intimidate, or physically abuse them simply because of their sexual orientation (Leinen, 1993).

In response to intense pressure and criticism, some police departments did begin to actively recruit gay and lesbian candidates as police officers, while others simply stopped excluding candidates solely on the basis of their sexual orientation. Some city governments came to view the inclusion of gays on the police force as a way to enhance its legitimacy within the gay community (Leinen, 1993). Even more importantly, however, the purposeful recruitment of gay and lesbian police officers, or at least the removal of discriminatory hiring barriers, was a response to the growing political power of groups demanding a greater say in the policies and operations of their police departments. For example, the first agency to actively recruit gay police officers was the San Francisco Police Department, which had an active gay community with substantial economic and political power. They represented an unusually high proportion of the population, and they were organized and active in local politics.

The initiative for the NYPD to recruit gay and lesbian police officers was launched largely through pressure from the Gay Officers Action League (GOAL). Sergeant Cochrane helped to create the organization and served as president. GOAL was "a movement for the acceptance of homosexuals in the New York City police and elsewhere" (Bartollas & Hahn, 1999, p. 329). Similar gay police organizations were organized in a number of large cities: Los Angeles; San Francisco; Denver; Seattle; San Diego; and Chicago. In 1987, the Boston Police Department began recruiting gays in direct "response to pressure from local gay activist groups" such as the Boston Lesbian and Gay Political Alliance (Leinen, 1993, p. 12). These groups testified in public hearings to 135 cases of physical or verbal attacks, some by police officers themselves. At the time of the hearings, both the activists and the police agreed that not one member of the Boston Police Department was openly gay or lesbian.

Impact of Gay and Lesbian Police Officers

For gay and lesbian police officers, the key to having a dramatic impact on police behavior and policy appears to rest on their ability to become visible members of the gay community:

> By taking no action when an assault is committed upon or a degrading comment is made to a gay by another cop, the closeted gay officer fails by default to protect the interests of the larger gay community . . . It is only when individual gay officers choose to take deliberate and decisive steps against police homophobia that any real progress can be made toward establishing support for the police. But this cannot occur until a more significant sector of the gay police population decides to come out of the closet. (Leinen, 1993, p. 15)

The vast majority of gay and lesbian police officers who come out are concentrated in large urban police departments, which represent only a small percentage of the police departments in the country (Meers, 1998). It is believed that these large urban departments are more likely to tolerate or accept diversity among officers than the more rural or suburban police departments. Most gay and lesbian police officers are careful to "prove their mettle," establish themselves as good police officers, and become "entrenched in the system, with allies" to support them before they let their sexual orientation be known (p. 32). Those who reveal their sexual orientation often realized substantial benefits. One officer stated, "so many things have happened for the better since I've come out. It's hard to look back now and see how many years I was so miserable." The liaison officer between the police department and the gay community in Los Angeles reported, "being openly gay allows me to stand in the middle and let both sides come together" (p. 28). In cities with large gay populations, police chiefs often find it preferable to have openly gay cops work on gay-bashing incidents and domestic violence cases between same-sex partners.

On a community level, having a substantial number of police officers disclose their homosexuality would send a positive and undistorted message that the police department reflects all members of society, including gays and lesbians (Leinen, 1993). If police executives want to improve the quality of law enforcement in the gay community and to gain the support of the members of that community, it is essential that they do much more than just eliminate hiring barriers or recruit a few gay police officers. They must ensure that their agency's work environment is not hostile to gay and lesbian police officers and that there are no negative repercussions for such police officers to clearly and publicly declare their sexuality.

If the state does not have a nondiscrimination policy, then the local government should pass one. If the local government does not pass such legislation, then the chief executive of the police agency should construct clear policies that prohibit harassment and discrimination. Violations of that policy should result in substantial discipline. Specifically recruiting gay and lesbian police officers can be a powerful mechanism for police officers to improve the quality of policing in the gay community, to break down stereotypes within and outside the police department, and to achieve greater legitimacy for the police in the eyes of the gay community.

Conclusion

Throughout much of U.S. history women and racial minorities have been denied participation in the political process. They have seized whatever means were available to shape the law and its enforcement to serve their interests more fairly. An important part of these efforts included achieving representation in the primary apparatus of social control—the police. While women were particularly concerned about the moral and physical exploitation of young women and girls by men, African Americans and other racial minorities attempted to gain representation on the police force to improve the quality of policing in their communities. The gay community in the 1980s and 1990s, much like racial minorities, hoped that having more openly gay police officers would lead to a decline in both overpolicing and underpolicing in their community.

Marginalized populations and marginalized police have sought to improve both the quality of their personal lives and that of their communities. Individuals worked to become police officers and then hoped to achieve full integration into the departments. Their appointments meant an opportunity for personal advancement and independence. Women, persons of color, and gays and lesbians believed that becoming police officers would improve their position in society and their ability to have an impact on the law and its enforcement. Choosing to work for the social control apparatus that was frequently oppressive and abusive to members of their communities often meant that these police officers found themselves alienated from both worlds. They have had to overcome numerous barriers and workplace hostility to achieve their goal of integration.

The integration of marginalized groups into policing has had some unanticipated results. To be accepted by the white male majority, many marginalized police officers have worked hard to look and act just like their white male counterparts. This phenomenon was largely shaped by the extensive recruitment, selection, training, and socialization process that occurs in policing. These processes have a tendency to force all police officers into a similar mold, regardless of their ethnic, gender, or personal backgrounds.

On the other hand, the mere presence of women, persons of color, and openly gay police officers is likely to have an impact on the level of overt racism, sexism, and heterosexism exhibited by the police. There may be some reality to the concern that the integration of these marginalized groups may undermine the camaraderie among police officers. Diversity may in fact undermine the police subculture that is so supportive of the cynicism, racism, sexism, gay bashing, and police brutality that has characterized much of the history of the police in the United States. Particularly as marginalized groups increase in number and rise to the supervisory and policy-making level, they may be able to effect qualitative change in police strategies and tactics that are particularly offensive to racial minorities, women, and homosexuals.

The structural constraints fundamental to the police institution appear to remain fully intact despite these changes in police personnel. Political officials and police executives who enacted changes in hiring were not necessarily interested in improving the fairness or quality of law enforcement in marginalized communities, since most had to be forced through public pressure or through legal action to appoint members of these traditionally marginalized groups as police officers. The two primary explanations for the eventual integration center around social control, the fundamental mission of the police. First, it was hoped that marginalized police officers would be able to enhance social control through their unique knowledge and connection with others like themselves, making them more effective at enforcing the law in their communities. Second, the hiring of members of marginalized groups as police officers was a strategy to obtain greater legitimacy in the eyes of marginalized people. Police executives wanted to obtain greater legitimacy for their police officers primarily because in a democratic society it is essential to have the support of the people to be effective and efficient in the enforcement of the law and in maintaining the social order.

The question arises whether the multicultural transformation of the police reflects fundamental change or is simply a part of the rhetoric of postmodern policing—producing a new image of police while retaining the central mission of social control and current relations of power. Claims that the police should be advocates for social reform collide with the structural foundation of the police as the primary agency charged with the maintenance of the current social order.

Afterword
Police and Society

We have attempted in this book to approach the subject of police and society from the point of view that police organizations and tactics do not simply spring forth from the minds of police executives or social theorists. We have also been guided by our view that the society in which the police operate is made up of many social, political, and economic relations that have played key roles in the historical development of the police and their policing strategies. An important assumption throughout has been that, while the police play a critical role in maintaining the social order by regulating the activities of individuals in society, members of society simultaneously shape the police practices utilized to maintain that social order.

The key to understanding the relationship between the police and society is to think critically about the role of power and interests. For example, descriptions of the police and what they do are often presented from a white, middle-class, suburban male perspective, with the police presented as neutral enforcers of the law. Although discussions of the role of the police officer as crime fighter are now often peppered with references to police as problem solvers, public servants, or even community organizers, the assumption that their efforts are designed to serve the general interests of all members of our society remains virtually unchallenged.

The fact is that the police primarily serve the interests of those groups and individuals in society who benefit most from current social, political, and economic arrangements. Certainly those at the highest levels of wealth and power in our society have the most to gain from the maintenance of the current social order. Just as certainly, those at the bottom rungs of society have the least to gain from things remaining as they are. The rest of us must determine for ourselves whether the role of the police in our society is one we can live with—both materially and morally. Police practices are, therefore, not class-neutral in a class society. Neither are they race-neutral or gender-neutral in a racist, sexist, and heterosexist society. Whether or not the actions of police appear neutral depends a great deal upon our point of view. In this book, we have tried to make it easier to see the police from different vantage points.

Power and Interests

Historically and currently, the relationship between the police and society is very closely tied to racial power and interests. Our book has focused largely on African Americans because their history in the United States has been so integrally connected with the history of police in this society. As we have seen, the very first municipal policing agencies were constructed primarily to regulate the activities of African people and to catch runaway slaves. Throughout most of the history of the police in the United States, the mission to maintain the social order and to enforce the laws of the land has resulted in the systematic and brutal repression of descendants of African people living in this country. African Americans have long struggled against this repression with whatever means available to them in an effort to transform the police. In other words, the police have long served the interests of White America by helping to preserve a system based on political, economic, and social white supremacy at the direct expense of people of color. White people, as the dominant racial group, constructed, maintained, and condoned a police force that served their personal interests. Despite great obstacles, African Americans and other people of color worked to shape the police to serve interests other than those of the majority.

African Americans were often very limited in their access to the power required to reconstruct the police, and consequently the entire social structure based on white supremacy. Africans had the least amount of power during the period of racial slavery. Thus, their options and their influence were very limited. Even so, African slaves resisted their repression in creative ways, sometimes with armed force. When racial slavery came to an end, the ideology of white supremacy continued to characterize the political and economic system. Freed Africans struggled to increase their political power, with varying levels of success, in order to transform the social system, which continued to work against their interests.

When they secured the power to vote, African Americans utilized the political process to influence politicians, to change racist laws, and to improve the quality of policing in African-American communities. When they gained access to the courts, African Americans also utilized this process to weaken racial oppression. Although the system of racial oppression left the vast majority of African Americans in a seriously economically disadvantaged situation, African Americans have frequently organized their efforts to utilize their economic buying power to initiate changes in the racist society. When political and economic efforts were unsuccessful, African Americans took their struggle to the streets through protests, civil disobedience, or physical confrontation.

The police, as the primary tool of racial oppression, were often the main target of these rebellions and the focus of much of the social reform that followed. The primary concerns among African Americans regarding the police have long involved both overpolicing and underpolicing in their communities. As soon as white Europeans gained physical and political control of the land which is now the United States, they created laws and law enforcement agencies that maintained white supremacy through the racial oppression of people of color. As the primary enforcement arm of this racist society, the police were heavily involved both officially and informally in the systematic and often brutal oppression of African Americans and other people of color.

Today, many African Americans accuse the police, both collectively and individually, of overpolicing. They observe that the police more aggressively regulate their freedom of movement, treat them more harshly, and are more likely to stop, frisk, and arrest them than they do white people. Underpolicing is also a direct result of the thrust to secure white supremacy. Laws and law enforcement agencies were formed that failed to protect the rights and freedoms of people of color. Today, many people of color including African Americans accuse the police, the criminal justice system, and the government of failing to take the victimization of people of color as seriously as they do white victimizations. The solution to both overpolicing and underpolicing is to change the fundamental role of police in society as we change society.

Compared to African Americans, white women and women of color in the United States have experienced both similarities and radical differences in their interactions with the police and the entire criminal justice system. During various periods of U.S. history, women have organized their efforts to improve the quality of policing. Women have expressed concerns about both overpolicing and underpolicing. White middle- and upper-class women first became involved in reforming the criminal justice system when they believed that women and girls were being treated too harshly and oppressively by men who operated the agencies within this system. Although women lacked official access to the political process throughout most of the United States, they used whatever influence or power that they had to promote change. These women organized to develop a number of civic groups and social movements that focused on temperance, sexual morality, and other social reforms. Sometimes these middle- and upper-class women were able to wield some economic power by themselves or through their husbands. At other times, they used the power of religious influence to motivate social change. Frequently these efforts were connected to various forms of social protests and demonstrations from suffrage marches to dismantling saloons.

At other times in the history of the United States, women's organizations struggled against underpolicing. Many women believed that the police were not taking their victimization seriously enough. As late as the 1980s and 1990s, women have formed such groups as Mothers Against Drunk Driving (MADD) to push the police to be more assertive in their efforts to catch and prosecute drunk drivers. They also organized to publicize domestic violence, in order to motivate the police to treat these assaults as criminal offenses and to arrest those who commit them. Women have used a variety of methods to motivate the police, but it was not until they received access to the political process that they have been able to consistently chip away at the systematic discrimination against women that has characterized U.S. society since its inception.

Gays and lesbians make up one more minority group that has emerged as a political force in many areas of the country in order to fight against systematic official and unofficial discrimination against them based on their sexual orientation. The success of gays and lesbians in altering legal discrimination and improving the quality of policing in their communities has come when they have been able to organize and wield a certain amount of economic and political power on the local level. However, such organizing simultaneously involves a risk. Unlike people of color and women, homosexuals can hide their minority status if they choose to do so. Organizing to secure civil rights means revealing an orientation that often encounters discrimination. Homosexuals are still waging battles against overt legal discrimination, a status already won by women and people of color.

An important strategy for any group in the struggle to eliminate overt legal discrimination and to improve the quality of policing has been to achieve a presence within the government and in police departments. Their right to vote affords the opportunity to support political candidates sympathetic to one's cause and to place candidates in policy-making positions. Activists have pushed political officials to eliminate barriers and quotas that have long excluded people of color, women, and homosexuals from serving as full-fledged police officers. Frequently they initiated legal action to secure their rights and to obtain representation in police agencies. None of these groups has been as successful as African Americans in obtaining representation at the highest levels of local governments. All these efforts have had a major impact on reducing overt forms of racial and gender discrimination by the police. However, the potential of these reforms to radically change policing is substantially limited by the structural conditions and inherent contradictions located in the foundations of policing in a class society.

Class

One theme that permeates this entire book, but has not been addressed as a separate topic, is economic class. Subordinate groups in society can transform the institutions that serve the interests of the dominant economic class only when they are able to secure enough political and economic power to do so. If it were possible to peel away the racial and gender barriers to equality, what would be laid bare is class power relations that continue to limit radical social change. Bittner (1980) described three structural characteristics of policing that help us understand the inherent contradictions of policing in a class society. First, police work is a "tainted profession," meaning that police forces were granted the legitimate use of violence in an effort to prevent the arbitrary use of violence by the public. In other words, in order to preserve the rights of certain citizens, police officers must choose to restrict the rights of others. Cultural diversity awareness training cannot change the fact that police officers serve the specific social control function of repressing certain activities and restricting freedoms.

The second characteristic of police work Bittner (1980) identified was that it is necessarily crude. The nature of police work requires police officers to reduce complex human conflicts and profound legal and moral questions to simple decisions. Police work involves a significant amount of crisis intervention, which requires definitive decision making and quick action. The removal of racist and sexist laws, the use of cultural diversity training, and the hiring of marginalized police officers may alter attitudes about some issues, but the officers will still be required to function as a crisis unit and to resolve conflicts in an inherently swift and crude manner.

Bittner (1980) noted that the third characteristic of police work was that it is discriminatory. It focuses primarily on the harmful acts of the lower classes. To the extent that particular minority groups are disproportionately concentrated in the lower classes, they will be disproportionately stopped, investigated, observed, searched, arrested, and killed by the police. The laws that police officers are assigned to enforce are structured in such a way that they criminalize the harmful acts of the poor and not the wealthy (Reiman, 1998). In addition, those with the least amount of political and economic power will also be those who have the least amount of influence on the local political system, as well as the police, to achieve greater police attention or a higher quality of policing. Neither the integration of marginalized police officers nor the implementation of cultural diversity awareness training will change the power relations that relegate certain segments of the population in the lower class.

We must emphasize here that we do not wish to subsume the significance of race or gender in the United States within conceptions of class. The material that has been presented in this book clearly establishes the significance of racism and racist violence in this country well beyond issues of class. The intersection of race, gender, and class in the United States creates a web of contradictions that permeates all aspects of life in the United States, including social control through criminal justice. Although the process of hiring African-American police officers and implementing cultural diversity awareness training involves efforts to assuage some of the injuries that result from the police role with regard to problem populations, it does nothing to resolve the fundamental contradictions that produce these injuries. The social relations that have contributed to the formation and development of police departments are left completely intact and, therefore, the contradictions of race and class relations continue to manifest themselves in the function of police, police community relations, and tensions between the police and minorities.

The concept of the "iron fist and the velvet glove" describes the contradictory nature of policing in a class society.

> The "hard" side has included the creation of SWAT (special weapons and tactics) teams, more technology such as audio-visual equipment and helicopters, more computer networks, and more weaponry and machinery. The "soft" side has included community relations programs, the hiring of women and minorities, and grants from studying social control

techniques. However, these new strategies have brought no change in the class or race arrested, and no drop in arrest and crime rates. As long as the police serve to enforce the class, racial, sexual, and cultural oppression that has been integral to capitalist development in the United States, attempts at reform can only result in repressive or superficial change. (Balkan et al., 1980, p. 101)

These two aspects of policing operate simultaneously, each supporting the other. Both are strategies of repression. Neither the conservative desire to develop more effective strategies of control nor the liberal desire to seek community participation challenge the structures of privilege and exploitation in the United States. Indeed, both support that structure "by making the system of repression that serves it more powerful or more palatable or both" (Platt et al., 1982, p. 49).

The police-community relations movement in the 1960s was motivated by the desire to pacify and control the poor and racial minorities (Balkan et al., 1980; Platt et al., 1982). The early community relations movement in policing was largely a reaction to the racial rebellions of the 1960s and the failure of the police to relieve the fears of White America:

The police were incapable of containing the violence; indeed, through overly brutal and ineffective methods, they seemed to contribute to the decline of legitimacy and stability of the system. Therefore, different strategies and forms of organization of organizing the police were necessary. (Balkan et al., 1980)

The different strategies were to mask police repression with a friendly face. "Behind the new 'pacification' approach is the conviction that the control of urban crime and violence must become far more subtle than the military model suggests" (Platt et al., 1982, p. 128). The critical element of these programs was that they had no real impact on the essential role of the police and only slightly altered the means by which that role was carried out. "Community-police programs glossed over the continuing repression and arrest of people in poor communities" (Balkan et al., 1980, p. 104). "The new community pacification strategies do not involve a real transfer of control of police work from the police themselves to the communities they affect" (Platt et al., 1982, p. 129).

The attempt to resolve the longstanding structural problems of police minority relations through the development of cultural diversity training for police officers is symptomatic of the historical pattern of criminal justice reforms in the United States. First, the initiative fails to seriously challenge the social structure's unequal distribution of wealth and power (Barlow et al., 1993). It is precisely this characteristic of social reform that appeals to more conservative organizations and makes its implementation possible.

Although criminal justice reforms help to appease various social activists who wish to improve the treatment of the disenfranchised, they do not fundamentally threaten the position of those in power. Thus, criminal justice reforms have historically strengthened existing relations of power in society by creating the false appearance that social change is taking place, thus reducing the potential for either violent rebellion or substantive change. This contradiction frequently found within criminal justice reforms explains the second way in which these training programs are reflective of many previous reform efforts.

Much like other criminal justice reforms, cultural diversity training programs are often initiated with good intentions, demanded by liberal individuals seeking to liberate people and improve the lives of those on the bottom of the social structure. During the process of implementation they tend to solidify the inequality of the social order by correcting its more disruptive aspects. Throughout the nineteenth and twentieth centuries, seemingly progressive criminal justice innovations have had decidedly conservative impacts, both in terms of preserving the status quo in relations of power and authority, and in their effects on immigrants and racial minorities, which have been particularly deleterious (Barlow, 1985; Barlow et al., 1993). For example, reforms in penal policy—such as institutionalization, indeterminate sentencing, probation, and community corrections—initially appeared to be progressive policies designed to make the criminal justice system more humane. Yet, a closer look at the impetus behind each of these reforms reveals a greater concern for enhancing the effectiveness of penal policy than for making it more humane. In the following excerpt, Miller (1980) noted this contradiction with regard to community-based corrections, arguing that "Increased use of community programs is not necessarily synonymous with an anti-incarceration movement. Furthermore, community programs are not necessarily more 'humane' or progressive" (p. 79). The same is true of other criminal justice reforms, such as the transition from private to public policing, police professionalization, the intervention of the federal government into street crime, and the expansion of defendants' and victims' rights (Barlow, 1985; Barlow et al., 1993).

A crucial element of all criminal justice reforms, including efforts to "reform" the police, is that they are incapable of resolving the fundamental contradictions that exist in a class society. Although efforts may be made to appease certain segments of the population or to make their situation in relation to the police more tolerable, the class structure that places them in jeopardy remains intact. No reform can change the fundamental class relations that produce the conditions calling for the reform.

As mechanisms of social control, police practices and strategies become outdated and ineffective, leading government officials either to improve upon them or to seek new mechanisms of control. Even if such alterations succeed in reducing racism and bigotry among those who are policing our communities, they will not alter the social conditions and power relations that produce social and economic injustice. Rather, the application and rhetoric of most police reforms tend to cloak existing injustice within the language and promise of fundamental fairness and equality before the law. The less offensive these practices and strategies are to democratic sensibilities, the better. Thus, changes in police personnel, practices, strategies, or philosophy have tended to amount to little more than system tinkering and have not produced significant changes in the fundamental nature of police in society.

Our conclusion, however, is not that efforts to reform the police, to eliminate racism, sexism, heterosexism, ethnocentrism, and bigotry among police officers and policies, and to improve police relations with people of color should be discouraged. It is the responsibility of White America to put an end to injustice. It is necessary to initiate community relations programs and cultural diversity training seminars and hire more marginalized police officers, to make the police more responsive to the needs of all community members, and to assist police officers in learning to understand diverse histories and perspectives. But these are only the very initial steps in the struggle for justice. They are not the end or the goal, but only small means toward achieving the goal of true criminal and social *justice*.

These reforms must be part of a much larger effort to implement broad-based social change. Without meaningful social change toward greater justice, police reforms such as community policing and training in cultural diversity are rightly criticized as attempts to obtain cooperation and support for the police from those who have no vested interest in cooperating and supporting a police structure that oppresses them. It is our hope that the movements to improve the quality of policing in the United States will proceed with a clear view of history, an understanding of their limits within present conditions, and a firm commitment to a larger agenda of social change for a future in which fairness and equality characterize the lived experiences of all members of U.S. society in relation to its system of justice.

References

Adamson, Christopher. (1983). "Punishment After Slavery: Southern State Penal Systems, 1865–1890." *Social Problems, 30*(5), 555–569.

Adamson, Christopher. (1984). "Toward a Marxian Penology: Captive Criminal Populations as Economic Threats and Resources." *Social Problems, 31*(4), 435-458.

Alex, Nicholas. (1969). *Black in Blue: A Study of the Negro Policeman.* New York: Meredith Corporation.

Axelrod, Alan and Phillips, Charles. (1992). *What Every American Should Know About American History: 200 Events that Shaped the Nation.* Holbrook, MA: Bob Adams, Inc.

Baldassare, Mark. (1994). "Introduction." In Mark Baldassare (Ed.), *The Los Angeles Riots: Lessons for the Urban Future* (pp. 1–17). Boulder, CO: Westview Press.

Baldwin, James. (1961). *Nobody Knows My Name: More Notes of a Native Son.* New York: The Dial Press.

Balkan, S., Berger, R. J., and Schmidt, J. (1980). *Crime and Deviance in America.* Belmont, CA: Wadsworth Publishing Compnay.

Barak, Gregg. (1991). "Cultural Literacy and a Multicultural Inquiry into the Study of Crime and Justice." *Journal of Criminal Justice Education, 2,* 173–192.

Barlow, David E. (1985). *An Historical Materialist Analysis of the Criminal Justice System in the United States.* Unpublished master's thesis, Florida State University, Tallahassee, FL.

Barlow, David E. and Barlow, Melissa Hickman. (1993). "Cultural Diversity Training in Criminal Justice: A Progressive or Conservative Reform?" *Social Justice, 20*(3–4), 69–84.

Barlow, David E. and Barlow, Melissa Hickman. (1994). "Cultural Sensitivity Rediscovered: Developing Training Strategies for Police Officers." *Justice Profesional, 8*(2), 97–116.

Barlow, David E., Barlow, Melissa Hickman, and Chiricos, Theodore G. (1993). "Long Economic Cycles and the History of Criminal Justice in the U.S." *Crime, Law and Social Change, 19,* 143–169.

Barlow, Melissa Hickman and Barlow, David E. (1995). "Confronting Ideologies of Race and Crime in the Classroom: The Power of History." *Journal of Criminal Justice Education, 6*(1), 103–122.

Barlow, Melissa Hickman, Barlow, David E., and Stojkovic, Stan. (1994). "The Media, the Police, and the Multicultural Community." *Journal of Crime and Justice, 17*(2), 133–165.

Barry, Robert J. and Cronkhite, Clyde. (1992, October 15). "Agency Management in the Post-King Era." *Law Enforcement News, 8.*

Bartollas, Clemens and Hahn, Larry D. (1999). *Policing in America.* Boston: Allyn and Bacon.

Bass, Jack and Nelson, Jack. (1984). *The Orangeburg Massacre.* Macon, GA: Mercer University Press.

Bayley, David H. (1994). *Police for the Future.* New York: Oxford University Press.

Bayley, David F. and Mendelsohn, Harold. (1969). *Minorities and the Police: Confrontation in America.* New York: Free Press.

"Beating of Undercover Cop Gets Two Fired." (December 31, 1992). *Law Enforcement News.*

Bennett, Lerone, Jr. (1993). *Before the Mayflower: A History of Black America* (6th ed.). New York: Penguin Books.

Benson, Katy. (1992, July). "Talking the Talk; Walking the Walk." *Police Magazine,* 40–43, 83.

Berry, Mary Frances. (1994). *Black Resistance, White Law: A History of Constitutional Racism in America.* New York: Penguin Books.

Bittner, Egon. (1980). *The Functions of Police in Modern Society*. Cambridge, MA: Olegeschlager, Gunn, and Hain.

Bittner, Egon. (1990). *Aspects of Police Work*. Boston: Northeastern University Press.

Bittner, Egon. (1996). Excerpts from "Popular Conceptions about the Character of Police Work" and "The Capacity to Use Force as the Core of the Police Role." In Brandl and Barlow (Eds.), *Classics in Policing* (pp. 111–129). Cincinnati: Anderson Publishing.

Blakemore, Jerome L., Barlow, David E., and Padgett, Deborah L. (1995). "From the Classroom to the Community: Introducing Process in Police Diversity Training." *Police Studies, 18*(1), 71–83.

Bobo, Lawrence, Zubrinsky, Camille L., Johnson, James H., Jr., and Oliver, Melvin L. (1994). "Public Opinion Before and After a Spring of Discontent." In Mark Baldassare (Ed.), *The Los Angeles Riots: Lessons for the Urban Future* (pp. 103–133). Boulder, CO: Westview Press.

Boesel, David, Berk, Richard, Groves, W. Eugene, Eidson, Bettye, and Rossi, Peter H. (1973). In Peter H. Rossi (Ed.), *Ghetto Revolts* (2nd. ed., pp. 39–58). New Brunswick, NJ: Transaction Books.

Bohm, Robert M. and Haley, Keith N. (1997). *Introduction to Criminal Justice*. New York: Glencoe, McGraw-Hill.

Bowen, Don R. and Masotti, Louis H. (1968). "Civil Violence: A Theoretical Overview." In Louis H. Masotti and Don R. Bowen (Eds.), *Riots and Rebellions: Civil Violence in the Urban Community* (pp. 11–31). Beverly Hills, CA: Sage Publications.

Brown, Lee P. (1984, August). "Community Policing: A Practical Guide for Police Officers." *The Police Chief*, 72–82.

Byrne, Edward C. (1996). "The Oneida Tribal Police: Politics and Law Enforcement." In Marianne O. Nielsen and Robert A. Silverman (Eds.), *Native Americans, Crime, and Justice* (pp. 114–117). Boulder, CO: Westview Press.

Capeci, Dominic J., Jr. (1977). *The Harlem Riot of 1943*. Philadelphia: Temple University Press.

Cashmore, Ellis. (1991). "Black Cops, Inc." In Ellis Cashmore and Eugene McLaughlin (Eds.), *Out of Order: Policing Black People* (pp. 87–108). New York: Routledge Publishing.

Chambliss, William J. (1994). "Policing the Ghetto Underclass: The Politics of Law and Law Enforcement." *Social Problems, 41*(2), 177–194.

Christopher Commission. (1991). *Report of the Independent Commission on the Los Angeles Police Department*. Los Angeles: The Commission.

Cizon, Francis A. and Smith, William H. T. (1970). *Some Guidelines for Successful Police Community Relations Training Programs*. Unpublished report. Washington, DC: U.S. Department of Justice.

Clark, Jacob R. (1992, May 31). "Keeping a Lid on Things." *Law Enforcement News*. New York: John Jay College of Criminal Justice.

"Dallas PD Ban on Gay Recruits is Overturned—For Now." (1992, February 2). *Law Enforcement News*, 3.

"Dallas PD to Open Doors to Gay Recruits." (1993, June 15). *Law Enforcement News*, 6.

Deloria, Vine, Jr. and Lytle, Clifford M. (1983). *American Indians; American Justice*. Austin: University of Texas Press.

Dubofsky, Melvyn. (1975). *Industrialism and the American Worker, 1865–1920*. Arlington Heights, IL: Harlan Davidson, Inc.

Duffy, Brian, Tharp, Mike, Streisand, Betsy, Guttman, Monika, and Cooper, Matthew. (1992, May 11). "Days of Rage." *U.S. News & World Report*, 21–26.

Dulaney, W. Marvin. (1996). *Black Police in America*. Bloomington: Indiana University Press.

Ehrenreich, Barbara. (1991, April 8). "Teach Diversity—With a Smile." *Time*, 84.

Feinman, Clarice. (1994). *Women in the Criminal Justice System* (3rd ed.). Westport, CT: Praeger.

Fletcher, Connie. (1995). *Breaking & Entering: Women Cops Talk About Life in the Ultimate Men's Club*. New York: HarperCollins.

Fogelson, Robert M. (1969). "White on Black: A Critique of the McCone Commission Report on the Los Angeles Riots." In Robert M. Fogelson (Ed.), *The Los Angeles Riots*. New York: Arno Press & The New York Times.

Fogelson, Robert M. and Rubenstein, Richard E. (1969). *Mass Violence in America: The Complete Report of Mayor La Guardia's Commission on the Harlem Riot of March 19, 1935*. New York: Arno Press and the New York Times.

Freer, Regina. (1994). "Black-Korean Conflict." In Mark Baldassare (Ed.), *The Los Angeles Riots: Lessons for the Urban Future* (pp. 175–203). Boulder, CO: Westview Press.

French, Lawrence. (Ed). (1982). *Indians and Criminal Justice.* Totowa, NJ: Allanheld, Osmun and Company.

Friedman, Lawrence M. (1993). *Crime and Punishment in American History.* New York: Basic Books.

"Friendly-Fire Shooting of Black Cop Probed." (1992, December 12). *Law Enforcement News,* 7.

Fukurai, Hiroshi, Krooth, Richard, and Butler, Edgar W. (1994). "The Rodney King Beating Verdicts." In Mark Baldassare (Ed.), *The Los Angeles Riots: Lessons for the Urban Future* (pp. 73–102). Boulder, CO: Westview Press.

Garbarino, Merwyn S. and Sasso, Robert F. (1994). *Native American Heritage.* Prospect Heights, IL: Waveland Press.

Genovese, Eugene D. (1976). *Roll, Jordan, Roll: The World the Slaves Made.* New York: Vintage Books.

Georges-Abeyie, Daniel E. (1989). "Race, Ethnicity, and the Spatial Dynamic: Toward a Realistic Study of Black Crime, Crime Victimization, and Criminal Justice Processing of Blacks." *Social Justice, 16*(4), 35–54.

Georges-Abeyie, Daniel E. (1991). "Forward." In Michael J. Lynch and E. Britt Patterson (Eds.), *Race and Criminal Justice* (pp. vii–x). New York: Harrow and Heston.

Goldstein, Herman. (1979). "Improving Policing: A Problem-Oriented Approach." *Crime and Delinquency, 25,* 236–258.

Goldstein, Herman. (1990). *Problem-Oriented Policing.* New York: McGraw-Hill.

Gonzalez, E. (1992). Repairing the Damage: The Metro-Dade Experience, 1980–1990." A paper presented at the "Unfinished Business: Racial and Ethnic Issues Facing Law Enforcement II Conference." Reno, NV.

Gordon, David M., Edwards, Richard, and Reich, Michael. (1982). *Segmented Work, Divided Workers: The Historical Transformation of Labor in the United States.* Cambridge, MA: Cambridge University Press.

Gratch, Linda. (1995). "Sexual Harassment Among Police Officers: Crisis and Change in the Normative Structure." In Alida V. Merlo and Joycelyn M. Pollock (Eds.), *Women, Law, & Social Control* (pp. 55–77). Boston: Allyn and Bacon.

Grennan, Sean. (1993). "A Perspective on Women in Policing." In Roslyn Muraskin and Ted Alleman (Eds.), *It's a Crime: Women and Justice* (pp.163–176). Englewood Cliffs, NJ: Prentice Hall.

Gurr, Ted Robert. (1980). "Development and Decay: Their Impact on Public Order in Western History." In James A. Inciardi and Charles E. Faupel (Eds.), *History and Crime: Implications for Criminal Justice Policy.* Beverly Hills, CA: Sage Publications.

Hagan, William T. (1966). *Indian Police and Judges: Experiments in Acculturation and Control.* New Haven, CT: Yale University Press.

Hagedorn, John M. (1991). "Gangs, Neighborhoods, and Public Policy." *Social Problems, 38*(4), 529–542.

Hale, Donna C. and Bennett, C. Lee. (1995). "Realities of Women in Policing: An Organizational Cultural Perspective." In Alida V. Merlo and Joycelyn M. Pollock (Eds.), *Women, Law, & Social Control* (pp. 41–54). Boston: Allyn and Bacon.

Hale, Donna C. and Menniti, Daniel J. (1993). "Discrimination and Harassment: Litigation by Women in Policing." In Roslyn Muraskin and Ted Alleman (Eds.), *It's a Crime: Women and Justice* (pp.177–189). Englewood Cliffs, NJ: Prentice Hall.

Hall, S., Critcher, C., Jefferson, T., Clarke, J., and Roberts, B. (1978). *Policing the Crisis: Mugging, the State, and Law and Order.* New York: Homes and Meier Publishers, Inc.

Haller, Mark H. (1976). "Historical Roots of Police Behavior: Chicago, 1890–1925." *Law and Society Review, 10:* 303–323.

Harring, Sidney L. (1983). *Policing a Class Society: The Experience of American Cities, 1865–1915.* New Brunswick, NJ: Rutgers.

Harris, Fred R. and Wicker, Tom (Eds.). (1988). *The Kerner Report: The 1968 Report of the National Advisory Commission on Civil Disorders.* New York: Pantheon.

Hawkins, Homer and Thomas, Richard. (1991). "White Policing Black Populations: A History of Race and Social Control in America." In Ellis Cashmore and Eugene McLaughlin (Eds.), *Out of Order: Policing Black People* (pp. 65–86). New York: Routledge.

Higgins, Lois. (1992). "Historical Background of Policewomen's Service" In Eric H. Monkkonen (Ed.), *Policing and Crime Control Part 3* (pp. 341–352). New York: K. G. Saur.

Hoare, Quintin and Smith, Geoffrey Novell (Eds. & Trans.). (1971). *Selections From the Prison Notebooks of Antonio Gramsci.* New York: International Publishers.

Horne, Peter. (1975). *Women in Law Enforcement.* Springfield, IL: Charles C. Thomas.

Iannone, Nathan F. (1994). *Supervision of Police Personnel* (5th ed.). Englewood Cliffs, NJ: Prentice Hall, Inc.

"In Rift Over Gays, Police Agencies Tell Boy Scouts to Take a Hike." (1992, November 30). *Law Enforcement News*, 5, 14.

Irwin, John and Austin, James. (1997). *It's About Time: America's Imprisonment Binge* (2nd ed.). Belmont, CA: Wadsworth.

Johnson, Bruce C. (1992). "Taking Care of Labor: The Police in American Politics." In Eric H. Monkkonen (Ed.), *Policing and Crime Control Part 2* (pp. 375–403). New York: K. G. Saur.

Kappeler, Victor E., Sluder, Richard D., and Alpert, Geoffrey P. (1998). *Forces of Deviance: Understanding the Dark Side of Policing.* Prospect Heights, IL: Waveland Press.

Katz, William Loren. (1992). *Black People Who Made the Old West.* Trenton, NJ: Africa Wold Press, Inc.

Katz, William Loren. (1995). *Eyewitness: A Living Documentary of the African American Contribution to American History.* New York: Touchstone.

Kelling, George L. and Moore, Mark H. (1988). "The Evolving Stragey of Policing." *Perspectives on Policing*, 4, 1–15.

Klockars, Carl B. (1991). "The Rhetoric of Community Policing." In Jack R. Greene and Stephen Mastrofski (Eds.), *Community Policing: Rhetoric or Reality* (pp. 239–258). New York: Praeger.

Koleas, John W. (1991). *Request for Proposals: Diversity Training for the City of Milwaukee Police Department.* Unpublished document.

Kraska, Peter B. and Kappeler, Victor E. (1997). "Militarizing American Police: The Rise and Normalization of Paramilitary Units." *Social Problems*, 44(1), 1–18.

Kuykendall, Jack L. and Burns, D. E. (1980). "The Black Police Officer: An Historical Perspective." *Journal of Contemporary Criminal Justice*, 4, 4–12.

Lane, Roger. (1971). *Policing the City: Boston, 1822–1885.* New York: Atheneum.

Latimer, D. and Goldberg, J. (1981). *Flowers in the Blood: The Story of Opium.* New York: Franklin Watts.

Leinen, Stephen. (1993). *Gay Cops.* New Brunswick, NJ: Rutgers University Press.

Leinin, Stephen. (1994). *Black Police, White Society.* New York: New York University Press.

Levy, Burton. (1968). "Cops in the Ghetto: A Problem of the Police System." In Louis H. Masotti and Don R. Bowen (Eds.), *Riots and Rebellions: Civil Violence in the Urban Community* (pp. 347–358). Beverly Hills, CA: Sage Publications.

Lipson, Milton. (1975). *On Guard: The Business of Private Security.* New York: The New York Times Book Company.

Liyama, P., Nishi, N. M., and Johnson, B. D. (1976). *Drug Use and Abuse Among U.S. Minorities: An Annotated Bibliography.* New York: Praeger Press.

Loewen, James W. (1995). *Lies My Teacher Told Me: Everything Your American History Textbook Got Wrong.* New York: The New Press.

Lohman, Joseph. (1968). "Law Enforcement and the Police." In Louis H. Masotti and Don R. Bowen (Eds.), *Riots and Rebellions: Civil Violence in the Urban Community* (pp. 359–372). Beverly Hills, CA: Sage Publications.

Lurie, Nancy Ostreich. (1980). *Wisconsin Indians.* Madison: The State Historical Society.

Lynch, Michael J. and Patterson, E. Britt. (1991). *Race and Criminal Justice.* Albany, NY: Harrow and Heston.

Maghan, Jess. (1992). "Black Police Officer Recruits: Aspects of Becoming Blue." *Police Forum*, 2(1), 8–11.

Mandel, Ernest. (1978). *Late Capitalism.* London: Unwin Brothers Press.

Mann, Coramae Richey. (1993). *Unequal Justice: A Question of Color.* Bloomington: Indiana University Press.

Manning, Peter. (1991). "Community Policing as a Drama of Control." In Greene and Mastrofski (Eds.), *Community Policing: Rhetoric or Reality.* New York: Praeger.

Marquis, Don. (1992, May 3). "Police Chief Joins 600 Reno Marchers." *Reno Gazette Journal.* Reno, NV.

Martin, Susan Ehrlich and Jurik, Nancy C. (1996). *Doing Justice, Doing Gender: Women in Law and Criminal Justice Occupations.* Thousand Oaks, CA: SAGE Publications.

Matthiessen, Peter. (1991). *In The Spirit of Crazy Horse.* New York: Penguin Books.

Mayor's Citizen Commission on Police-Community Relations. (1991). *A Report to Mayor John O. Norquist and the Board of Fire and Police Commissioners.* Unpublished Report.

McCone Commission. (1965). *Violence in the City—An End or a Beginning? A Report by the Governor's Commission on the Los Angeles Riots.* Los Angeles: The Commission.

Meers, Erik. (1998, March 3). "Good Cop, Gay Cop." *The Advocate*, 26–34.

Meyer, John W. and Rowan, Brian. (1977). "Institutionalized Organizations: Formal Structure as Myth and Ceremony." *American Journal of Sociology, 83*(2), 340–363.

Miller, Jerome G. (1996). *Search and Destroy: African American Males in the Criminal Justice System.* New York: Cambridge University Press.

Miller, M.B. (1980). "At Hard Labor: Rediscovering the 19th-Century Prison." In Anthony M. Platt and P. Takagi (Eds.), *Punishment and Penal Discipline: Essays on the Prison and the Prisoners' Movement.* San Francisco: Crime and Social Justice Associates.

Miller, Wilbur. (1977). *Cops and Bobbies: Police Authority in New York and London, 1830–1870.* Chicago: University of Chicago Press.

Milton, Catherine. (1972). *Women in Policing.* Washington, DC: Police Foundation.

Minerbrook, Scott. (May 11, 1992). "A Different Reality for Us." *U.S. News & World Report*, 36.

Mirandé, Alfredo. (1987). *Gringo Justice.* Notre Dame, IN: University of Notre Dame Press.

More, Harry W. and Wegener, W. Fred (1990). *Effective Police Supervision.* Cincinnati, OH: Anderson Publishing Company.

Moore, Mark H., Trojanowicz, R. C., and Kelling, George L. (1988). *Crime and Policing.* Washington, DC: National Institute of Justice.

Morgan, P. A. (1982). "The Legislation of Drug Law: Economic Crisis and Social Control." In J.C. Wissmand and R.L. DuPont (Eds.), *Criminal Justice and Drugs: The Unresolved Connection.* Port Washington, NY: Kennikat Press.

Morrison, Peter A. and Lowry, Ira S. (1994). "A Riot of Color: The Demographic Setting." In Mark Baldassare (Ed.), *The Los Angeles Riots: Lessons for the Urban Future* (pp. 19–46). Boulder, CO: Westview Press.

Muwakkil, Salim. (2000, March 13). Cops doing the dirty work of American tradition. *Chicago Tribune*, p. 13.

Nabokov, Peter. (Ed.). (1992). *Native American Testimony: A Chronicle of Indian-White Relations From Prophecy to the Present.* New York: Penguin Books.

"Navajos & Sheriff in Cross-Deputizing Pact." (1998, September 30). *Law Enforcement News*, 5.

NOBLE and PERF. (1993). *Unfinished Business: Policing an Increasingly Diverse America.* An advertisement flyer distributed by the Police Executive Research Forum.

Ohlin, Lloyd E. (1973). *Prisoners in America.* Englewood Cliffs, NJ: Prentice-Hall, Inc.

Ostrom, Vincent, Bish, Robert, and Ostrom, Elinor. (1988). *Local Government in the US.* San Francisco: ICS Press.

Peak, Kenneth J. "African Americans in Policing." In Roger G. Dunham and Geoffrey P. Alpert (Eds.), *Critical Issues in Policing* (3rd ed., pp. 356–362). Prospect Heights, IL: Waveland Press.

Palmer, Edward. (1973, October). "Black Police in America." *The Black Scholar.*

PERF. (1992). *Subject to Debate: A Newsletter of the Police Executive Research Forum.* Washington, DC: Police Executive Research Forum.

Petersilia, Joan and Abrahamse, Allan. (1994). "A Profile of Those Arrested." In Mark Baldassare (Ed.), *The Los Angeles Riots: Lessons for the Urban Future* (pp. 135–147). Boulder, CO: Westview Press.

Piven, Frances Fox and Cloward, Richard A. (1971). *Regulating the Poor: The Functions of Public Welfare.* New York: Vintage Books.

Piven, Frances Fox and Cloward, Richard A. (1979). *Poor People's Movements: Why They Succeed, How They Fail.* New York: Vintage Books.

Platt, Tony, Frappier, Jon, Gerda, Ray, Schauffler, Richard, Trujillo, Larry, Cooper, Lynn, Currie, Elliot, and Harring, Sidney. (1982). *The Iron Fist and the Velvet Glove: An Analysis of the U.S. Police* (3rd. ed.). San Francsico: Synthesis Publications.

Poter, Bruce and Dunn, Marvin. (1984). *The Miami Riot of 1980: Crossing the Bounds.* Lexington, MA: Lexington Books.

Quarles, Benjamin. (1989). *The Negro in the Civil War.* New York: Plenum Publishing Company.

Quinney, Richard. (1973). *Critique of Legal Order: Crime Control in Capitalist Society.* Boston: Little, Brown and Company.

Rabinowitz, Howard N. (1992). "The Conflict between Blacks and the Police in the Urban South, 1865–1900." In Eric H. Monkkonen (Ed.), *Policing and Crime Control Part 2* (pp. 593–607). New York: K. G. Saur.

"Rank Objections: Study Calls Growth in Policing 'Alarmingly Slow.'" (1998, May, 15). *Law Enforcement News,* 1, 10.

Reiman, Jeffrey. (1998). *The Rich Get Richer and the Poor Get Prison: Ideology, Class, and Criminal Justice* (5th ed.). Boston: Allyn & Bacon.

Richardson, James F. (1974). *Urban Police in the United States.* Port Washington, NY: Kennikat Press.

Richardson, James F. (1980). "Police in America: Functions and Control." In James Inciardi and Charles E. Faupel (Eds.), *History and Crime: Implications for Criminal Justice Policy.* Beverly Hills, CA: Sage Publications.

Roberts, David. (1992, October). "Geronimo." *National Geographic, 182*(4).

Rossi, Peter H. (Ed.). (1973). *Ghetto Revolts* (2nd ed.). New Brunswick, NJ: Transaction Books.

Rudwick, Elliott M. (1972). *Race Riot at East St. Louis, July 2, 1917.* New York: Atheneum.

Rustin, Bayard. (1969). "The Watts 'Manifesto' and the McCone Report." In Robert M. Fogelson (Ed.), *The Los Angeles Riots.* New York: Arno Press & The New York Times.

Samora, Julian, Bernal, Joe, and Peña, Albert. (1979). *Gunpowder Justice: A Reassessment of the Texas Rangers.* Notre Dame, IN: University of Notre Dame Press.

Schulz, Dorothy Moses. (1995). "Invisible No More: A Social History of Women in U.S. Policing." In Barbara Raffel Price and Natalie J. Sokoloff (Eds.), *The Criminal Justice System and Women: Offenders, Victims, and Workers* (2nd ed., pp. 372–382). New York: McGraw-Hill.

Schwartz, Martin D. and Friedrichs, David O. (1994). "Postmodern Thought and Criminological Discontent: New Metaphors for Understanding Violence." *Criminology, 32*(2), 221–246.

Scott, Kody. (1993). *Monster: The Autobiography of an L.A. Gang Member.* New York: The Atlantic Monthly Press.

Shusta, Robert M., Levine, Deena R., Harris, Philip R., and Wong, Herbert Z. (1995). *Multicultural Law Enforcement: Strategies for Peacekeeping in a Diverse Society.* Englewood Cliffs, NJ: Prentice-Hall.

Silver, Alan. (1967). "The Demand for Order in Civil Society: A Review of Some Themes in the History of Crime, Police and Riot." In David J. Bordua (Ed.), *The Police: Six Sociological Essays.* New York: John Wiley and Sons, Inc.

Silvergate, Harvey A. (1974). "The 1970s: A Decade of Repression?" In Richard Quinney (Ed.), *Criminal Justice in America: A Critical Understanding.* Boston: Little, Brown, and Company.

Skolnick, Jerome H. and Fyfe, James J. (1993). *Above the Law: Police and the Excessive Use of Force.* New York: The Free Press.

Snyder-Joy, Zoann K. (1996). "Self-Determination and American Indian Justice: Tribal Versus Federal Jurisdiction on Indian Lands." In Marianne O. Nielsen and Robert A. Silverman (Eds.), *Native Americans, Crime, and Justice* (pp. 38–45). Boulder, CO: Westview Press.

Soloman, T. and McCarthy, D. (1989). *Fear: It Kills. A Training Guide for Law Enforcement in the 1990s.* Arlington, VA: International Association of Chiefs of Police.

Sonenshein, Raphael J. (1994). "Los Angeles Coalition Politics." In Mark Baldassare (Ed.), *The Los Angeles Riots: Lessons for the Urban Future* (pp. 47–71). Boulder, CO: Westview Press.

Spitzer, Steven. (1981). "The Political Economy of Policing." In David F. Greenberg (Ed.), *Corrections and Punishment*. Beverly Hills, CA: Sage Publications.

Spitzer, Steven. (1995). "Toward a Marxian Theory of Deviance." *Social Problems, 22,* 641–651.

Spitzer, Steven and Scull, Andrew T. (1977). "Social Control in Historical Perspective: From Private to Public Responses to Crime." In David F. Greenberg (Ed.), *Corrections and Punishment* (pp. 265–286). Beverly Hills, CA: Sage Publications.

Stewart, Pearl. (1992). "Black and Blue: The Oakland Cop Who Would be King." In Don Hazen (Ed.), *Inside the L.A. Riots* (pp. 58–60). Los Angeles: Institution for Alternative Journalism.

Sullivan, Peggy S. (1989). "Minority Officers: Current Issues." In Roger G. Dunham and Geoffrey P. Albert (Eds.), *Critical Issues in Policing: Contemporary Readings* (pp. 331–345). Prospect Heights: IL: Waveland Press.

Takaki, Ronald. (1993). *A Different Mirror: A History of Multicultural America.* Boston: Little, Brown, and Company.

Taylor, Nancy. (1991). *Bias Crime: The Law Enforcement Response.* Chicago: Office of International Criminal Justice.

Thomas, R. Roosevelt. (1990, March–April). "From Affirmative Action to Affirming Diversity." *Harvard Business Review,* 107–117.

Tierney, Kathleen J. (1994). "Property Damage and Violence: A Collective Behavior Analysis." In Mark Baldassare (Ed.), *The Los Angeles Riots: Lessons for the Urban Future* (pp. 149–173). Boulder, CO: Westview Press.

"To Keep the Peace." (1992, March 2). *The Milwaukee Journal*, pp. 1–4.

Trojanowicz, Robert and Bucqueroux, Bonnie. (1990). *Community Policing: A Contemporary Perspective.* Cincinnati, OH: Anderson Publishing Company.

Tuttle, William M., Jr. (1970). *Race Riot: Chicago in the Red Summer of 1919.* New York: Atheneum.

Wachtel, David. (1982). "Indian Law Enforcement." In Lawrence French (Ed.), *Indians and Criminal Justice* (pp. 109–120). Totowa, NJ: Allanheld, Osmun and Company.

Walker, Samuel. (1977). *A Critical History of Police Reform: The Emergence of Professionalization.* Lexington, MA: Lexington Books.

Walker, Samuel. (1980). *Popular Justice: A History of American Criminal Justice.* New York: Oxford University Press.

Walker, Samuel. (1984). "Broken Windows and Fractured History: The Use and Misuse of History in Recent Police Patrol Analysis," *Justice Quarterly, 1,* 77–90.

Walker, Samuel. (1990). *In Defense of American Liberties.* New York: Oxford University Press.

Walker, Samuel. (1992a). "The Origins of American Police-Community Relations Movement: The 1940s." In Eric H. Monkkonen (Ed.), *Policing and Crime Control Part 3* (pp. 813–834). New York: K. G. Saur.

Walker, Samuel. (1992b). "The Rise and Fall of the Policewomen's Movement, 1905–1975." In Eric H. Monkkonen (Ed.), *Policing and Crime Control Part 3* (pp. 847–857). New York: K. G. Saur.

Walker, Samuel. (1998). *Popular Justice: A History of American Criminal Justice* (2nd ed.). New York: Oxford University Press.

Walker, Samuel. (1999). *The Police in America: An Introduction* (3rd ed.). New York: McGraw-Hill.

Walker, Samuel, Spohn, Cassia, and DeLone, Miriam. (2000). *The Color of Justice: Race, Ethnicity, and Crime in America* (2nd ed.). Belmont, CA: Wadsworth Publishing.

Washburn, Wilcomb E. (1971). *Red Man's Land/White Man's Law: A Study of the Past and Present Status of American Indians.* New York: Scribner.

Waskow, Arthur I. (1971). "The Washington Race Riot, 1919." In Thomas R. Frazier (Ed.), *Underside of American Hisotry: Other Readings* (pp. 113–126). New York: Harcourt Brace Jovanovich, Inc.

Watts, Eugene J. (1992a). "Black and Blue: Afro-American Police Officers in Twentieth Century St. Louis." In Eric H. Monkkonen (Ed.), *Policing and Crime Control Part 3* (pp. 870–907). New York: K. G. Saur.

Watts, Eugene J. (1992b). "The Police in Atlanta, 1890–1905." In Eric H. Monkkonen (Ed.), *Policing and Crime Control Part 3* (pp. 908–925). New York: K. G. Saur.

Weaver, Gary. (1992). "Law Enforcement in a Culturally Diverse Society." *FBI Law Enforcement Bulletin*, 1–7.

Weckler, J. E. and Hall, Theo E. (1944). *The Police and Minority Groups*. Washington, DC: The International City Managers' Association.

Wilbanks, William. (1987). *The Myth of a Racist Criminal Justice System*. Monterey, CA: Brooks/Cole Publishing Company.

Williams, Hubert and Murphy, Patrick V. (1990). *The Evolving Strategy of Police: A Minority Perspective*. Washington, DC: National Institute of Justice

Wilson, James Q. and Kelling, George L. (1982, March). "Broken Windows: Police and Neighborhood Safety." *The Atlantic Monthly, 249*: 29–38.

Witkin, Gordon, Tharp, Mike, and Arrarte, Anne. (1992, May 11). "What the LAPD Ought to Try." *U.S. News & World Report*, pp. 27–35.

Wright, Eric Olin. (1979). *Class, Crisis and the State*. London: Verso Editions.

Wright, Richard. (1945). *Black Boy*. New York: Harper & Brothers Publishers.

Zangrando, Robert L. (1980). *The NAACP Crusade Against Lynching, 1909–1950*. Philadelphia, PA: Temple University Press.

Zinn, Howard. (1980). *A People's History of the United States*. New York: HarperCollins.

Index